21 JAN 2019
4-APRIL-19

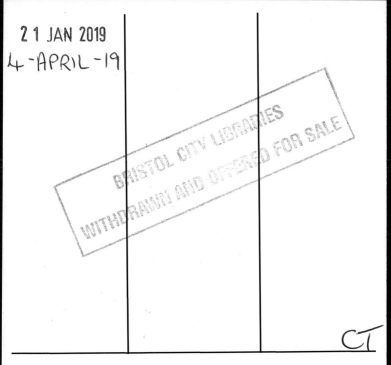

CT

Please return/renew this item by the last date shown on this label, or on your self-service receipt.

To renew this item, visit **www.librarieswest.org.uk** or contact your library

Your borrower number and PIN are required.

Dramatic Exchanges

The Lives & Letters *of the* National Theatre

THE OLD VIC

The National Theatre Company

Dramatic Exchanges

The Lives & Letters *of the* National Theatre

Selected and edited by
Daniel Rosenthal

P

PROFILE BOOKS

For Lyn Haill and Gavin Clarke

First published in Great Britain in 2018 by
Profile Books Ltd
3 Holford Yard
Bevin Way
London WC1X 9HD
www.profilebooks.com

10 9 8 7 6 5 4 3 2 1

A CIP catalogue record for this book is available from the British Library.

ISBN 978 1 78125 935 1
eISBN 978 1 78283 397 0

Text design and layout by Nicky Barneby

Printed and bound in Italy by L.E.G.O. SpA

Photograph facing title page: The Old Vic in the 1960s. It was home to the National Theatre Company from 1963 to 1976. Photo: Chris Arthur

Contents

Foreword

What this book shows is that letters have the power to transport us, just as theatre does. Many of us have a stash of envelopes somewhere, containing letters that tell love stories, crack open secrets or rekindle old memories. Similarly, the correspondence in these pages gives us access to privileged information that ignites curiosity – the impression is sometimes of peeking around a curtain when one shouldn't. Yet, while many of these letters were originally intended for private consumption, they tell a story that in some ways belongs to us – after all, the National Theatre is publicly funded; its history and legacy are for us all.

This correspondence is part of an actor's life, as much as the letters, and now emails, discussing scripts or offering roles. *Dramatic Exchanges* brings together hundreds of these missives, and offers a thrilling insight into other people's lives and creative practices. It's fascinating to read the correspondence behind plays I've watched and loved, and particularly to read letters from actors, writers and directors with whom I've worked, such as Richard Eyre, Nick Hytner, Peter Brook, Michael Gambon and Ian McKellen.

For many years, I was a member of the audience at the National Theatre, rather than a player on its stages. Among many other plays, I remember watching *The Recruiting Officer* and *Othello*, both with Laurence Olivier, in the Old Vic and later *The Royal Hunt of the Sun* on the South Bank. I have sat amid the expectant pre-show hubbub in the Dorfman, Lyttelton and Olivier, waiting for the lights to dim and the magic to start. Over the years I visited friends in their dressing rooms, where postcards, telegrams and notes wishing them well fringed their mirrors.

In the 1970s I became involved in the larger story of the NT through a letter I wrote to the *Guardian* about overspending in theatres – my follow-up letter to Lord Birkett is included here,

Opposite: Helen Mirren rehearsing the title role of *Phèdre*, 2009. Photo: Catherine Ashmore

and several of the points I made then remain close to my heart, among them the closure of regional theatres, which is still an ongoing problem today, and the lack of inclusiveness which affects both theatregoers and performers.

But the NT itself has changed, and there is a range of programmes – from £15 tickets to EntryPass for 16–25-year-olds, to NT Live – designed to help open its productions to a wider audience, keeping the art of the theatre alive and relevant.

In 2009, eleven years after my debut at the National, I was honoured to be involved in the very first NT Live broadcast, playing the title role in *Phèdre*. That night, our performance in the Lyttelton was broadcast live to 72 cinemas around the country; faced by an audience of around 800 in the auditorium, we were suddenly performing to many thousands of people.

Dramatic Exchanges effects a comparable expansion in the audience for these letters: often intended for an intimate audience of one, they may now be read by us all. It's illuminating to discover how my contemporaries and predecessors have grappled with some of the big questions of our craft during the first 55 years of the National's production history – and exciting to wonder what is now being said over email, what groundbreaking NT projects are in development, and how the next half-century will play out. Whatever happens, though, I doubt if we'll ever stop sending cards on opening night.

Helen Mirren
July 2018

Introduction

In 1981, the dramatist Peter Shaffer and director Peter Hall exchanged letters concerning Hall's discovery that, having triumphantly staged Shaffer's *Amadeus* at the National and on Broadway, he would be denied the chance to direct it for the screen. Shaffer's remorse at this turn of events was matched only by Hall's disappointment, anger and indignation.

At the NT Archive more than 20 years later I read this exchange, in which Shaffer curses his own 'hesitation and drift', and Hall accuses him of 'cowardly' and 'appalling' behaviour. It was my first close encounter with the power of theatrical correspondence, and the inspiration for the book you now hold (Shaffer and Hall's letters appear on pp. 170–71). I was used to actors, directors and playwrights expressing themselves forcefully in biographies or memoirs, in newspaper and on-stage interviews, but in gathering correspondence for this book I discovered that the raw, unmediated candour of private letters, in which practitioners attempt to reconcile the demands of art, commerce, friendship and ambition, is more affecting and revealing.

On *Amadeus*, the (temporary) souring of Shaffer and Hall's professional collaboration pushed them to expressions one might otherwise expect only in love letters. And much of the correspondence in this volume shows actors, designers, directors, literary managers, playwrights and stage managers experiencing, and articulating, intense emotions (a passionately committed Helen Mirren; joyful Judi Dench and James Corden), sometimes confirming, sometimes contradicting carefully honed personae: John Osborne, writing back in anger; Laurence Olivier, sometimes flattering, sometimes wounding, always florid; Alan Bennett, a study in self-deprecation.

The cards, letters, memos, telegrams and emails assembled here not only provide glimpses of the writers' lives, they also animate the performance history of the National Theatre: year by year, show by show, a choric, epistolary diary. It illuminates key relationships and pivotal moments in the history of the NT.

The correspondence captures dramas both on-stage and off: the frustration, satisfaction and disappointments endemic to all theatrical collaboration; its subtext is the fact that practitioners who work at the National – created by Act of Parliament, partly funded by taxpayers, subjected to intense media scrutiny – must also contend with what Genista McIntosh, its former executive director, characterised as 'boundless expectation, generated by the organisation and the outside world, of what it could provide'.

This book covers the four ages of the NT – as a dream, a campaign, a company and a building. The dream first shaped by Harley Granville Barker and William Archer in 1904 gave impetus to a stop–start campaign waylaid by decades of theatrical infighting, political inertia and two world wars. These two phases are summarised in the Prologue.

The National Theatre Company, with Laurence Olivier as founding Director and prime box office draw, took up residence at the Old Vic in 1963, and performed a huge variety of work, including new plays, Shakespeare, and classics of American and European drama.

Since March 1976, 'National Theatre' has meant Denys Lasdun's vast complex beside Waterloo Bridge, with three theatres, capable of accommodating up to 2,500 people a night. This National Theatre's raison d'être – to produce 20 or more new shows a year – explains why the pressures on NT Directors and their colleagues are so relentless (they must finalise plans for next year's shows while this year's are being cast, designed, rehearsed and performed), and why the archives hold such enormous quantities of correspondence. For every play or musical that reaches an NT stage, there will probably have been half a dozen alternatives considered for the same production slot in the same auditorium. These plans may have been dropped because, say, a commissioned script needed to be reworked; a West End producer turned out to hold the rights to the Arthur Miller play that an associate director longed to revive; a leading actor's provisional availability evaporated when they accepted an irresistible offer from Hollywood. Abandoned revivals or rejected scripts tell their own story, however, and so correspondence about almost 30 of them is included here.

The selection gathers some 800 items (the vast majority previously unpublished), which I considered to be the most engaging and illuminating among more than 12,000 pieces of correspondence read over the last two years, in institutional archives and personal holdings.

This correspondence between theatre practitioners holds special value because the myriad decisions that shape a stage production are mostly taken by phone or face-to-face, in meetings, auditions and rehearsals, over coffee or drinks. Letters or emails written by directors or playwrights after a casting session, or a first preview, are not only suggestive of long-lost discussions in NT offices or canteen; they also demonstrate how people feel compelled to write when matters of principle or taste need clearer, lengthier articulation than is generally possible in conversation.

Living dramatists come to the fore in what follows because the NT's New Work (previously Literary) Department has dealt with almost every British dramatist of note since 1963. The selected readers' reports, and memos from literary managers, contain what are, in effect, the first 'reviews' of dramas such as Pam Gems's *Stanley*, Tony Kushner's *Perestroika* and Michael Frayn's *Copenhagen*, months or years before NT audiences first saw them.

Premieres dominate this book partly because a new script's inherently experimental nature often generates intricate correspondence between agents, dramatists, literary managers and directors that is seldom, if ever, required before rehearsals begin for revivals of classics, when the script's worth has been proven time and again. The selected exchanges map the development of powerful, sometimes controversial, dramas and comedies, including *The Romans in Britain*, *The Invention of Love*, *The History Boys* and *The Effect*. We find some of the most acclaimed British and American playwrights of their generations prone to self-doubt, cherishing a hit, or lamenting the critical assault on what they believed to be their finest work to date. This material also illustrates why Tony Kushner believes that 'the director/playwright relationship is the most difficult in theatre.' The correspondence of partnerships such as Michael Blakemore/ Peter Nichols and Richard Eyre/David Hare finds them prone to highs and lows, argument and reconciliation.

Among performers, several letters serve as self-portraits of the actor as a young man or woman, notably Eileen Atkins, Derek Jacobi, Ian McKellen and Lynn Redgrave, all writing to Laurence Olivier in their twenties, close to the start of careers that we know – as they could not – would prove exceptionally successful.

The pleasures of being in a new play's original cast are captured in cards and letters from, among others, James Corden (*One Man, Two Guvnors*), Emma Fielding (*Arcadia*) and Nigel Hawthorne (*The Madness of George III*). Conversely, we find actors – including Alan Bates, Maureen Lipman and Paul Scofield – rejecting parts, whether in a premiere or a classic, that many of their peers would have seized.

'There's nothing better than good honest audience appreciation!' So wrote Tamsin Oglesby in 2010, after reading a stranger's response to her NT play *Really Old, Like Forty Five*. Audience members are frequently heard from in these pages, to showcase the delight and dismay inspired by the National's work (who bothers writing to star, author or director when a play has provoked only indifference?). There are also many cards and letters from creative practitioners-as-audience: actors, directors, playwrights (also novelists) responding to NT shows they were not involved in. Their analyses of stage performance and dramatic writing are among the most vivid and perceptive of their kind – private assessments often at odds with the newspaper and magazine reviews that generally determine a production's place in performance history.

Many of the selected letters, packed with unpretentious guidance and stoic reflections, might be reproduced verbatim in theatrical handbooks: 'Dramaturgical advice and encouragement for playwrights' (see, for instance, Nicholas Hytner reassuring Alan Bennett that his latest script paints 'a wonderful portrait of two dying men'); 'Directors' tips for actors' (Patrick Marber reminding Anna Friel and the rest of the Broadway cast of *Closer* to let their characters' thoughts 'tumble out like they do in real life – unguarded, uncensored'), or 'How to meet with triumph and disaster and treat them just the same' (Michael Frayn suggesting that 'criticism and opposition sharpen you up; praise and approval weaken you').

The space devoted to each show reflects my evaluation of the relevant correspondence (rather than any judgment on the quality of the production). I have attempted to ensure that coverage of each tenure included a fittingly varied mixture of new plays, revivals and pivotal off-stage events (notably the all-important Directorial successions), and quantified the intimidating, twin responsibilities of the Director: as producer of other people's shows, and director of their own. Olivier shouldered a third burden, as leading actor.

Hundreds of letters that made my initial selection did not make the final cut for reasons of space. Some playwrights and directors with multiple NT credits on their CVs do not feature because I could not find, or was not given access to, suitable correspondence about their work at the National. Among NT directors and dramatists in this volume, a dearth of female correspondents, and black, Asian and minority ethnic men and women (especially before the late 1990s) is in large part a regrettable matter of history.

The Cottesloe had premiered more than 30 new scripts by men before Debbie Horsfield had two performed, in 1985; the Olivier had presented more than 50 productions before one was directed by a woman (Sheila Hancock in 1985); not until 2000 did a woman have her original play premiered in the Lyttelton, Yasmina Reza's *Life X 3*; the same milestone was passed in the Olivier in 2008, by Rebecca Lenkiewicz with *Her Naked Skin*. The NT had been on the South Bank for 15 years before its first world premiere of an original play by a black or Asian dramatist: Mustapha Matura's *The Coup* in 1991.

The gender and ethnic balance among those who write and direct for the NT has in the past decade become notably more representative of Britain, and the National recently made the commitment that by March 2021, half of the directors and living writers working on its stages will be women, and 20 per cent will be people of colour; similar targets for performers are already being met. Initiatives are also in place to widen the involvement of disabled artists. In future, NT correspondence will have increasingly diverse authorship – and we can be certain there will still be a great deal of it.

Philip Larkin, in a letter to an old friend in 1981, predicted: 'We may be the last generation to write to each other.' The second half of this book demonstrates that Larkin was wrong: the urge to correspond remains strong, albeit now predominantly in a form, email, that Larkin did not live to use. Methods of communication evolve, but the challenges posed by each stage production, and the life of a producing theatre, will always generate moments of crisis, inspiration or jubilation when only writing will do.

Daniel Rosenthal
London, May 2018

A note from the editor

- Plays and musicals produced on a National Theatre stage are listed in simple chronological order, according to the production's NT press night (the first date given in each production's subheading). Complete credits for all productions are available via the NT Archive's online catalogue.
- Two asterisks next to a play's title indicate:
  - a revival mooted for, but not ultimately staged by, the National
  - a new play commissioned by, or submitted to, the National, but not ultimately produced there.
- Deletions of words within a sentence, and/or deletions of a complete sentence within a paragraph, have changed neither the sense nor the meaning of the unedited letter, and are *not* indicated with ellipsis.
- […] denotes the deletion of one, or more, complete paragraph/s from the unedited letter.
- … denotes an ellipsis that appears in the original correspondence.
- Editorial interpolations are indicated within [square brackets].
- 'National Theatre' has often been shortened to '[NT]'.
- Rather than include many instances of '[sic]', spelling errors in the original correspondence have been corrected. Therefore '[sic]' has only been used when incorrect, odd or archaic spelling occurs in the original letter for deliberate (e.g. comic) effect.

Six Decades of False Dawns

—

1903–1963

SCHEME & ESTIMATES

FOR A

NATIONAL THEATRE

by

William Archer & H. Granville Barker

LONDON
1904

For some, the origins of the National Theatre lie with the publisher William Effingham Wilson, and his A House for Shakespeare, written in 1848. In this pamphlet he called for the purchase 'by national subscription on the part of and for the people' of a theatre in which the works of Shakespeare would be constantly performed, at ticket prices 'within the reach of all'.

But Wilson's plan was not taken up, and it would be half a century before the true founding fathers of the National Theatre emerged on to the London drama scene: William Archer (1856–1924) and Harley Granville Barker (1877–1947). As leading figures in the English Stage Society, Archer translated the plays of Ibsen, and Granville Barker took leading roles in three Bernard Shaw premieres, including Mrs Warren's Profession (1902), wrote plays of his own and directed. Archer and Granville Barker believed that theatre should always provide more than mere entertainment.

Harley Granville Barker to William Archer, 28 April 1903

Dear Mr Archer,

Thank you for having that long talk with me. It is helpful to me in my impatience to get under the wing of your knowledge and experience sometimes.

I do hope the National Theatre will hurry up and fall into Liberal or even Radical hands and deliver us to some extent from the [commercial theatre] manager with the wooden head before another generation of actors (mine in this case) has gone to the devil artistically. […]

Very sincerely yours,
H. Granville Barker

Archer and Granville Barker compiled Scheme & Estimates for a National Theatre (1904), an extraordinarily detailed plan for the construction, endowment and management of a purpose-built, repertory theatre with a permanent company of 66 actors (42 men and 24 women). It would 'break away, completely and unequivocally, from the ideals of the profit-making stage'; it would 'bulk large in the social and intellectual life of London' and be 'unmistakably a popular institution'. The Scheme's navy-coloured covers saw it nicknamed 'the Blue Book'. Its authors sought support from eminent literary figures.

Thomas Hardy to Archer, 1 November 1904

My dear Archer,

I have read the Blue Book so far as is necessary for understanding the general principles; and I can say that it seems to be a desirable one in its main points.

It is most praiseworthy devotion in you to theatrical art to labour so sincerely in its cause.

A humorous feature in the movement has been the earnestness in supporting it of those living English dramatists who, by writing bad plays, are piling up vast fortunes through the absence of such a theatre. They are like smugglers who should earnestly entreat the Government to establish a more efficient system of coastguarding.

Believe me,
Yours sincerely,
Thomas Hardy

Opposite: 'The Blue Book': front cover of Scheme & Estimates for a National Theatre

Between 1904 and 1907, Granville Barker directed seasons at the Court Theatre, Chelsea, which revolutionised the scope and ambition of English drama: 32 plays (28 of them premieres) by 17 dramatists. Here was National Theatre repertory in all but name, but – without private endowment or state subsidy (not yet available for the performing arts in England) – the seasons lost money. Granville Barker was left with scant hope of establishing the National Theatre of his dreams.

Archer to Herbert
Trench (director),
15 December 1907

My dear Trench,

In the National Theatre business Granville Barker is quite clearly *the* indispensable man; and he, despairing of anything here, is in active negotiation with the New York millionaire's theatre, who are offering him a fabulous salary to start their concern. Now, if we let him go to America, we practically lose him altogether. […]

When Barker and I tried to get someone to realise the scheme in our Blue Book we were handicapped by the fact that we could not point to a desirable and available manager. I knew all the time that Barker was the man; but he was little more than a boy. Now he has *donné ses preuves*, and circumstances have shown that even he, with his genius [as a director], and his tremendous power of work, cannot make an artistic theatre without endowment otherwise than a *most* precarious undertaking.

What we want is the promise of a substantial sum on condition that such and such another sum is raised.

Really, really the time is ripe, and will soon be over-ripe. We have all the materials for a dramatic literature, but we lack the right machinery for developing it. Let us make up our minds not to die, on any pretext whatever, until we have seen an English theatre worthy of the name.

Yours sincerely,
William Archer

In 1908, the NT campaigners merged with a distinguished group determined to build a memorial to Shakespeare in central London – the Shakespeare Memorial National Theatre Committee (SMNTC) was born.

It included Archer, Granville Barker and Shaw. They needed half a million pounds – equivalent to £54 million today – to build and endow their National Theatre, which would 'keep the plays of Shakespeare in its repertory; prevent recent plays of great merit from falling into oblivion; produce new plays'. For this 'idealism' they were castigated by leading actor-managers, led by 71-year-old Sir Charles Wyndham.

Sir Charles Wyndham
to the editor,
Daily Telegraph,
26 March 1908

Sir,

A National Theatre would be a type of institution alien to the
spirit of our nation and of our age, which has always believed in,
and relied on, individual effort and personal competition as a
healthier stimulus than the motherly or grand-motherly fostering
of a State nurse.

> Sincerely,
>   Charles Wyndham

*The NT movement found no support from government, and little from the general public
– which explains why, in 1913, Shaw had this letter read out by William Butler Yeats to the
audience at the Court Theatre, before a matinee by the visiting Irish Players.*

Bernard Shaw
to W. B. Yeats,
14 July 1913

My dear Yeats,

[My promised] speech will not be delivered. I can only beg the
audience to bear this bitter disappointment with fortitude. It
is not my fault; it is that of the English nation which has just
enthusiastically given a huge sum of money to buy the Crystal
Palace for the sake of the cup finals, but absolutely refuses to
endow a national theatre.

What a contrast with our own country! In Ireland we have
a national theatre, a national drama and a national school of
acting. […]

A meeting of the executive committee of the Shakespear [sic]
Memorial National Theatre has been called for three o'clock this
afternoon to settle business of no importance except to the few
who have sense enough to understand its importance. They are
so few, in fact, that if I stay away there may be no committee.
But I am bound to be present to make a proposal to add to the
scheme of a national theatre, a football ground and racecourse. If
this proposal be adopted, we shall get the half-million we require
quite easily. Until then, England will have to get on as best she
can with the help of an occasional visit from our Irish players. If
the band would here strike up 'Rule Britannia' it would form an
appropriate end to this letter.

> Yours ever,
>   G. Bernard Shaw

*In 1914, on the outbreak of war, all fundraising efforts for a National Theatre were
suspended. Granville Barker accepted a commission from the Red Cross for a book about
their battlefield service, and wrote to Archer from 'KPO of the British Expeditionary Force
(in France and Belgium)'.*

Granville Barker
to Archer,
4 February 1916

My dear W. A.,

[…] Do you know if the millionaires had taken up that Blue Book of ours when it was written [and built a National Theatre] I'm not sure we [the British Public] shouldn't have found it a little easier to win this war.

Yours,
H. G. B.

When peace came, a war-battered British economy made it even harder for the SMNTC to raise funds, leaving Archer to confide in one of its most devoted members.

Archer to Edith
Lyttelton,
25 August 1922

Dear Mrs Lyttelton,

My mind is a sort of maelstrom of conflicting ideas and suggestions. I think we ought to send £100 to Germany (where it would be equivalent to several millions of marks) and in a few weeks they would ship us a National Theatre in sections, with Director and all complete. Why is it that they can do these things there and we can't? […]

Yours sincerely,
William Archer

Max Beerbohm to
Granville Barker et
al., 19 February 1923

My dear Harley,

In these lean times the ennobling discipline of poverty has not, alas, fixed the public eye on those upper radiant clouds behind which, no doubt, a complete National Theatre is lurking. And you surely aren't quite so mad as to suppose that H. M. Government is going to help you in any way? It wouldn't dare, even if it could be got to care. […]

Yours affectionately,
Max Beerbohm

When the government refused the SMNTC's request for land, the Duke of Westminster offered them an isolated site which, scoffed Shaw, would once 'have proved an ideal site for a gibbet'; it was declined.

In 1938, the SMNTC spent £75,000 on a plot in Cromwell Gardens, South Kensington, and commissioned Edwin Lutyens to design the theatre – only to have construction postponed by the outbreak of the Second World War.

When peace came, the SMNTC was superseded by the Joint Council of the National Theatre and Old Vic. Cromwell Gardens was exchanged for land donated by the London County Council (LCC), on the South Bank of the Thames, just upstream of Waterloo Bridge. Following the death of Lutyens, the NT had a new architect, Brian O'Rorke.

Brian O'Rorke
to Kenneth
Rae (secretary,
Joint Council),
23 November 1946

Dear Mr Rae,

[…] On Monday I went down to the site – it happened to be
a fine morning and standing on the edge of the river I was
deeply impressed by the wonderful possibilities the site offers.
I had thought that, with the site lying low between the two
bridges, there might be a shut-in feeling, but the closeness to
the water and the openness due to the river bend, give a sense
of space that I have never felt in central London. Looking
downstream and framed under the south arch of Waterloo
Bridge is the city with St Paul's in the centre. Upstream, when the
new Charing Cross Bridge is built and obstructions
cleared, the view will be to the Houses of Parliament. If the site
and waterfront can be developed sympathetically and the
Theatre is built in a human way – not as a heavy monument but
as a place to be enjoyed in the fullest sense – London will be the
richer. […]

Yours sincerely,
E. Brian O'Rorke

*Clement Attlee's Labour government introduced National Insurance and the
National Health Service, and, via the newly formed Arts Council, invested in the
performing arts, including theatre. A National Theatre Bill, committing £1 million of
taxpayers' money towards the construction of O'Rorke's South Bank theatre, would
go before the Commons on 21 January 1949, partly thanks to lobbying by Lord Esher,
chairman of the Old Vic, and Oliver Lyttelton (Edith's son), Joint Council chairman and
a Tory former cabinet minister.*

Oliver Lyttelton
to Rae,
24 December 1948

Dear Kenneth,

[…] The Whips are not going to be put on. It is lucky that our
Chief Whip is a determined supporter of the [NT] movement. I
think a very large majority of our Party are in favour of it, and it is
unlikely that there will be more than some sniping.

Yours,
Oliver

The National Theatre Act became law with overwhelming cross-party support.

On 13 July 1951 the Queen laid the NT's Foundation Stone. It had to be moved in 1953, a few months after the LCC shunted the putative NT along the South Bank, to a new location beside County Hall. As Lord Esher prepared to attend Queen Elizabeth II's Coronation at Westminster Abbey there were signs that actual foundations might soon be laid.

Rae to Lord Esher,
29 May 1953

My dear Oliver,

Oliver Lyttelton agrees that the time when we may hope to build is drawing swiftly nearer. He thinks it essential that you write to Mr Attlee himself. He was Prime Minister when his party introduced the [NT] Bill which became law without a dissentient voice and now [Labour] seems to be going back on the scheme.

You will have plenty of time to draft your letter while waiting in the Abbey on Tuesday! By the way, I am told by several of the functionaries that the heat is quite unbearable owing to the number of powerful stage lamps being installed to make television possible. So I should advise you to wear nothing under your robe! […]

Yours ever,
Kenneth

Six years passed without construction work on the National. Enter Laurence Olivier, aged 51, Britain's foremost stage and screen actor. He became a trustee of the Joint Council and rallied his peers.

Laurence Olivier
et al. to the
Editor, *The Times*,
23 February 1959

Dear Sir,

[…] [In 1949] the Treasury was empowered to subscribe up to one million pounds for the erection of a National Theatre. Since then no progress has been made and, due to inflation, the building will now cost nearer two million pounds.

[…] May we plead most earnestly that Her Majesty's Government makes the bold decision to release the funds required for the [NT], so that Great Britain may be put on an equal footing in this respect with other countries.

We are, Sir,
Yours faithfully,
Peggy Ashcroft, Lewis Casson, Edith Evans,
John Gielgud, Alec Guinness, Laurence Olivier (Trustee),
Michael Redgrave, Ralph Richardson, Sybil Thorndike

Opposite: First page of
The National Theatre Act

CHAPTER 16

An Act to authorise the Treasury to contribute towards
the cost of a national theatre, and for purposes
connected therewith. [9th March 1949.]

WHEREAS arrangements have been made between the
Trustees of the Shakespeare Memorial Trust (in this
Act referred to as "the Trustees") and the London
County Council for reserving to the Trustees as a site for the
erection of a national theatre by way of memorial to William
Shakespeare, certain land in the borough of Lambeth belonging
to the Council and for the transfer to the Council of certain
land in the Royal Borough of Kensington previously acquired by
the Trustees for the purpose aforesaid :

And whereas it is expedient to make provision for authorising
the payment out of public funds of contributions towards the
erection and equipment of such a theatre by the Trustees:

Be it therefore enacted by the King's most Excellent Majesty,
by and with the advice and consent of the Lords Spiritual and
Temporal, and Commons, in this present Parliament assembled,
and by the authority of the same, as follows:—

1. Upon the submission to the Treasury of a scheme satisfactory to them for the erection by the Trustees of such a theatre
as aforesaid on the site reserved to them for the purpose in
accordance with the said arrangements, and for the equipment
and management thereof, the Treasury may undertake to make,
and may make out of moneys provided by Parliament, upon such
terms and subject to such conditions as they think fit, such contributions to the funds of the Trustees as they think fit (not exceeding
one million pounds) in respect of the cost of erecting and equipping
the theatre in accordance with the scheme.

*Power of
Treasury to
contribute to
cost of national
theatre.*

1

That spring, Olivier would play Coriolanus *for the new artistic director of the Shakespeare Memorial Theatre in Stratford-upon-Avon, Peter Hall, who was just 29 and had made his name by staging Samuel Beckett's* Waiting for Godot *in London in 1955.*

Hall would later recall how, in a lunch break during Coriolanus *rehearsals, the pair had spoken of shared ambitions:*

Olivier: *'I'm going to have a go at making the National. Will you join me as Number Two?'*

Hall: *'I'm very flattered, Larry, I'd love to. But I'm going to make my own company, as Number One.'*

Olivier to Peter Hall, 3 July 1960	Private and Confidential

My dear Peter,

It doesn't seem easy to meet, so I'm going to try to put my thoughts down on paper.

I feel that the central duty of my career should be bent towards the establishment and erection of the National Theatre.

Until the [Old Vic Company] and Stratford have expressed themselves in entire unity in the National Theatre movement by your company playing at the Vic it would not be to the main interest for me to work for either party.

Any desire I might have to do this I find to be hampered by two considerations,

  a) The Vic and Stratford alone are not enough to form the schools of acting necessary to make the foundation of a company large enough to fill the needs of a National Theatre Company, which should be able to draw on about 150 people in three years' time. ([Shakespeare's] birthday 1964 – 400th Anniversary – is the selling date of opening to the Treasury and the public.)

  b) my own desire to have one more independent fling at it before incarcerating myself in State service.

To service both these ends, my ambitions are directed towards the 'Met Scheme' to engender a theatre policy at the Metropolitan in Edgware Road. I remember telling you of these sort of ambitions in the restaurant at Stratford during *Corio* rehearsals [last year] at which time you conceded that you had similar ambitions for your Strat. Co. It did not seem at all productive to me to plunge on in rivalry to you since you had such overwhelming production advantages, workshops, etc. and working actors all to hand. But now that the idea seems to have a contributive usefulness to our common aim I find myself back with it.

I should always want to feel that I had one leg free to shake in another camp if I wanted to, and this would apply to my [NT] contract should I ultimately have one. I realise that everybody couldn't expect that sort of freedom but I have served the business for 35 years now, and it's possible that sort of privilege could be extended to a very few of a certain record.

I have put these thoughts very bluntly, without any 'do you see what I mean' or 'if you'll pardon me for saying so'. I hope you accept them in this spirit which you know is very close to your own in comradeship and friendship ever.

Your
Larry

**Hall to Olivier,
1 August 1960**

Private & Confidential

My dear Larry,

Forgive my long delay in answering – it's been caused by nothing but lack of time. Because of internal troubles, I finally had to do the whole of *The Shrew* & *Troilus*, so I nearly went demented with work! However, it is all over now, and quite successfully at that, thank God.

Although I was very depressed by [your letter], I was very glad that you were so open with me.

There has got to be a marriage between Stratford and the Old Vic if the [NT] is to be built. You are the only person capable of making such a union. In forming a third company you will dissipate the talents available so that the formation of [an NT] Company will be even more difficult and unlikely. There just isn't enough talent available, and we shall all be pulling in three separate directions. This is why your decision to form a third company is very disturbing. Quite apart from the sadness I personally feel about your inability to work with Stratford again, your action will increase the fragmentary nature of our important theatre work. Believe me, I don't say this out of a mere personal ambition to have you work in my company, but because I believe passionately in a National Theatre.

I am now free of rehearsal and will come anywhere, anytime for a chat if you would wish it.

Yours ever,
Peter

The Met Scheme did not happen. But in 1961 Olivier became founding artistic director of Chichester Festival Theatre, a 1,200-seat, open-stage auditorium that would open in 1962.

Hall, meanwhile, transformed the Shakespeare Memorial Theatre company into the Royal Shakespeare Company, and expanded its operations from Stratford into London, with West End bases at the Aldwych and Arts theatres.

Then the government, hoping to save money, proposed merging the RSC and the Old Vic Company into the putative NT. The question of whether Olivier or Hall would run this unified entity became moot when the RSC's governing council withdrew from the merger plan.

My dear Larry,

I'm terribly unhappy about the state of Stratford's position over the [NT].

When we lunched in November, I thought you & I were in complete agreement. Now I find people thinking that we are not.

My Governors withdrew because

1. They were trying to be constructive and clear the way for [an NT].
2. They believed that the Wells/Vic/Stratford package was administratively unworkable.
3. Because the scheme was <u>not</u> the one envisaged in Dec. 1960.

I find to my infinite distress that our withdrawal has been represented to the Chancellor in much more dubious terms. The implication is that we have walked out, been unconstructive, and should be cut off without a shilling [in government subsidy].

Why is this? – because it's not the truth.

I want [an NT] just as much as you, and you know that it was my hope to work in it one day with you, but obviously my first loyalty must be to Stratford and what my Governors decide.

But why is federation – which is Stratford's suggestion – dismissed? If your new empire is going to set out to kill Stratford and my Company, then what will have been achieved except the usual British waste?

Stratford & the Aldwych is and must remain a small thing compared to the [NT]. Yet with a little money, we could do a lot. I have never believed that [an NT] should try to create a monopoly – otherwise you must eliminate the Royal Court & the Provincial Repertory Theatres.

Can't we work in harness somehow? – otherwise the foundations which I've fumblingly laid at Stratford during the last two years might just as well not have happened.

Michel Saint-Denis is planning to join me as General Artistic Adviser. I offered him co-directorship, because quite frankly I can't go on alone. I'm too isolated, too overworked – with nobody I can turn to for advice. But Michel wants to be an influence – not in the ring except when he wants to be.

When you are back in England, perhaps we can all meet. I find it a very worrying time.

Yours ever,
Peter

Olivier replied from Dublin, where he was playing an alcoholic teacher accused of assaulting a pupil in the film Term of Trial.

My dear Peter,

The Nat. Theatre is a horribly formidable spectre to me, but one that I can and must put aside if I am ever going to know my words and give a decent show in this film, <u>all</u> other time I must devote to Chich. or I am going to make a botch of that. I have managed to live with that Nat. Th. as a safely locked away black cloud. This is how I would like to continue if I could, but I am stopped by the thought that such would naturally be regarded as prevarication by you with overtones of hedging and duplicity.

It is possible that some of your statements to the Press have given the impression of grievance and dissension. I always consider the Press to be a thoroughly unreliable means of expressing oneself, and my present determination to resist the use of it is principally to avoid misunderstandings and also to avoid looking a cunt. I have explained to you that any statements you make about the Nat. Th. are bound to be embarrassing to me, and have indeed advised you never to talk to the buggers on any subject for your own sake, but you seem determined to enthrone yourself among the decoy ducks.

'My Governors withdrew to be constructive.' Forgive me, dear boy, but that is absolute rubbish. They withdrew entirely for their own reasons, entirely to do with their own *amour propre.*

You know very well that I do not want and never would allow anything to 'kill' Stratford except over my dead body and you really mustn't throw up words like 'Empire' to me, not you, with Strat, Aldwych and now Arts. So it would appear that you are not against monopoly unless it is held by the NT instead of Stratford!

Your letter carries to me a slightly hysterical tone (if I may say so without meaning to be the tiniest bit offensive) – which worries me and makes me feel you are not in a good state – or else you are pulling wool over my eyes, which I don't like much better (!) (Never shit a shitter).

Finally – the statement which, to me, represents the kernel of your feelings: 'otherwise the foundations I have fumblingly laid at Strat. during the last two years might just as well not have happened.' That's it, isn't it? And my God I understand it completely.

I assure you I will help you if I can, and when I can. But you must understand that when and if all the burdensome horrors of NT do in the order of things confront me – Stratford's worries about it probably cannot take absolute priority.

At the moment it looks like the most tiresome, awkward, embarrassing, forever-compromise, never-right, thankless fucking post that anyone could possibly be fool enough to take on and the idea fills me with dread.

This has been written scattily through two or three days and between shots, so forgive its shortcomings. Tell me if there is ought mistaken, unfair or untrue in it.

Ever,
Larry

Pieter Rogers
(Chichester Festival
Theatre general
manager) to Leslie
Evershed-Martin
(CFT Founder),
9 August 1962

My dear Leslie,

Larry thought you would like to have copies of the two announcements that will be put out this evening in London:

'At a preliminary meeting of the newly appointed National Theatre Board held today, it was decided to invite Sir Laurence Olivier to be first Director of the National Theatre.

Sir Laurence has intimated that he would be delighted to accept. [This] appointment will not affect the continuance of his present commitments with Chichester Festival Theatre at least for the next two years. […]'

Larry has officially commented on the above as follows:

'I shall strive my utmost to lay the foundations of a National Theatre that will finally justify its long wait for existence and be a source of pride to my profession and to the country as a whole.'

All good wishes,
Yours,
Pieter

Soon after Olivier's appointment came news that the new South Bank Board would assume responsibility for building the National, and invite architects to apply for a new commission – a terrible blow for Brian O'Rorke, after 17 years' fruitless labour on the project.

O'Rorke to Rae,
March 1963

Dear Kenneth,

I'm afraid I had really given up long ago except in moments of wishful thinking. I am now 62 and with no partners and a small office and I could not really see the [South Bank Board appointing me] – especially after all the delay. I would have liked to have had a go at the theatre – and it all seems a waste. I could have designed a good building – perhaps more reticent than present fashion demands but after a few years none the worse for that.

I am lucky to have the new hotel [the Berkeley, in Kensington] to occupy my thoughts and must now forget the NT and get on with life.

Yours, and with thanks for all your help,
Brian

That November, Denys Lasdun, best known for the concrete campus at the new University of East Anglia, would become NT architect, tasked with creating a complex housing a 1,000-seat auditorium (capable of proscenium and amphitheatre staging), a 400-seat, 'experimental' space, offices, rehearsal rooms, workshops and catering facilities. It was expected to open in 1969.

Olivier began recruiting performers under his two headings: 'Renowned', including Joan Plowright (his wife), Colin Blakely and Michael Redgrave; 'To Be Renowned', including Derek Jacobi, Lynn Redgrave and Robert Stephens. The question was whether the 'Renowneds' could include actors who were already movie stars.

Rex Harrison to
Olivier, 20 March
1963

My dear Larry,

I really think that *Wild Goose Chase* [an 1867 comedy by Dion Boucicault] could be a wonderfully funny, gay and bawdy piece [for me at the National].

I have been wondering whether it's a full evening or could not with good advantage be half an evening.

I feel careful editing would enhance it and highlight its comedy – what do you think?

I have therefore been manfully plowing my Jonson, Dekker, Massinger et al. ... to find a companion for it but so far without any great success. My work continues!

I do very much want to find more than one play to do in a season, it's so much more fun, and so I have been reading myself silly.

My dates during the coming [tax] year April to April are controlled by the Inland Revenue to three months [in England] – if I have to come back [to shoot] certain exteriors on *My Fair Lady* the three months would be minus that time – let us say two weeks – I could come back the middle of January, 1964, and carry on three months the other side of April 5th to July without endangering my tax position.

We shall be [in New York] about five weeks, thence to California for *Fair Lady*. [...]

I love the *Wild Goose* – a marvellous part for me and a divine part for a very young and beautiful girl, and a great improvement on the usual masquerade comedies of the period – and anyway it's very intriguing dear Larry and forgive me for not answering sooner – but I have not been idle – and I would <u>love</u> to do it.

You must be very hard pushed at the moment – but I envy you.

Great love as always,
    Rex

Olivier to Harrison,
23 May 1963

My dear Rexie,

[...] Please don't think that it's 'putting off' of me to view it realistically. We cannot really do much for you at the National in such a short total stay. Once we have opened our first season, plays are going to take longer than they usually do to rehearse, owing to the fatigue that sets in on the company, and the limit on their rehearsal time imposed upon them by performance times, so that we are considering ourselves pushed if we allow less than seven weeks' rehearsal.

It is impossible for us to hope to get the standard up by licking a thing on a normal West End three to four weeks rehearsal basis. This makes your performance period look a bit skimpy, doesn't it?

For the sake of the *amour propre* of the company I do not want to practise more than I can help a constant settling on top of them of visiting stars. Occasionally is alright, but more than this begins to get disheartening, and they will wonder if they are ever going to get anywhere themselves.

I am sure you will appreciate that the old 'happy and efficient ship' attitude is important in the properly delicate handling of an ensemble, but I plan to keep the Chichester season as stellar as I can, and if you would like to do it there, that might be the answer. […]

Thank you so much, dear fellow, for your enthusiastic work. […]

All love, as ever,
Larry

Harrison did not join the National or Chichester. Olivier's reluctance to bring him into the Company was influenced by his having cast Peter O'Toole – who had found global fame in Lawrence of Arabia *in 1962 – in the title role of the NT's opening production:* Hamlet.

The Laurence Olivier Years

—

1963–
1973

The start of the Olivier years

Laurence Olivier would send many hundreds of letters to actors and directors over the next decade, attempting to reconcile their ambitions, schedules and whims with his own tastes, and with those of his associate directors, initially William Gaskill and John Dexter, and his literary manager, the brilliant drama critic Kenneth Tynan – as well as with the National's relatively meagre production budgets, and the fact that, until the South Bank complex was ready, it had just one theatre at its disposal.

That theatre was the Old Vic, near Waterloo station, where the NT Company would, from October 1963, perform in the 880-seat, proscenium auditorium. They would also mount summer seasons at Chichester, in 1964 and 1965.

Many letters from Olivier on the following pages were dictated and typed in the National's cramped, spartan administrative base at The Archway, 10a Aquinas Street, a three-minute walk from the Old Vic. Home to 18 full-time staff, this HQ was a row of prefabricated Nissen huts, containing offices, a board room, rehearsal room and canteen – colloquially referred to as 'the huts'. Under their tar-paper roof, recalled Donald MacKechnie, one of Olivier's assistant directors, 'we froze in the winter, we roasted in the summer and the slightest rainfall made even a routine telephone conversation quite an adventure in phonetic comprehension.' Olivier's office was 'woefully inadequate' for the head of such a high-profile enterprise, but, at last – 60 years after Granville Barker and Archer first dreamt of a National Theatre Company – audiences were about to see it perform.

Hamlet (c.1601)

by William Shakespeare
Director: Laurence Olivier
Old Vic, 22 October to 4 December 1963 (27 performances)

Olivier had played Hamlet in 1937, and starred in and directed an Oscar-winning film version in 1948. His Old Vic revival would have a set by Sean Kenny and costumes by Desmond Heeley.

Olivier to Desmond Heeley, 27 May 1963

Dear Desmond,

I am burning to talk to you about *Hamlet*.

It is terribly difficult to feel glossy or new when one has done a thing more than once, and then made a film – one really does not feel one has much more to say.

I do not think it any good my trying to join the Brechtian ranks in the presentation; that would only be a lame follow-on to a trend upon which others have put their stamp, with far more authority than I could. So I suppose the aura of the play which still exists with me is what would be thought today a romantic one – with [Peter] O'Toole as the principal it would be hard to think otherwise.

Opposite: Laurence Olivier as Edgar in *The Dance of Death*. Photo: Zoë Dominic

The set that Sean and I have concocted is an abstract shape on a revolve, a ramp curling round the perimeter, which covers a little more than half of the circumference, so that the blunt side, presented to the audience, represents the ramparts, and when it is turned round becomes an interior SO you and I have simply got to costume it in a fashion that spells 'Hamlet'.

What I have in mind is to use period for character; Michael Redgrave would like [Claudius] sort of Henry IV, a more romantic type of Henry VIII. One wants the Queen redolent of the most voluptuous period of womanhood, Ophelia to have a Victorian feeling. I tried to convey this in the film, and it was perfectly alright, but I would love to know how you feel. […]

I wish to God you were here so that we could talk and talk all night long – it would help so much. […]

Yours ever,
Larry

In the West End a few months earlier, Olivier had played an insurance salesman in David Turner's comedy Semi-Detached, *with Eileen Atkins, then 28, as his daughter.*

Eileen Atkins to
Olivier, 14 June 1963

Dear Sir Laurence,

I've no doubt that Ophelia is cast, signed and sealed by now but I have to write as I've been reading and reading the play since [my audition on] Monday and I see how wrong I was about the part – I was so frightened of it I had no confidence to do the simple thing.

If you are seeing any girls a second time round will you please see me a second time round – oh dear, I know you must be the busiest man in England and how dare I ask to waste even more of your time.

Love,
Eileen

Olivier to Atkins,
5 July 1963

Darling Eileen,

It was angelic of you to take such trouble in studying and reading Ophelia for me, and you were as good as you could possibly be.

Please try to understand that when a person is so familiar with something as I am with Ophelia's scenes, there is hardly anything to choose between the people he hears. Particularly if they are obviously clever and accomplished actresses.

There is a whole library of choices of business – readings, expressions, attitudes, already in existence, and it is only really a question of pressing the right buttons to get a formula.

This sort of tired and useless knowledge has perplexed me terribly in deciding what on earth it is I really want out of a part, and therefore there has been nothing for me to do but to sit in hopes that somebody will tell me what it is that I wanted; the answer being in some wavered and probably quite simple alchemy that the person themselves would provide it very possibly unconsciously and intuitively.

I am really quite sincerely sorry not choosing you, but reading the thing is not really the answer. One should cast it instinctively, just as it should be played instinctively.

I am awfully sorry to have imposed upon your kindness, and so very grateful for your splendid willingness.

All love, as ever,
Larry

Atkins to Olivier, 10 July 1963

Dear Sir Laurence,

I was so touched by your letter. I know <u>exactly</u> what you mean. When I first came to see you I felt that if you didn't instinctively have a feeling for the part it would never be right, but I was so mad to work with you that I simply <u>had</u> to see if I couldn't make it mine.

I felt an awful cheat wasting your time, but I wouldn't have missed reading Ophelia to your Gertrude for anything!

I shall look forward enormously to seeing *Hamlet.*

Much love,
Eileen

Olivier cast Rosemary Harris as Ophelia. Tom Courtenay, 26, star of the films The Loneliness of the Long Distance Runner *(1962) and the just-released* Billy Liar*, had accepted parts in forthcoming NT productions of* Andorra *and* Hobson's Choice. *On 13 August, the* Daily Mail *ran a news story noting that Courtenay had declined to replace O'Toole when he left* Hamlet *in December to shoot the feature film* Becket.

Tom Courtenay to Olivier, 20 August 1963

Dear Sir Laurence,

You probably saw that awful bit in the *Daily Mail.* At the press lunch for *Billy Liar* one of the reporters asked me was it true that I'd been offered Hamlet after Peter. He knew it was true all right, people have known about it for months: these little tit-bits get round very quickly. I told him it was true – I should really have said 'No', and smiled knowingly, or something.

Anyway, one of the press boys pricked his ears up and decided here was an opportunity for a sour little piece and wrote something that was not much to do with what I went on to say. I should really have said nothing, but one doesn't always have time to think that quite reasonable remarks can be made to look really loaded when in print. […]

I can't wait to start *Andorra*, and today have to decide whether to do a <u>commercial</u>!! film in between now and then.

Billy Liar seems to have gone down very well. That should surely help both our causes.

Please don't bother to reply to this – you must be terribly busy.

Yours,
Tom (Courtenay)

Olivier to Courtenay,
29 August 1963

Dear Tom,

[…] It is almost impossible to learn how to deal with the Press boys. I sometimes think I have mastered the problem and then immediately find that I've boobed it again. […]

Larry

Peter Hall to Olivier
and Joan Plowright,
31 August 1963

Dear Joan & Larry,

[…] Now that the [RSC's] third [*Wars of the Roses*] history is launched, I feel like one about to be demobilised!

Next Tuesday I go off for three months to recuperate from this ghastly summer. Among my chief regrets is that ill-health kept me from Chichester, and that I won't be there to cheer the beginning of the [NT]. I do wish you a <u>triumphant season</u> and not just out of love & admiration, but because this project is vital to the whole future of our Theatre. I'll be rooting from a foreign shore.

Yours ever,
Peter

Hamlet *had sold out before it opened, but garnered lukewarm-to-poor reviews, including a* Daily Mail *notice headlined 'After a wait of 100 years, this will do for a start'.*

Uncle Vanya (1899)
by Anton Chekhov

Translated by Constance Garnett (1923)
Director: Laurence Olivier
Old Vic, 19 November 1963 to 1 August 1964 (45 performances)

In Olivier's production, first seen at Chichester in 1962, he played Dr Astrov and Joan Plowright was Sonya, who is forlornly in love with Vanya (Michael Redgrave).

Kenneth Rae (NT
board secretary) to
Michael Redgrave,
20 November 1963

Dear Michael,

I have now seen your performance of Uncle Vanya four times and can truthfully say that nothing in the theatre has ever moved me more. It is utterly heart-breaking in its beauty. Were I to attempt to tell you in person all I felt, I should merely stammer and blub – hence these poor inadequate few lines of gratitude and grovelling admiration.

Yours,
Kenneth

This does not, repeat NOT, require an answer.

Opposite: Rosemary Harris (Ophelia)
and Peter O'Toole (Hamlet) in the NT's
opening production. Photo: Angus McBean

Marion Hatcher to Redgrave, 3 June 1964

Dear Sir Michael,

I enjoyed *Uncle Vanya* so much tonight, but surely you feel you are beating your head against a brick wall when the audience laughs like a drain at every word. I was so infuriated that I seethed all the way home in the train [to Chislehurst, Kent]. For a large majority your performance must have been absolutely wasted as they probably saw Ivan Petrovitch as a rather mixed-up funny-man. Apart from the ignorance of it all, it kills the atmosphere stone dead. When the Professor's wife said to the Doctor 'I shall take this pencil as a reminder of you' it seemed so poignant, and yet the sniggers of the audience destroyed the feeling completely. Does this happen at every performance? But I must not let this over-rule the play itself. I wouldn't have missed it for anything.

    Yours sincerely,
      Marion Hatcher

Michael Redgrave in the title role of *Uncle Vanya*. Photo: Angus McBean

Redgrave to Hatcher,
8 June 1964

Dear Marion Hatcher

The line about the pencil <u>should</u> not produce a snigger but it's
only the lunatic fringe who snigger – even those who have never
read Freud can recognise a piece of phallic symbolism nowadays
– and those who do snigger do so because they are excited and on
the verge of both laughter and tears.

You were not on the verge of laughter that evening, it seems.
But I don't see how one can help being. The pathos and the
humour and fun of <u>life</u> are very closely entwined. Less than a
minute after Vanya has been laughing with the doctor he is in
tears because Sonya looks at him 'So like your dear Mother'.

You say 'your performance must have been absolutely wasted as
they probably saw Ivan Petrovitch as a rather mixed-up funny-man.'

Well, that phrase doesn't sum up all of Vanya but it's not
so wide of the mark, you know. As Astrov says of him, he is
something of a buffoon. There's no getting round that. Each one
of the characters has an element of absurdity. I won't enumerate
them – but if you study the play you will find you can't contradict
this. That is one reason why the play is so universally appealing
and why the audiences laugh as they do and weep as they do: they
are recognising aspects of themselves.

There is nothing solemn about Chekhov. Perhaps that's why
Tolstoy thought so little of Chekhov's works. But Chekhov is the
most compassionate of writers and though he pin-points our
absurdities he dismisses them or cleanses them with laughter.
There is not one laugh in this production – excepting the
fortuitous one about the pencil – which I would try to erase. To
act in it has been the greatest joy of my professional life. 'Beating
my head against a brick wall'? Never.

I have written all this not because I wanted to start a
correspondence but to see if I could make clear to myself in words
what I intuitively aim for when playing Vanya. With you – <u>on
that evening</u> – I evidently didn't succeed entirely, even though
you say you 'wouldn't have missed it for anything'. Or could it
not perhaps have been something in <u>you</u> that evening? A lack of
response to the laughter? A longing to shed more tears? A touch
of solemnity which Chekhov would, most gently, have mocked?
Or a simple misliking of the crowd of people around you?

Please drop me a note to say you have or have not understood. I
would be interested to know. But I have nothing more to add.

Best wishes,
Michael Redgrave

The Recruiting Officer (1706)
by George Farquhar

Director: William Gaskill
Old Vic, 10 December 1963 to 5 December 1964 (60 performances)

Set in the early 1700s, The Recruiting Officer *featured Robert Stephens as philandering Capt. Plume and Olivier as bombastic Capt. Brazen, who compete for army recruits in Shrewsbury; Maggie Smith took the part of Silvia, Plume's beloved. They were watched by John Gielgud, who had acted with Olivier many times, including as Clarence in Olivier's film of* Richard III *(1955).*

John Gielgud to Olivier, 29 June 1964

Dear Larry,

Bravo for Brazen. I loved your performance, as usual, and much of the play, though it is a bit cumbersome here and there. Liked Colin Blakely so much, also Lynn Redgrave, [John] Stride and of course Maggie [Smith], who is brilliant. [Robert] Stephens plays well but somehow seems to lack the charm needed for so long a part. Lovely décor. I didn't come round, thinking you would want to get away to Brighton. […]

> Love as ever,
> John

Marvellous your business with the [eye] patch – and all the kissing and clubbiness – and the walk and the bows in your hair.

Olivier to Gielgud, 31 June 1964

Dearest Johnnie,

You are an angel, thank you infinitely much, dear one, for your kindness, your generosity and your trouble.

Time is so woefully short that I find myself constantly approaching things clumsily to approach them at all; so please forgive me if the following suggestion seems to come from any sense of gratitude for your sweet letter.

How overjoyed I should be, if you would consider working for us at the National.

This should have been said long long ago, but because all one's energies have been so strongly devoted to matters actually in hand, it has been neglected. I ask you to forgive me and to accept this word now, in case a further prolonged silence might make you suspect a lack of interest. This would not only be tragic but utterly wrong.

If, in default of our having anything to suggest, you might find yourself in possession of an idea, I should be overjoyed.

Again, please forgive me for wrong approach, wrong method, wrong timing, everything wrong.

> Always your devoted & grateful,
> Larry

Gielgud to Olivier,
23 September 1964

Dearest Larry,

I have thought a great deal about *Love for Love*, but I don't really feel I could take it on. I spent nearly two years with it in the war, and long before that had done it at Oxford, and do not think I could shed any new light, only strive to do it differently for difference's sake, never a good plan. I love the play, and was a bit tempted as I would love to work with you again, but even if the Albee play does not come through, as I hope it will, I just don't feel it is a good idea to go back on my tracks.

I saw John Dexter [NT associate director] in Venice the other day and he murmured something about Shylock, but I felt that I did not bring that off in 1938, and doubt if I would now either. In spite of my nose I have never managed to have much success in Jewish parts! […]

My love as ever,
John

Olivier to Gielgud,
1 October 1964

Dearest Johnnie,

Do you think you would consider [the Christ figure] in Johnny Osborne's adaptation of Lope de Vega's play *La Fianza Satisfecha* a modern enough departure for you? This is a much more exciting project than it may sound.

You are grossly under-estimating your Shylock. I remember thinking it was marvellous and goodness, gracious me, I would not like any memories there might be of my Macbeth to be confined to my effort of 1938!

Time does such wondrous things in increasing our observation and broadening our outlook, as well as sharpening our intuition, that as we grow older I always think we ought to be more inclined to say 'What have I got to lose' rather than what I might be losing.

However, don't let me dare to preach at you. This is really simply to say how very deeply I hope one day to catch you, either by a mixture of things ancient and modern, or some other concoction. The National Theatre earnestly needs your stature.

Yours always with love,
Larry

That December, Gielgud appeared in the premiere of Edward Albee's Tiny Alice *in New York. In 1965, Peter Wood directed* Love for Love *for the National.*

1964

Play (1963)
by Samuel Beckett

Director: George Devine
Old Vic, 7 April to 31 July 1964 (20 performances)

Play, first staged in French in Paris, lasts less than 20 minutes. A husband, his wife and his mistress – Man (Robert Stephens), First Woman (Rosemary Harris) and Second Woman (Billie Whitelaw) – look back on their lives while placed inside large urns; only their faces, caked in thick make-up, are visible. Beckett had assigned production rights to his plays in England to George Devine, who had been artistic director of the English Stage Company (Royal Court) since 1956.

Kenneth Tynan to George Devine, 31 March 1964

Dear George,

I must try to explain more clearly to you and Larry what is worrying me about *Play*. I wouldn't do so if I didn't feel that many of my qualms were shared by others.

Before Sam B. arrived at rehearsals, *Play* was recognisably a work we all liked. The delivery of the lines was (rightly) puppet-like and mechanical, but not wholly dehumanised and stripped of all emphasis and inflections. It seems that Beckett's advice on the production has changed all that – the lines are chanted in a breakneck monotone with no inflections, and I'm not alone in fearing that many of them will be simply inaudible. I suspect that Beckett is trying to treat English as if it were French – where that kind of rapid-fire monotony is customary.

We are not putting on *Play* to satisfy Beckett alone. It may not matter to him that lines are lost in laughs; or that essential bits of exposition are blurred; but it surely matters to us. Beckett has never sat through any of his plays in the presence of an audience: but we have to live with that audience night after night!

Play – our first experimental work – follows straight on [from the critical and box-office failure of] *Andorra*. If it fails to get over with maximum impact, it may jeopardise our future plans for experiment and put a weapon into the hands of those people who think the [NT], like the Proms, should stick to the popular classics and not cater for minority tastes. It may even provoke the more conservative members of the NT Board to start interfering in the choice of plays – which would be disastrous!

I trust the play completely, and I trust your production of it. What I don't especially trust is Beckett as co-director. If you could see your way to re-humanising the text a little, I'll bet that the actors and the audience will thank you – even if Beckett doesn't!

Yours,
Ken

cc Laurence Olivier and William Gaskill

Devine to Tynan,
9 April 1964

Dear Ken,

The presence of Beckett was of great help to me, and to the actors. I assume you read the stage directions: 'Voices toneless except where indicated. Rapid movement throughout.' Any other interpretation is a distortion. You do not seem to realise that rehearsing a play is an organic process. To play the play as you indicate would be to demolish its dramatic purpose and turn it into literature. The simple truth appears to be that you got into a panic about *Play*, in case it did not 'come off'. You'll have to have a bit more guts if you really want to do experimental works, which, nine times out of ten, only come off for a 'minority' to begin with. I certainly would never have leased the play to the [NT] if I had thought the intention was to turn it into something it isn't, to please the majority.

    Yours,
      George

cc Laurence Olivier

Olivier to Devine,
12 April 1964

My dearest Georgie,

I am deeply sorry that you have been upset. What you also know is that anything of this nature is something for which I must be blamed and what you know too is that this doesn't absolutely mean that it is my fault.

    You of all people in the world, and probably only you, know and appreciate the job that is mine and however furious incidents and mistakes may make me, and justifiably so, that if I had really hoped to have a smooth-running perfect machine in six months, I would by now have shot myself. […]

    You, dear love, have been justifiably angry and I am very sorry about it. I have been just as angry with everybody in the whole organisation from time to time, but I am not going chopping off heads right left and centre until I have decided that what is in them is not worth keeping, or that others are going to give me more.

    From all the various opinions that I have gleaned, and in spite of some of them, it would seem to me that your work on *Play* has been shrewd, correct and wise. I die to see it.

    I am in the car at this moment, on my way to a dress rehearsal [of *Othello*] in Cardiff which will not, I fancy, be remarkable for its sang-froid.

    My love to you, dearest one.
      Larry

In a memo to Tynan on 12 April, Olivier wrote: 'I like you. I like having you with me. But you can be too fucking tasteless for words.'

Othello (c.1604)

by William Shakespeare

Director: John Dexter
Old Vic, 23 April 1964 to 4 February 1967 (89 performances)

It was Kenneth Tynan who had persuaded Olivier to take on Othello, at a time when it was still standard – and unchallenged – practice for white actors to, in Olivier's words, 'go into blackface' to play Shakespeare's Moor.

Geraldine McEwan to Olivier, 8 April 1963	Dear Larry,

Of course I would love to play Desdemona with you.

However, this does seem to be quite a long way off, if you are not putting *Othello* into the repertory until the Spring, and so I feel that I need to be pretty keen on *The Recruiting Officer* to want to play just that for several months. […]

Give my love to Joan and congratulations to you both on the arrival of your baby daughter.

Gerry

McEwan to Olivier, 15 April 1963

Dear Larry,

I have read *The Recruiting Officer* and I must say I do wish that Silvia were a more exciting role. It would be quite fun to do as one of a line of parts, but I don't feel it would be interesting or challenging enough to keep me occupied until I did Desdemona in the Spring. […]

With love,
Gerry

In 1955, Claire Bloom had played Lady Anne in Olivier's film of Richard III. *In June 1963, she asked him to consider her for Desdemona.*

Olivier to Claire Bloom, 11 June 1963

Darling Claire,

I'm sorry it was difficult to write, but there is nothing but tenderness from the reader.

I absolutely understood your attitude last year and am very sorry now to disappoint you about Desdemona, but it is cast.

Thank you so much for writing and of course, I'll remember you, my dear, as and when.

Always, with love,
Larry

Olivier had cast Maggie Smith as Silvia and Desdemona after McEwan turned him down; Bloom never acted for him at the National.

Joan Plowright watched her husband as Othello in a run-through at the Old Vic, then wrote to him in Birmingham, where Othello *was about to try out at the Alexandra Theatre.*

Joan Plowright to
Olivier, 20 March
1964

Dear Larry,

[...] Just want to send all my love and thoughts and energy to you.
Don't let any doubts creep in about your Othello; I know this is
about the time one begins to bite one's fingernails and think only
of the bits one is still dissatisfied with. No harm in that as long
as you remember also that in the greater part of the play you are
wildly exciting, beautiful, superb and head and shoulders above
anyone living today. Don't know about those who went before,
but I'm pretty sure you are way above them too!

Your characterisation is fascinating, original and absolutely
valid in human terms, the split personality of a man who has had
to overcome one powerful part of his nature in order to achieve a
certain position in the world. [...]

Am going to jot down random thoughts and impressions
which might ring a bell somewhere and, if they don't, no harm
has been done! [...]

I think you are maybe trying to believe Cassio's kisses have
been on [Desdemona's] lips, instead of trying to stop yourself
believing. [...]

This is probably just something I feel, but I have felt each time
I've seen it that your passion is too great and openly displayed for
Maggie to top it and try to pretend it is a game. [...]

No other suggestions, my love. And I bet you don't like those!

Oh ... I do love you.
Joan

*Most drama critics agreed with Plowright's assessment, and the NT box office was
overwhelmed – the* Daily Express *called a ticket to* Othello *'the most difficult piece of
paper to get hold of in Britain today'.*

On 1 May 1964, Life *magazine ran a 16-page spread headlined 'The Great Sir Laurence'.
In it, Olivier observed of Peter Brook's 1962 RSC* King Lear, *starring Paul Scofield:
'I wasn't one of its admirers. He rid Lear of his glamour, kingliness; made him down to earth.
People nicknamed the play "Mr Lear".' The magazine appeared while Brook's production,
still with Scofield as Lear, was on a US tour that would conclude in New York, from
18 May to 6 June.*

Peter Brook to
Kenneth Tynan,
21 May 1964

Dear Ken,

I'm writing to you not as friend to friend, but as co-director of the
Royal Shakespeare Company, to you in your official capacity as
I believe that it carries a responsibility for the statements of the
National Theatre.

Larry's article in *Life* magazine has aroused a great ill-feeling.
It is surely obvious that like a Cabinet Minister, the Head of the
National Theatre can no longer be 'just a private individual' at the
same time.

It is obvious that when he goes into print in a major American
periodical on the eve of the first appearance of the Stratford
Company ever in New York, his words take on considerable

weight. Naturally, objective criticism coming from him at the right time and in the right place would be treasured. However, for his one public comment on *Lear*, and, by implication on Paul's performance to have picked this moment and this journal, seems to many people here [in Stratford] either very irresponsible, or malicious towards a fellow actor and a rival organisation. I cannot believe either, but I feel I must let you know this.

> Yours,
>   Peter

cc Peter Hall

Olivier to Brook, 26 May 1964

My dear Peter,

I am quite horrified and a good bit flabbergasted at the effect that passage in the *Life* interview seems to have made.

You must, please, believe that when I gave that interview (sporadically, over some weeks) there was no premeditation whatsoever regarding the Stratford visit to New York.

I can't believe that you could really think otherwise, any more than I can believe that you, or any other thinking friend, could seriously think that I would ever want to be malicious to a fellow actor, let alone one whose talents I admire as much as you well know I do those of Paul.

As to the question whether I am an artist or a Cabinet Minister, I think that is a large and vexatious one that we could leave until we see each other, don't you?

> Yours ever,
>   Larry

Hay Fever (1925)

by Noël Coward

Director: Noël Coward
Old Vic, 27 October 1964 to 12 June 1965 (51 performances)

When Olivier invited Coward to direct Hay Fever, *they had been friends since appearing in the premiere of Coward's* Private Lives *in 1930.* Hay Fever *is set in June, in the Cookham home of actress Judith Bliss and her family; their weekend guests include Myra Arundel, who has designs on Judith's son, Simon.*

Noël Coward to Olivier, 12 February 1964

Dear Larry,

I don't want Joyce Redman as Myra. I <u>long</u> for Maggie Smith. My wild author's eye has always envisaged Myra as tall and svelte. As it is going to be a season opener, it ought to be as glamorous and star-crossed as possible – just a collection of good actors will not be quite enough.

> Noël

| Coward to Olivier, 15 April 1964 | Dearest Larry-Boy,

I'm bitterly disappointed to have to tell you that I can't direct *Hay Fever* for you. I enclose a fairly sharp letter from my doctor which explains why. I am terribly sad about this because I was so flattered and pleased to have been asked to work for your National Theatre. *Hay Fever*, as you know, is one of my pets, but if you feel like dropping it from your programme I shall quite understand. If, on the other hand, you want to go on with it with another director I will do anything I can to help in discussing cast etc, etc. […]

I hate letting you down like this and please believe that I wouldn't unless it were absolutely unavoidable.

It is being slowly and painfully beaten into my skull that I am no longer a precocious boy of nineteen, although when I look in the mirror at this lovely little heart-shaped face with all those pretty little jowls hanging from it, I find it hard to believe. […]

Please cable me or write to me when you get this letter saying that you understand and forgive your loving old

Noelie.
My fond love to Joan and a very great deal to you. |

The 6 April note from Edward Biggs MD, of Chicago, advised Coward to 'spend at least one year in a relatively quiet environment, avoiding such stressful situations' as directing. Olivier replied on 27 April ('It's no good crying over milk that never got into the jug'), then invited Dame Edith Evans, 76, to play the middle-aged Judith Bliss.

| Edith Evans to Olivier, 21 May 1964 | Dear Larry,

I must confess my heart jumped a beat when I got your letter.

With regard to Judith Bliss I absolutely love it and adored doing it on Television about four years ago, but I am getting too old for the part as it is written. Would Noël be able and willing to make it that I could play it without looking ridiculous? I would love to do it if we can in honour work out something.

With love – and hopes,
Edith |

Coward ignored medical advice and staged Hay Fever *with Evans (denied a rejuvenating rewrite) as Judith, and Smith as Myra, alongside Derek Jacobi and Robert Stephens. At the first rehearsal Coward declared: 'I'm thrilled and flattered and frankly a little flabbergasted that the National Theatre should have had the curious perceptiveness to choose a very early play of mine, and to give it a cast that could play the Albanian telephone directory backwards!'*

The Royal Hunt of the Sun (1964)
by Peter Shaffer

Directors: John Dexter and Desmond O'Donovan
Old Vic, 8 December 1964 to 4 February 1967 (105 performances)

Peter Hall to Olivier,
17 April 1961

Dear Larry,

[…] You may have heard of Peter Shaffer's play about the conquest of Peru called *The Royal Hunt of the Sun*. I read a first draft last year, and though I found it very cold and rather over-preoccupied with history I must say its quality appealed to me. I therefore commissioned him to rewrite it entirely. A commission which he accepted, and which is now producing results. He has nearly finished his rewrite, and it looks most exciting.

It centres round Pizarro, the man who dethroned the last of the Inca kings – a titanic bull of a man, a rough-hewn warrior with the most extraordinary megalomania and strength of spirit. I can't imagine anyone else playing it save you. It's possibly the best modern part I've ever read for a great heroic actor.

Can I at least send it to you as soon as it's finished? […]
Leslie [Caron] joins me in w love to you both.

Best wishes,
Yours ever
Peter

By the time Shaffer delivered, Hall had decided that The Royal Hunt… *was now 'exactly' the kind of play the RSC were not interested in. It was eventually acquired by the National, and, with Colin Blakely as Pizarro and Robert Stephens as Inca god-king Atahuallpa, opened at Chichester in July 1964 and was hailed by the* Daily Mail *as 'the greatest play of our generation'.*

*Dingo***
by Charles Wood

To comply with the Theatres Act (1843), Charles Wood's Dingo *– like all other NT scripts earmarked for production – had to be submitted to the Lord Chamberlain's office in St James's Palace, with a request for a performance licence. The following correspondence demonstrates the strictures from which British theatre would not be freed until the Lord Chamberlain's powers of censorship were abolished by a new Theatres Act in September 1968.*

T. B. Howard's
report on *Dingo*,
6 December 1964

This is a provocative parody/satire in the classic anti-establishment manner, a bitter, pungent attack on war and heroism.

It purports to present the whole of the Second World War by concentrating on a small part of the Western Desert (Act I), and then on a POW Camp (Act II). It uses a highly stylised symbolist presentation in which the dead mingle with the living, and characters are deployed like marionettes to demonstrate the author's argument. It is all very unusual, but good theatre.

Realism, the authentic crudities of other ranks, often brutal and gruesome imagery convey the author's message: that (in the words of Tanky) 'I don't hold with heroes' – or war. [...]

It is a systematic devaluation of the conventional military values of the Second W.W. [...]

Dingo is a model anti-hero, whose sole motivation is to avoid action and to direct all comers to the nearest minefield. Mogg, his 'civilian' friend, has romantic military aspirations. Tanky joins Dingo and Mogg when his tank is [hit by enemy fire]; he is haunted by his failure to release his friend Chalky, who is burned to death inside. The Comic appears every now and again as an entertainer to the troops. He is in part a caricature of FM Lord Montgomery whose desert homilies are parodied. [...]

Attention is directed to:

I/7: ...these **fucking** Eyties haven't got the stamina [*Alter*...]

I/12: **I haven't had a good toss off in months** [*Alter*]

II/2/6: You're a collaborating **shagnasty** [*Alter*]

II/2/8: Morale is shot to **buggery** [*Alter*]

II/2/28: **'kin hell** ... [*Alter*]

II/2/32: **Right up his arse** [*Alter*]

II/2/36: Ghoulish **buggers** [*Alter*] [...]

Ronald Hill (secretary to the Lord Chamberlain), memo to the assistant comptroller, December 1964

Asst. Comptroller,

I have had time only to skim through.

As the reader says, it falls into the patter of the 'avant-garde' of this country which now secures such disproportionate publicity for its efforts to undermine in every way the nation's will to resist. The ghastly effects of propaganda of this sort were seen in the abject surrender of France to the Germans, and the effect could be just as serious here.

Assistant comptroller to the Lord Chamberlain, 14 December 1964

[*Dingo*] is a terrible play with a sinister theme and dreadful dialogue. I would like to recommend that you refuse a licence, but we shall have to make do with cuts.

1/3–1/5: I think the screaming of the burning soldier must be toned right down.

1/18: Presumably it will be a dummy of an incinerated corpse, but is bound to be a fairly disgusting sight. If it is cut out we may be accused of trying to hide the horrors of war etc. [...]

Unsigned and unaddressed note, 26 January 1965

Sir Laurence Olivier and Mr Kenneth Tynan came to see [the L.C.] today to discuss *Dingo*.

The [L.C.] expressed his desire not to have an open row with the National Theatre over a controversial play that might receive publicity in the press. [...]

It was decided [they] would consult further with the author, who has the sole copyright, and re-submit it with the words and phrases that are so obviously unacceptable deleted.

Tynan, memo to
Olivier, 11 February
1965

Dingo

The Lord Chamberlain's office will not licence the play in
its present form. The changes he would require fell into the
following categories:

1) Deletion or substitution of all the obvious four-letter words.
The same applies to p.17: the sexual image about grease in the
breech block.

2) More explicit stage directions to clarify the action in
passages he considers needlessly horrific. This includes Chalky's
screaming (which mustn't be continuous), the charred corpse
(which mustn't be realistic), the bayonetings in Act 2.

3) The blasphemy: the L. C. objects to the frequent use of 'Jesus'.

4) *Lèse-Majesté*: the L. C. doesn't like the reference to George
VI not wanting to be king. The medal pinned to the blonde's
knickers should not be the DSO.

5) Impersonations of living persons: a composite general is
okay but he mustn't be identifiable as Viscount Montgomery.

I told [him] that we had postponed any further action until
John Dexter had returned to London and discussed the position
with myself and Charles Wood.

K. T.

cc John Dexter, William Gaskill

Peggy Ramsay
(Wood's agent) to
Tynan, 22 April 1965

Dear Ken,

Thank you so much for telephoning and saying that provided
Albert Finney wants to play in [*Dingo*], the National will do it in
March next year.

If Finney wants to do it, and John Dexter is still keen, then of
course you must keep the play and do it. Charles wholly endorses
this.

Ever yours,
Peggy

Ramsay and Wood waited another two years for the NT to produce Dingo, *but finally
gave up hope and withdrew it. It was premiered at Bristol Arts Centre in April 1967. That
November, Geoffrey Reeves's production moved to the Royal Court, where its audience
included film producer Otto Plaschkes.*

Otto Plaschkes
to Charles Wood,
28 November 1967

Dear Charles

I saw *Dingo* last week and genuinely loved it. It is a super play, so
beautiful theatrically, and so effective and, indeed, so moving.
Not only I but the entire audience loved it and left the theatre
feeling 'now <u>there's</u> a play'.

Congratulations.

Sincerely yours,
Otto

1965

The Crucible (1953)
by Arthur Miller
Director: Laurence Olivier
Old Vic, 19 January 1965 to 2 March 1966 (54 performances)

Laurence Olivier and Arthur Miller got to know one another when Miller's then wife, Marilyn Monroe, starred opposite Olivier in the film The Prince and the Showgirl *(1957).*

In The Crucible, *Miller's dramatisation of the 1692 witch trials in Salem, Massachusetts – his allegorical response to anti-communist 'witch-hunts' – John Proctor has been unfaithful to his wife, Elizabeth, in a brief affair with their young maid, Abigail Williams. Abigail, with Mary Warren and other girls, is accused of witchcraft.*

Olivier to Arthur Miller, 15 August 1964

Dear Arthur,

I'm delighted to be doing the play. I feel like a young chap in love for the first time. I think and I pray that we shall do the thing well, and I hope to your satisfaction. The dialogue seems absolutely to dictate, in most instances, a countrified lilt of some sort.

I have never thought that Abigail's line [to Proctor] in Act I 'I know how you clutched my back' really indicated the extent of the thing that had really occurred, which we learn from Elizabeth and later from Proctor, is a complete act of sex. Do you think you might strengthen Abigail's line into meaning all that it should mean?

Ever,
Larry

Miller to Olivier, 17 August 1964

Dear Larry,

You delighted? Not half as much as I am to think that at last the play will be done by a man who actually is concerned with its language instead of trying to figure out how to make it sound 'unobtrusive'!

I have always felt that English actors were closer to this play than Americans who have to don its speech with their costumes.

Now you mention these things I imagine I must have been a more delicate creature when I wrote this years ago. I will apply my latter-day indelicacy. Joe Harris directed the play at the height of the McCarthy hysteria. Whether the times or his temperament dictated it, the attitude created a 'classic' ballet-like production in which the heat of passion hardly entered except by remote implication. The play was done again some seven years later off-Broadway, by a much less accomplished cast, but this time with an unimpeded thrust of feeling. The first production was called cold, and quite rightly; the second ran two years. I'm only sorry that you aren't Proctor, but the news of your directing it lit up the sky.

> Ever yours,
> Arthur

Lynn Redgrave, the youngest of Michael's three actor children, was 21, and had played five small parts with the Company when she wrote to Olivier.

Lynn Redgrave to Olivier, 2 August 1964	Dear Sir Laurence,

Ever since I learned that *The Crucible* is being done next season I have felt slightly sick!

This is because ever since I first read the play aged 10 – and later saw a production of it – I have coveted the part of Mary Warren.

I have never felt so strongly about a part as to feel actually jealous in advance that 'someone else' might play it – till now.

You have probably cast it already – or maybe don't think I am suitable. If so – so be it! But I had at least to ask you to consider me.

Forgive me.

> Love,
> Lynny
> (Redgrave)

Mary, 17, and described in Miller's stage directions as 'subservient, naïve, lonely', was played by Jeanne Hepple, perhaps because Crucible *rehearsals clashed with those for* Much Ado About Nothing, *in which Redgrave was Margaret, Hero's maid.*

Richard Hatton, telegram to Olivier, 19 August 1964	OUR CLIENT SEAN CONNERY WOULD LOVE TO PLAY PROCTOR IN THE CRUCIBLE WHICH HE DID VERY SUCCESSFULLY ON TELEVISION IF YOU WANTED HIM AND WE THINK DATES COULD BE ARRANGED ARE YOU INTERESTED SINCERELY
RICHARD HATTON

Olivier was 'touched' that Connery – who had already appeared as James Bond in Dr. No *and* From Russia with Love – *should 'offer his services', but had already chosen Colin Blakely as Proctor. Miller later told Olivier that this was the best* Crucible *he had ever seen.*

Arthur Miller (left) is greeted by Laurence
Olivier at the NT 'huts', ahead of the press night
for Miller's *The Crucible*

Much Ado About Nothing (c.1598)

by William Shakespeare

Director: Franco Zeffirelli
Old Vic, 16 February 1965 to 19 June 1966 (113 performances)

In Much Ado…, *Ian McKellen, then 25, made his NT debut, as Claudio, and had also been
cast as Captain de Foenix in* Trelawny of the Wells, *and as The Evangelist, one of the
leading roles in* Armstrong's Last Goodnight; *both would open during the forthcoming
(and final) NT residency at Chichester.*

Ian McKellen to
Olivier, 22 April 1965

Dear Sir Laurence,

After a week's thought, I have decided not to accept your offer of
a three-year contract. I think that refusal of so generous a contract
needs explanation.

First I am aware of the advantages of working with the [NT].
Of these advantages, the security doesn't appeal to me at this
moment in my career and life. Having spent most of my few
years as an actor with three good repertory theatres, I know I can
work well in a permanent company and enjoy it tremendously.

But perhaps, and of course I have doubts, now is the time to be on my own and explore a little. My temperament is generally too unadventurous.

The crux of the decision, though, is my ambition: my ambition to achieve the recognition as an actor which will help me to be eventually a senior member of a company like yours. You can't promise, and I didn't expect you to, any certainty of that recognition over the next three years. The [NT] will enhance an actor's reputation but not obviously make it. I think there is more chance of establishing my ability publicly elsewhere and this I shall now try and do.

Again my thanks to you for your offer and for having me in the company at all! I enjoy *Much Ado* as much as the part allows and look forward enormously to Chichester.

And I really hope that my absence from the National Theatre will be only temporary.

All best wishes,
Yours ever,
Ian McKellen

Olivier to Elspeth Cochrane (McKellen's agent), 29 April 1965

Dear Miss Cochrane,

I am very unhappy about Ian McKellen's decision.

I feel that after so short an engagement – indeed it is barely two months since he opened for us – there has been no time allowed either for him to do well by us, or for us to do well by him.

I have a very strong instinct that his future with the National would be a happy and bright one.

He has made a very good start, and although there is nothing of a dazzlingly striking nature [yet] in his collection of repertoire, the collection itself has started, and it is a shame to let this go now because as time goes by such collections are perforce going to be made more and more slowly by anybody who joins the Company, the later that they join it or re-join it.

I recognise that anybody is entitled to second thoughts, and I will not deny to you that the practical considerations that drive me towards making this plea now, present me with many difficult problems for the next few months, which are appallingly jammed up, but this apart, it is really the spectre of lost opportunity that haunts me.

The question of [leaves of absence for] films is one consideration with which we can cope, but West End jobs, or commercial theatre successes, are going to do nothing to help him in [an NT] career; for which I truly believe he is best suited, both for the sake of the development of his talents and for his artistic happiness.

Yours sincerely,
Laurence Olivier

McKellen did not change his mind. After leaving the National, he was named Plays & Players' *Most Promising Actor of 1966, for Arnold Wesker's* Their Very Own and Golden City *(Royal Court); he did not return to Olivier's Company.*

*Virtue with Bottles***

by Ken Campbell

Ken Campbell was just 23 when he first submitted a play to the National.

Ken Campbell to
Kenneth Tynan,
25 September 1965

Dear Mr Tynan,

Please find enclosed my play *Virtue with Bottles.*
    It seems at first as if it's 'way out'. In fact it's 'quite near'. Far be it from me to tell you how to read scripts – just this script. Take the first act gently and meet the guests of Amelia's Hotel through the eyes of the outsider, Sigmund Cott, and then I think you'll find it all falls neatly into place. Perhaps an added word about Sigmund Cott would be helpful. Cott is a witty, intellectual alcoholic. Due to the slightly contrived circumstances of his meeting with Amelia's eccentric guests, he believes them to be madder than they are. In fact they are not mad at all. But Cott revels for the most part in the madness, as he sees it, of these people. He is a man who is never happier than in utter chaos. Also he is a lonely man. He is a wit with no one to be witty to. Hence he is inclined to play his life to an imaginary audience.
    I look forward to hearing your reactions.

Yours sincerely,
  Kenneth Campbell

Campbell's work was not produced during the Olivier tenure, but his epic Illuminatus! *(1977) would open the Cottesloe.*

1966

Black Comedy (1965)

by Peter Shaffer

Director: John Dexter
Old Vic, 8 March 1966 to 1 February 1967 (46 performances)

Black Comedy is set in a struggling young artist's London flat, which is plunged into darkness by a blown fuse. Audience enjoyment of the ensuing farce depends on a visual conceit: when the stage is blacked out, the flat's electric lights are assumed to be on; when it is fully illuminated, we accept that the characters are fumbling in a blackout.

John Bird to Kenneth Tynan, 6 May 1965

Dear Ken,

[…] I'm bound to say, even after (mainly) your gallant salvage attempts, that I'm still tremendously pessimistic. I am more and more convinced that no amount of hasty doctoring is going to rescue this script from its fundamental difficulties. This idea is so original I don't think it is matched at any point by this slim and rather pointless comedy of manners and I don't think that playing about with the characters is going to alter that basic weakness.

The visual idea <u>is</u> brilliant, there's no doubt about that, and must be built on, by author, director and actors, very slowly, very carefully, with lots of time for experiment, necessary false starts, and revision. The National/Chichester season [doesn't] seem remotely to allow that, and the more I think about it, the madder it appears to go on with it.

As Larry seems determined to go on with Peter's play come what may, and as I'm pretty convinced I won't like the rewrite that miraculously much more, the best thing is for me to withdraw right now, as it will give you more time to find a director who does like it. I don't feel so bad about the NT, as they were prepared to drop the whole thing (and me) a week or so ago, but I don't want to drop you in the shit, you who suggested me in the first place (and doing the brilliant grinding away at it since then). But it would be completely suicidal to add to the problems a director out of sympathy with the piece. Apart from anything else, this immediately communicates itself to the actors, thus making 13 people miserable instead of only two (you and me).

I'm writing this very late at night, so I'll drive up now and drop it in to you. Sorry this letter is so illiterate, but I'm a bit clapped out.

Yours ever,
John

Opposite: *Black Comedy,* featuring (on table)
Derek Jacobi and Maggie Smith.
Photo: Zoë Dominic

Olivier immediately cabled John Dexter, who took on Black Comedy *as his second Shaffer premiere.*

**Peter Shaffer to
Olivier, 7 June 1965**

Dear Larry,

I'm so glad you like *Black Comedy*. It was written in nine days during a break from work on *Public Eye* [film] script. I hope it's alright. Naturally I'm nervous about anything written at such a speed, particularly something for an illustrious company to be performed in a now very famous theatre. It couldn't have had more inventive sweat poured over it if it were *Royal Hunt*! They were nine days of very hard work – largely because of the mechanics. Farce is hard, hard, hard to write. (To act, no doubt, even harder.) All those stage directions, and constant visualisation of what is going on with everybody on stage at the same time, etc. etc. I only hope the net result will be a credit to us all. […]

I'll be back next week, for those no doubt mad rehearsals.

Love,
　　Peter

In Chichester, Black Comedy *was acclaimed as 'a landmark in laughter' (*The Sun*), and Shaffer wrote to Olivier: 'Audiences seem to love it, and that is the main thing. But also it really does provide a stylistic exercise for the company, and that is surely a good thing too.'*

A Bond Honoured (1966)

by John Osborne

Based on *La Fianza Satisfecha* (*c*.1612) by Lope de Vega
Director: John Dexter
Old Vic, 6 June 1966 to 1 February 1967 (40 performances)

As Observer *drama critic, Kenneth Tynan had helped make John Osborne's reputation, with a rave review of* Look Back in Anger *(1956). When the NT* Hamlet *opened in October 1963, Tynan had already commissioned Osborne to adapt de Vega's play.*

John Osborne to
Kenneth Tynan,
4 November 1963

Dear Ken,

I am sorry to complain or sound ill-used but I do seem to be getting a whole lot of shit from the [NT]. I think you should know about it because I fancy I am not the only one to experience it. In fact I know it.

First: I understand about the difficulty of getting seats for the plays – *Hamlet* in particular – but this sort of thing should be provided for in a properly run box office. Anyway, I got nix from trying. My secretary spent an hour and a half trying to get two tickets (I asked for three). Her diction is quite good but she spelt my name out slowly and carefully to Renee Gilmore, who had never heard of me. Fair enough. But she didn't seem very interested.

Miss Gilmore: 'In what way is he connected with Sir Laurence?'

My secretary: 'He's writing a play for the National ...'

Gilmore rang back later saying they'd found a pair but it was all very difficult etc., apparently she is sending me an application form.

I haven't had the seats yet but I fancy they'll be behind the only pillar in the place. It might have seemed inappropriate, or perhaps no one thought of it at all, to have put my name on the list in the first place, particularly when I think of all the sycophants, time servers and layabouts who were. I know the Vic now is a small theatre but it's rotten policy, unnecessary and unfriendly.

Part of the explanation may be my discovery that [your administrator] Stephen Arlen doesn't exist. Perhaps I shall find him playing the Player King – that is if he's visible from my seat.

It is last May since you approached me about a play. Since then I've not had a letter, let alone a contract from the Management. Margery Vosper [Osborne's agent] says no one answers the 'phone, or when they do, no one seems to know what's going on and Stephen Arlen is rehearsing the Player King and unavailable. I don't really give a stuff but it doesn't seem exactly serious. I know Brecht never answered letters but I could go into his theatre without having to ring bells.

Sorry to complain, hope all is well.

Yours,
    John

**Tynan to Osborne,
5 November 1963**

Dear John,

[…] I have convened a midnight coven of the Vic–Wells supporters club to conjure Stephen Arlen [formerly of Sadler's Wells Opera]. He appeared spitting brimstone and ticket stubs – belligerently shouting 'Contracts? Contracts? Tommy Beecham never had a contract in his life. My handshake was good enough for Tommy' I don't know if you know Stephen Arlen's handshake. If you see it lying around, tread on the fingers. I have shown him your letter and he promises to write to you. I've proposed to him that the play should be regarded as 'based on Lope de Vega' and that you should receive the same royalties as for an original play.

I have also asked him about the extra ticket but I gather that he really has run out of house seats. Perhaps one day he will run out of the house and never come back. […]

Love,
Ken

On 22 May 1964, Tynan asked Osborne when he might deliver the de Vega script, explaining that Peter O'Toole and Paul Scofield were being 'heavily discussed' for the lead, Leonido, who attacks a priest, blinds his father and seduces his sister, before being miraculously redeemed by a Christ figure, and crucified.

**Osborne to Tynan,
29 May 1964**

Dear Ken,

Only just got back. I've been working at a tremendous rate on two other things for quite a long time, so perhaps I'm a bit demented. However, I have been brooding over the Lope, doing my usual notes bit and hope you will have it by October or November […]

Penelope sends love.

As ever,
John

In London in 1946 Alec Guinness had played the Fool to Olivier's King Lear, in a production which Olivier also directed.

**Olivier to
Alec Guinness,
28 August 1964**

My dear Alec,

I have been longing to get you in the National, and I have spied out an opportunity.

Would it appeal to you, to open in Chichester as The Merchant and as the Christ figure in a new adaptation by John Osborne of *La Fianza Satisfecha*, and then bring them into the following season at the Vic?

Please let me hear from you.

Yours as ever, with love,
Larry

**Guinness to Olivier,
8 September 1964**

Dear Larry,

I am very honoured and delighted by your kind suggestion, though I have a feeling I am not going to be able to accept. I owe Columbia Pictures a film and there is a possible [Columbia] project for next summer. If I do it, I will then be free of all my film contracts which have saddled me for the past ten years, and then I shall be free to come and go as I please. In any case, I am not sure that I would be very keen to play Shylock (if that was your idea). Old Gobbo, yes. My great regret in feeling I must say no on this occasion, apart from disappointing you, is missing the chance to act in the Lope de Vega play.

I am so very sorry to be missing your Othello of which I hear the most tremendous things from all quarters.

Marula and I will be back in England in late September. I then have a month's holiday before going to Germany to film. I do hope you have a wonderful and refreshing holiday. And no doubt we shall be bumping into each other, sweating, groaning and trembling at that very expensive gymnasium.

Affectionately,
Alec

Guinness saying no allowed Olivier to ask John Gielgud to portray the Christ figure, but this role went to Graham Crowden. Robert Stephens was Leonido.

**Neil Fitzpatrick,
accident report,
12 May 1966**

During rehearsal, on Old Vic stage, Wednesday 11 May 1966, for *A Bond Honoured*, I accidentally struck actor Robert Stephens on back of left hand, with a sword to be used in production, causing a cut which severed a tendon on this hand and resulting, among other things, in Mr Stephens being unable to perform in current productions involving him, until further notice.

This incident occurred during a sword fight required by the play under rehearsal.

Neil Fitzpatrick

The injury postponed the Bond Honoured *press night from 31 May to 6 June. It opened to largely hostile reviews. The Times's (unbylined) critic, Irving Wardle, argued that Osborne had 'gone to work more in a spirit of self-indulgence than of re-interpretation'.*

**Nellie Osborne,
telegram to Osborne,
7 June 1966**

MY DEAR SON HOW DARE THESE CRITICS PULL TO PIECES SUCH FINE WORK, FOR TEN YEARS THEY HAVE INSULTED YOUR ART IN THE THEATRE, TO ME THEY JUST SMELL, I HATE THEM, KEEP UP YOUR COURAGE AND GUTS AND DON'T LET THEM HURT YOU. PLEASE FORGIVE THIS MESSAGE I AM SO MAD REALLY MAD JOHN AND SAD, KNOWING HOW KIND AND LOYAL YOU ARE TO SO MANY, HOW CRUEL CAN THESE LITTLE WEE MEN GET HOW I HATE THEM YOUR SAD MUM LOVE TO YOU BOTH.

The *Daily Mail* reports
Osborne's reaction to
the reviews for *A Bond
Honoured*

Osborne declares war on critics

By Daily Mail Reporter

Osborne, telegram
to Irving Wardle, and
Daily Telegraph and
Daily Mail, 8 June
1966

THE GENTLEMAN'S AGREEMENT TO IGNORE PUNY CRITICS
AS BOURGEOIS CONVENTIONS THAT KEEP YOU PINNED
IN YOUR SOFT SEATS IS A THING THAT I FALL IN WITH
NO LONGER. AFTER TEN YEARS IT IS NOW WAR. NOT A
CAMPAIGN OF CONSIDERATE COMPLAINTS IN PRIVATE
LETTERS BUT OPEN AND FRONTAL WAR THAT WILL BE AS
PUBLIC AS I AND OTHER MEN OF EARNED REPUTATION
HAVE THE CONSIDERABLE POWER TO MAKE IT.

Wardle to Osborne,
8 June 1966

Dear Mr Osborne,

Thanks for the bumper telegram. I don't suppose there's
much point in replying to it as I now seem to have swung into
position as THE ENEMY and anything I say will be read as
further evidence of my treacherous, parasitic, and cowardly
nature: no doubt the fact that I'm only spending 4d on replying
to you will be added confirmation of my fear of risks. But here
goes.

It beats me why you, with your contempt for my profession
whose support you no longer need, should be so upset by a piece
in *The Times*. The only reason I can think of is that you don't
judge reviewers according to whether or not they talk sense (how
could we, we don't understand), but according to their loyalty to
you personally. I've been loyal until this week; so no doubt you've
been prepared to tolerate my other shortcomings, waiting for me
to confirm your mistrust of critics by turning with a knife in my
hand.

But from the reviewing end, it can't work for that: not for me
anyway. I think you're the best dramatist we've got, but I feel no
loyalty whatever to you personally. I don't know you. All I know
are the plays. Now I find one that sticks in my craw. What the
hell am I supposed to do – ignore the immediate response and
write some piece of soft-soaping equivocation because I admired
your work last time? I don't call that living dangerously. Maybe
you're right; perhaps there are marvels of technique and language
in the play that I was too dim to recognise. If your work creates
appetites, then presumably it will do so in spite of people like me.
All I can do is try to make sense of it with the limited equipment
I've got. As for English sadism, I didn't say you were writing to
gratify it: I said I thought it was on the wane. But you surprise me
if you say that you have no appetite for cruelty; how else can you
write about it if you haven't got the appetite to begin with? I don't

know what you mean by open war; but I'm told you used to be a boxer, and if you fancy a gentlemanly British punch-up I'm more than ready to oblige.

Yours,
Irving Wardle

THANK YOU FOR YOUR NICE NOTE. STOP. I STILL THINK YOU WERE UNCHARITABLE NOT PERSONALLY THAT IS UNIMPORTANT BUT ABOUT WORK SERIOUSLY UNDERTAKEN AND I DON'T THINK THE TIMES SHOULD BE AS FRIVOLOUS AS ALL THE OTHERS. STOP. AFTER TEN YEARS' GRIND IT DID SEEM RATHER A BOOT IN THE FACE FROM AN UNEXPECTED QUARTER. STOP. HOWEVER IT'S ALL A BIT LARKY. STOP. I'M BIGGER THAN YOU BUT I'M SURE YOU'RE STRONGER SO LET'S FORGET IT – JOHN OSBORNE

My dear Johnnie,

You may regard this letter as a carefully put off piece of apologia stuff, but please do believe me it isn't any kind of shenanigan. [...]

I did have every single intention of bringing back *Bond* with *Black* [*Comedy*] during the summer, and I must not claim that Maggie [Smith]'s earlier-than-expected departure has really made all that [much] difference in that her understudy [Carolyn Jones], who played a couple of times, turned out to be a very promising replacement – and Joanie [Plowright] could have taken over in *Black*, but due to circs beyond our [control] I have had to switch the productions of *Three Sisters* and *As You* [*Like It*] around. This gives us not a cat's chance of getting [*Bond*] back in.

I am terribly disappointed about it. It is my job to be disappointed most of the time so I would rather disappoint myself than you but now that I am disappointing both of us I am really wretched. Please don't be too cross with us.

All my love, as ever
Larry

A handwritten note added to the bottom of this letter reads: 'John's reply – thanks but what he expected!!'

Three years later, Robert Stephens was rehearsing the NT Hedda Gabler *with his wife, Maggie Smith, who had played Leonido's incestuous sister in* A Bond Honoured.

My dear Robert,

[...] What I have always felt about the [NT] and all who sail in her, including yourself [is that] it is full of schoolgirlish commercialism, over-weening ambition, one-shot competitiveness (with its hangers-on and pushers), but, above all, ultimate and complete timidity as well as third rate politicking and treachery. I shall do all the little I can to draw attention to it. However, it all matters little enough, I dare say.

What is baffling about you, Robert, like others, is your consistently faulty character reading. Perhaps it comes of living in a world of professional parochial fantasy. Quite a long time ago, as you will remember, hordes of hacks and plush nonentities used to go into Larry's dressing room [at the Royal Court when he was playing Archie Rice in Osborne's *The Entertainer*] and complain about the inadequacies and what Margaret [Smith] would no doubt call 'the disappointment' of *The Entertainer*. Why you should imagine I should be affected at this stage by this kind of dressing room lizard does surprise me a little. It was only too easy to ignore. Larry and Vivien [Leigh]'s sycophants, in the event, are not much different from yours and Margaret's. What is strange is that you should be unable to recognise it.

> Indeed, as ever,
>   Yours,
>   John

Stephens to Osborne, 11 June 1970

My dear John,

Everything you say about the NT is perfectly true.

As to our Director, he is a vain, jealous and ageing man who, and God knows who ever permitted it, has total artistic control despite the advice of his associates and his board. I however am no longer fearful of him nor impressed by him and I shall do my utmost to change the system. I thought and think still that *The Entertainer* is one of your most marvellous plays. Margaret has never seen it.

Neither Margaret or I have ever entertained, for one second, any kind of sycophants. Margaret is too Scots and too sharp and too intelligent and I don't need or want that kind of attention.

What is of the utmost importance is that [*A Bond Honoured*] which was, despite my desperate pleas, dropped, by Larry, from the repertoire should now be seen by as many people as possible. I have talked to the director who is more than keen and obviously understands the play better than John Dexter and, from our conversation, better than I did. The casting must be done with the utmost care and attention. We shall rehearse it for 3–4 weeks then shoot it on film rather than tape. Please let us meet soon.

I love you very much and I never want to lose your affection for me: people and circumstances have, it seems, worked hard to destroy it, we must not allow that to happen.

> Always,
>   Robert XXX

The proposed film of A Bond Honoured *never materialised.*

The Burning Man**
by Pam Gems

Pam Gems was 41 when she sent Kenneth Tynan The Burning Man. *Set in the 1950s, it follows a school English teacher (and frustrated writer), Elizabeth Swann, her science lecturer husband, and her most intelligent pupil, Christina.*

Pam Gems to
Kenneth Tynan,
1 November 1966

Dear Mr Tynan,

Will you read the enclosed for me? It is a play about the nature of work, about what to do with the best of oneself. I reckon it should run about two hours. I have written about eight plays for television, not all performed. This is the first time I have tried to do a stage play. I must say I have found it very hard to do. Perhaps you can tell me whether I am anywhere near it.

    Yours sincerely,
    P. Gems

Bembridge,
Isle of Wight.
November 1st. 1966

Dear Mr. Tynan,

    Will you read the enclosed for me?
It is a play about the nature of work, about what to do with the best of oneself. I reckon it should run about two hours. I have written about eight plays for television, not all performed. This is the first time I have tried to do a stage play. I must say I have found it very hard to do. Perhaps you can tell me whether I am anywhere near it.

    Yours sincerely,
    P. Gems

Jean Benedetti,
report on *The
Burning Man*, 15 [?]
December 1966

This author has a gift for naturalistic dialogue. Unfortunately too much of the play takes place in a class-room or a lecture room. The structure aimed at seems to me more suited to a TV treatment. I think this writer should be encouraged.

1967

The Dance of Death (1901)
by August Strindberg
Translated by C. D. Locock (1929)
Director: Glen Byam Shaw
Old Vic, 21 February 1967 to 25 July 1969 (79 performances)

Strindberg's play, set in an artillery fortress, explores the tempestuous marriage of Alice, a former actress, and Edgar, the fortress Captain – a role Olivier hoped might appeal to Paul Scofield, who (despite telling Olivier he wished to join the Company) had turned down The Royal Hunt of the Sun.

Olivier to Paul Scofield, 13 May 1964

My dear Paul,

[…] I am burningly desirous that you should be attached to the [NT], if that doesn't sound too much like a prison sentence, and that we in our turn should be useful to you in contributing to your stage career by forming an interesting and attractive pattern of life which might at once relieve you of worry and provide you with all you might desire. […]

I have nothing more fascinatingly original to suggest than *The Dance of Death* or *Edward II.*

News of your fabulous personal success [as King Lear] comes clocking in from various parts of the world as regular as signals from Night Stage Door Keepers to the Central Fire Station. […]

Yours ever,
Larry

Scofield to Olivier, 7 July 1964

My dear Larry,

[…] I have to tell you straight away that I do not at this time want to do it. […]

You have been so welcoming and your suggestions so exciting, I hope for the opportunity to be able to meet & match them.

I feel a little crazy writing this letter, I hope you will understand my ill-expressed state & feelings.

A thousand congratulations on what you have already achieved & all my good wishes for what follows.

Thank you.

Yours sincerely,
Paul

Scofield would eventually play Edgar on ITV in a Dance of Death *broadcast in 1966.*
Olivier approached a director who had staged other Strindberg scripts in his native Sweden.

Olivier, cable to
Ingmar Bergman,
7 February 1966

DEAR MR BERGMAN

I HAVE OF COURSE A GREAT AMBITION THAT YOU MIGHT
ONE DAY DIRECT A PLAY FOR THE BRITISH NATIONAL
THEATRE
    WOULD IT BE POSSIBLE FOR YOU TO CONSIDER THE
DANCE OF DEATH FOR THIS COMPANY OPENING EARLY
SEPTEMBER STOP […]

YOURS WITH EVERY GOOD WISH AND ADMIRATION
    LAURENCE OLIVIER

*Bergman cabled back that, although 'very happy and honoured' to be asked, prior
commitments obliged him to say no (he would revive Ibsen's* Hedda Gabler *for the NT in 1970).
Olivier turned to Glen Byam Shaw, his director on* Macbeth *in Stratford in 1955.*

Olivier to Glen Byam
Shaw, 15 February
1966

Dear One,

Here is [*Dance of Death*] – For my money the translation is as
good as I think we get, but you may have other ideas.

    I am having trouble, just at this moment, in nailing down [Leo]
McKern, and so the date has temporarily become unstuck but as I
am not going to be able to latch on to Gerry [Geraldine McEwan]
indefinitely without this part [Alice] the dates most desirable
would still seem to be Rehearse 18 July (7 weeks), Open 5 Sept.
But this feast is as moveable as may be required to get you for it,
my darling.

    Ever your devoted,
      L

Byam Shaw to Olivier,
20 February 1966

Dearest Larry,

Oh what a joy about the play. Strindberg! A most agonising and
brutal, but completely true, interpreter of human relationships.
Having read the play I said to Angela 'No one in the world
could portray the Captain except Larry. McKern can't do it in a
thousand years.'

    The Captain is all that is terrible, and also true and even good,
in the male. Only a great actor could possibly play such a part.

    It is all positive.

    Alice is monstrously feminine. Kurt is the eternal good friend,
who is awful.

    And then the young people!

    The girl! Marvellous! How Strindberg hated women of any
age.

    Well he was a genius, and that's for sure.

    I can never thank you enough for asking me to direct this
remarkable play in your theatre, and – thank god – with you.

    Angela joins in sending fondest love to you both.

    Yours as ever,
      Glen

Dance of Death opened with Olivier, McEwan, and Robert Stephens as Kurt.

Olivier to Oliver Lyttelton (NT chairman), 23 February 1967

My dear Oliver,

I am so infinitely grateful to you for writing to me such a perfectly lovely letter, which makes me feel both proud and happy.

I enjoy the Captain, much less of a brain-tease than the Ibsen [Solness in the NT *Master Builder* in 1964–65], though both authors seem to know an uncomfortable amount about <u>me</u>! There's hardly a thing I haven't been guilty of saying or feeling towards some or other marriage partner; I think he was a passionate young man, as I was, and many are, or have been, and sometimes when the nature of a passion is changed by life's cruel hand, it has to find for itself another medium, as it were, like the desire to hurt, and the power to wound becomes the obsession.

I think both Gerry McEwan & Bob Stephens deserved a much more glowing reception by the press than they got, and it only makes me sad that the critics' present (and God knows, temporary) preoccupation with me should make them indulge me at other people's expense and make it appear that our National Th. is a secure home for my own opportunities, as you know well, that is the very antithesis of all that I desire.

Perhaps the [Sunday newspaper critics] will do something to restore the equilibrium. Let's hope so anyway. [...]

Yrs. Always,
Larry

Rosencrantz and Guildenstern Are Dead (1966)

by Tom Stoppard
Director: Derek Goldby
Old Vic, 11 April 1967 to 22 October 1970 (151 performances)

The action of Rosencrantz and Guildenstern Are Dead runs concurrently with that of Hamlet. Apart from brief scenes lifted from Shakespeare, it imagines the title characters en route to and inside Elsinore, and on the ship that carries them to execution in England.

Tom Stoppard was 29 when his play was first produced by Oxford University students, at the Edinburgh Festival in 1966. Kenneth Tynan secured the professional rights, and it was staged by Derek Goldby, at 26 the NT's youngest director to date, with Edward Petherbridge (Rosencrantz), John Stride (Guildenstern) and Graham Crowden (The Player).

Olivier, postcard to Edward Petherbridge, 11 April 1967

Dear Edward,

I am completely and delightedly confident in the deserved success of your brilliant performance. Just remember that nerves are a self-indulgence, and something of nothing. You have a job to do and it is going to be a good one. I wish I could see it tonight. Please give your room-mates a sip of this [champagne] from me.

Loving wishes,
L. O.

Derek Goldby to
Olivier, 12 April 1967

Dear Sir Laurence,

Thank you for allowing me to do this production. I cannot tell you
what it has meant to me to be given such an opportunity at the
NT. [Thank you for] your tremendous help and encouragement,
without ever making me feel that I had lost your confidence.

> Best wishes,
> Derek

*Rosencrantz… secured (mostly) rave reviews, and attracted Broadway producers, among
them David Merrick, whose credits included* Look Back in Anger *and* Oliver!

David Merrick, cable
to Olivier, 4 May 1967

DEAR LARRY, I AM ABSOLUTELY MAD ABOUT
ROSENCRANTZ AND GUILDENSTERN STOP PLEASE DO
EVERYTHING YOU CAN TO GET IT FOR ME STOP TERMS NO
OBJECT STOP YOU FELLOWS CAN WRITE YOUR OWN TICKET
STOP. […] BEST REGARDS
DAVID MERRICK

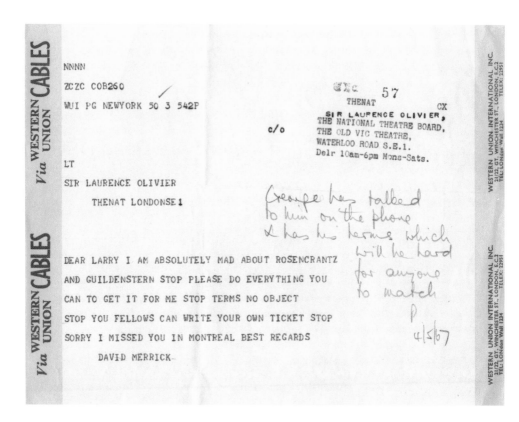

*Merrick secured the rights, and news spread of the New York transfer. It was also public
knowledge that Olivier was being treated for prostate cancer.*

Julian Glover to
Olivier, 4 July 1967

Dear Sir Laurence,

I do hope you'll pardon my writing to you personally like this, at a time which must be of especial strain for you, but I'm so anxious that I felt I must leave no stone unturned.

I've written to Tom Stoppard and Mr Goldby separately asking them to consider me as a replacement for John or Edward Petherbridge in *Rosencrantz…*, which I gather is to go to America. My desire to do this play is intense. I cannot remember being so excited in the Theatre as when I saw the public dress rehearsal and have lusted for the opportunity to say those lines ever since. I only say this to make it clear that my interest is not a mercenary one – I'm not simply asking for a job, I'm asking to be considered for this one!

I do hope you're better now. We've all watched your progress with great pleasure.

Yours sincerely,
Julian

Glover did not receive a reply. While Rosencrantz… *continued in London, Goldby, with Stoppard beside him, redirected it in America with a new cast. It reached Broadway's Alvin Theatre in October without Robert Eddison (The Player during the try-out in Washington DC), who had been replaced by Paul Hecht.*

Goldby to Olivier,
October 1967

Dear Sir Laurence,

The play is a smash hit. Business is fantastic. The only sad feature has been the replacement of Robert Eddison, a decision I had to take on my own shoulders and I am very glad I did. He was a mistake, your instinct was right. I hope it is clearly understood at the NT that the dismissal remained entirely in my hands throughout. [David Merrick] has behaved admirably.

Best wishes,
Derek

Tom Stoppard to
Olivier, 5 November
1967

Dear Larry,

We have come – wife and child – to this opulent hermitage for wrung-out writers and other refugees from the market-place [the Boca Raton Hotel and Club, Florida], to recover from two months with *R and G* and I have now recomposed myself to the point where I can put my mind to such pleasures as thanking you for your cabled luck and love, and congratulating you on the Company's enormous success in Canada. I'm very pleased that we managed to keep the NT's North American stock high, after some fears, and some good times. We could not have been better served by David Merrick – I gather he does have another side, but with us he was unobtrusive, helpful, pertinent, patient and a good provider. He spotted very early the coming-home-to-roost of your reservations about poor Robert Eddison (*mea culpa* – but in truth both our expectations were fulfilled, in that Robert got a very good press in

Washington for a rich but subtle performance which, however, by its muted intelligent reading had the oblique effect of slowing and lengthening the play). *R and G* is now starting to come out of my ears – I attended every rehearsal and every performance, and was still rehearsing last week – having promised the actors to continue on my return to New York next week fixing the odd kinks which still remain. Derek and I co-operated very satisfactorily.

Well, it's nice to be warm in November – this is a vast pink Moorish palace. We swim every day at a private beach half a mile away (we have bicycles – <u>purple</u> bicycles) and eat the best food so far encountered in America. On Friday we return to New York, and plan to stay in America for Christmas – so far we have had no opportunity to do or see anything much, so I'm taking my chance now, not knowing when there'll be another. I am beset with Chances of a Lifetime – i.e. offers to write films all over the shop, so far resisted, though <u>am</u> intrigued by the notion of doing *The Canterbury Tales*, which I had <u>never</u> read, and which I bought in Palm Beach, along with Ken Tynan's new collection of articles (good stuff for the beach). Plans are afoot for a London production of my early – first – play (which I have also re-read on the beach, rather dubiously) and a one-acter. So I suppose it will be a busy '68 , but I retain the hopes of getting on with a new play amid it all and leave the phone off the hook.

I met Terence Rattigan, briefly, when he came to see the play – found him very charming and got a kick out of it. <u>Nearly</u> met Sugar Ray Robinson, <u>nearly</u> met Walter Winchell, two myth figures out of my adolescence. Success here is very good for meeting people, or nearly meeting them. A dual radio interview with Peter Finch ended up riotously at his hotel. I suspect that my current potential for living loudly and socially in NY is limitless – but fortunately it has no attraction, and I'm looking forward to six weeks of gentle work and family life and tourist-ing. We were very lucky to get a lovely apartment in New York – on Riverside Drive, very London-ish and homely, though huge. We were offered it through friend of friend of friend of Ben Gazzara, who owns it but lives in Calif. Having a good base made all the difference – especially as the first apartment we were shown was 26 floors up, which was too frightful. It'll be a good place to give Xmas dinner to all the lonely actors.

Wednesday the rains came – warm rain, of course full of Vitamin C no doubt – but rain. And a school or flock or herd of stinging jellyfish have invaded the beaches. We return to New York in high spirits.

My fondest love to you and yours,
Tom

In May 1968, Stoppard won the Tony Award for Best Play and Merrick won Best Producer of a Play. Rosencrantz… ran on Broadway until October 1968, by when Stoppard's 'one-acter', The Real Inspector Hound, had opened in the West End. At the Old Vic, Edward Hardwicke replaced Stride as Rosencrantz, but Petherbridge continued as Guildenstern, until, after six years with the Company and three in Rosencrantz…, he left both.

Olivier to Petherbridge, 2 May 1970

My dear Edward,

I am so sorry I can't come over to say goodbye to you tonight – just as well as I should probably burst into tears! It is very sad to come to the parting of the ways and I do want you to know how sorry we are that you are leaving us and how grateful we are for all the fine work you have given us.

You take with you our very best and warmest wishes for success in 'the outside world' and high hopes that one day you will be back with us again.

And love,
Larry O.

Lord Olivier?

When the prime minister, Harold Wilson, wrote to Olivier, no actor had ever been made a peer.

Harold Wilson to Olivier, 8 May 1967

HONOURS – IN CONFIDENCE

Dear Sir Laurence,

I have it in mind on the occasion of the forthcoming list of Birthday Honours to submit your name to The Queen with a recommendation that the dignity of a Barony for Life be conferred upon you. I should be glad to know if this would be agreeable to you and I will take no steps until I have your reply.

Should The Queen approve such a recommendation, your new title would be settled on a recommendation from Garter King of Arms.

Yours sincerely,
Harold Wilson

Wilson to Olivier, 8 May 1967

HONOURS – IN CONFIDENCE

Dear Sir Laurence,

I do want you to understand that there is nothing political in the recommendation conveyed formally to you in the attached letter.

As you know, I do not regard recommendations for Life Peerages as Honours for services rendered to the State, but as a job of work. I think that you have something very important to say and I would like you to have this particular forum in which to say it.

If you are willing to accept you will of course please yourself whether to take any Whip – or sit on the cross-benches.

Yours sincerely,
Harold Wilson

Dear Prime Minister,

I am so grateful for your two letters, particularly for your very kind consideration in troubling to write the second, and for the warm sense of gratification which your gracious and kindly way of putting things gives to me.

Please understand that my life and its interests are entirely wrapped up in the National Theatre and it is the thoughts proceeding from this fact which guide my every footstep; and it is only after gruelling heart-searching that I feel I should, however reluctantly, decline this great honour.

I am a workman, certainly; an artist, hopefully; but I should be a Lord, only very uneasily.

Only from one of your gargantuan output could I hope it might not be dismissed as an impertinence, if I said, I honestly feel I have not got time for it.

You refer to, 'a job of work', and of course, I entirely appreciate the point, but consequent to it, I must reckon with the new burdens that that involves.

The extra feeling of responsibility to my new Peers; the endorsed free-for-all of distractions from my real work; social obligations and expectations stepped up a hundred-fold. I really don't think I can manage, Sir. I would have to give up acting altogether, with no time to learn or give due study to my roles – (an increasing worry at my time of life), and I don't think, perhaps, I ought to do that quite yet, or take from my growing company that companionship, or rob myself of it.

Paradoxically, I feel that my position all round might be weakened, not strengthened by accepting this enviable step up. I doubt if I should find myself more strongly placed with my future Peers, and I fear some strange loss of face with my fellow artists and with the man in the street; and it is to these last two that I feel most sense of responsibility for the conduct and image of their National Theatre.

I am aware that there is much weakness and naivety in my arguments and that far cleverer ones could demolish them easily; but though there has not really been an abundance of time for consideration, I feel certain enough that the conviction which my poor reasonings struggle to fortify will remain.

There are many considerations which will, no doubt, combine to make me regret this decision, not the least of which would have been the sensation of jostling next to my revered uncle [Sydney], the first Labour Peer, I believe, and Secretary for India in 1926.

I am deeply sensible of the honour you have done me, Sir, and shall feel most humbly grateful for it all my life.

Yrs. sincerely,
  L. Olivier

Three Sisters (1901)

by Anton Chekhov

Translated by Moura Budberg (1967)
Director: Laurence Olivier
Old Vic, 4 July 1967 to 26 April 1969 (73 performances)

Anthony Hopkins, then 29, had understudied Olivier in The Dance of Death, *performing four times as Edgar when the Director had appendicitis, and, in Olivier's words, seizing the role 'like a cat with a mouse between its teeth'. In* Three Sisters *Hopkins was the title characters' brother, Andrei.*

Sunny Amey (NT repertory manager) to Anthony Hopkins, 1 November 1967	Dear Tony,

I understand you have been experimenting with growing a beard for your film.

I am so sorry but I did say that it wouldn't be possible for you to do this at this stage.

Obviously it is wrong for the part of Andrei to appear looking scruffy at the beginning of the play, which I believe he did look last night. […]

Your release was certainly not conditional upon your being allowed to grow a beard. I think we could agree to allow you to start growing one after 16th November, provided you were prepared to tidy it up for *Three Sisters*. But I shall certainly have to ask Sir Laurence's permission. […]

Sincerely,
Sunny Amey

Katharine Hepburn to Olivier, November 1967	Dear Larry,

I am sitting here in the hills of Delgany [Ireland] near the Ardmore Studio – about to begin a movie with Peter O'Toole – *The Lion in Winter* – One of your actors – Tony Hopkins – is playing our son Richard – Apparently they signed him with the full understanding that from time to time specifically – November 28 and Dec 1st for *Much Ado* – for Dec 8, Jan 10, Jan 11, for *Three Sisters* – he would rush back to play for you –

Now faced with it – it is of course an agony for all concerned – as most of us are ever present in every scene – The boy naturally is not a bit bothered by rushing back and forth – being 23 [sic] – But we think of the fog and my stop date as I have to begin *Mad Woman of Chaillot* on February 5 –

Don't you have some remarkable understudy whom you could put on in his place – I know I've not a damn bit of shame – writing you this sad letter – but I simply wanted to suggest that if there were a possibility that it would not be too difficult for you – it would certainly make a hell of a difference to all of us –

Dear Larry, – Don't even answer this if you think – Oh my God – but if – only if it's practical and you have someone –

[The producers] haven't a leg to stand on – just a dumb arrangement – I am writing on my own – just in case – you are in a position to help the stupid –

How thrilled Irene Selznick was with you in Canada – it's a long way from [you appearing in] *The Green Bay Tree* [on Broadway in 1932] – What a remarkable fellow you turned out to be – – – –

My love,
K H

Olivier to Hepburn,
30 November 1967

Darling Girl,

I am awfully sorry to seem unsympathetic. The letting go of this boy, Tony Hopkins, has caused us all an untellable history of agonies of worry, elaborate re-shufflings, and gallons of midnight oil. I would claim before all the world far greater depths of inconvenience than could ever happen to any of you dear creatures, fog and your stop date and all.

There is certainly no time left to get anybody ready to take his place as understudy (we have never yet foisted understudies on the public so that somebody may do a film) before his replacement [Robert Stephens] goes in on January 30th.

Sorry to scream, darling, but we really have been through quite a bit of hell to oblige this lad and your film people, to help a situation from which we get no benefit at all.

All love, as ever,
Your
Larry

In Three Sisters, *Derek Jacobi had played Baron Tusenbach, until Olivier asked him to take over from Stephens as Andrei.*

Derek Jacobi to
Olivier, February/
March 1969

Dear Larry,

During the last few years I believe that we have become friends over and above our purely professional relationship, and this is why I find it difficult, paradoxically, to discuss my future with you, without feeling that I am imposing on that friendship. I know that in discussions in your office, I have rarely voiced those feelings which, afterwards, I felt I should have done. This is why I have decided to write.

One of the main promptings is your suggestion of my switching parts in *Three Sisters*. The mental contortions involved in reaching a decision have made more immediate my general problems concerning my life as an actor. My thoughts go back to pre-National days, almost to pre-professional days, when I could achieve great impact in roles which stretched and tested my abilities to give, for want of a better word, a 'star' performance. That instinct I still believe I have; but now I've acquired a technique which I need to use on a larger scale. I don't intend this letter to be a list of boring and outworn grievances, but my great happiness in this company is strongly tinged with an inhibiting frustration – and I need your help and counsel.

I have great loyalty to you personally and to the Company, but I no longer feel that I am developing as an actor along the path which makes me an individual performer. Perhaps I should blow my own trumpet more often; a self-deprecatory attitude has bugged me for too long. I must know your views before I can decide what to do next. I'm very well aware that with the Company I have increased my technical skill and stature tremendously, but I firmly believe that if I am to make the next step I must have a role that makes demands on me emotionally and gives me an opportunity to use fully [my] potential.

It may sound unworthy to you that have it, but I need some kind of success beyond the respect and congratulations of my fellow actors, to give me the confidence to act with the kind of broadness, courage and daring that makes really splendid performances. I have begun to think of myself recently as a competent-adequate-professional-supporting actor who can be relied upon to turn in an acceptable piece of work – and I think that that is a very unhealthy state to be in.

If the Company has no place for me in the kind of role I need, I will with reluctance and fear have to risk the cold outside world. Please don't think that this is some kind of threat to extort compensation or whatever – it's only a plea for survival as a major actor, which I still believe it's possible for me to be.

I would love to talk with you, and to try to be clear-headed about something that concerns me so much – perhaps we could try? I leave it to you, but please let me know something soon.

Love,
Derek Jacobi

After finally claiming a leading role, Prince Myshkin in The Idiot *in July 1970, Jacobi left the Company the following spring, and soon landed his first major television part, in* Man of Straw *(1972), a six-episode BBC adaptation of Heinrich Mann's novel.*

As You Like It (*c.*1600)
by William Shakespeare

Director: Clifford Williams
Old Vic, 3 October 1967 to 16 July 1969 (77 performances)

Word that As You Like It *would have an all-male cast reached Britain's most famous drag artiste.*

Al Parker to Olivier, 15 September 1966

Dear Larry,

I understand that *As You Like It* is one of [your] contemplated productions and I heard 'Rosalyn' [sic] will be played by a man.

If so, how about Danny La Rue, whom we act for? He would be a woman and would be a man. [...]

All best wishes,
Al Parker

Parker to Olivier, 29 September 1966

PRIVATE AND CONFIDENTIAL

Dear Larry,

When I suggested Danny La Rue, it was a leg-pull and if it annoyed you, please accept my apologies.

All good wishes,
Al Parker

Kenneth Tynan to Paul McCartney, 28 September 1966

Dear Mr McCartney,

Playing 'Eleanor Rigby' last night for about the 500th time, I decided to write and tell you how terribly sad I was to hear that you had decided not to [write the music for] *As You Like It* for us. There are four or five tracks on *Revolver* that are as memorable as any English songs of this century – and the maddening thing is that they are all in exactly the right mood for *As You Like It*. Apart from 'E. Rigby' I am thinking particularly of 'For No One' and 'Here, There and Everywhere'. (Incidentally, 'Tomorrow Never Knows' is the best musical evocation of L.S.D. I have ever heard.)

Won't you reconsider? John Dexter [slated to direct *As You Like It*] doesn't know I'm writing this – it's pure impulse on the part of a fan. We don't need you as a gimmick because we don't need publicity: we need you simply because you are the best composer of that kind of song in England. If Purcell were alive, we would probably ask him, but it would be a close thing. Anyway, forgive me for being a pest, but do please think it over.

Oppostite: Charles Kay (Celia) and Ronald Pickup (Rosalind) in *As You Like It*. Photo: Zoë Dominic

Yours sincerely,
Kenneth Tynan

McCartney explained his decision in a letter to Tynan: 'I don't really like words by Shakespeare … Maybe I could write the National Theatre stomp sometime! Or the ballad of Larry O.'

<table>
<tr>
<td>Olivier to John Dexter, 4 January 1967</td>
<td>

Dearest Johnnie,

[…] In view of the following considerations I would feel safer in postponing *As You* for two weeks.

Orlando is proving a stickler. I feel rather sorry you can't see Bob Stephens in the part as his size would at least help with a six foot one Rosalind [John Stride]. Dare I suggest Neil Fitzpatrick? He has shown such remarkable improvement and I could work with him on the speech if you like. His height could still be thought a disadvantage but at least he is husky and has in some ways the same sort of 'bonny boy's' quality as John Stride. […]

Altogether, the June 20th [*As You…*] opening date would help us use the Company economically. Please let me have your answers by wire, if you will, no matter how cryptic.

Love,
  Larry

</td>
</tr>
<tr>
<td>Dexter, cable to Olivier, 22 January 1967</td>
<td>

DEAR LARRY IN VIEW OF CASTING PROBLEMS I FEEL I CAN NO LONGER UNDERTAKE AS YOU STOP THE CASTING SEEMS TO ME DESPERATELY THIN THE NON EXISTENCE OF A SUITABLE ORLANDO CELIA AND PHEBE ALONG WITH OTHER SMALLER COMPROMISES RENDER MY TASK IMPOSSIBLE

I HAVE NO OBJECTION TO THE PROJECT BEING HANDED TO ANOTHER DIRECTOR OR IF POSSIBLE POSTPONED UNTIL A FULL STRENGTH CASTING MIGHT BE POSSIBLE AT PRESENT IT SEEMS UNDERNOURISHED AND MERELY EXPEDIENT ALTERNATIVES WILL I BELIEVE EVENTUALLY REFLECT MORE CREDIT ON THE COMPANY THAN THE PRESENT FEEBLE AND BOTCHED PROJECT YOURS ALWAYS JOHN

</td>
</tr>
</table>

Olivier accepted Dexter's withdrawal 'with great reluctance' and hired Clifford Williams, whose As You Like It *cast included Ronald Pickup (Rosalind), Charles Kay (Celia), Richard Kay (Phebe) and Anthony Hopkins (Audrey), alongside Jeremy Brett (Orlando), Robert Stephens (Jaques) and Derek Jacobi (Touchstone). They opened while Olivier was on tour with the Company in Vancouver.*

<table>
<tr>
<td>Olivier, cable to *As You Like It* cast, 3 October 1967</td>
<td>SUCCESS TO THE WITH IT LOT FROM THE WAY OUT LOT</td>
</tr>
</table>

Olivier, cable to
Ronald Pickup,
3 October 1967

RON DEAR HAVE A LOVELY BASH TONIGHT
   IT IS VERY IMPORTANT THAT YOU SET YOURSELF ONLY
TO ENJOY IT JUST TAKE OFF NOW ON A LOVELY LYRIC
FLIGHT
   LOVING AND STRENGTHENING THOUGHTS
   L. O.

Danny La Rue,
telegram to *As
You Like It* cast,
3 October 1967

COME ON IN THE WATER IS FINE BEST WISHES FOR A
GREAT SUCCESS — DANNY LA RUE

Sunny Amey to
Olivier, 8 October
1967

My dear Larryo,

As You really is the talking point in London & bookings are
improving. […]
   HOW ARE YOU? We miss you all terribly. The company is in
good heart here – the reception helped. To indicate what good heart
let me tell you that Mark Cullingham & I have achieved a scoop with
the understudies for *Tartuffe*. Derek Jacobi has agreed to cover Sir
John (don't be rude) Charles Kay = Robert Stephens, Sheila [Reid]
(after innumerable conversations) for Joan [Plowright]. Richard

Kay for John McEnery (as Damis) & Ron Pickup has practically agreed to U.S. Jeremy [Brett] as Valère. We want to prove to other seniors that there's nothing anti-status about understudying. [...]

Danny La Rue & pint-sized Ronnie Corbett did Othello & Desdemona on the David Frost [TV] show in reference to *As You*. Quite amusing. Finished up with a song to the tune of 'Chicago':

'Iago, Iago, what do I care, what do I care'

etc etc. finishing

'Though you may think the set-up is queer

Wait 'til you see Dame Sybil as Lear!' & so on. [...]

Joan's party was very nice after the opening. She looked absolutely lovely in an apricot chiffony dress with beading round the neck.

Much Ado reopens Tuesday & then on to *Tartuffe* rehearsals. Thinking of you very much. Are you catching up on your sleep? Canadian champagne is not up to much – so I should let it alone.

Much love,
Sunny [...]

Tartuffe (1664)

by Molière

Translated by Richard Wilbur (1967)
Director: Tyrone Guthrie
Old Vic, 21 November 1967 to 19 July 1968 (39 performances)

Tyrone Guthrie had directed several of Olivier's most celebrated performances, including Hamlet *and* Henry V *at the Old Vic in 1937. In June 1964, Olivier hoped Guthrie would do one of the plays that Paul Scofield was then studying, including* Danton's Death *and* Tartuffe.

Tyrone Guthrie to Olivier, 1 July 1964	My dear Larry,

Alas I am not free to accept. I have another year to do here [at the Guthrie Theater, Minneapolis]. That sounds like an old lag writing from jail, but, in fact, I have loved it here.

Please give me another chance at a later date. Though considerably enfeebled, I don't think I am yet entirely senile.

Love,
T. G.

In November 1966, Olivier offered Guthrie Tartuffe *again, this time with John Gielgud as Orgon, Robert Stephens as Tartuffe and Joan Plowright as Elmire or Dorine, imploring: 'If only you knew how bored I am with not having you here.' Guthrie accepted these three actors (Plowright as Dorine), but also evidently asked permission to cast from outside the Company.*

Olivier to Guthrie,
30 March 1967

My dear Ty,

[…] The two parts you bring up, Elmire and Cleante, are not the sort that anybody is going to give their back teeth to play – by which I mean 'anybody who is anybody'. A person of note not already in the Company is not going to be anxious, even with the bait of you directing them, to come in at considerable sacrifice in salary to play either, unless given something a great deal more sterling to follow it up.

This plan would be possible but some people in the Company will not understand why they weren't thought good enough. As the years go by the opportunities in a Company like this do not increase, in fact they gradually tail off. Our first season we put on ten plays: that was natural in that we had to sift the good and the bad and get in a stock of some sort.

With due regard to <u>two</u> <u>things</u>:

a) not to snatch your successes before the public has had a chance to see them, and
b) to bring in enough new stuff to keep the ball rolling and bright.

These two things point to about five new productions a year. As we have to divide the company roughly into two halves to cope with touring problems, this means the average expectation cannot be more than about two and a half parts a year, and in some cases far short of this.

Study and observation of the last 30 years has led both Peter Hall and myself to [conclude] that a permanent ensemble is the only way to keep the standard consistently on a high rise. There will be some star visitations but you will not get any actor in a troupe nowadays (unless he is above a certain age) to accept that his level is Benvolio throughout. There are a handful of stars which may come season by season, viz. Godfrey Tearle, Sir John, Sir Ralph, Sir Michael, Scofield and myself. You wear them out quite quickly. In the meantime, you have done absolutely nothing whatever to promote continuity or unity of purpose and spirit in the rest of the Company, which is the only thing that a permanent ensemble has to offer.

If I were to cast all the leading parts for the next year or so out of the people that I know you would really rather like in *Tartuffe* and *Volpone*, I should lose: Colin Blakely, Peter Cellier, Paul Curran, Frank Finlay, Edward Hardwicke, Derek Jacobi, Robert Lang, Kenneth Mackintosh, Geraldine McEwan, Anthony Nicholls, Ronald Pickup, Joan Plowright, Louise Purnell, Maggie Smith, Robert Stephens, John Stride in a very few months indeed, as soon as they saw how the land lay.

There are people who regard my engagement here as a clumsily camouflaged process of the most old-fashioned type actor-management. This is not true. Out of 26 plays I have played in six – only three of which could be called star parts – and have [directed] only four.

You have seen nothing of [the Company's] work, but its name as a troupe has a high place. Occasionally we get a wigging, usually on account of the play being a flop, but it is known as a Company, and one of up to now unique achievement.

Out of the original 35 people we still have 14 after four years, all good. I must not put its nose out of joint unless it is absolutely vital that I do so. They are – most of them – much more than can be described by your word 'promising'. They have all worked marvellously hard and well.

I don't want to have to engage almost an entirely new Company every year, the results of which have been seen all these years past, with nothing built, nothing maintained and nothing constructive to the future except some young shaver like I was with you stretching himself and knocking off some rough edges playing Hamlet, Henry, Toby Belch, etc. Such a job as mine has worn out many a good soldier, who finally leaves with nothing but a past both for himself and his actors. The prospect simply does not interest me and I would feel that I had simply wasted my time and everybody else's.

I don't think Binkie [Beaumont] could cough you up a better threesome than John Gielgud, Joan Plowright and Robert Stephens in *Tartuffe*. […]

All love as ever,
    Larry

Guthrie to Olivier,
7 April 1967

My dear Larry,

After [your] really HORRID crack about my h'writing guess I'd better TYPE. It probably won't be much more legible. I type hugely fast but rather wild – Bobby Helpmann playing a Chopin Mazurka.

Your letter was – no surprise – hugely sensible. I do realise the need for quite a high degree of permanence in a co. We are trying just the same thing at M'polis and the co. there though not bad is also not a galaxy of world-fame. I suppose one could argue that a scarcely supported (other than by its customers) repertory group in a comparatively obscure corner of the American provinces is one thing, whereas … but I really don't intend to bore us both by pursuing the matter another inch.

[I] have no use for [actors] content to go plodding on as Benvolio decade after decade. But, alas, compared to, say, I.C.I. our profession just doesn't offer a regular ladder up which the deserving can climb and, unless grossly unreliable, can eventually reach, not necessarily the topmost pinnacle, but always a respectable eminence. In fact, people in your or my position are forever being compelled (ironically, by our own consciences) to promote talented riff-raff over the heads of their (less talented) betters. […]

I don't want you to think, because I write these sort of letters, that I don't realise your difficulties; or that I shall arrive and be the pouting discontented 'artistic' type of director. You know me too well for that. I shall do m'inadequate best with the material placed in front of me; and I realise ABSOLUTELY that managerial diplomacy, rather than solely artistic considerations, MUST dominate all casting. […]

I am boring myself to death reading, with ceaseless wet-finger flicking of dictionary pages, a French commentary about *Tartuffe*, which takes it all as desperately seriously as an American college professor; and a rather lively commentary on his own production by a French actor-cum-producer. The latter has millions of diagrams – dotted lines and arrows and mystic signs tell where everyone is supposed to go at any given moment. It's prodigiously tedious. But I'm so anxious that we shouldn't just have a high-spirited romp. I know so clearly the way I think it ought to go: the MOST outrageous high jinks supported on a frame-work of sober, solid credibility. […]

Love,
Ty

Guthrie to Olivier,
23 November 1967

My dear Larry,

Thank you very much for my bott of whiskey – a gracious & acceptable offering.

I'm sorry the press [for *Tartuffe*] wasn't more enthusiastic. But I really don't think, at all events in the Wilbur version, that the play has much more than curiosity value. Perhaps, after all, we should have just gone for merry pranks and jolly jinks. But I think the Serious Approach had to be tried. […]

Lastly, I enclose a tout for our jam, in the hope that you & Joan might think it wd make dainty Xmas gyftes. We started the factory four years ago. Now we employ 1/3 pop. of village [Newbliss, County Monaghan] & have 50/60 farmers growing fruit under contract. It's still a very small enterprise but just beginning to thrive.

Finally, let me say that I've loved working with your Co. & have been very impressed with the 'esprit'.

See you soon.

Love,
T.G.

John Gielgud to
Richard Sterne,
10 January 1968

Dear Richard

[…] *Tartuffe* is miscast in my opinion. I have not had a success in it and only enjoy it as a sort of exercise. Now we are rehearsing *Oedipus* (Seneca) with Peter Brook – 10½ weeks' rehearsals, which ought to produce something interesting, I hope.

Ever yours,
John

1968

Oedipus (55–60 AD)
by Seneca

Adapted by Ted Hughes (1968) from a translation by David Anthony Turner
Director: Peter Brook
Old Vic, 19 March to 3 August 1968 (42 performances)

Sunny Amey, memo
to Olivier et al.,
12 October 1967

PETER BROOK

Peter Brook is still ill in Paris, I spoke to him on the telephone on
10 October. The following is a report of the main points as near
as I could get it down:

My only interest in doing it would be to attempt something
extremely difficult, this needs conditions which will have to be
discussed with your production and costume departments.

SCENERY AND COSTUMES
Do we need an outside designer? I don't think so. My ideas are
simple but they would have to evolve during rehearsals; a flexible
organisation is necessary if I am to do *Oedipus*.

LONG REHEARSAL
Ten weeks is essential with everyone. We shall be breaking new
territory and a unified style for this kind of experiment needs
time. We have to grow together.

CHORUS
Can be of both sexes, but must be very flexible people of
high quality. This kind of production needs either very young
promising actors or superb actors like John Gielgud [Oedipus].
My aim is there should be no difference in style and quality
between Gielgud and the others, everyone must be modest and
prepared to help one another. The chorus will need to work as a
principal and not be rehearsed away from the others as with an
opera. […] I must be extremely demanding about the quality of
the raw material, for example, John McEnery interests me (he is
going to be a sensation as Mercutio in Zeffirelli's film [of *Romeo
and Juliet*] by the way) […]

FURTHER NOTES ON ACTORS
I shall have to speak individually to each actor to warn him of
what my demands will be. This play is not going to be fun, it will
come to a point where it is an acute, unforgettable experience.
We shall work step by step towards a greater intensity. If the actor
himself is not determined that no power is going to stop him
then he must not come. I will say at my first rehearsal this is an
expedition, anyone in this room who is not prepared to go all the

way must leave now, if you don't go now you are in for it. When it comes to the difficult peak there will be no turning back. […]

JOCASTA [wife and mother to 63-year-old Gielgud's Oedipus] He very much wants Joan Plowright [then 38], says age does not enter into. It is the nature and calibre of the actress which is important.

CREON
He says this is a problem, there isn't one in the Company unless Colin Blakely. He says it really needs an Olivier or that strength. […]

Brook was able to cast Blakely as Creon, and for Jocasta chose Irene Worth, then 51; she had been Goneril in Brook's RSC King Lear.

Ted Hughes to Peter Brook, 5 December 1967

Dear Peter Brook,

Here are six pages. I've stuck pretty close to the Turner trans for most of the way. I didn't want to lose the naked odd quality of his version – though I think I may have done. The slightly scatty over-breathless strain I have gone against. Tell me if you think I have chilled it with a bit too much style. Trying to deepen the general note of it, I realise I've formalised it a little. I hope not too much. From this draft – if you think there's any point in it – I'll be very ready to adjust in any direction. I must say, the further I get from the Turner version, the freer I feel. Some places I've expanded a bit, others compressed.

I missed out the first long chorus – I'm pretty sure I could do that O.K.

If you feel it's better to go back to the Turner and make far fewer changes – changes perhaps only of odd words and phrases – I shall see what you mean.

If I am on the right lines, I could do the play pretty quickly.

Yours sincerely,
Ted Hughes

Hughes to Brook, ? December 1967

Dear Mr Brook,

I'll try and get the rest to you by Monday.

I shall come to the first rehearsals – expect to change the text quite a bit.

Yours sincerely,
Ted Hughes

Hughes to Brook, ? February [?] 1968

Dear Peter,

Here is Oedipus' last lines versified – no words or order altered. Perhaps it will help formalise it a little for Sir John – help him to get it further removed from just personal exclamations, etc. as we were saying. Also it will make him more sure of the emphases – to hit those last words terribly hard, to separate the lines definitely however lightly, to float the whole thing more level and more intensely contained. If you think the punctuation might throw him (I thought it might help at this stage in this form) you could get it copied with none. That's if you think it's worth showing to him at all.

I look forward to Sunday,

Yours,
Ted

**Hughes to Brook,
? February/March
1968**

Dear Peter,

This is only an idea – I heard very briefly the actors producing some of those sounds you described. How if – either somewhere among the chorus or through loudspeaker there were some sort of drumbeat – very soft and low to begin with – to come under this moaning singing they produce, and this be the beginning of the chorus to Bacchus – which quickly works up louder and more agitated till it begins to break into words – phrases etc. superimposed on the singing noise, and the beat, gradually becoming almost entirely words – but the beat and the singing going on under (singing from all who are not at that actual moment speaking). I imagine this could be hair-raising. It would

Irene Worth (Jocasta) and John Gielgud (Oedipus) in *Oedipus*. Photo: Zoë Dominic

come naturally from under the mourning etc. – it would be the natural course for converting despair into exultation through a sort of cumulative frenzy. The beat and those weird singing sounds would carry the whole feeling of it, and would bring any effect within range.

Also, at the end, a similar thing – perhaps beginning before the end of Oedipus's last speech, growing louder and dragging the chorus up out of the depths onto the stage and flinging them up finally into whatever it is.

It's that singing noise I felt which holds the possibilities for those difficult transitions – and which can carry the right sort of half animal devilish feeling to really overthrow the play, with something as powerful and from the same world as the play.

Anyway, I thought this might just be another ingredient in the general mix at this stage.
John Gielgud's description of how he imagined the scene behind the chorus was exactly as I'd been imagining it.

The snake image is a fundamental one to Bacchus/Apollo, to the mother, to blood, to the oracular hole in the earth, to the fundamental immortal quality of energy that's too pure ever to be affected by negations (as Kundalini and the Voodoo Damballah, Ouroboulos etc. passim). Tiresias and the coupling of snakes, also Cadmus founded Thebes and killed a great snake, as Apollo founded Delphi after killing the great snake there (which was Dionysus). The snake, in fact, loses the first battle and wins the last in all the great collisions. Presumably after the nuclear holocaust it will rear its head or its fifty heads perhaps inside some pioneering single cell quite undaunted.

> Yours,
> Ted

Bryan Robertson (Director, Whitechapel Art Gallery) to Brook, 20 March 1968

Dear Peter Brook,

Your production of the *Oedipus* of Seneca is one of the greatest creations in the history of the European Theatre. I had not known before that your musical intelligence and sensibility, which charges every second of the play with tension, is matched only by Balanchine's. It would be absurd for me to comment on the intellectual force that you have brought to bear on this production and which so clearly informs, articulates, and throws into dazzling relief every emotional nuance. I have never known such agony of feeling so magnificently disclosed, with such dignity and precision AND SPLENDOUR. Visually, your production is one of the greatest revelations of my lifetime: I sat in an agony of English self-embarrassment, with tears pouring down my face, even before the play started, with the drumming, the spatial use of sound, the great gold box slowly turning, flashing light at Thebes: us, the audience. There were many times during the performance when I could hardly watch or listen for tears, and strong feeling.

The total impact of sound, speech, action, vision – and meaning, never obscured – was not unlike a great performance of *Le Sacre du printemps*. Stravinsky should have been fortunate enough to have you to extend and realise his dramatic concept, if he ever had one.

For the past year, I have been on the verge of emigrating, and working abroad (personal despair at English dullness and the shabbiness of my own professional context – & its ignorance) but what you and that great company of young actors and actresses have created has made me believe in England all over again, and I think I shall stay (who cares – pompous arse that I am, but I do want you to know what the experience last night meant to me: this isn't fan mail guff).

The convulsive, straddled, diagonally swinging, irregularly paced and timed, slow lurch across the stage of Jocasta is shattering. Grief, horror, physical agony, reversal to animal behaviour – and the alarming monkey king in oriental drama. This Jocasta <u>sits</u> like a queen. The way in which some kind of imposed rhythm illuminates/disrupts so eloquently and beautifully all the great speeches, is tremendously exciting. The <u>sound</u> of the chorus flickering and hurtling round and round or in counterpointing echo across the entire theatre is electrifying. Creon's change of pitch and intonation after the oracle's disclosure is a master-stroke.

The speech from Pickup [as Messenger, describing Oedipus blinding himself] is one of the most agonising revelations I've ever known from an actor. Everything Creon does is flawless, too – the mounting urgency, the passion and crescendo – masterly. The terrible slow death you've devised for Jocasta, with that great gaping mouth hanging open like a terrible wound – what a device to symbolise the manner of her death – is a stroke of genius. Gielgud's restraint, pride, fear, obtuseness, mental blindness self-induced, regality, everything – beyond praise. His changes of voice after blinding, agonising. I shall never forget Gielgud's bald domed head, bird-like face, the intensity of his physical presence, the sheer intelligence of our greatest actor's imaginative projection of a <u>Roman</u> concept of a Greek victim. He is lucky to have your genius to work with, and so is everyone. I have never known such a fusion of space; time; dramatic sequence; rhythm; musical pitch in subtlest variation; meaning; lighting; and visual device. You must take this production all over the world. I wish I could read this letter to every member of the company: please accept it as a token of my regard for your animating genius.

Bryan Robertson

Brook's production ended with a bacchanalia, emulating the ancient tradition that tragic action should be followed and leavened by humour and licentiousness: the Oedipus *actors danced around a 12-foot phallus, as a jazz band performed a Dixieland arrangement of 'Yes We Have No Bananas'. On the eve of the press night, Brook had refused to cave in to Olivier's demand that he omit the phallus, which the Director claimed could alienate audiences and the Board.*

**Brook, memo
to Frank Dunlop
(associate director)
et al., 20 March 1968**

I make no bones about being deeply mistrustful at the moment so I would like to put everything on record. I received a request from George Rowbottom to consider eliminating the phallus from *Oedipus* for the school matinee [tomorrow]. The following points were the essence of my reply:

1. To ask if it could be explained to me very simply on what grounds we might fear having a phallus seen by children between the age of 12 and 16. Was our concern that it might provoke certain questions? If so, would such questions be in any way contrary to the general practice of sex education in schools today?
2. As a help to accepting the genuineness of such anxiety, could I be assured that certain lines of Shakespeare had been omitted in the past from school performances?
3. I naturally applaud the theatre's sense of responsibility towards its young audience.

Consequently, I can safely assume that before rushing into accepting bookings from school parties, the question of the possibly disturbing effects on young adolescents of the themes of this play have been thoroughly discussed and weighed. I admit that, learning for the first time about school parties, I am very concerned to know whether the horrors described by the Messenger and the profoundly horrible event of [Jocasta] sticking a sword up her vagina might not be genuinely traumatic.

I hope this question is being given attention.

P.B.

After that matinee, Kenneth Rae, board secretary, reported: 'The performance was stopped before the messenger's speech. Mr Brook then explained to the audience how the play ended, giving them full details. Educational officials were present and, after a request that anyone under 16 should leave the theatre, the performance proceeded at the request of the audience.'

**Richard Roud
(*Guardian* film critic)
to Brook, ? March
1968**

Dear Peter Brook,

Just to tell you that I think your *Oedipus* is one of the greatest things I have ever seen in a theatre. Unlike Hope-Wallace [*Guardian* drama critic], I have NO reservations.

Yours,
Richard Roud

P.S. KEEP THE PHALLUS FLYING!

**Mrs S.P. Maunsell to
Kenneth Rae, 29 April
1968**

Dear Mr Rae,

I am writing to protest about the final scene in *Oedipus*.

I have seen most of the plays that the [NT] has staged recently, and have been generally impressed; but I have never before experienced the shock of gratuitous obscenity that I received at the appearance on the stage, as the focal point of an irrelevant finale, of a large gilt penis.

This I consider inexcusable, because it had no dramatic point and no connection with the play itself. It compares shabbily with the scene of Jocasta's suicide, which was also shocking, but because it had a dramatic point, acceptable. The last scene was superfluous, disgusting and an insult to the audience, and should be omitted from subsequent presentations. [...]

Yours sincerely,
Susan Maunsell

On 3 May, Olivier wrote to all 16 members of the Oedipus *chorus asking if, after a three-week August holiday, they wished to continue in repertoire until late November. Seven declined, several gave a conditional 'yes', asking for better parts in other shows, or more money; one, recalling Brook's rehearsal exercises, said 'Yes, as long as it doesn't mean being a snake for three weeks.'* Oedipus *was not extended.*

The next letter came from a 17-year-old, south London schoolgirl, passionate about theatre, who saw the Oedipus *matinee on Thursday 13 June, the day of her Art A-Level exam.*

Jenny Beavan to
Brook, 1 July 1968

Dear Mr Brook,

I saw *Oedipus* about 3 weeks ago and I thought that its effect would wear off in time, but it hasn't. You see, I didn't understand the end (jazz band onwards) at all. The build up of horror was so intense and the design was so perfect and it was so right to have the chorus in the auditorium (except for the fact that the hatted American lady in front obviously didn't want to miss anything and therefore had to turn abruptly every time anyone behind spoke) but the ending completely destroyed for some time as far as I was concerned everything that had become so increasingly intense before. Presumably this is what you intended? If you did, it was a total success but why? Someone I met muttered something about Aristotle and Alienation, but they seemed to know little more about it and on looking up Aristotle (about whom I know little) it mentioned no possible solution and Alienation seems more to do with Brecht.

Looking back on *Oedipus*, it has become a little easier to remember although it is still rather muddled owing to the fact that my strongest memory is still of a fancy dress King's Road party before midnight.

Please don't bother to reply if you're very busy, which, knowing the theatre, you probably are – I did think that the beginning was quite brilliant, especially being blinded by the revolving cube, it made one feel very much part of it all.

Yours sincerely,
Jenny Beavan

P. S. Please excuse the muddled sentences – a sentence always seems too short.

Beavan passed her art exam – and went on to become the Bafta- and Oscar-winning costume designer of A Room with a View, Gosford Park *and* Mad Max: Fury Road.

An autobiographical new play**
by Dennis Potter

Dennis Potter had made his name with scripts for the BBC's Wednesday Play.

Kenneth Tynan, memo to Olivier, 16 July 1968

PROSPECTS FOR 1969

[…] d) The Dennis Potter – He refuses to show it to us in its present form because 'it isn't a play, it's a scream of pain'. He promises that by October 31 he'll show us either (i) a revised version, or (ii) the original scream.

    K. T.

Clive Goodwin (Potter's agent) to Tynan, 6 November 1968

Dear Ken,

Dennis would like to cancel his commission to write an autobiographical stage play and he will return the money (£200). […]

    I have reminded him of his agreement that in the event of him not completing the agreed play he would show [us] the draft. He remembers the conversation but because of his present delicate state, both physically and mentally, he would like to return to [it] later.

    Yours sincerely,
    Clive

1969

The Way of the World (1700)
by William Congreve
Director: Michael Langham
Old Vic, 1 May to 26 July 1969 (59 performances)

Maggie Smith played nine leading roles for the NT from 1963 to 1966. When she took an extended break from the Company, Olivier programmed The Way of the World, *and gave Geraldine McEwan its leading role.*

Olivier to Maggie Smith, 29 October 1968

Darling Mageen,

I am so very sorry I have not been able to keep Millamant for you. It just fulfils the needs of the time and there just isn't anything else that does that so well.

Nov. 2nd

Dear Larry,

what on earth
do you expect me to say?
I am absolutely
heartbroken by your decision
but what can I do? You
must know that I have now
no chance at all to play
the one part you have
always told me I should.
I wish I could
accept your reasoning but
I cannot even do that —
there must be some play
you could do —
Well, what is the point

Maggie Smith writes to Laurence Olivier about
The Way of the World

of trying to tell you my
feelings. They obviously
count for so very little —
It was nice of you to
say you will devote your
energies to my return but
really I do not think it
would be wise of me to
believe that either —

Margaret.

I do promise we shall devote all energies to building a lovely return for you and hopefully so that you will not miss that particular lady. [...]

Please let's see you again very soon. We love you and yours so very much.

Always your,
Larry

Smith to Olivier,
2 November 1968

Dear Larry,

What on <u>earth</u> do you expect me to say?

I am absolutely heartbroken by your decision but what can I do? You must know that I have now no chance at all to play the one part <u>you</u> have always told me I should.

I wish I could accept your reasoning but I cannot even do that – there must be <u>some</u> play you could do.

Well, what's the point of trying to tell you my feelings. They obviously count for so very little.

It was nice of you to say you will devote your energies to my return but really I do not think it would be wise of me to believe that either.

Margaret

Smith did return to his Company, as Hedda Gabler, and Mrs Sullen in The Beaux' Stratagem, *in 1970. She starred as Millamant in Ontario in 1976, and in Chichester and London in 1984.*

The National Health (1969)
by Peter Nichols
Director: Michael Blakemore
Old Vic, 16 October 1969 to 25 February 1971
(122 performances, incl. ten at Cambridge Theatre)

Olivier to Peter
Nichols, 24 May 1967

Dear Mr Nichols,

[...] I write to tell you how very much I admired [your play *A Day in the Death of Joe Egg*] and to say that if you could find time to have a look at this Company and let gently germinate possibly the idea for another play for us here, we would be overjoyed.

Yours sincerely,
Laurence Olivier

**Nichols to Olivier,
31 May 1967**

Dear Sir Laurence,

Thank you for your most kind and encouraging letter. […]
    Two plays for the stage have been knocking about in my head for some years now and your kind interest is all I need to push me into starting on one.
    Thank you again,

    Yours sincerely,
    Peter Nichols

Nichols expanded and reworked his earlier, unproduced television play, The End Beds, *into* The National Health, or Nurse Norton's Affair. *Set in a London NHS hospital, and based closely on observations he made while in hospital in Bristol and London for several weeks in 1960–61, with a collapsed lung, it shows patients, doctors, nurses and surgeons in realistic scenes, juxtaposed with extracts from* 'Nurse Norton's Affair', *a pastiche of hospital TV soap operas. Nichols sent the script to his friend, the painter and sculptor Francis Hewlett.*

**Francis Hewlett to
Nichols, 27 February
1969**

Dear Peter,

I enjoyed it very much and have not seen or heard anything very like it – except perhaps you, describing certain events and things. It is quite baffling in the way it leads strongly in all kinds of what appear to be clear directions, like farce and tenderness, and pity, and every time leaves the direction looking disenchanted and brittle. [It] has the kind of clarity of deadpan poetry which I think is in all your writings, but the texture is richer because of the great chunks of theatricality in it and the final feeling I had is really one of acceptance, which is both beautiful and bitter.
    The absolute mythic quality of being in a hospital, which to all of us is irredeemably linked to pre-death, or a pre-death condition of illness – a new kind of universal limbo – should give it the same kind of basic gut-appeal that the *Joe Egg* had in its attitude to parenthood.
    I think the farts are great moments, really great, and Sir Laurence must keep them in. […]
    I think it is a moving, truthful, and unsentimental play. […]

    Best wishes,
    Yours,
    Francis

The National Health *would be directed by Michael Blakemore (who had staged* Joe Egg *in Glasgow and London). The play is narrated by a hospital porter, Barnet, who delivers running commentary on what hospital staff are really feeling ('We show every conceivable respect the deceased is due. We may hate the sight of them when they're living.'), addressing the audience like a vaudeville comedian …*

Olivier to Frankie
Howerd, 24 February
1969

Dear Frankie,

It is some time since you and I acted together at the Coliseum in a show for the Green Room Club. We were a brilliant pair with Nigel Patrick as our feed.

I am sending you this play with some trepidation. Barnet is only the leading [part] if one chooses to think of it like that, and the part of the Chorus in any Greek tragedy is always regarded as pivotal. Shakespeare himself, we are told, probably did this bit in the original *Henry V*. […]

Barnet has to have some evil as well as those brilliantly witty aspects of his character of which you are the master. He does, after all, slip a brandy bottle into the dipso's pocket before he goes off for his cure, and he does tell Ash [another patient] that he is queer, which he might perfectly well have gone on kidding himself about not being, without doing himself or anybody else any harm.

If you didn't like, or got bored with, his stories, one or two of which you may find a bit too crude, you could change these and vary them from time to time.

[I] fear that I may conceivably be asking too much of the play to have you in it. Although the part requires above all the easiest kind of audience relationship, it may possibly be that a person of your eminence and brilliance might swamp the piece. […]

If this whole idea should be a mistake, I ask you to forgive me and understand that I have a very strong ambition for you to be part of the National. After all, you haven't been seen on the Old Vic stage since your Bottom was (what have I said).

Yours ever,
Dictated by Laurence Olivier and signed in his absence.

Howerd declined, citing a prior commitment to making a film. Barnet was Jim Dale, who had spent years as a stand-up comedian before finding screen fame in the Carry On *series.*

When The National Health *opened, the* Evening Standard *praised Blakemore for 'brilliantly' integrating fantasy and reality in 'one of the most corrosive, cynical and coruscating' plays of recent years. The* Daily Telegraph *dwelt on Nichols's 'revelatory wit and brutal compassion', but in* The Sunday Times *Harold Hobson found 'the passion of Mr Nichols's hatred of life interesting but saddening also'. The* Sunday Times' *deputy literary editor, and occasional theatre reviewer, disagreed.*

John Peter to
Nichols, 17 October
1969

Dear Mr Nichols,

I hope you will forgive me if I intrude with a note: *The National Health* is the most moving, humane and intelligent play I've seen for a very long time. I can't think of any other playwright today who can combine so much compassion and understanding with so much humour. I hope everyone whose opinion is worth having will think it a great play (I choose the word with care) – which it is.

No need to acknowledge.

Yours sincerely,
John Peter

**Nichols to Olivier,
23 October 1969**

Dear Sir Laurence,

Thank you for your kind gift and your greetings on the first night.

The show, at least, seems successful, even if the play itself is being misunderstood, by Left and Right, as an advertisement for BUPA. As a Socialist, I suppose I should find this amusing, but really it must point to some wrong emphasis either in play or production that Michael and I might think about quite seriously. […]

Yours sincerely,
Peter Nichols

**Sybil Habermel
to Nichols,
15 November 1969**

Dear Mr Nicholls [sic],

I saw *National Health* yesterday and thought it in altogether extremely bad taste, insulting to the nursing profession and lacking in any human sympathy or warmth.

Added to these were very many medical inaccuracies some of which were –

a) nurses do not usually shake down thermometers after taking temperatures
b) surgeons do <u>not</u> handle X Rays with gloved hands before operation
c) human orifices are <u>not</u> plugged after death (although this used to be so many years ago)
d) the penis is not tied with a reef knot or any other knot in the laying out procedure.

Your characters were stereotyped – especially the nurses – and behaved like automatons. I think the entire play could aptly be described as 'sick' and very offensive.

I may just add that I enjoyed immensely your *Joe Egg* and expected to see in your new play some of this quality. I am very disappointed.

Yours truly,
Mrs Sybil Habermel

In December, Blakemore flew to Tel Aviv to stage Brecht's The Resistible Rise of Arturo Ui *in Hebrew, as the opening production at the new home of the Habima, the Israeli National Theatre.*

**Olivier to Blakemore,
24 November 1969**

<u>Private and Confidential</u>

My dear Michael,

I do hope things are going spiffingly for you in Tel Aviv. I always chuckle when I remember years ago when Tony Guthrie had been at the Habima, Judy Guthrie saying 'My <u>dear</u>, their very most dazzling costume is black hessian with one brown button.' Also, for the purposes of his production Tony learnt two phrases in Hebrew

a) Too much, – much, much, much too much,
and
b) Fuck off.

I am not clear as to whether you are going to be able to re-create *The National Health* for us [next season] but I feel I ought to tell you that I would like to alter some of the casting which at present worries me quite a lot. […]

Do you think you could talk to Peter Nichols and see if he would not do a bit of reconstruction and eliminate the [Chaplain scene]. We have had quite a few slaps at God and religion without going in at this late hour of the evening for this means of doing the same thing. […]

As you know, I think that the opening of the Second Act scene out on the balcony takes us down to a point from which the play can never quite get off on to its feet again. As it isn't by any means a short evening, would you not consider please eliminating this scene. […]

> Yours affectionately, as ever,
> Larry

**Blakemore to Olivier,
11 December 1969**

Dear Larry,

I was just on the point of writing to tell you about certain cuts and emendations that I discussed with Peter before I left London. They are less radical than your own but have the advantage of clearance with the author.

I have to disagree about the Chaplain scene, which is very much part of the agnostic and sceptical bias of the play.

Nor do I think it a good idea to lose the Veranda scene completely. It's not just that it's necessary for the developing relationship between Ash and Loach. Foster's subsequent death is much diminished without his moment on the Veranda. Again, though (Peter disagrees), I think some cuts could be made.

Perhaps we can discuss all this [in] London in mid-Jan. Total confusion this end with the theatre nowhere near built and the first night already postponed twice. Victory in the Six Day War is beginning to seem as much a Miracle as the parting of the Red Sea. […]

> Every good wish,
> Yours,
> Michael

In January 1970, The National Health *was named Best New Play at the* Evening Standard Theatre Awards, *but Blakemore and Nichols were infuriated by how few performances it was allocated. Nichols wrote in his diary of 'a sustained campaign against* The National Health *carried on by enemies* within *the company'. After learning that its run would end in February 1971, Blakemore privately briefed* Times *critic Irving Wardle and invited him to revisit the production; Wardle's second* Times *review denounced the NT's 'indefensible' decision to close the play.*

Olivier to Nichols, 2 February 1971

My dear Peter,

I have not been untouched by the complaint set up publicly by Irving Wardle over the apparent limitations put on *The National Health.*

Let me say that we have decided to [extend the run] as it were 'by public demand' in the booking period after the next one. This is not as munificent as all that. Although I adored the play myself, still do and always will, I was not unworried by its prospects owing to its subject matter which might conceivably prove a little much for the stomachs of some, and I could just see the banners across the newspapers 'Do we really want to see blood mixed with urine upon our stages'.

This seemed to be borne out on the first night by our Chairman, who really behaved very badly to me indeed. I was absolutely thrilled for its success and needless to say over the moon over the prizes. […]

I am sending you a précis of all the [play's box-office percentages] so that you may see perhaps that my conduct has not been so culpable as I am sure you must have felt. […]

I wanted only to tell you that it has never been a question of carelessness or lack of respect for a work that I am absolutely mad about.

Your telly play the other night [*Hearts and Flowers*] made me long for another work from you.

Yours in admiration, and warmest wishes,
   As always,
      Larry

Nichols to Olivier, 10 February 1971

Dear Sir Laurence,

[…] I wanted to go to the press some time ago, after both Peggy Ramsay's protests and my indirect grumbles went unheard. But Michael and Peggy thought I should wait and see how things turned out. It was only when we heard the play was being taken off that Michael was roused to ask Wardle if he'd re-review. I'm very happy his notice has resulted in a few more performances. […]

I've no wish to keep flogging this horse and had decided to try to be thankful for a marvellous production and a happy experience but must take this opportunity to suggest that perhaps better liaison might make for a happier and more efficient ship.

Mutinous mutters could be heeded and grievances appeased before they have to be publicised.

Playwrights do forgo the possibility of larger rewards by writing for the National or RSC and this could be acknowledged by letting them know the fate of their work in the current season.

The high standards of your troupe more than make up for this hypothetical sacrifice and I am delighted that you have renewed your invitation to work with the company.

Thank you again and best wishes,

Yours,
    Peter

Peggy Ramsay
(Nichols's agent), to
Olivier, 5 March 1971

Dear Lord Olivier,

The National Health – Peter Nichols

It was most kind of you to send me a copy of your [2 February] letter to Peter Nichols.

I hope you won't mind my telling you what I think is the basic reason for Peter's anxiety about his play. He didn't break through as a playwright until he was 40, and he feels that he is 'behind' the other playwrights, particularly the playwrights we represent.

I know this is foolish, but you, who blazed to glory in the full bloom of your youth, will understand how Peter feels that the fruits of success are eluding him, so that he must compensate by an intensification of effort.

I know it's a romantic notion that youth and success go hand in hand, but it does help.

He told me he had replied, and I do hope he replied with the grace you displayed when you wrote to him.

With many thanks and good wishes,
    Sincerely yours,
        Peggy Ramsay

Ramsay is one of the dedicatees of Nichols's autobiography, published in 1984 – and entitled Feeling You're Behind.

1970

The Merchant of Venice (c.1594)

by William Shakespeare
Director: Jonathan Miller
Old Vic, 28 April 1970 to 29 July 1971
Cambridge Theatre, 8 June to 13 August 1970 (100 performances)

Laurence Olivier hoped that Orson Welles, who had directed him in Ionesco's Rhinoceros
(Royal Court, 1960), might stage The Merchant of Venice.

Kenneth Tynan to
Olivier, 28 April 1969

Dear L.,

Still no word from Orson. I called Paula twice and she had heard
nothing except that he was finishing a film [*Waterloo*] near Rome.
    Working on the bird-in-hand theory, I would recommend
going for Jonathan Miller.

        Love,
            K.

Orson Welles, cable
to Olivier, 29 April
1969

DEAR LARRY,

FILM I'M WORKING ON DISASTROUSLY OVER SCHEDULE
SO CANNOT COME LONDON FOR ANOTHER THREE WEEKS
STOP OBVIOUSLY I CANT PRESUME ON YOUR PATIENCE ANY
LONGER STOP REGRET THIS MORE THAN I CAN SAY BUT
VIRUS AND SLOW DIRECTOR TOO MUCH FOR ME.
    ALL FONDEST ALWAYS,
    ORSON

Paul Scofield to
Olivier, 31 May 1969

My dear Larry,

[…] I've thought a lot about Shylock, and I honestly don't want
to play him. I'm sorry if it seems that I could have said this earlier,
but I wasn't sure.
    It obviously still isn't my moment to work with the National. I
wish it were & I look forward to the time when it is. […]

        Most gratefully & with love,
            Paul

*Only after Scofield and, in 1964, John Gielgud and Alec Guinness, had all said no, did
Olivier decide to play Shylock himself. Miller directed, updating the action to the 1890s.*

Jonathan Miller, postcard to Olivier, December 1970

Dear Larry,

Here are a few Jewish snaps. They give a rough idea I think. I look forward to starting work in the New Year.

Yrs
  Jonathan

Miller enclosed a Spy *caricature of Sir Albert Sassoon in waistcoat, dark jacket and tie and photographs of three Rothschilds, including Lord Rothschild, in top hat and tails. Olivier's Shylock was costumed to resemble a late nineteenth-century banker.*

Baron Olivier of Brighton

Harold Wilson to Olivier, 11 May 1970

HONOURS – IN CONFIDENCE

Dear Sir Laurence,

I am very pleased to hear from the informal soundings that you may now be ready to accept a Life Peerage. In sending you the enclosed somewhat formal letter, I feel I should write to you personally again to make it clear that I regard Life Peerages as a means of enabling people who have a contribution to make to public debate to do so in this particular forum. […]

Yours sincerely,
  Harold Wilson

Richard and Elizabeth Burton, telegram to Olivier, 14 June 1970

BY THE LORD HARRY LARRY ITS ABOUT TIME YOU WERE SEPARATED FROM THE HERD WE ARE DELIGHTED AND VERY PROUD MUCH LOVE FROM US AND MANY THANKS FOR YOUR LETTER NOW FOR AN EARLDOM

RICHARD AND ELIZABETH BURTON

Bette Davis, card to Olivier, June 1970

How marvelous, <u>Sir</u>! How deserved –

Love,
  B.D.

Terence Rattigan, telegram to Olivier, 15 June 1970

I SHALL LIFT UP MY EYES UNTO THE LORD AS I DID UNTO THE KNIGHT AND EVEN UNTO THE MISTER STOP I ONLY HOPE TO LIVE LONG ENOUGH TO LIFT THEM UP UNTO THE DUKE OLD AND MAD OF COURSE STOP MUCH LOVE MANY KISSES

TERRY RATTIGAN

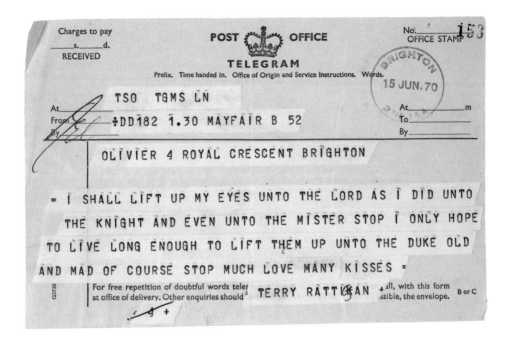

POST OFFICE

TELEGRAM

Charges to pay

____s.____d.

RECEIVED

No. 153
OFFICE STAMP

Prefix. Time handed in. Office of Origin and Service Instructions. Words.

BRIGHTON
15 JUN. 70

TSO   TGMS LN

At____

From____ +DD182 1.30 MAYFAIR B 52

By____

At____m

To____

By____

OLIVIER 4 ROYAL CRESCENT BRIGHTON

= I SHALL LIFT UP MY EYES UNTO THE LORD AS I DID UNTO THE KNIGHT AND EVEN UNTO THE MISTER STOP I ONLY HOPE TO LIVE LONG ENOUGH TO LIFT THEM UP UNTO THE DUKE OLD AND MAD OF COURSE STOP MUCH LOVE MANY KISSES =

For free repetition of doubtful words teler
at office of delivery. Other enquiries should

TERRY RATTIGAN

all, with this form
ssible, the envelope.

B or C

Olivier sent the following letter to every member of the acting company, including Cleo Sylvestre, then appearing in The National Health.

Olivier to Cleo Sylvestre, 15 June 1970

NOT FOR PUBLICATION PLEASE

Dear Cleo,

Please forgive this form letter. Of course I am enormously honoured by what was announced on Saturday, but it was not altogether an easy decision for me. I have, in fact, been resisting it for nearly three years now.

My resistance was not due to an over-developed sense of humility, but that something about the title really did, and still does, and probably always will, make me feel a bit awkward. Perhaps there is still enough of the urchin in me to feel a little mockingly about it.

I would like it to make absolutely no difference whatever to the way you, my friends and colleagues, address me, whether you are used to calling me Sir Laurence or Sir or Sir Larry or Larry. Please don't change that or even think about me any differently.

My personal feelings would incline towards something not so committing or classy-sounding, and my vainglory would have preferred something with two or three initials, let us say. [*O.M. for Order of Merit, or C.H. for Companion of Honour?*] When I explained that I would rather have almost anything other than the thing at present provided, it was patiently explained to me that nothing other could do anybody any good at all apart from myself. Thus was my conscience – habitually and quite properly a guilty one – quite cunningly appealed to, and I fell for it.

I would like to feel that the new title is only to be used as an entrée to the House of Lords which could be for me possibly the useful forum that the Powers-that-be are determined that somebody of our profession should have.

In other words, 'Your call, Sir Laurence' is one thing, while 'Your Lordship's call' is another – so please let us have no truck with anything other than that which has been before.

However you should find your feelings – either for or against the decision – please help me to make it a good one.

L. O.

1971

The Two-Character Play (1967)**
by Tennessee Williams

First performed in London in 1967, and described by Williams as his 'most beautiful' work since A Streetcar Named Desire *(1947),* The Two-Character Play *is the story of actor-manager Felice, and his sister and leading lady, Clare.*

Kenneth Tynan,
memo to Olivier,
15 January 1971

I think *The Two-Character Play* is very poor indeed. Having run out of material, Tennessee looks inward at his own dreads and anxieties and cannot dramatise them. The style is all under-lining and exclamation marks – the mood of hysteria would get fearfully monotonous long before the evening ended. Also it's soft-centred. […]

Amorphous construction – a pointlessly baffling plot (Tennessee doesn't dare to dispense with plot, like Beckett; no, he wraps up the play in coils of it, like the snakes around Laocoon) – and a self-pitying style. However well played, this combination would make a deadly evening.

Love,
Ken

No Williams script was staged by the NT in the Olivier/Tynan decade.

The Captain of Köpenick (1931)

by Carl Zuckmayer

Adapted by John Mortimer (1971)
Director: Frank Dunlop
Old Vic, 9 March to 27 November 1971 (60 performances)

*Zuckmayer's comedy persuaded Paul Scofield to make his long-awaited NT debut, as the
ex-convict who enjoys a few glorious hours masquerading as the titular officer.*

**Oliver Lyttelton
to Paul Scofield,
10 March 1971**

Dear Scofield,

Let me add one more cheer to the chorus of praise for your truly
fascinating performance. You made it into a glittering evening.

There was one other thing, which was that the enthusiasm of
the cast, and the obvious affection with which they worked with
you, came across the footlights at the end in an unmistakable and
moving fashion. I am not sure that this was not worth even more
than the critics.

No answer.

Yours,
Oliver [Lyttelton]

From June, Scofield alternated The Captain… *with Pirandello's* The Rules of the Game,
playing Leone Gala, who convinces his wife's lover to take his place (fatally) in a duel.

*Olivier, having waited seven years for Scofield, was determined to keep him, offering
Alceste in* The Misanthrope *(in Tony Harrison's new translation), Brutus in* Julius Caesar
and Gaev in The Cherry Orchard. *Scofield first dismissed Harrison's verse as 'rather crude
cracker', and then, three weeks later, wrote again.*

**Scofield to Olivier,
14 March 1972**

My dear Larry,

Thank you for all your good suggestions but I want to call a halt
to my association with the National. It is always very difficult to
explain the reasons in terms practical and understandable, and I
loved doing *The Captain* & the Pirandello.

It must rest rather baldly in that I don't want to continue; and
I would like to thank you for the experience of 1971, and to send
you my hopes and wishes for the company, and much love to you
and Joan.

Always most gratefully,
Yours,
Paul

**Olivier to Scofield,
30 March 1972**

My dear Paulie,

It is with something of an empty heart that I write this.

It is sweet and dear of you to be so gentle in removal of yourself
from us (or me). But it would be idle to pretend that it does not
leave an aching gap in my deep concerns at the Nat.

'Cut off' – in the blossoming youth of our association is what I feel, and I can only half apprehend your feelings, but of course I must accept them at their inferred value!

I cannot have been a v. satisfactory partner – 'So shaken as we are, so wan with care', we are also, I'm afraid, a bit of a cunt as an administrator.

If a man carries a load a bit too heavy for him, his condition perhaps makes him sparing of his courtesies to his friends he meets in the street. This isn't really an excuse, there can't be one but it is hopefully reasonable enough as a reason?

It would be just ghastly if I really thought you could turn your back on us for good.

Always with loving wishes,
Larry

Scofield did not return to Olivier's Company.

1972

Jumpers (1972)
by Tom Stoppard

Director: Peter Wood
Old Vic, 2 February 1972 to 5 July 1973 (132 performances)

The protagonist of Stoppard's play is George Moore, a professor of moral philosophy, who, along with his wife Dottie, a former musical-comedy performer, is caught up in the murder of a policeman.

The role of George left Olivier 'green with envy' when he offered it first to John Neville, then Alan Bates.

Alan Bates to Olivier,
15 October 1971

Dear Sir Laurence,

I do wish I had had the opportunity to read [*Jumpers*] when I wasn't feeling quite so bloody. Please forgive me if I sounded dismissive with what is obviously a very fine piece of work.

I wish you all the success in the world with it. There are splendid acting opportunities for the company.

My thanks once more,

Yours sincerely,
Alan Bates

Olivier to Louise
Purnell, 15 October
1971

Darling Lou,

Thank you so very much for coming in to read [Dottie] so
splendidly for me – and with me – for Tom Stoppard.

I am afraid the way things are now going it looks as if this part
will definitely be cast outside the Company. As you know, it was a
long shot, but all the same I am sorry it didn't come off.

Yours,
Larry

The same day, Olivier sent an identically worded letter to Gillian Barge.

*Stoppard had envisaged George as 'between 40 and 50' and Dottie as ten or 15 years
younger; Bates was 33 and Neville 46, but George was eventually played by Michael
Hordern, at 61 old enough to be the father of 33-year-old Diana Rigg's Dottie. They enjoyed
a triumph;* Jumpers *would win the* Evening Standard *award for Best Play.*

Tom Stoppard to
Olivier, 9 May 1972

Dear Larry,

I gather that a premature mutter from the RSC has prevented
me from telling you first that I have agreed informally to write a
play for them next year. I am very well aware of how much I owe
to you and the [NT] – as much as any playwright around owes to
any theatre – and I would not wish to seem to be contradicting
that indebtedness. But I don't think a playwright should be
expected to be either a Capulet or Montague, and for my part I
hope that I will return to the National with a new play. I have for
years been vaguely promising a play to Trevor Nunn whom I have

Diana Rigg (Dottie)
and Michael Hordern
(George) in *Jumpers*.
Photo: Michael
Childers

known since before he took over the [RSC], and I had told
him that I would try to give him one after *Jumpers* – so the next
one is it.

> Kind regards,
> Sincerely,
> Tom

A year later, Olivier called on Stoppard to fulfil that hope.

Olivier to Stoppard,
2 April 1973

Dearest Tom,

Before the scorch marks disappear from my long residence in the
hot seat I would want to ask [you for] a play, please, for the new
theatre on the South Bank.

You will have a wide choice of directors at your disposal,
among whom will number your very humble, but don't let that
put you off. […]

So, dear friend, proscenium or amphitheatre, whichever you
like, it would be simply marvellous to have one of You in the
opening seasons.

> Yours ever,
> L. O.

Stoppard replied that, assuming he could 'come up with something', he would be delighted:
'Meanwhile it's nice to know that while I have my eye on the new NT, the new NT will have
its eye on me.' Olivier referred to leaving the 'hot seat' because his days as Director were
numbered.

Peter Hall, NT Director Designate

After resigning as head of the RSC in 1968, Peter Hall had directed four feature films,
including the drama Three Into Two Won't Go *(1969), starring Rod Steiger. Hall then*
returned to the stage, with Harold Pinter's Old Times *(RSC, 1971) and three productions at*
the Royal Opera House (RoH), where he was due to become Director of Productions from
September 1971 – only to resign that summer, convinced that Covent Garden's board would
not endorse his plans for radical change. John Tooley, RoH general director, sensed, too, that
Hall 'wanted to be seen to be free' to run the National.

Despite Olivier's declining health, and the repeatedly postponed opening date for the
South Bank theatres (which had slipped from 1969 to 1974), he failed to provide for his own
succession. 'Larry had passing through the Old Vic all the younger talent the British theatre
had to offer,' recalled Michael Blakemore, 'and he never, ever decided on their succession.
Any of us could have been chosen – Bill Gaskill, John Dexter, me, Jonathan Miller. He didn't
want to think about it: death or retirement.'

Early in 1972, it emerged that the NT Board, now chaired by the property tycoon Sir Max
Rayne, had chosen Hall as the next Director. This news was leaked to The Observer *on Sunday*
9 April. Two days later, Olivier addressed the Company in the Old Vic stalls and told them he was
heartbroken, and had not been properly consulted. The Evening Standard *ran stories headlined*
'Now the National Theatre is torn by successor crisis' and 'I will fight, says Olivier'.

Max Rayne to Olivier, 12 April 1972

Dear Larry,

[…] I am indeed sorry about the unfortunate publicity which appears to have developed around the question of your eventual successor, particularly in view of the most agreeable and constructive manner in which our own discussions have been conducted and the complete harmony which exists between us on this subject.

Incidentally, Ken Tynan telephoned and asked to see me in order – as he put it – to try and clear up some of the confusion which the press reports appear to have created. We have arranged to meet tomorrow afternoon.

Yours ever,
Max

Olivier to Rayne, 12 April 1972

Dear Max,

Thanks for your very nice letter and it's good of you to see Ken.

Wouldn't it be just lovely if <u>nobody ever</u> made a fuss about anything? I do very much resent these stirrer-uppers.

Ever,
Larry

On 18 April the NT informed the press that discussions between Hall, Olivier and the Board 'have now been satisfactorily concluded': Hall would join the NT as Director Designate in 1973, and become Director after Olivier led the Company, which included Denis Quilley, onto the South Bank.

Denis Quilley, to Olivier, 18 April 1972

Dear Larry,

[…] About the company meeting the other day. What we all thought, and all said to each other afterwards (but being stupid & British & reticent didn't actually open our mouths to say so at the meeting) is that we all love and admire you very much, and we are all disappointed – both on your behalf and our own – that you won't be in sole charge when we go into the new building.

As far as I personally am concerned, the National Theatre means Larry Olivier, and always will.

Much love,
Denis

Olivier to Rayne, 7 May 1972

My dear Max,

I have long been wishful to lay the dust of discordant feelings haunting the air between us. The foolishness of my position starts to obsess me, having regurgitated the calm acceptance with which I at first condoned it. Shock, however icily controlled, turns out to have the same symptoms upon inspection. Perhaps discourtesy is not the right word which I should ascribe to this treatment. 'Brusque, cavalier, opportunist, insensitive' come nearer; and maybe 'imprudent' since my informed judgment would have brought an insight to your deliberations that no outside viewer could possess.

It was, and is still, strange that these were not invited and makes me think that the Board's view of me must be a low one. [...]

Yours ever,
Larry

My dear Larry,

[...] While I respect your very natural sensitivity regarding the publicity unfortunately generated around the appointment of Peter Hall, I cannot help feeling that none of it is helpful to any of us – least of all yourself – and that the sooner we direct our thoughts to the future, rather than the past, the better for everybody concerned – and the [NT] most of all.

Now the clouds of dust are settling, there seems to be general agreement within the Company as to the actual choice. [...]

It seems to me that we do now have a successor designate between yourself and whom there is the greatest mutual respect and regard, as well as a common interest in taking to new heights of success the splendid [NT] which you have done so much to establish. [...]

With kindest regards,
Max

Private and Confidential

My dear Larry,

[...] Long talk with Tynan as promised.

He made it easy for me. Very early in the conversation he volunteered that he thought perhaps the time might be coming for him to leave. He had, after all, done ten years with the National and was perhaps feeling that when you finished as Director, he should finish too.

I told him that I was glad he felt like that because although I had a great respect for what he had done and for his brilliance, I wasn't sure that he and I could work together.

He denied this, but the situation was not, at least on the surface, unpleasant or tense.

I think you would have been pleased.

Anyway, there is no need for gossip or crises. [...]

Thank you for the meetings this week, which I have really enjoyed. I look forward to more talk.

Best wishes,
Yours ever,
Peter

1973

Equus (1973)
by Peter Shaffer

Director: John Dexter
Old Vic, 26 July 1973 to 8 February 1975 (131 performances)

In Equus, *a disillusioned psychiatrist, Martin Dysart (Alec McCowen), investigates why his young patient, Alan Strang (Peter Firth), blinded six horses at the stables where he worked. The attack took place on the night Alan tried, and failed, to have sex with a stable girl, Jill (Doran Godwin).*

Kenneth Tynan, memo to John Dexter and Peter Shaffer, 16 July 1973	Production Notes – *Equus* […] The passage from the abortive fuck to the murders needs restructuring. I think Alan should see in his mind the looming heads of the horses peering in at his attempt to fuck the girl; he should react to them with guilty panic, which prompts Jill to think he must be crazy, and this is what sends her scurrying offstage. He must surely not put on those briefs (they look like a last-minute concession to prudes): he must remain naked because he is hypnotised by the horses' accusing eyes, because he expects punishment, because he sees himself as a sacrifice to the horse-god, because single combat in the ancient world was always carried out in the nude – find your own reason, but please keep those knickers off.

Tynan to Dexter, 23 July 1973	Dear John,
	
	Congratulations. I saw the show with Kathleen on Saturday night, and when I led her round to Alec's dressing-room afterwards she was crying almost too hard to speak. It's the best thing you have done for years and Peter [Shaffer] possibly ever. […]
	
	    Love and blessings,
	    Ken

Equus *was a smash at the Old Vic, transferred to the West End and also Broadway, where Dexter rehearsed with Anthony Hopkins as Dysart, alongside movement director Claude Chagrin, who again choreographed the actors who represented Alan's worshipped horses.*

Dexter to Joan Plowright, 1 October 1974	Dear Joan, All goes well here and I am very happy. Tony Hopkins is on the way to being superb in *Equus*. He is calm, disciplined and every word is crystal clear. On the whole, [the play] seems more

interesting than in England, but I am still only half way through rehearsals.

Claude Chagrin has gone slightly mad and left New York saying that the play is immoral and Peter Shaffer is a wicked man. As it has taken *her* two years to discover this, how long will it be before the public finds out? […]

Love,
John

Peter Firth as the horse-obsessed Alan in *Equus*

The Bacchae (405 BC)

by Euripides

Adapted by Wole Soyinka (1973)
Director: Roland Joffé
Old Vic, 2 August to 20 September 1973 (20 performances)

Olivier had been planning to revive The Bacchae *since 1971, when he offered it to one of the actors who had auditioned as Ophelia in 1963.*

Eileen Atkins to Olivier, 25 August 1971

Dear Lord Olivier,

I'm writing because [I want to] explain properly how I feel about your offer.

I didn't know either of the plays – I've now read them both several times – I think that *Lysistrata* is a poor camp joke – I think Aristophanes needed some quick cash – it's almost a play about peace – but I can't rise above those erections!

The Bacchae is of course a great play – very right to do it now – but please forgive me for being presumptuous – I would have thought if it were done properly it would be so powerful one couldn't possibly take anything else.

I'm selfish enough an actress to want to attempt *The Bacchae* if it's to be the first play of the evening – and let someone else cope with *Lysistrata* – but if it's the second half I think they'd be worn out before I came on.

I would love to come to the National and I do realise that in a company one has to play parts sometimes that one doesn't necessarily want to play – but I feel it would be foolish to make a start in this uncertain manner.

Maybe something can be worked out – or maybe having waited so long – I should wait & hope for parts more immediately appealing – for although I think Agave [mother, and unwitting killer, of Pentheus, King of Thebes] a stunning part I <u>do</u> think it would be more touching if played by a woman clearly past childbearing.

Forgive me if I sound less than enthusiastic – I do so <u>want</u> to join the company – but I want it to be right.

I know you'll understand.

Love,
    Eileen […]

In The Bacchae, *Constance Cummings, then 63, played Agave; Atkins would have been 39.*

The end of the Olivier years

Writing to Peter Hall in 1960, Laurence Olivier described the twin goal of establishing and building the National as 'the central duty of my career', one which would necessitate 'incarcerating myself in State service'. His exhausting dedication to the National between 1963 and 1973 meant forgoing huge income from the television, film, West End and Broadway roles that would undoubtedly have come his way had he remained a free agent.

Olivier could not escort the Company on to the South Bank, but, at a press conference in March 1973, which confirmed that Hall would become Director on 1 November, Kenneth Tynan rightly observed: 'When Laurence Olivier asked me to work for him, the National Theatre was merely an idea. Now it is an institution. Not bad in ten years.' He could not resist adding: 'Our welcome to Peter Hall is heartfelt, but we would be more than human if it were not tinged with a distinct overtone of "follow that."'

The Olivier Theatre under construction
in October 1972

Act 2

The Peter Hall Years

——

1973–
1988

The start of the Hall years

The first, two-and-a-half-year phase of Peter Hall's tenure included a triumphant Harold Pinter premiere and acclaimed performances from Peggy Ashcroft, John Gielgud and Ralph Richardson. Administratively, it left the new Director in a torturous limbo.

Hall and his colleagues were obliged not only to programme the Old Vic, but to secure, in good faith, binding commitments from directors, designers and actors for a 'shadow' repertory for the South Bank – only to shred these plans when the South Bank opening date was postponed yet again. 'All the contractors are blaming each other and I am having to wind up the Company,' Hall wrote to John Dexter in 1974. 'It is a nightmare of the first proportions. And an unbelievable farce. I am feeling quite well because I'm so angry.'

Between The Party *(1973) and* Watch It Come Down *(1976), many letters written by Hall may be read with 'Will we ever move in?' as plaintive subtext.*

The Party (1973)
by Trevor Griffiths

Director: John Dexter
Old Vic 20 December 1973 to 21 March 1974

The Party takes place on Friday 10 May 1968, in the London home of a television producer, Joe Shawcross, whose guests include a heavy-drinking playwright, Sloman (Frank Finlay), and a Glaswegian, John Tagg, National Organiser of the Revolutionary Socialist Party, played by Laurence Olivier – his final stage role.

Kenneth Tynan to Hall, 29 September 1973

Dear Peter,

I've just had a very disquieting talk with Trevor Griffiths and, since I commissioned *The Party* and shepherded him through the writing of it, I can't help writing to you about the ugly situation that seems to have developed. Because of the large number of new productions you have planned for 1974, and because Larry and Finlay are leaving in March, it won't be possible to give the play more than 34 performances.

This strikes me as simply appalling. It is quite unprecedented. The [NT] has never imposed a guillotine on a play's run before it opened. It is terribly damaging to Trevor's reputation, not to mention his purse, that the National should write his play off as a flop (34 performances equals a month's run in the West End) before it is even in rehearsal.

Has Harold Pinter's widely known dislike of the play got anything to do with this? Or has the play other enemies with other motives? I cannot see how one can justify spending public money on a <u>predetermined</u> flop. And although the choice and timing of the production was not your responsibility, the decision to close it certainly is.

I hear there has been talk about the possibility of permitting a West End transfer. This sounds to me what Larry calls chimera-department talk.

I cannot recall a greater blow dealt to a talented writer at such a crucial stage in his career. Welcome to the big league, we say, and then slap his face and show him the door. Is there no way of repairing at least some of the damage before the repercussions begin to spread?

Yours,
Ken

Hall to Tynan,
3 October 1973

Dear Ken,

There is no conspiracy against the play, no new broom being wielded, no purge that is in need of exposure in the public interest. Harold expressed uneasiness about certain characters in the play being close to those he knew in real life. But to say that he dislikes the play is very wide of the mark.

I have proposed to Trevor that as soon as the play has opened, we will plan for its return on the South Bank in March 1975. This will probably be without Larry. As an earnest of my good intentions and to avoid it being 'chimera-department talk' I have suggested that we pay Trevor in 1974 a reasonable advance on his royalties for 1975. […]

I find it hard to believe that Trevor shares your suspicions.

I hope there will not be a public wangle over this, although you fear that there may be.

Yours,
Peter

John Dexter, memo
to Hall, 9 October
1973

I had a very good meeting with Trevor. No problems. He regards K. T.'s letter as hysterical and over stated, and told Ken that if he (Ken) wrote, he would be writing on his own behalf and not Trevor's. Trevor still working out what to do, but no personal problem in relation to National Theatre

JD

1974

The Tempest (1610)
by William Shakespeare
Director: Peter Hall
Old Vic, 5 March to 29 June (46 performances)

As Prospero in Hall's first production as Director, John Gielgud returned to the Old Vic for the first time since Oedipus *in 1968.*

John Gielgud to George Pitcher and Ed Cone, 2 March 1974

Dear George and Ed,

We rehearsed eight weeks for *The Tempest*. I think it will be a beautiful production, but very elaborate – designed for the new theatre (next year), so is a bit cramped on the small stage at the Old Vic. Flying goddess and Ariel too – a brilliant young boy [Michael Feast] who sings counter-tenor and manages to be convincing also as Ceres in the Masque and the sea-nymph who brings Ferdinand on in the first act.

I nearly killed myself (and Ferdinand) when they rashly opened a trap door I was standing on at the dress rehearsal. I fell about 4 ft. on top of the young lovers who were waiting to come up, and neither one of us was hurt at all – miracle really – but a slightly alarming experience, to say the least. We have had two previews – the first a bit shaky, but last night went splendidly and I had a real ovation at the end, which, of course, delighted and encouraged me very much.

Yours ever,
John

The National under fire

On 15 October 1974 The Times *published a letter headlined 'National Theatre's Needs', signed by Oscar Lewenstein of the Royal Court and 12 other artistic directors of subsidised theatres.*

Oscar Lewenstein et al., to William Rees-Mogg (Editor of *The Times*), 14 October 1974

Sir,

Quite naturally, the aims and ambitions of Britain's new National Theatre have attracted a great deal of public attention. The ambitions are high, attractive and extensive. They are also going to cost a great deal of money. While wishing Peter Hall all the good fortune he will certainly need to fill his three theatres with performances of quality, we feel that it is important at this stage to make it clear that serious dangers may well arise from so elaborate a complex.

First, there is danger in the demand which will be made by the NT on the resources of the Arts Council. Next year these demands seem likely to absorb something like 25% of the council's annual drama budget. The arts are still severely under-subsidised in this country, particularly outside London. The NT must receive the subsidy it needs – but never at the expense of the nation's other subsidised theatres. And if, as seems probable, we must face the prospect of cuts in the real value of grants, this must be 'across the board'. The National's name, and its huge initial ambitions cannot exempt it from the same obligation to economise as the rest of us.

Perhaps an even more important danger is the drain, which can already be felt, on resources other than financial. To staff its three auditoria, the NT is said to be seeking 140 skilled technicians. It is doubtful whether there are many more than that number working in [this] country. The National has been busy for some time already, endeavouring to attract technicians and staff from other theatres with salaries far in excess of anything these theatres can afford. The implications of this are unhealthy.

The NT is [our] largest single theatrical venture. Its work will doubtless conform to the highest standards. But this does not mean that equally worthwhile, equally important work will not continue to spring from all sorts of different, sometimes unexpected, sometimes less celebrated sources. Only thus will the theatre flourish.

Mr Hall has said that he wishes to make the National 'the nation's theatre'. This is an effective slogan; but the nation has many good theatres already. Big is not always beautiful. The size and the status of the New NT must not be allowed to drain or to enfeeble the other theatres of the nation. This, we suggest, is now a dangerous possibility.

Yours faithfully,

Oscar Lewenstein, Lindsay Anderson (Associate Artistic Director, Royal Court), Peter Cheeseman (Artistic Director, Victoria Theatre, Stoke-on-Trent), Michael Croft (Director, National Youth Theatre), Frank Dunlop (Director, Young Vic), Michael Elliott (Joint Artistic Director, '69 Theatre Company, Manchester), Richard Eyre (Artistic Director, Nottingham Playhouse), Howard Gibbens (Director, Bush Theatre), John Harrison (Director, Leeds Playhouse), Ewan Hooper (Director, Greenwich Theatre), Peter James (Crucible, Sheffield), Joan Littlewood (Theatre Royal, Stratford East), Charles Marowitz (Artistic Director, Open Space Theatre), Toby Robertson (Prospect Theatre).

In his diary, Hall wrote: 'I am terribly hurt about it, although pretending not to be.' His lengthy response, insisting that the NT needed no more than 70 technicians, was published on The Times *Letters page on 17 October: 'If adequate funds for the new National can only be provided by starving others, then that is a negation of what the NT is about.'*

On 13 November, The Guardian *published a letter from Helen Mirren, then playing Lady Macbeth for the RSC, in which she argued that 'the expenditure on costumes, sets and staging in general' in RSC and NT shows 'has been excessive, unnecessary and destructive to the art of theatre'.*

RSC trustee Michael Lord Birkett (soon to become NT deputy director) had produced Hall's film of A Midsummer Night's Dream *(1968), with Mirren as Hermia.*

Helen Mirren to Lord Birkett, 29 December 1974

Dear Lord Birkett,

A friend sent me a copy of the House of Lords Official Report Thursday 21 November [when] you spoke on the National Theatre Bill [lifting the cap on the government's capital contribution to the new building], indirectly referring to my letter to *The Guardian.*

You say 'Unless the arts can maintain their level through thick and thin, every form of national life, and every form of popular art will be impoverished.' I support these words wholeheartedly, but disagree with the methods of maintaining the level. There can be no 'ill-chosen moment' for re-appraising, criticising, re-forming the stuff on which an artist works. That is a never-ending process, or indeed the artistic level deteriorates rapidly, witness the USSR.

I believe if, as [trustees] of the RSC, you spent any time in and around the theatre, the rehearsal room, the workshops, the wings; if you involved yourself at all with the real workings of a theatrical event rather than the economical indications of it, you would get closer to an understanding of the views of myself and many other people, and be more qualified to speak on the subject at the Lords.

We both know that the silly sarcasm of a yard or two of taffeta dismaying an actor is avoiding an all-important issue; that is whether the large expenditure on glossy tourist-attracting theatres is the best method of keeping the art of the theatre alive and kicking and indeed a popular art. Theatres in the provinces are being closed and cut back – like Peterborough and Hull, sometimes beautiful new theatres, all in towns that now and especially in the dark future of unemployment, need art and culture as their only means of expression. Small theatres with reputations for good, far-reaching work, like the Young Vic, the Bush Theatre, the King's Head, the Soho Theatre are all facing extinction – is this maintaining the level of the theatre? While a dead piece of expensive spectacular is playing to expensive seats filled with upper middle class 'theatre-goers', or a matinée of bored schoolchildren who cannot relate to the play because of the circumstances in which it is played.

For me it is not a question of the expense of a production, but what it is done at the expense of. No-one involved in theatre would assume something can be achieved for nothing – nothing

will come of nothing – but neither can something be achieved
by making nothing hugely expensive. Peter Brook's work now
[in Paris] is exciting not because of the star actors, nor because
of the expense of converting the [Théâtre des Bouffes du Nord],
but because for the last eight years or more he has worked, with
the exception of an occasional invasion, outside the walls of
bourgeois theatre, in a state of learning rather than smugness,
using a great deal of money, effort, imagination, sweat, thought,
energy and emotion in the discovery of <u>how</u> to turn nothing into
something. The only chance for the arts in England is for every
person involved in them to take his example.

Yours sincerely,
Helen Lydia Mirren

One of the Lewenstein signatories, Richard Eyre, brought Trevor Griffiths's Comedians
from Nottingham Playhouse to the Old Vic in September 1975. Interviewed in the Sunday
Telegraph *to promote the London run, Eyre confessed to 'a justifiable fear' that the South
Bank NT, 'with a large subsidy and three theatres, may have to absorb everything. It's too
large for a single policy … the more you do, the less good it is.'*

Hall, postcard
to Richard Eyre,
22 September 1975

Dear Richard,

I wish you hadn't found it necessary to add to the Lewenstein shit
in the *Sunday Telegraph*. 'It's too large for a single policy.' How do
you know yet?
    Frankly I'm fed up with people like you praising the NT
to my face and doing dirt behind my back. I would be better
off to ignore your remarks. But why should I? Even so, I hope
Comedians goes well. You've made sure it will not help the cause
of the NT.

Sincerely,
Peter

The Freeway (1974)
by Peter Nichols

Director: Jonathan Miller
Old Vic, 1 October to 26 December (32 performances)

After their success with The National Health, *Michael Blakemore had felt let down by
Peter Nichols, first when he lost out to another director on the film of* National Health
(the same thing had happened with A Day in the Death of Joe Egg*). Then, having worked
with Nichols on the script of his comedy* Chez Nous, *its West End premiere was given to
Robert Chetwyn.* Chez Nous *was in rehearsal when Nichols wrote to Blakemore about* The
Freeway, *a dystopian vision of England in the near future, in which the government cuts
expenditure on social services to fund universal car ownership, and drivers are threatened by
anti-motor terrorists, the Scrubbers.*

Peter Nichols to
Michael Blakemore,
10 January 1974

Dear Michael,

Peggy [Ramsay] has now forwarded a copy [of your letter explaining that you did not want to direct *The Freeway*]. I am completely taken by surprise and don't know which way to turn. Though you didn't seem knocked out by the play when we came to see you in Biarritz, well, that's been your reaction to all my plays. I have a record of how you first saw *Joe Egg*, *National Health* and *Forget-me-not Lane* and you were properly circumspect. This approach, though difficult for the author, has proved a proper one for you. You look at the work with every suspicion and if it survives that, it's probably alright. So I assumed that was the case with *The Freeway*.

I also thought that by working apart we'd proved our independence and could now happily resume a partnership that came up with the goods. I wrote last year, saying I thought we ought to swallow our differences and try to work together again because we were able to produce work both intelligent and entertaining.

If I take your letter at face value, there isn't much to say, except that I believe *The Freeway* to be my best so far and can think of no one else who could direct it half as well as you. I am re-writing it and it is less arbitrary and more clear-sighted than anything I've done.

I can only ask you whether you really need to 'feel strongly' about the plays you direct? I'm not sure you felt all that strongly about the others at the time. Perhaps working on them involves you.

If there is any other reason for your turning it down, like some disagreement at the National, let's for God's sake do the play elsewhere.

That said, I'll certainly let Peter [Hall] read it. The fuel crisis gives the situation an extra point and the play becomes a description of what's happening now. This, you must see, is very helpful, because I don't want people thinking it's only about a traffic jam. I intend that it will move from the bright comedy of Act One, ending with the picnic, to a more gory climax. […]

Of course it is tricky dealing with this and rehearsals and my only reproach is that you might have told me earlier. It might be friendly if we met in town one day. You're rehearsing *Knuckle* [by David Hare], I imagine.

Chez Nous looks promising. Good cast. […]
Good luck with the Hare.

Love to Shirley and Con,
    Peter

Blakemore to Nichols, 13 January 1974

Dear Peter,

In a first draft of my letter to Peggy I put: 'I think it's better to preserve a friendship than maintain a professional collaboration.' I cut it subsequently because it covered an area not really proper to bother her with. But this, rather more than my response to the play, is at the root of my not wanting to direct *The Freeway*.

Too much has happened. I'm pretty sure the friendship need not be affected by it, but it will be if we persist in the working relationship. I'm sure eventually we'll do a play of yours again.

Love to the family.

Yours,
Michael

Hall to Blakemore, 17 May 1974

My dear Michael,

I managed to effect an agreement between Jonathan [Miller] and Peter Nichols that Jonathan should do *The Freeway*.

John Bury is designing it, so at least I am happy that it is being presented by the home team.

I think everybody in our group is very sorry that you did not feel that you could undertake the play, although we all understand the complex reasons that led you to the decision.

Jonathan was particularly anxious that you should hear what is happening from us rather than rumour. […]

Best wishes,
Peter

For Nichols's play, designed by John Bury, Miller had a 28-strong cast, including Irene Handl as Nancy, elderly mother of an influential peer; they join other characters forced by freeway gridlock to spend a weekend camped out on a grass verge: provisions run scarce, tempers fray.

Nichols to Hall, 21 August 1974

Dear Peter,

[…] My feelings are still that a black surround could be disaster for this play. John assures me the black will be so far away we shan't see it as black. But how about in the wing areas? Nor do I really think that black ever looks anything but black.

Let's hope I'm wrong.

Rehearsals are going well, though it's too early to say more. We shall have to wait for the routine drudgery and drill to see. At the moment it's good fun and Jonathan's laughing at the jokes. Irene hasn't so far complained but I intend to try to write her a bit of an aria in the last scene, partly because she's worth it and also because the play may need something of the sort at that point. […]

Yours,
Peter

On the first night, Hall wished Nichols good luck and thanked him for his 'utter professionalism', but the play was dismissed as 'a dismally facile, predictable affair' (The Guardian), in a 'wretchedly muddled and amateurish' production (Daily Telegraph).

Ann Bernard to Nichols, 2 October 1974

Dear Mr Nichols,

As someone completely unknown, my opinion bears no weight. Nevertheless, I would like to congratulate you. I thought the critic in *The Telegraph* had completely missed the boat and was not surprised, judging by the amazingly unresponsive audience near me on the first night, of whom he must have been one!

We thought *The Freeway* superb. As always, you have a fine ear for dialogue and this makes your characters entirely believable. There was nothing 'patronising' about your treatment of these characters. Les and May [a Ford factory supervisor and his wife] were real, generous, warm-hearted people, who had been manipulated completely and unsuspectingly by the system and, as such, they represent the majority of us.

I have been brought up on such writers as Chekhov and Ibsen and I go to the theatre to shed blood. You are the only living playwright that makes me do so.

I do hope the Sunday critics show a little more perception.

Yours sincerely,
Ann Bernard

Andrew Ellis to Nichols, 13 November 1974

Dear Mr Nichols,

Yesterday evening I [saw] *The Freeway*.

I did not expect a high standard of acting and direction – because the last several plays I have seen at the Old Vic have been deficient in those areas – so I was not disappointed on that count.

I did go hoping for originality and invention in the writing – and I based this hope on my happy experiences of *Joe Egg*, *The National Health*, *Chez Nous* and *Forget-me-not Lane*. And *The Gorge*.

I believe I saw *The Gorge* three times on television. The fact that it was repeated indicates that many people must be very familiar with it.

But I went to see a new play called *The Freeway*. Not a reworking (and a distortion) of a previous play. I didn't want to see that picnic scene again, or meet again those four central characters, or hear again about the ballroom dancing, the hamster, 'acquiring property' and – above all – that toilet.

How did you have the nerve?!

I really would welcome your comments.

With disappointment,
Andrew Ellis

Dear Mr Ellis,

I'm pleased to have the chance to speak up for *The Freeway*, which in script form was considered both by me and all who read it to be my best play to date. Since it opened, not a good word has been said for it.

I've often used my television plays as starting points for stage plays. Certainly there are scenes from *The Gorge* in *The Freeway* and I would, if you twisted my arm, admit that they're the least successful on the stage and, if the production were revised, might cut them out. But if you didn't notice that there was a really extensive growth in the people and the situation, you can't really have given the play your full attention.

There was no traffic jam in *The Gorge*, no Motor Home, no stranded toffs, no futurist extrapolation, no linking of political freedom with technical chaos, no ministerial visit, no helicopter, no Wreckers, no Scrubbers, no crisis at all.

I have obviously thought a lot about the reasons for our bad press and poor response. I believe it may be that the play makes gloomy predictions in a cheerful way. People prefer their futurism to be more like *Nineteen Eighty-Four*. They don't want social comedy to be hereafter. But why not? People change slower than techniques. The people in my play are of today, their attitudes are today's, while they are being overwhelmed by tomorrow's junk.

Yours sincerely,
Peter Nichols

Hall closed The Freeway, *replacing it with additional performances of* Equus.

1975

Happy Days (1960)
by Samuel Beckett

Director: Peter Hall
Old Vic, 13 March to 19 August 1975 (34 performances)
Lyttelton, 20 March 1976 to 22 September 1977 (10 performances)

In Happy Days, *which opened on tour in Liverpool in November 1974 before coming to the Old Vic, Peggy Ashcroft was Winnie, buried up to her chest, then neck, in a mound of earth.*
Hall had hoped that, before appearing in his revival of John Gabriel Borkman *from January 1975, Ashcroft might have played Nancy in* The Freeway.

The National Theatre at the Old Vic

The National Theatre receives financial assistance from the Arts Council of Great Britain and The Greater London Council

Happy Days

by Samuel Beckett

Peggy Ashcroft / Alan Webb
Director Peter Hall / Designer John Bury
Assistant Designer Timian Alsaker
Lighting David Hersey

Peggy Ashcroft as Winnie in the poster
for *Happy Days*

Peggy Ashcroft to Hall, 31 May 1974

My dear Pete,

Just arrived here & found your letter & copy of *The Freeway*. Before reading it I think I should write my immediate and very strong reaction. I really do not want to postpone *Happy Days* any longer; not only because of our commitment to Sam but I feel now <u>so</u> committed in every way & am thinking internally & constantly about it & about to learn it. Also – I am more & more convinced that we came to the right, & for me, essential, decision – to do it <u>first</u>. I have always dreaded tackling it when I am already playing, however intermittently, another piece – & I <u>know</u> I need the freshness of energy to do it, <u>not</u> after a heavy work like *J. G. B.*

The over-riding reason is that *H. D.* is what I know I must be 'on' & I would find it impossible to deflect from that. [...]

So – I will read the *Freeway* for interest but even if it were the greatest comedy of all time, I <u>couldn't</u>, in view of all this, consider it. Feel sure you will understand. [...]

　Love,
　　Peg

Ashcroft would perform Happy Days *in the NT's opening South Bank season from March 1976. Hall had known Beckett since directing* Waiting for Godot *in 1955.*

Hall to Samuel Beckett, 18 February 1976

Dear Sam,

I know you are going to say no to this letter but we all felt we had to ask you!

We have all agreed to do a [70th] birthday celebration for you – including *Happy Days* and readings etc., here in our new building.

We are therefore inviting you to be with us – but we know you won't want to be. Nonetheless this is the invitation with our love and respect.

　Best wishes,
　　Peter

Beckett replied on 24 February, profoundly grateful for the invitation, deploring the element in his 'unfortunate composition' that habitually prevented him from attending such events, and relieved to know that Hall would forgive him.

No Man's Land (1975)
by Harold Pinter

Director: Peter Hall
Old Vic, 23 April to 28 June 1975, 40 performances

No Man's Land was Hall's fourth world premiere of a Pinter play. John Gielgud was Spooner, who visits the elegant Hampstead house of a wealthy writer, Hirst (Ralph Richardson), who is attended by Briggs (Terence Rigby) and Foster (Michael Feast). Richardson was already at the Old Vic as Ibsen's John Gabriel Borkman.

John Gielgud to Harold Pinter, 28 September 1974

Dear Harold,

Impossible to get on to you by telephone! … thank you for letting me read the brilliant play and to say how really delighted and flattered I am that you and Peter should think I could play Spooner. You know how greatly I have always hoped to be in something of yours – and this should be the most exciting event I could possibly look forward to.

Best regards and congratulations. I am mad about the script.

Ever yours,
John Gielgud

Lillian Hellman to Pinter, 5 November 1974

Dear Harold,

That's a mighty, mighty interesting play. I, who don't much like to read plays, started very late at night and went straight through, and then started over again the next morning. I am afraid to say that I understood it. But somewhere deep down I think I did. In any case I am an old and increasing admirer, and I can't tell you the good luck that I think you deserve with the play.

My affection,
Lillian

Ralph Richardson to Pinter, 18 November 1974

Dear Mr Pinter,

Thank you very much for telephoning me and inviting me with such charming welcome. This has given great cheer to me: it has long been my ambition to act in a play of yours – Hirst is a splendid part – I pray I may be able to hold the bat.

EVER
Yours very sincerely,
Ralph Richardson

Elia Kazan was preparing to direct Pinter's screen adaptation of F. Scott Fitzgerald's The Last Tycoon, *for producer Sam Spiegel.*

Elia Kazan to Pinter,
5 December 1974

Dear Harold,

Bursts of laughter from seat 6C on the Boeing 707. An anxious look from the stewardess. Your play is hilarious. Then very touching. Poor England, I thought! Still, how extraordinary, and caught perfectly! It will be a great success. Those two old boys you've got to play it will be brilliant. I thought the two younger parts might have a little firmer line drawn between them. But maybe I didn't get it, must read the play again.

Otherwise nothing critical. And lots of affection.

Send me, or have Sam's people send me, the new script as soon as you get it done. Better send me two.

Yours,
Mike
Elia Kazan

Gielgud to Irene
Worth, 14 February
1975

Dear Irene,

We read [*No Man's Land*] on Monday, blocked the whole action on Tuesday, if you please, and walked through it on Wednesday with our books in our hands! It all seemed to fall into place with almost terrifying felicity and Pinter was simply delighted. I only hope we are not being too optimistic. We have three weeks off now to study and learn, and begin rehearsing properly on March 3rd for five weeks. Very exciting, I must say.

Wonderful press [for *Borkman*]. Ralph (who will be wonderful in the Pinter) begs me not to come till he has settled down, but I think he is touchingly and secretly delighted at the success and seems in wonderful form.

Love,
John

Michael Feast to
Pinter, April 1975

Dear Harold,

I just want to say thank you for your invaluable help and that I am enjoying totally, working with such a fucking great play.

My love and sincere admiration,
Mickey Feast

Gielgud to Worth,
29 April 1975

Dear Irene,

The Pinter play went wonderfully on the opening night and everyone seems very pleased with both Ralph and me. I dried up stone dead in my long speech at the end of the last preview – tried to replace a line I had left out, and fumbled the whole thing badly, so I was in terror of doing it the next night, but God – or proper concentration – was with me, fortunately. Very good press all round – all a bit baffled by the obscure passages and whatever moral one takes away – or leaves behind? But it is funny, menacing, poetic and powerful, though possibly the blending of the components is a bit startling and confusing to the audience. But this is true to some extent with all the Pinter plays.

Love,
John

With Michael Kitchen having replaced Feast, No Man's Land *transferred to Wyndham's Theatre in September 1975. A year later, it played in Toronto and Washington DC before opening on Broadway, and concluded its run back in London, at the Lyttelton in January–February 1977.*

Terence Rigby to Pinter, 24 October 1976

Dear Harold,

[…] From where I stand each night [Eisenhower Theater, Washington DC] the play is going well – RR and JG have both had colds but soldier on tremendously.

I have developed a sort of 'super affection' for RR – he is a tremendous human being.

I think that Mike Kitchen has done well with Foster – he is a talented chap who took on an enormous task – all he needs is a little French polish.

The Washington audience seems rather sour and are for me worrying. Quite different to Toronto where I thought they were superb. I am therefore looking forward to New York. […]

As ever and thanks,
Terry x

Richardson to Pinter, 21 January 1977

Mon cher Harold,

Thank you very much for your kind GREETINGS TELEGRAM for our 3rd 4th I'm not sure FIRST NIGHT – but always remembered by you.

I am very proud, privileged and happy to be in your beautiful play and you are A JOY TO DRIVE WITH.

With affectionate best wishes,
EVER,
Ralph

Queen Christina**
by Pam Gems

The heroine of Pam Gems's play ruled Sweden from 1632 until she abdicated in 1654.

Clive Goodwin to John Russell Brown (NT associate director – literary), 8 December 1975	Dear John,
	
	Would you consider this excellent play? I am sure it could work extremely well. It probably still needs some architectural adjustment but it's brimming with theatrical life and zest and tells an amazing true story.
	
	    Yours sincerely,
	      Clive

Russell Brown to Goodwin, 2 June 1976	Dear Clive Goodwin,
	
	I find that I cannot recommend [*Queen Christina*] for production.
	    Pam Gems has a lot of ability and flair and a great deal of the writing is brave and strong. But there's little to offset a laboured quality that I sense in the writing. I suspect the script is more a basis of studio work than a finished play.
	    Thanks for sending it.
	
	    Yours ever,
	      John Russell Brown

The RSC premiered Queen Christina *in its Stratford studio theatre, The Other Place, in September 1977.*

1976

The Rape of the Sabine Women (1885)**
by Franz & Paul von Schönthan

Rex Harrison to Hall, 12 January 1976	My dear Peter,
	
	There is nothing in the world I would rather do than act for you at the National.
	    The material is, I agree, of the essence. I saw a play at the Burgtheater in Vienna called *The Rape of the Sabine Women*. As far as I could tell it was a very funny original farce with some excellent parts. Certainly the audience adored it.
	    I am getting my [tax] affairs in order so that I can return to live [in England] after April 5th. I will however be in London

for four or five days because the *Evening Standard* have asked me
to introduce the 21st anniversary of their Awards at the Savoy
lunch of February 4th. Perhaps we could get together for a drink
and some ideas over those days? I shall quite understand if you
cannot, because goodness knows you must be up to your eyes
in work. It's a gigantic thing you have on your hands – but how
exhilarating for you.

> With every good wish,
>   Rex

Harrison never appeared at the National, which has yet to revive The Rape of the Sabine
Women.

Watch It Come Down (1975)

by John Osborne

Director: Bill Bryden
Old Vic, 24 to 26 February 1976 (10 performances; first preview 18 February)
Lyttelton, 20 March to 7 September 1976 (29 performances)

Hall to John Osborne,
7 August 1974

My dear John,

Thank you for our meeting.
    You may regard this letter as impertinent – perhaps I am taking
things too far.
    But theatre agreements are very much like human relationships
– somebody has to make the first move.
    I would very much like you to consider [the NT] as your house.
This means anything you write will be performed by us, though
if I have reservations or doubts, the play might only be in the 400-
seat theatre, the Cottesloe. Otherwise we will be performing you
in the 900-seater [Lyttelton]. […]
    Am I going too far?

> Best wishes,
>   Yours ever,
>   Peter

Within a fortnight, Hall had read, and committed to producing, Osborne's Watch It Come
Down. *It features an agonising portrait of Osborne's stormy marriage to Jill Bennett, who
nonetheless agreed to play her alter ego, Sally, estranged novelist wife of film director Ben
Prosser. The play ends with Ben shot dead by local residents.*
    *In October, Hall informed Osborne that Albert Finney did not wish to appear as Ben,
but added: 'I am in the middle of a flirtation with Alan Bates about coming to the National.
I think he would be very good.' Bates knew Osborne well: he was Cliff in the premiere
of* Look Back in Anger *in 1956, and Archie Rice's son, Frank, in the 1960 film of* The
Entertainer.

Alan Bates to Osborne, November 1974

Dear John,

Peter Hall sent me your play. I think it's terrifically powerful writing, although I found the end hard to accept. I'd like to talk to you about it. I've had recently a rather awful experience with Peter Hall which makes me very wary altogether of the National.

I'm glad to have read it & it would be terrific to do something of yours again. I think this play is Sally's play really – typical actor's reaction. I'll try to contact you when I get back. I'm filming in Germany for a month on a piece of hopefully high-class rubbish called *Royal Flash*.

Love & to Jill,
Alan

The 'awful' experience appears to have been Hall's invitation to Bates to play Marlowe's Tamburlaine – the role eventually given to Albert Finney.

Hall to Osborne, 7 November 1974

My dear John,

The director on our strength who is available and who is mad about your play and makes a lot of sense about it is Bill Bryden.
I think it would be an excellent idea. Bill has balls.

Best wishes,
Yours ever,
Peter

Hall to Osborne, 10 June 1975

My dear John,

[…] We will present *Watch It Come Down*. Press Night 24th February 1976.
We guarantee to do the play unless matters outside our control which I believe are loosely described in contracts as acts of God, fires, or lockouts, prevent us.
Please don't be suspicious of our intentions.

Best wishes,
Yours ever,
Peter

Osborne to Hall, 11 June 1975

My dear Peter,

How God ever came into this particular transaction I can't quite understand. I have tried though unsuccessfully to do without Him in these things. Although I have hoped for His loving eye in the enterprises in which I have been involved. […]

Ever,
John
    cc Robin Dalton [Osborne's agent]

**Hall to Osborne,
13 June 1975**

My dear John,

As to the acts of God etc., may I urge you to comfort yourself as I do with Sam Beckett's observation, 'God, the bastard; he doesn't exist.'

> Best wishes,
> > Yours ever,
> > > Peter

After the National rejected Peter O'Toole's offer to play Ben at the Old Vic for only three weeks, Frank Finlay was cast, and he, Bennett and Bryden were part of the first group to use one of the new South Bank rehearsal rooms, where they read the play on 16 January 1976.

**Hall to Osborne,
18 January 1976**

My dear John,

I thought the play read wonderfully well. The humour of the first act opens up the audience to be chilled by what follows. And I liked the cast very much.

I hope you'll be happy with us.

Now that I'm about to have three theatres to fill, I begin to feel credible again. So I'm saying, and saying strongly: any hope of a new play?

> Ever,
> > Peter

**Osborne to Hall,
20 January 1976**

My dear Peter,

Thank you so much for the nice welcoming atmosphere the other day. Any first reading is a nightmarish experience usually. But you certainly turned it into something quite different.

I thought it was going to be somewhat awesome and first-day-at-school stuff but the whole atmosphere and working conditions are so remarkable that even I have vowed to give up making jokes about the 'Colditz of the South Bank'. […]

With very best wishes for it all,

> Ever,
> > John

P. S. As for another play, I would be delighted when the present clouds have lifted a bit more from my head.

**Hall to Osborne,
1 March 1976**

My dear John,

I hope you felt, as I did, that the critical reaction on Sunday was a little less crass [than the daily press]. Not much, it's true. But a little.

As you well know, I want another play from you.
What is the best way of us serving you?
A straight commission?
A deadline?

I'm sorry to nag, but after such a good experience, we must not stand still.

> Best wishes,
> Yours ever,
> Peter

Osborne to Hall, 3 March 1976

My dear Peter,

I was agreeably surprised by the Sunday press which at least gave the impression of some historical event taking place. You certainly don't have a theatrical Concorde on your hands with the new building. Indeed, for myself, I don't think I can ever remember having had such 'good' notices. It's interesting how much they hedge their bets. They certainly don't want to be on the wrong side later on, and made it pretty clear. […]

Hope to see you sometime after you have survived the rigours of your launching. Anyway, very best wishes for it.

> Ever,
> John

Osborne, telegram to Hall, 8 April 1976

HELLO SAILOR YOU CAN PENCIL IN NUREMBERG ON THAMES RIGHT AWAY FOR JULY 1977 IF YOU WISH LOVE AND THANKS J. O.

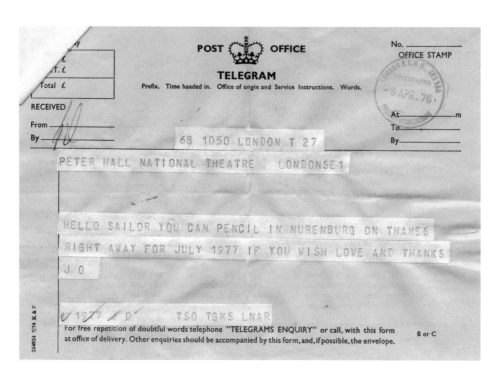

Osborne wanted to write about the Third Reich. Hall commissioned him immediately.

Osborne to Hall, 12 April 1976	My dear Peter,

I have got over my post-natal blues, and indeed am feeling a kind of muted euphoria that I haven't felt for a very long time indeed, perhaps not 20 years.

I shall start working on the Nuremberg Rally sometime in the summer of this year which will give me about six months to do my homework. [...]

> Yours ever,
> John

Osborne to Robin Dalton, 10 May 1976	Me dear Robin,

I get the impression from the [NT] that they are panicking slightly in their choice of repertory by putting on a lot of plays which might easily be done by commercial managements in the West End. Apart from the fact that I see no reason why the tax payer should be in fact subsidising Shaftesbury Avenue through the building of the [NT], it seems to me also extremely unfair if they are indeed contemplating taking *Watch It Come Down* out of the repertory, especially in view of the fact that it is a commercial success – not that this should be the criterion. George Devine's words about the right to fail still should have their relevance in such an enterprise and be pursued as hotly as ever.

[So] I am having second thoughts about being commissioned if one is going to be treated in this rather cursory way. Naturally I see it in my interest that all the juice that is in [*Watch It...*] should be used and if they don't want to carry on with it at least until the end of the summer, one might think of possible alternatives. I don't think this should be held up as some sort of ultimatum but I should like my position made clear and if you have reason to be dealing with P. Hall about, say, my undertaking a commission, you might put these points to him. [...]

> Love,
> John

Osborne to Hall, 9 June 1976	My dear Peter,

Third Reich

The very nature of the subject is pretty vast and needs a great deal of time and thought in reading, etc. I shall not have got very far for at least six months. If it then takes fire, I can only expect that one of my last minute dashes to the final post might take place. I have said to you pencil in July 1977. I certainly would not advise using an indelible pencil. [...]

> Ever,
> John

Hall to Osborne,
11 June 1976

My dear John,

I really think that we should have another working lunch together. I feel – I hope wrongly – that our relationship has become a bit bruised.

I would like to talk some more about *The Third Reich* (we are all of course paranoically wondering if you've changed your mind against the commission). [...]

I want you to use us as something that provokes you to write. Not as a prison.

Best wishes,
Yours ever,
Peter

Osborne to Hall,
17 June 1976

My dear Peter,

Our relationship has become somewhat bruised. Whether or not this could be put right on a personal basis I don't know.

1. *The Third Reich*: I am sorry that Michael Hallifax [NT company administrator] is wondering what to do but I do think that this whole attitude about when I should deliver any script portrays a complete misunderstanding of the creative process of most writers. This may sound a little pompous but I am sure you will understand what I mean. In fact, I have never been so harried about a script in my entire professional career, which spans something like 30 plays and ten films ... There is really no point in my discussing *The Third Reich* at this stage with anyone, as I have not sorted it out for myself yet. I do not even know whether such an ambitious project will even work. [...]

Ever,
John

cc Robin Dalton

Hall to Osborne,
17 July 1976

Dear John,

I was afraid that I was going to have to write to you saying that because of declining business *Watch It Come Down* would have to finish in August; but we weren't happy about this.

So we have included its last performances in the September schedule, thus bringing the total to 40.

Assuming that business holds at 53% we will have played to over 25,000 people. So I hope you'll feel that this is a satisfactory run.

This is an explosive subject at the best of times, and in view of our recent meetings and correspondence I feel it may be more than usually so today. We have done the best we possibly can for a play which I think has benefited all of us, and I hope it will be the foundation for even more productive work together. I am here to be talked to or shot at whenever you feel the need. [...]

Best wishes,
Peter

cc Robin Dalton

Osborne to Hall,
19 July 1976

My dear Peter,

Just got your note about the play. Clearly, when you decide to take it off is your decision. I can only say that it seems a hasty, Shaftesbury Ave-like decision and if that is the way the NT is going to carry on, playing SAFE with Coward revivals, Ayckbourn, Travers, old Uncle A. Finney and all, the whole exercise is absurd from my point of view. George's real dictum about the 'right to fail' etc., is obviously buried and talk of commissions etc., quite pointless. Tell Michael H. am taking up weaving.

Ever,
John

Osborne made notes for the Third Reich play, but never completed it.

The South Bank NT

Denys Lasdun's magnificent concrete complex beside Waterloo Bridge contains six floors of offices; five rehearsal rooms; workshops for sets and props; bars, cafés and restaurants. And three theatres: the open-stage Olivier, with 1,065 seats; the Lyttelton, a proscenium-arch auditorium seating 890; and the Dorfman (until 2014 the Cottesloe), a flexible studio, seating up to 450.

But in March 1976 only the Lyttelton was ready to host performances; the Olivier would not open until July (with Hall's production of Tamburlaine The Great*), the Cottesloe not until February 1977.*

Lasdun's building transformed the scale of NT production. Olivier's Company had enjoyed its busiest calendar year in 1971, with ten press nights; in other years it launched only five shows. In 1977–78, the first financial year in which Hall could programme all three theatres, 25 NT productions opened.

In the Director's office – on the fourth floor, with a panoramic view of the Thames – Hall had to confront the same basic questions as Olivier: which new plays and revivals to stage; who should direct and star, at what cost, for how many performances – but far more of them. Conversations and correspondence also had to be devoted to an issue that, by default, never troubled Olivier: whether a particular script would be best suited to Cottesloe, Lyttelton or Olivier.

Consider, too, the increased managerial workload, as the National, which had begun life with 18 full-time staff at Aquinas Street, took on hundreds more administrative and backstage employees. Hall would later sum up the move from 'the huts' and the Old Vic to the South Bank: 'We didn't just expand, we exploded.'

Michael Blakemore resigns

In January and February 1976, NT associate director Michael Blakemore's revival of the farce Plunder *(1928) had packed out the Old Vic. But, in the week the NT opened, Peter Hall was angry that Blakemore's first South Bank production had yet to be programmed.*

Hall to Michael Blakemore, 8 March 1976

My dear Michael,

I have heard from the RSC that they want you to do Peter Nichols' new play *Privates on Parade* at the Aldwych. […]

I must record though my extreme anxiety about this situation. I feel that we've lost Peter Nichols mainly because of my failure to persuade you to do *The Freeway*. For you now to leave us to do a Nichols at the RSC is very upsetting. I really do not want you to go the RSC.

There are many things you should do here.

Yours ever,
Peter

On 17 March, at the associates' monthly meeting, in the NT's fourth-floor conference room, Blakemore handed out copies of a six-page paper in which he challenged many aspects of Hall's leadership. He read this inflammatory document aloud to the group, which included Hall, Harold Pinter and Bill Bryden. The meeting ended without resolution, and with each associate handing back his copy, in support of the Director.

On 12 April, Hall was heavily criticised in a large feature in the Evening Standard.

Blakemore to Hall, 11 May 1976

Dear Peter,

The waters have now got so muddied with misunderstandings and mistrust that I think the best thing I can do is to resign as an Associate Director. If you want me to continue with the National on a freelance basis I'm happy to do so, though you may think we have got a little beyond that.

I would, however, like to get the record as straight as possible :

1) The confidentiality of the paper I read on March 17 was; and has remained, absolute.

2) Although I knew in advance of the article in the *Evening Standard* on April 12, I neither encouraged it, nor furnished it with the least information. I was disturbed and embarrassed by it, because I knew it would be entirely counter-productive to what I hoped to achieve with my paper from within.

Two actions on my part certainly haven't helped. One was agreeing in principle to do the Nichols play at whatever theatre he chose without first talking [to] you. I can see that my acceptance of the play, even as an understanding between friends, could be interpreted as hostile. Similarly, it was unfortunate that I was out of the country when the *Standard* piece appeared. […]

Finally, though my departure is of some consequence to me, it is a lesser matter than the continued welfare of the [NT].

So I would like to wish you and the Associates purpose and exuberance in the days ahead.

Yours ever,
Michael

On 14 May, Hall accepted Blakemore's decision with 'regret'. Pinter wrote to Blakemore, 'disturbed' by his resignation.

John Schlesinger had missed the associates' meeting in March because he was in the US, finishing his thriller Marathon Man, *starring Dustin Hoffman and Laurence Olivier.*

Blakemore to John Schlesinger, 14 May 1976

My dear John,

I don't know if you will be interested in obscure wrangles across the water but the enclosed correspondence tells quite an interesting story. I have resigned. The resignation became a foregone conclusion the evening I read the [enclosed] paper. I have been meaning to write you a long description of [that] wonderfully melodramatic occasion – just like the play scene in *Hamlet* and, alas, once the court had dispersed, about as effective. However, I tried. But it was time I left anyway. After five years I was getting a little institutionalised and grumpy. But I'm sorry that my departure may have been the result of some engineering a shade on the squalid side. Extremely foolish, too, in the light of the paper.

Love,
Michael

Schlesinger to Blakemore, 23 June 1976

My dear Michael,

Thank you for sending me [the paper]. A lot of what you say is worth careful consideration and I can only imagine that the cat was really put amongst the pigeons because, perhaps, it was not the best moment to deliver this particular bombshell. Had I been present, perhaps my feelings might have been different, but I hope not. It seems to me that it was written with a great deal of thought and perhaps would have been better read by the individuals privately rather than have it read to them.

All this, alas, is water under the bridge and I am very sorry that you are no longer part of the team, because I thought you brought a great deal of experience, talent and judgment, but I hope you will be back. All told, this is such a difficult profession, fraught with conflicts of personality which are inevitable, I suppose. […]

Love,
John

Blakemore directed Privates on Parade *in 1977 (for which Nichols won Best Comedy at the* Evening Standard *Awards that year). But he did not take on another production at the NT until Hall was no longer Director.*

Weapons of Happiness (1976)

by Howard Brenton

Director: David Hare

Lyttelton, 14 July to 23 October 1976 (41 performances)

Soon after Howard Brenton's The Churchill Play *opened at Nottingham Playhouse in 1974, Peter Hall read this 'magnificent' script, and immediately commissioned Brenton to write for the South Bank. The result was* Weapons of Happiness, *which dramatises a strike in a London crisp factory, whose young employees – Ken, Janice, Billy, Liz and Stacky, who is profoundly deaf – form a bond with their new co-worker, Czech dissident Josef Frank, who was executed by the Communist regime in Prague in 1952, but is 'reincarnated' by Brenton as a decrepit exile.*

Brenton was on holiday with his wife, Jane, and eight-month-old son, Sam, at Montisi in Siena in June 1975, when he wrote to his agent.

Howard Brenton to Peggy Ramsay, 4 June 1975

Dear Peggy,

Your letter and telegram came yesterday and also a telegram from Peter Hall saying he likes *Weapons of Happiness* very much.

Your letter is <u>invaluable</u> to me for it is crucial that the play can be understood without any political knowledge and on a level of passionate response and simple human story.

Reading the play again this morning. You are <u>right</u> about the [strikers'] trip to Wales [in Act Two]. I will rewrite it. But – not for a time. It is immensely difficult, for it's a scene – underneath – of heady, perhaps foolish optimism. The play ends with something real being handed on by [the dying] Frank to that benighted, chaotic band of people. And there is a chance for them at the end of the play – or, less but still hopefully, a way forward for them. The theatre – the actual form, the assumptions congealed around 'modern writing' are so full of negations – stasis, pessimism is so peaceful, fashionably beautiful on our stage – that to get played-out <u>simply</u> that there really is a way of changing the world needs a finely honed dramatic action, credible, memorable – and not a speech. I've not found that action for the scene yet. […]

I want to be very disciplined with any reworking. David [Hare] and I have a similar approach to our texts. If they can be made better – make them better. But with *Magnificence* [Royal Court, 1973] – I made a great error in that I rewrote in public, delivering three versions of the play in all. This constant boiling of the text fed the enemies of the play and made its acceptance a tangled affair. With *Weapons* I don't want to breathe a word about rewriting to the National – I'm prepared to let the play stand or fall exactly as it stands. If they say 'Yes' to it and decide to put it on and a firm production is offered – then I will feel free to say 'Great you've said YES. Now say – YES but…' It comes down to – I can only discuss the play with people who are committed to it. You and David at the moment. (And anyway – if someone doesn't like the play when you rewrite you only emphasise what they hate!) So – I'll listen, store and think before touching the play again.

Yes it's the best play so far. It's the closest to life. Though there aren't character sketches from real people I did work in a crisp factory, when I was bumming with no money, and with Ken, Billy, Janice, Stacky, Liz … Alf …

This is written in the sun, nature buzzing, in the grass, a cat watching lizards on the farmhouse wall. Olive groves all around. Jane sends her love. Snoo [Wilson, playwright] is here. I've recklessly prophesied a NO vote in the referendum tomorrow [on continued UK membership of the European Community] (See – never trust a writer's opinions!) If I'm right Snoo had promised to build me a pair of hydraulic, golden cothurni – to rise above you all in prophetic wisdom …

Jane sends her love. Sam is wonderfully well. The poison of the London winter draining away …

And – THANK YOU, Peggy, for delivering the play so firmly and getting it read so fast. We'll talk a lot, I'm eager for all the discussion you can give. We're in with a chance for a wonderful show with *Weapons*, eh?

Yours sincerely,
Howard

Ramsay copied this letter to Peter Hall in confidence.

Ramsay to Hall, 26 September 1975

Dear Peter,

Hare is being ruthless with Howard over the final rewrite, and if he can pull it off it will be wonderful.

Kind regards,
Ever yours,
Peggy

Hall to Brenton, 30 December 1975

Dear Howard,

The new work is all gain. The play is harder, clearer, the issues more complex, the paradoxes more searching. And the last scenes are now very sure.

Yours ever,
Peter

After Paul Scofield and Alec Guinness rejected invitations to play Josef Frank, the part went to Frank Finlay.

John Russell Brown, memo to Hall, 7 July 1976

First Night of *Weapons of Happiness*

Talking to Peggy Ramsay I became very aware that this is very important for her (as, of course, for Howard).

In a theatre which increasingly disappoints her, she sets great store by us and by Howard. I know she has been doing a lot of 'preparation' among critics and the like. She is more than usually 'excited'.

Perhaps you would have done this anyway, but could you write to her for the first night?

JRB

My dear Peggy,

Tonight is very important for all of us. A major new play by a young author of great stature.

You know how much I believe in the venture, and in Howard and David. I just want to wish you success with it too; and to thank you for making it possible.

Much love,
Peter

Weapons… was acclaimed as an 'austere, mind-engaging political study of revolt' (Daily Express)*, but the* Daily Mirror *castigated Brenton for presenting working-class characters who are 'a bunch of phonies. Caricatures every one.'*

Dear Peter,

Thank you for your letter.

I'd very much like to talk with you about the idea for a big play. I'll telephone in the next few days to see when you're free.

The *Evening Standard* has decided to give the best new play award this year to *Weapons of Happiness*. It's a secret, so please do keep it to yourself, Peter, until it's announced on February 2nd.

But, in these crabbed paranoid times, let's for once thump on the ceiling and congratulate ourselves, eh?

Best wishes,
Howard

16th. December, 1976

Dear Peter,

Thank you for your letter.

I'lld very much like to talk with you about the idea for
a big play.   I'll telephone in the next few days to
see when you're free.

The Evening Standard has decided to give the   best new
play award this year to WEAPONS OF HAPPINESS.   It's a
secret, so please do keep it to yourself, Peter, until
it's announced on February 2nd.

But, in these crabbed paranoid times, let's for once
thump on the ceiling and congratulate ourselves, eh?

                    Best wishes,

                         Howard

<u>CONFIDENTIAL</u>

Blithe Spirit (1941)

by Noël Coward

Director: Harold Pinter
Lyttelton, 19 June 1976 to 15 January 1977 (65 performances)
Olivier, 9 February to 28 May 1977 (23 performances)

Hall, memo to The
Company, 30 June
1976

PRESS NIGHTS

At the Old Vic we found that new productions which had
previewed very well tended to suffer on their press night because
the audiences were consistently comprised of what one can only
describe as the traditional and unchanging first night faces – I'm
sure you know what I mean. Thus the play was denied a truly
typical audience on the night it most needed one.

So we invented a Guest Night into which we encouraged the
exciting first nighters, and tried strenuously to sell the Press
Night only to the ordinary public. It worked well.

But we noticed many familiar faces reappearing on *Blithe Spirit*'s
press night, and I don't think the play, though it went well enough,
was helped. It had gone better before and it's gone better since.

So can I please urge you all to invite your agents, friends in the
business etc. to the Guest Night, usually the final preview? Please
leave the Press Night to public and performers, so that critics
can see the play working the way it's going to go on working and
make a judgment uninfluenced by an untypical audience.

Peter

The Royal Opening

*The Queen would officially open the NT on 25 October 1976. Twelve months earlier, Peter
Hall and his deputy, Michael Birkett, were desperate both to ensure that Laurence Olivier
took a full part in the evening's ceremonies, and acted in the new building.*

Michael Birkett,
memo to Hall,
23 October 1975

STRICTLY PRIVATE

OLIVIER

It seems clear to me that he wants badly to be let off and doesn't
want to be associated with us whilst he is re-forging himself with
television and films. It's going to be very difficult to keep on inviting
him [to act here] when he's so obviously determined not to come.

B.

Birkett to Hall,
2 September 1976

Larry is back today, so John Schlesinger tells me, so I'll go and
see him with timetables, guest lists, etc.; tell him tactfully that the
Palace turned down [his] idea of a ball [on the Olivier stage].

Schlesinger tells me [Larry's] still unapproachable on the
subject of the NT in general, obviously harbouring many

bitternesses, and that he's being coy about doing Big Daddy [in *Cat on a Hot Tin Roof*] for John. John's going to keep plugging it, though, and I'm sure it's better in his hands than in ours.

B.

At the Royal Opening, Olivier delivered a rapturously received speech in the auditorium that bears his name – but he would never act on the South Bank.

Counting the Ways (1976)
by Edward Albee

Olivier, 6 December 1976 to 6 January 1977
Lyttelton, 21 January to 25 February 1977 (12 performances in total)

Peter Hall knew Edward Albee well, having directed his A Delicate Balance *(1969) and* All Over *(1972) for the RSC.*
   Bill Bryden staged Counting the Ways, *with Michael Gough and Beryl Reid as 'He' and 'She', whose word games explore love and memory. It received scathing reviews. In* Punch, *Sheridan Morley noted that it was 'not Mr Albee's fault … that a two-character vaudeville is being staged in a space which might seem over-large for* Ben Hur *on ice.'*

Edward Albee to Hall,
13 December 1976

Dear Peter,

I believe I should share a few of my thoughts with you about *Counting the Ways* before time and distance cloud the issue for me.

   I think we discussed the fact that a good deal of the press hostility to the play was caused by extraneous matters – primarily the running battle between the press and the National Theatre. I'm sorry the battle is going on and even more sorry to have gotten caught in the middle of it.

   I agree with you that the play will be happier in a small theatre and that the Olivier – for all its wonders – did not serve it well.

   Most certainly I don't feel that the play was served well all by itself in that vast space. It is, after all, a curtain raiser, Peter, and while I understand your point in wanting to perform it by itself on the *Tamburlaine* and *Hamlet* matinee days, I fear I should have insisted that it be performed with its sister, *Listening*, or not at all. […]

   While I think both Beryl and Michael are intelligent and sensitive actors and could have performed my play as I wrote it, they were not asked to do so.

   I'm fond of Bill Bryden, but I am not cheerful about what he did to my play, though I remain convinced about the excellence of his intentions.

   The play I wrote was a 40-minute, fast-moving, light-hearted, existentialist comedy. What emerged was 70 minutes of slow-moving, leaden sentimentality, punctuated occasionally by slow-motion attempts at humour.

I told Bill over and over in rehearsal my feelings about briskness, about pace, about 'attack'. He just didn't seem to be able – or is it willing? – to transform his syrup into my champagne. […]

Perhaps I was too gentle in my suggestions. Perhaps saying 'Tempo! Pace! Lightness! Vaudeville!' was not enough. Perhaps I should have done what I resisted, which was stepping in and saying, 'Look here, this is how it is supposed to be done.' – taking over, in other words. […]

No sour grapes, Peter, just candour and, I hope, usefulness. I think Bill has the makings of a very, very, good director but I don't think that he should be pushed too fast and certainly not in directions that are unfamiliar to him. […]

My love to you, and keep up the battle,
    Edward

Hall, postcard to Bill Bryden, 28 December 1976

My dear Bill,

Here's the Albee letter. I think you must see it. But <u>please</u>, never say you have, to a living soul.

    And don't be upset. I'm behind you, – 100%.

Ever,
    Peter

Telephone
01-928 2033

National Theatre
South Bank
London SE1 9PX

NT
NATIONAL
THEATRE

My dear Bill,   28 Dec 76

Here's the Albee letter. I think you must see it. But <u>please</u>, never say you have, to a living soul.

And don't be upset. I'm behind you, — 100%.

Ever, Peter.

Hall to Albee,
5 January 1977

Dear Edward,

I thought [your letter] honest, rational and fair.

You have been badly treated by the British press. We went out of our way to explain why we were doing such a short play, but they didn't listen because they didn't want to hear.

Half the troubles the production encountered were due to Beryl's health and her current inability to learn lines.

[But] I understand your dissatisfactions. I have spoken with great care to Bill Bryden about the contents of your letter. And he accepts them and understands them. […]

I am sorry, because I hope you know the value that I've put on your work and on our relationship. And I desperately want it to continue. As far as Britain is concerned, this should be your theatre.

Ever,
  Peter

Albee to Hall,
2 March 1977

Dear Peter,

[…] *Counting the Ways* and *Listening* have had a full-house, six-week run [at Hartford Stage Company, Connecticut] with the reviews split as I thought they would be – the bright, sensitive folk good; the Philistines awful. It might interest you to know that *Counting the Ways* plays consistently at 41 minutes. […]

Best wishes,
  Edward

A new play**
by Ted Hughes

Ted Hughes to John
Russell Brown,
2 November 1976

Dear John Russell Brown,

Sorry to be so delayed answering your invitation to talk about work for the National Theatre.

I very much hope to produce some kind of drama, sooner or later. But I'm reluctant to promise anything, or enter an engagement that would add to the heap of things I'm trying to clamber over at the moment.

What I would prefer would be to come to you in my own time with something done, or some scheme all mapped out.

Meanwhile, thanks for the invitation.

Sincerely,
  Ted Hughes

Hughes did not write for Peter Hall's NT, but his version of The Oresteia *was staged by Katie Mitchell in the Cottesloe in 1999, a year after Hughes's death.*

North Tawton
Devon
2nd Nov. 76

John Russell Brown
Associate Director (Scripts)
National Theatre

Dear John Russell Brown,

Sorry to be so delayed answering your invitation to talk about work for the National Theatre.

I very much hope to produce some kind of drama, sooner or later. But I'm reluctant to promise anything, or enter an engagement that would add to the heap of things I'm trying to clamber over at the moment.

What I would prefer, would be to come to you in my own time with something done, or some scheme all mapped out.

Meanwhile, thanks for the invitation. Sincerely, Ted Hughes

Ted Hughes writes to
John Russell Brown

1977

Tales from the Vienna Woods (1931)
by Ödön von Horváth

Translated by Christopher Hampton
Director: Maximilian Schell
Olivier, 26 January to 25 August 1977 (57 performances)

Peggy Ramsay to Hall, 10 December 1976

My dear Peter,

Could I suggest something which I hope you won't think too hopelessly sentimental.

Last year in Paris I was strolling through Père Lachaise, and passing Molière's grave I noted an actor had put his acting script, with a little flower, on his grave.

Horváth is buried in a neglected and uncared for grave in St Ouen, and I wondered whether you might perhaps sign an NT card of 'hommage' & post it to me, and I will ask someone in Paris to buy a little bunch of flowers & put it on his grave on the first night of the play.

I'll ask the Ionesco family to perform the ceremony, if you approve.

Love,
Peggy

A wreath from the National was flown to Paris at Ramsay's expense and placed on Horváth's grave on the evening of the first preview of Tales from the Vienna Woods.

Bedroom Farce (1975)
by Alan Ayckbourn

Directors: Alan Ayckbourn and Peter Hall
Lyttelton, 16 March 1977 to 17 July 1978 (185 performances)

When Bedroom Farce *opened at the Lyttelton, it was a first NT credit for Alan Ayckbourn, artistic director of the Library Theatre, Scarborough, and the most commercially successful English playwright of the 1970s. It was also the culmination of long wooing by Peter Hall.*

Hall to Alan Ayckbourn, 29 August 1973

Dear Alan Ayckbourn,

I saw *Absurd Person Singular* last night. Thank you for a most remarkable evening.

The mastery of your architecture didn't surprise me – I have seen that in your work before. An added excitement was the totally unblinking exposure of the characters. And the audience sat there recognising themselves with laughter that made them think about themselves.

I hope one day you will think of writing a play for the [NT]. Otherwise you will have to wait 40 years until your West End successes are revived here and you have become a classic. This will assuredly happen.

>   Best wishes,
>   Yours ever,
>   Peter

Dear Peter Hall,

[…] It's particularly gratifying that your enjoyment embraced [the play's] two levels. It's the type of writing I've been aiming to produce – not always successfully – for some time and I feel at last it's beginning to gel together.

I'd certainly love to think about writing a play for you.

All my plays have been written and directed by me here in Scarborough. I hope you'd have no objection, should there be a collaboration between us, to my continuing to work in this way.

Meanwhile, thank you again for writing. Whenever I hit one of those unavoidable patches of self-doubt that afflict writers – and, I suppose, most of us, it will be an enormous morale-booster, believe me!

>   With very best wishes,
>   Yours,
>   Alan Ayckbourn

Ayckbourn's Absent Friends, *in which Colin and his friends gather at a tea party to reflect on the recent death of his fiancée, opened in Scarborough in June 1974.*

Dear Alan Ayckbourn,

I liked [reading] *Absent Friends* very much. I laughed uncontrollably and disturbed several well-meaning passengers in my railway train.

It has made comedy out of the last great taboo left – death.

If it isn't done in the West End, you can be assured of a home for it here. And I would be in the queue to direct it, however low down.

>   Best wishes,
>   Yours ever,
>   Peter Hall

Ayckbourn to Hall, 23 July 1974	Dear Peter Hall,

Regarding *Absent Friends*, I'm afraid I have sold it to Michael Codron. […]
    Your enthusiasm is very encouraging. It's alarming but the more one writes, the less confident one becomes. Probably [because] there are so many more wrong ways open to one to choose from.

> Best wishes,
>> Yours,
>>> Alan

Hall to Michael Codron, 13 September 1974	My dear Michael,

This is a cheek but I may as well try. I think [*Absent Friends* is] magnificent.
    No doubt you are making plans to present it as soon as maybe.
    It just occurred to me that with your four Ayckbourns running, you might not want to add it to the West End very soon.
    If there was any chance of the [NT] doing [it] I would be overjoyed.

> Best wishes,
>> Yours ever,
>>> Peter

Codron replied: 'It is an unusual request and one that I cannot see being granted if it were the other way around!' He produced Absent Friends *in the West End in July 1975.*
    Hall and Ayckbourn finally met, for lunch in February 1975, when the latter promised to send Hall his new play as soon as it was ready, which, 'if I work to my normal deadlines, won't be till right before the first day of rehearsal in Scarborough on 26th May!'

Hall to Ayckbourn, 9 June 1975	Dear Alan,

I like [*Bedroom Farce*] very much. I shouted out loud with laughter twice while reading it.
    But more important, I love the serious observations underlying the comedy.
    I'll certainly come up to Scarborough then begin laying plans with my colleagues for a production. […]

> Best wishes
>> Yours ever,
>>> Peter

Peggy Ramsay to Ayckbourn, 10 June 1975	*Bedroom Farce* Dear Alan,

Peter Hall had agreed to a 10% royalty (which is what Harold Pinter gets) but when I told him that Scarborough also has to be paid 1% of the gross, he was deeply disturbed, because this would make it more than the National could possibly afford. Would you agree to a 9% royalty from the National [while] Scarborough requires 1%?

The National have got to watch every penny terribly carefully to survive, and as they will give you a remarkable production and cast it is well worth your waiving the extra 1%.

I'm also confirming that you are happy that this should be a truly [NT] production, with, we hope, Peter free to direct or, otherwise Michael Blakemore or John Schlesinger. Peter thinks he can get a better cast at the National than we could even get in the West End.

I'm sending a copy of this to Peter, because I know he is concerned.

Yours,
Peggy

Ayckbourn agreed to pay Scarborough from his 10 per cent, and to co-direct Bedroom Farce *with Hall. Unfolding over the course of one night and the next morning, it sees Trevor (Stephen Moore) and Susannah (Maria Aitken) wreak havoc in the bedrooms of three other married couples: Trevor's parents, Ernest (Michael Gough) and Delia (Joan Hickson); Nick (Michael Kitchen) and Jan (Polly Adams), who is Trevor's ex-girlfriend; Malcolm (Derek Newark) and Kate (Susan Littler).*

The Daily Express *review on 21 March noted: 'There has not been laughter like this since the National Theatre opened its doors.' The* Evening News *welcomed 'a gloriously funny piece of work'.*

**Hall to Ayckbourn,
21 March 1977**

My dear Alan,

Well, that's over happily. And even Bernard Levin [in *The Times*], though demonstrating in a masterly fashion how to give another bad notice to the National by giving a good one to your play, has at least not been entirely blinded.

Just to say:

It has been an entirely joyous experience for me, which I always suspected would be the case.

I think we make a good team, and I'd be very happy to do it again.

Please can we have a new play from you for Autumn 1978?

The play is an enormous success and even our eight paranoids [the NT Board] are raising a wintry smile. […]

Yours ever,
Peter

**Ayckbourn to Hall,
22 March 1977**

My dear Peter,

Well – I guess we did it! I've never, personally, had nicer reviews – all round.

I hope the play does do well, in the long term as I would like for once to support a Nationalised Industry I believed in – my efforts for British Leyland have been very disappointing after all the money I have personally poured into it. […]

Love & thanks for everything –
Alan

Michael Kitchen to Ayckbourn, 31 March 1977	Dear Alan,

It was a pleasure working with you & I'm very pleased it's turned out O.K. Not easy rehearsing comedy is it? I found it difficult: I've not done a lot and I'm glad you were around.

Things are much the same – people are laughing & Newark's no subtler.

The bedroom has begun to attack me – the floor gives me one in the side when I fall on it now & that monstrosity at the back of the bed gives me one in the elbow when I hit it. It never used to happen. […]

Yours,
Michael K.

Ayckbourn to Hall, 10 June 1977	Dear Peter,

A bird has told a bird who has told Peggy Ramsay as all birds ultimately do that Maria and Derek may be going over the top in the bedrooms. Since I don't stand a chance of getting near the show for at least a month, I wondered if next time you were passing the door of the Lyttelton, you might murmur something to them. Actually, it's probably safe enough to say something to Derek without seeing him since he's bound to be going over the top. I feel he may resent a telegram from Scarborough telling him so by a director who hasn't seen it. Newark. National Theatre. Stop going over the top stop. I know you are. Ayckbourn.

You might see what Maria's doing though. I promise I will come down and do my whack when I can.

Yours,
Alan

Hall replied that Ayckbourn's request had 'been acted on instantly'.

The National was now hit by a walk-out of stage staff, in support of a sacked NT plumber – a strike which led to the cancellation of several performances.

Hall to Ayckbourn, 12 July 1977	My dear Alan,

I don't run a theatre any more, I am running a training school in industrial relations concentrating on Section V sub paragraph (ii) c – Plumbers. It's pretty bloody boring.

Would like to see you soon. I need a ray of light in this gloomy Thameside bunker.

Ever,
Peter

Hall to Ayckbourn, 18 July 1977	My dear Alan,

[…] Maria is leaving in September and I would like to give the part to Sara Kestelman who is in the company. You may remember her as Titania in Brook's [*Midsummer Night's Dream* in 1970]. She's an excellent girl. Is this OK? […]

> Ever,
>   Peter

My dear Alan,

Sara Kestelman went in last night and was quite brilliant. She's very alarming, and somehow very touching. And she gets a lot of character laughs. I think you'll be pleased.

> Yours ever,
>   Peter

Michael Stroud took over as Nick; Polly Adams continued as Nick's wife, Jan.

Dear Alan,

The [revised] 'Did you have a nice evening?' scene went beautifully on Saturday.

Polly & I rehearsed 'the fall' before the matinée and I duly fell across her like a sperm-whale on a rock & moved nary a muscle throughout the scene.

I endeavoured to wham the lines out, Groucho-like as instructed, & it was a dream to play! Indeed Joan remarked, in the interval, that it had never gone better.

No doubt, when next you see it, it'll be about as interesting as a snowflake on a hot shovel. But Saturday 24th July we <u>did</u> enjoy!

Many thanks for all your help & guidance. […]

> Ever,
>   Michael

Bedroom Farce transferred to the Prince of Wales Theatre, then Broadway. Finally, it was filmed by Granada Television, and Hickson – the one ever-present cast member – was reunited with Kitchen, Adams, Newark, Moore and Aitken from the original line-up.

My Dear Alan & Heather,

We have just returned from recording *Bedroom Farce* at Granada, & we all are hoping for it to turn out beautifully. I felt very ephemeral & negative & ineffective without all those gales of laughter, & learning to speak so very softly (comparatively), & it was awful to say goodbye to all those loved ones, – they really <u>were</u> loved ones, & we all always got on like a house on fire.

All my love to you & Heather

> as always
>   from
>   Joan

Julius Caesar (c.1599)

by William Shakespeare

Director: John Schlesinger
Olivier, 22 March to 3 September 1977 (52 performances)

The National's first Julius Caesar *might have taken place in 1970, after John Gielgud's appearances in* Oedipus *and* Tartuffe.

John Gielgud to Laurence Olivier, 24 September 1969	Dear Larry,
	
	[…] Did Ken [Tynan] speak to you of my idea of *Caesar* – you as Julius – such a short part, but I am told when Ralph did it on a record, the importance of a great personality helped the whole play immeasurably – and [Robert] Stephens (?) as Cassius. I always thought I might do something with Brutus – he is usually so dull and priggish – and could not one think of an Antony (*not* Laurence Harvey, but that kind of arriviste personality). […]
	
	       Yours ever,
	       John

Eventually, Caesar *was John Schlesinger's second Shakespeare production, after* Timon of Athens *(RSC, 1965).*

Hall, memo to Michael Birkett, 1 December 1975	I spoke to Alec McCowen.
	    He's always expressed a desire to play Cassius – and I think he would be very good. I mentioned that we were toying with a production and his eyes lit up. They dimmed slightly when I said that John Schlesinger would be directing it – or so I thought. I think there is a past history over John turning him down for [a film].
	    Could you ask John if he would take McCowen as Cassius and then find out if Alec would like to do it.
	    PH

Birkett, memo to Hall, 3 December 1975	*Julius Caesar* [John] loves the idea of Alec McCowen and is hovering on the brink of explaining how he wants to do the toga-less but classical production: something to do with its being not quite real – more a collection of power-hungry actors than a reproduction of Ancient Rome. Won't say more yet, but is very happy that John Bury [designer] is trying to help. B

Birkett, memo to Hall,
27 May 1976

JOHN SCHLESINGER

Caesar: He still wants to do it and is confident of being able to
cast it once he has the right Brutus, Cassius and Antony. He
would be happy with Alan Howard and Brian Cox if the right
Brutus were forthcoming. He would have liked Peter Finch,
but Finch won't leave his pineapple farm. He would consider
Richard Johnson, but finds Denis Quilley too uncomplicated a
creature. […]

B

Hall to John
Schlesinger, 26 July
1976

Michael tells me you were very upset at our [Ralph Richardson
for Caesar and Ian Holm for Cassius] suggestions [and] saw it as
a lack of confidence on our part with the concept and some kind
of betrayal. This really isn't so. Can I explain?

Ralph has just signed a three-year contract with us. He came to
me and suggested that he should play Caesar. I personally think
it is a good idea, because you would have an enormous, powerful,
sick tyrant in the centre. But you are the director, and if you think
it's wrong, it's wrong. […]

I am utterly miserable about the state of the Olivier and the
attitude of the contractors. But somehow I'm going to get it open.
It's a time for determination. And for strength.

I hope all is well with you.

Best wishes,
Peter

Schlesinger to Hall,
29 July 1976

My dear Peter,

I got very stroppy when Michael Birkett called me in the
middle of mixing a reel (which was not going too well) with the
[Richardson] news.

The play would take on a quite wrong tone were Caesar to be
the grandfather of most of his political colleagues. I would love
to work with Ralph, and hope you make this clear to him, but the
balance would be terribly harmed by having him. […]

We are on the home stretch, thank God, with *Marathon Man*.

I hear things are going well with rehearsals for *Tamburlaine* but
less well with getting into the [Olivier]. Good luck!

Thinking of you all,

Love,
John

*Schlesinger's objections to 74-year-old Richardson on grounds of age seem odd, because his
eventual Caesar was John Gielgud, 72.*

John Gielgud to Irene Worth, 17 February 1977

Dear Irene,

We have started [rehearsing] *Caesar* which will, I think, be very interesting. I like Schlesinger immensely, and Brian Cox as Brutus and Ronnie Pickup as Cassius seem both to be promising. Hardly any crowd, nondescript period clothes – semi-uniforms, no togas – and I find my small part full of tiny indications which may, I hope, justify my trying to play it. Then I do a small part in *Volpone* – Sir Politick Would Be. We finish *No Man's Land* next week for good. It will be sad to leave the part, and part with Ralph. […]

Love,
John

Gielgud to Ralph and Meriel Richardson, 24 March 1977

Dear Ralph & Mu,

The notices were pretty brutal and naturally I found it a bit embarrassing to meet the company last night – and John Schlesinger is, I think, bitterly disappointed. I fancy he thought the Bard had an easy wicket, and he says he wanted [Colin] Blakely, [Alan] Howard and Alec McCowen but they all turned it down! I would have thought Albert Finney and Paul Scofield nearer the mark but one does realise the awful difficulties of juggling casting at the National. But *Caesar* ain't much good without big personalities and really powerful *speaking*. All that black, and meagre crowds don't help much either. Of course that [huge Olivier] stage needs a big Reinhardt crowd, which seems nowadays to be absolutely out of the question. Ah me!

Love,
John

John Schlesinger (third from left) rehearses *Julius Caesar* with John Gielgud (second from right) in the title role. Photo: Michael Childers

Piaf**
by Pam Gems

Pam Gems's agent, Clive Goodwin, submitted Piaf *as a vehicle for Julie Covington, who had just played Eva Perón on the hit double-album of Andrew Lloyd Webber's* Evita.

John Russell Brown,
***Piaf* report to Hall et al., 14 April 1977**

Takes us through the entire life of Piaf, from destitution through success to failing powers and nerve. Many, many scenes and a huge cast. Stands or falls by the enactment of Piaf as character and performer, and the actress would have to simulate extreme youth and decrepit, aged failure.

Quite a number of scenes are well presented and the authenticity of what Piaf says is generally credible. But the play pauses nowhere so no scene gets much further than the immediate surface of things.

Julie Covington could do [it] better than anyone I can think of, but I do not think this text offers sufficient support for the impersonation. It is more a first draft for a film script than a play.
JRB

Rejected by the National, Piaf *was produced by the RSC in Stratford in October 1978, starring Jane Lapotaire. It transferred to the West End and Broadway, where Lapotaire won a Tony as Best Actress in a Play.*

Notes from Underground (1864)**
by Fyodor Dostoevsky
Adapted for the stage by Hanif Kureishi

Hanif Kureishi to John Russell Brown, 30 March 1977

Dear Sir,

I am a young writer [aged 22] trying hard to get on.

Last year a play of mine was given one Sunday performance in the Royal Court's Theatre Upstairs.

Since then I have been working on this adaptation – which I enclose – of Dostoevsky's short novel *Notes from Underground*.

I think it might be suitable for one of the National's early evening performances (with the sets etc. suitably simplified), or perhaps for a full, later evening production.

I'd be grateful if you could give the play your kind attention and give me your decision as soon as possible, since I probably won't sleep until I receive your reply.

Yours faithfully,
Hanif Kureishi

30 March 1977.

Dear Sir,

     I am a young writer trying hard to get on.

     Last year a play af mine was given one Sunday
performance in the RoyalXx Court's Theatre Upstairs,
where it was directed by David Halliwell.

     Since then I have been working on this adap-
tation - which I enclose - of Dostoevsky's short
novel "NOTES FROM UNDERGROUND."

     I think it might be suitable for one of the
National's early evening performances (with the sets etc
suitably simplified), or perhaps for a full, later
evening production.

     I'd be grateful if you could give the play
your kind attention and give me your decision as
soon as possible, since I probably won't sleep until
I receive your reply.

     Yours faithfully,

(Hanif Kureishi.)

State of Revolution (1977)
by Robert Bolt

Director: Christopher Morahan.
Lyttelton, 18 May 1977 to 21 January 1978 (85 performances)

Peggy Ramsay
to Hall, 26 September
1975

Dear Peter,

I'm awfully worried about the pressures on Bob's life, and I think it tremendously worth your while helping him with his new play, because the public have a passion for his work. The important thing is to raise it a little above the earnest middle-brow. He has been asked to write a film on Augustus John, which is a good idea. I'm trying to steer him away from writing a film on Stalin (which, obviously, will never be made). Bob values your friendship and concern greatly, Peter. It's quite important to him. This, of course, is not twisting your arm to say you should do the play, but your interest in it will get it done, and there is always David Jones standing on the side lines [at the RSC].

> Kind regards,
>   Ever yours,
>   Peg

Hall committed to producing Bolt's epic dramatisation of the Russian Revolution. With Michael Bryant as Lenin, it was Christopher Morahan's NT debut; he joined Hall's team after many years producing and directing plays for BBC television.

Hall to Christopher
Morahan, 5 May 1977

Dear Chris,

Again many congratulations on last night. I think it is a clear and brilliant production, totally devoid of sentimentality bullshit. If it does nothing else, it has clearly established you with the Company as a major director …

I woke this morning with my feelings … reinforced. It *is* too long and the overall impression of the play is too soft. You must make it the anti left-wing play which it sets out to be. That is what one must carry out of the theatre. Otherwise we shall be thought to be trying to have it both ways.

I'm sure Bob will do it. And I'm bloody sure you can.

> Best wishes,
>   Yours ever,
>   Peter

As State of Revolution's *run came to a close, Bolt was staying at The Beachcomber Hotel on Tahiti.*

Robert Bolt to Hall,
3 January 1978

My dear Peter,

Beat that for an address! The Island Paradise is enjoying its rainy season just now; it's like standing under the gutters of Heaven just after God has taken a bath. I'm writing a big film [about the mutiny on *The Bounty*] for David Lean and the lovely money. Wanting terribly to be home, feeling very isolated and sorry for myself. Twenty years ago my present locale and activity would have seemed the peak of desirability. That's life for you. What I say is fuck it.

I wasn't overjoyed to hear that Lenin and the lads are coming to the end, but there's no appeal from the Box Office Returns; if it's failing there it's failing. Do you think it has had any impact at all? I mean, what do people say about it? I found it amazing that most of the critics thought it 'uncommitted'. They can't know much about Marxism. I suppose the fact that I admired the people while hating what they did and attacking what they were impelled by was seen by the critics as having it both ways. I was trying to say that personal merit won't surmount an evil creed, nor a good intention an evil man. Talking about the critics is a waste of time which one constantly returns to, like the *Times* crossword.

Love to you both,
Bob

Hall to Bolt,
24 January 1978

My dear Bob,

I'm sorry to hear that life on The Island of Paradise isn't quite all it should be.

Nothing has changed dramatically here in SE1. There are threats that the Thames is about to burst its banks so we'll all have to move up a floor. I'm deep in rehearsals for *The Cherry Orchard* [and] overworked as usual. But apart from that life isn't too terrible.

State of Revolution had an excellent final performance on Saturday, playing to a near capacity house. It has certainly provoked a great deal of discussion and interest. We're all very proud to have had it here.

I hope the David Lean film is going well and you'll be back soon. I would like to talk about the future.

Best wishes,
Yours ever,
Peter

**Bolt, postcard to Hall,
21 December 1978**

Dear Peter,

Today is the longest day of the year, thank God, so it should presently begin to be cooler and, eventually, less wet. I am still horribly here and like to be so this many a moon more. My relationship with David [Lean] approximates that of the man in [Evelyn Waugh's *A Handful of Dust*] with the other man who liked to have Dickens read aloud to him daily. But at least it was Dickens, not the tedious doings of Cap. Bligh & Mr. C.

Love,
Bob

State of Revolution *had played to 85* per cent *capacity, impressive for a new play. Lean's* Bounty *film was never made; nor has another Bolt script been staged by the NT.*

1978

The National under fire – again

**Peggy Ashcroft to
Mr Turner (*Evening
News*), 3 April 1978**

Dear Mr Turner,

Enclosed is the piece I have written which my secretary has already mentioned to you. I would be very pleased if it could be printed as a short feature, in full.

Yours sincerely,
Peggy Ashcroft

Last week your paper carried on its front page in banner headlines, 'A National Disaster – Theatre Chief Peter Hall Accused'

The lurid headlines were the result of a book by John Elsom, *The History of the National Theatre*. I have not yet read the book. I am concerned, therefore, only with the report of it, and quotations from the author, by your writer James Erlichman.

What emerges is a lamentable misrepresentation of many facts about the National, and an attack on Peter Hall, the man who has had the far from enviable task of following in the steps of a national hero, Laurence Olivier, who established the Company in the much loved Old Vic. What has been grave has been the escalation of costs, due to building delays and inflation, of a building conceived in the affluent early '60s; and even now, through what inadequacies of techniques it is hard to understand, the actual machinery of the stages is still incomplete and therefore the cause of vastly increased labour costs – labour in itself having bedevilled the running of the theatre in wage demands and strikes both threatened and implemented.

Peter Hall has shouldered these problems and the vast undertaking of moving a relatively small company from the Old Vic, into a 3-auditoria giant citadel, at a time when the economics of the country were in an increasingly grave state. […]

John Elsom's other main charges are Peter Hall's 'style of leadership', and his 'commercial judgement which is driving the National wildly off the course set by Olivier'. That course is described as 'good classical repertory'. Yet Olivier is surely the last man to want our [NT] to be a museum of only classical repertory. He put on the work of modern writers – Arden, Osborne, Shaffer. Were his [NT] productions of *Hay Fever* or *Hobson's Choice* so totally at variance with the new National's productions of *Blithe Spirit* or *The Guardsman*? Are we to deplore the fact that such leading playwrights as Pinter, Bolt, Ayckbourn, and Beckett, have their plays produced by [Hall]? And surely the new NT's *Hamlet, Tamburlaine, The Madras House, The Country Wife*, to list a few, fulfil the demands of classical repertory?

Elsom is quoted as saying, '[Hall] is a man of enormous energy and intellect who is immensely well liked by many of his staff.' (I would add, and loved and admired by hundreds of actors.) 'But he is also a man driven by ambition and frightened – frightened of failure.'

Here, I admit, I become outraged. Ambition is surely a necessary ingredient for a man who above all wishes to establish a leading world company. As to Fear, having worked with Peter Hall for over 20 years I can say it is almost unknown to him.

In my fairly long experience of theatre, the three men who have given their lives and energies to it in the greatest degree have been the late George Devine, Laurence Olivier, and Peter Hall.

It is a sad thing that in this country we should be so ready to blame, criticise, and never to celebrate achievements. It would amaze many foreigners, and dismay our own theatregoers, who visit the National in their thousands with enormous enjoyment, to have it labelled 'a National disaster'. Fortunately, they know better.

The Evening News *ran Ashcroft's article on 7 April.*

Plenty (1978)
by David Hare

Director: David Hare
Lyttelton, 12 April to 4 November (75 performances)

Plenty *charts the life of a bright, volatile Englishwoman, Susan Traherne, from 1943 to 1962; from her exhilarating work as a courier with the Special Operations Executive in Nazi-occupied France, to her disillusionment and mental breakdown in post-war London, marooned in a stultifying marriage to an underachieving diplomat.*

David Hare to Hall, March 1977	Dear Peter,

The member of your company I had in mind [for Traherne] was [Diana] Rigg (who is pregnant?). She did once write to me, by the way, saying how much she wanted to do one of mine, & I do think she would be sensationally well suited to it.

David

Hall to Diana Rigg, 21 March 1977	My dear Di,

Here is the first draft of a play by David Hare which he'd like us to do at the NT. No one has seen it yet except me.

I wonder if somehow we can combine this with [your playing Maggie in *Cat on a Hot Tin Roof*] and *The Guardsman* [Ferenc Molnár's comedy], when you are coming to us after the baby.

It's a hell of a part, and the play manages a very comprehensive view of what's been happening to us all since the war. I think it could be magnificent.

I hope you're flourishing.

Peter

Michael Hallifax, memo to Hall, 30 March 1977	DIANA RIGG

We had a long talk about plans.

Her baby is due on May 13th.

I asked her first about the David Hare play. She said she thought it was 'super', although it was too long. [...]

Michael

Hare to Hall, April/ May 1977	Dear Peter

[...] Directors. I would value your advice on [John] Dexter, [William] Gaskill and [Peter] Gill. I am not sure in my own mind and really need your help. I am against Schlesinger because I was nauseated by *Marathon Man*, an Englishman trying to out-nasty the Americans at their own game, and succeeding as far as I'm concerned. I don't think I'd work easily with him after that. [...]

David

Rigg's daughter with Angus Stirling, Rachael Stirling, was born on 30 May 1977. Almost at once, Rigg had second thoughts about playing Traherne, and Hare immediately wanted to cast Kate Nelligan, who had taken the lead in Licking Hitler, *the television play he had just written and directed.*

Hare to Hall, 5 June 1977	Dear Peter,

Our package is very volatile. Gaskill rejecting, Rigg rumoured to be defecting to the West End and both you and I in six minds about who should direct. Can I tell you what I am thinking ?

You may say I have no right to change my mind, and that we've made a commitment; but Peggy had also heard of Rigg's departure, was greatly relieved and asked why we had never offered Nelligan the part in the first place. I said, because she was too young. She said pooh.

Kate's problem would be with the age, although the rewrite will bring the span down from 19 to 37, which I don't think is outside her range. She is the best actress in England apart from Edith Evans, and she's dead: and she is the most brilliant player of my work.

I don't like the alternatives.

I also don't identify too strongly with the directors we're discussing; and Peggy bullied me heavily into saying I should do it myself.

A script which isn't yet written. A writer who believes he can direct his own work. An actress five years too young and who sells no tickets. If you say you are no longer interested, then I would quite understand.

I do look at your face very closely when we meet, Peter, and think – is there anybody he really desperately wants me to accept for this project ? Actress? Director? And I can't really say you've so far been any more definitive in your passions than I am in mine.

This is the best formula I have heard yet, but I am quite willing to be trumped if it is possible. It goes without saying I have not mentioned anything to Kate.

David

Kate Nelligan, note to Hare, April 1978

I am honoured to play Susan Traherne in the play *Plenty*. Life will never be so good again. And I thank you. I do sincerely thank you, David.

Kate

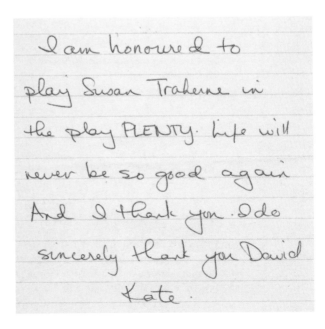

My dear David,

[…] You've doubtless heard that [Kate]'s got the *Evening Standard* Drama Award for *Plenty*.

I think those awards are always full of shit as I don't believe the best of anything exists. But it's like good weather; you might as well enjoy it. […]

Yours ever,
Peter

Betrayal (1978)

by Harold Pinter

Director: Peter Hall

Lyttelton, 15 November 1978 to 8 September 1979 (71 performances)

Betrayal traces the affair between Jerry, a married literary agent, and Emma, an art gallery owner whose husband Robert, a publisher, is Jerry's best friend. It unfolds with reversed chronology, starting in 1977, two years after the end of the affair, concluding in 1968, at the party where Jerry first reveals to Emma his passion for her.

Early in 1978, Pinter sent typescripts to the NT, and to his publishers, fellow writers and directors, and his mother-in-law, Elizabeth Longford. They responded while he was directing Simon Gray's The Rear Column, *for a 22 February press night in the West End.*

Dear Harold,

First, I want to thank you for sending me your play. Secondly I found it riveting to read and therefore read it in one sitting. Like a time-bomb likely to go off, it felt. Thirdly there are many things both subjective and objective that I would like to talk to you about (in) it. It does as you can imagine raise passions in one. Fourthly I shall wonder who will play it, and how and when. But most of all I want to congratulate you and say that you're in the ring, fighting and fit.

My best wishes and *molto* congratulations,
Edna

See you soon I hope.

Dear Harold,

I couldn't resist reading *Betrayal* one more time before handing it on to Geoffrey [Strachan, Managing Director] and also can't resist writing you a fan letter! I think the whole device of playing the action backwards works triumphantly, totally validating what might so easily have been merely a gimmick: the last two scenes pack more poignancy than I've experienced for a long time because you've already let us in on what's to happen to these people.

Further poignancy for me, as someone with growing children watching my friends' children also grow yearly less childlike, came with that recurrent image of Charlotte [Robert and Emma's daughter] being tossed up into the air surrounded by a circle of benevolent grown-ups. *Betrayal* prompted in me a richer mixture of laughter and near-tears than any previous play of yours. It's going to be marvellous on stage: it's already super on the page.

Many cheers,
Yours,
Nick

Elizabeth Longford to Pinter, 16 February 1978

Dear Harold,

You already know from Antonia how much I enjoyed it – or <u>almost</u> how much, as since telling her I have re-read it twice, each time with even more enjoyment & understanding (I hope!). It is so amazingly economical & also packed with subtleties that I found it was necessary to read it again, at intervals, before writing to thank you.

Now I do, most fervently, & with very very many congratulations. It will be wonderful acted, & of course Sir P. will snatch it.

My final thought on the ever-intriguing concept of betrayal is that, at any rate <u>here</u>, it does not exist. I felt more & more that this was so as I read along, & absolutely convinced in the last scene when Robert '*clasps Jerry's shoulder, briefly*'. That clasp seems to me to be one of the universal symbols meaning 'Get on with it'. It could I imagine be given by a father to a son before he leaves home on the morning of the exam, or by the sports master before the boy goes in to bat, or by the best friend before his best man seduced his wife. […]

I must stop myself, or I'll soon have gone through it scene by scene with enthusiastic annotations.

Very best luck for the 22nd and a million thanks for sending us the tickets.

Once more my thanks & love,
Elizabeth

Ronald Harwood to Pinter, 18 February 1978

My dear Harold,

I wish I could properly express the pleasure I've had reading *Betrayal*. The inner life of the work is electrifying: so original and mysterious in the profound sense. Also, the play is theatrical and comic and sad. Something tells me that it is a leap in a new direction and that's the most exciting thing in art.

Albert [Finney] spent the last weekend with us, and we talked at length about your play. He understands the world you've created and has real insights into it, and it seems to me you couldn't want for a better actor.

I've also had a lovely time reading Antonia's new book [*King Charles II*].

All good things with Simon's play.
Betrayal is superb.

Love,
Ronnie

By March, Daniel Massey and Penelope Wilton (then husband and wife) had been cast as Robert and Emma, but Hall and Pinter had yet to find the right Jerry. Pinter, after desperately scouring the Spotlight *directory, offered Hall nine names, including Edward Fox, Ian McShane and Martin Shaw. He was delighted when, in June, the role went to someone he had not suggested, Michael Gambon.*

**Hern to Pinter,
15 November 1978**

Dear Harold,

Saw a pretty good play at the Lyttelton last night. Even better than it had seemed on the page. And the whole thing beautifully and faultlessly orchestrated to the last breath. Brilliant.

There was one point last night when Michael Gambon tripped over a word. Not a bad fluff by even the most exacting standards but enough to disrupt the rhythm, and, for a moment, by its very absence one realised what razor-edge precision there was governing every aspect of gesture, delivery, position, the lot!

I do most sincerely congratulate all of you. I had a <u>wonderful</u> time.

All the very best,
    Yours,
        Nick

Penelope Wilton
(Emma) and Michael
Gambon (Jerry)
in *Betrayal*. Photo:
Michael Mayhew

Betrayal *was named Play of the Year at the SWET (now the Olivier) Awards. In January 1980, Hall directed it on Broadway, with Roy Scheider (Robert), Blythe Danner (Emma) and Raul Julia (Jerry). Its audience included Mike Nichols, who had been attached to direct Pinter's* Last Tycoon *screenplay, and worked with him on it in 1974.*

Mike Nichols to Pinter, 3 February 1980

Dear Harold,

I can't stop thinking about *Betrayal*. I think it's as good as anything you've ever written. The thing I love in the theatre above all others is the theatricality of a scene in which the audience and one character know something which the other character doesn't. I was very moved by the play; by the kitchen memory and the repeat of the kitchen memory, which are more like life than life. So are the whiskey and water, and the *prosciutto* and *melone*, and, of course, the last scene. But really every second of it. My jaw dropped from the first moment and stayed thus to the last, save when I was snuffling. It also has that strange quality of having been plucked out of one's own head. […]

I think it's a movie. I would like very much to talk to you about it. I would like to talk to you about it soon. I will call you.

I read an interview with you in some New York magazine which moved me a lot because you simply said the way things were. I also saw an interview by Dick Cavett with Antonia in which I admired her immensely and she made me laugh. There it all is. I guess I should leaven all this with some tart criticism. Let's see. I wish you'd call me sometime. How's that?

Love,
Mike

In 1983, Betrayal *was filmed by David Jones from Pinter's screenplay.*
Nichols directed Betrayal *on Broadway in October 2013 – his final stage production; he died in November 2014.*

1979

The longest strike

After unofficial walk-outs by NT stage crews in 1976 and 1977, a third strike had almost caused the press night of Betrayal *to be aborted. In March 1979, stage staff rejected the NT Executive's latest proposal for new working patterns and a 4.8 per cent pay rise, and launched their fourth strike in consecutive years.*

Michael Elliott
(NT general
administrator),
statement to
employees, 21 March
1979

Dear _____

There has been an unofficial stoppage of work by Stage staff
since the evening of Friday, 16th March 1979. Whilst this action
continues both management of the [NT] and NATTKE union
officials are requesting all employees to continue normal working
and where necessary to cross picket lines.

We have already stated that where employees do not cross
picket lines, they will not be paid. However, we now understand
that not only are you not crossing the picket lines, but you are also
taking this action in total support of the Stage staff's action.

Unless you report for work on Friday 23rd March, then we shall
be forced to suspend your employment forthwith.

Signed by the appropriate Administrator

Unsigned memo,
26 March 1979

DETAILS REGARDING DELIVERIES/ORDERS FOR THE NT
CATERING DEPARTMENT: FRIDAY 16TH MARCH – MONDAY
26TH MARCH 1979

Monday 19/3
Express Dairy – Came through picket lines and left milk etc.
outside Goods Inwards Door as usual. Later found all containers
pierced and milk (10 galls) was consequently lost. […]

Wednesday 21/3
Paul Allen & Co. – Managed to deliver, using <u>unmarked private</u> car.

Panificio Italiano (Bread) – Verbally threatened on picket line
but managed to deliver.

C. S. T. (Butchers) – Went through regardless of threats,
intimidation and abuse. Van was followed by strikers to Stage
Door. Whilst unloading (helped by Catering Management)
strikers damaged [van] and put matches etc. into all locks,
consequently setting off the van's alarm system. […]

Monday 26/3
Sonny's (Cheesecakes) Ltd. [and] Phelan's Ltd. (Quiches
etc.) – In view of the increased number of pickets, abuse and
intimidation which their drivers were exposed to, they are not
prepared to deliver anymore.

Tom Pate (theatre
manager), memo to
Elliott, 26 March 1979

[…] On Saturday morning Jimmy Hannah [stage door keeper] was
advised by someone he refuses to name that it was 'hardly worth
his while continuing to work at the NT'. Jimmy felt no doubt that
the statement amounted to a threat. On leaving the building on
Saturday night he was struck by an apple core (thrown by a person
unknown), and was also the victim of some verbal abuse.

Jimmy is now 'on holiday'. He does <u>not</u> want the above
incidents formally investigated. […]

TP

DATE	SUPPLIERS	COMMENTS
Friday 16/3 and Saturday 17/3	All suppliers delivered normally.	Came through picket lines (not well organised).
Monday 19/3	Express Dairy	Came through picket lines and left milk etc. outside Goods Inwards Door as usual. Later found all containers pierced and milk (10 galls was consequently lost.
	Kierley & Tongue (Dry Goods/Groceries)	Turned away at picket lines.
	Foster Probyn (Youngs Breweries)	Turned away at picket lines.
	Woodhouse Hume (Butchers)) Philips & Co. (Butchers)) Youngs Seafoods) Panificio (Bread)) Paul Allen) Farmer Giles)	Tried to cross picket line, threatened and intimidated and consequently turned away.
Tuesday 20/3	No orders and no deliveries.	
Wednesday 21/3.	Express Dairy	Managed to deliver, albeit asked not to do so.
	Paul Allen & Co.	Managed to deliver using unmarked private car.
	Panificio Italiano (Bread)	Verbally threatened on picket line but managed to deliver at Goods Inwards Door. (Catering Management and driver unloaded car).
	C.S.T. (Butchers)	Went through regardless of threats, intimidation and abuse. Van was followed by strikers to Stage Door. Whilst unloading (helped by Catering Management) strikers damaged car and put matches etc. into all locks, consequently setting off the van's alarm system.
	Turnell & Co.) Greengrocers Hawkes & Co.)	Did not cross picket lines, mainly because at that time (i.e. 9.00 am) no police were in evidence.
	Bulmer's Cider	Turned away at picket lines.
	Modeluxe Linen Services Ltd.	Managed to deliver (for the last time) but was again followed and driver was physically threatened and abused.
Thursday 22/3 Friday 23/3 Saturday 24/3	No orders – no deliveries	
Monday 26/3	Sonny's (Cheesecakes) Ltd. Phelan's Ltd. (Quiches etc.)	In view of the increased number of pickets, abuse and intimidation which their drivers were expose to, they are not prepared to deliver anymore.

R. C. Osborn,
solicitor, Denton Hall
& Burgin, to Elliott,
30 March 1979

Dear Mr Elliott,

[…] There can be no doubt that many of the incidents, which you and your colleagues have described to us, amount to unlawful picketing and that therefore you have a *prima facie* case for an *ex parte* injunction restraining such conduct. […]

The difficulty is entirely evidentiary, in that it has been impossible to identify particular defendants and attribute specific incidents of unlawful picketing.

I appreciate your frustration and the feeling that the law is impotent to help you. […]

You are as aware as I am of the imperative need to find hard evidence. No reasonable effort should be spared, even to the extent of adopting somewhat unconventional methods. The most obvious possibility of a confrontation is when drivers try to cross the picket lines. It would be helpful if someone could actually stow away in the cab of the vehicle and take a tape recording of any conversation. Witnesses should be in attendance near the picket lines to observe what happens and it may be sensible to engage a professional photographer with a zoom lens to take photographs, which can be produced in court. […]

Yours sincerely,
R. C. Osborn

Shop stewards to
Elliott, 30 April 1979

Dear Michael Elliott,

We wish to record our regret that the South Bank Theatre Board found it necessary to issue writs against six strikers. We feel it was an added provocation to an already explosive situation.

The issuing of these writs prompted the collapse of the strike: the picket lines disappeared in early May. Since 1979, the National has not lost a single performance to industrial action.

Close of Play (1979)

by Simon Gray

Director: Harold Pinter
Lyttelton, 24 May to 22 October (47 performances)

The nine characters in Gray's family drama include a married GP (Michael Gambon), who is having an affair with a patient; his alcoholic brother (John Standing), and their father (Michael Redgrave), a retired literature professor, now silent and chair-bound.

Because of the strike, its original press night, 11 April, was repeatedly postponed; it finally opened on 24 May. 'It's been a terrible strain on everyone,' Pinter told the Evening Standard, *and paid tribute to Gray, 'the poor bloody author, his spirit has been so encouraging to the company. He could have despaired but he didn't.'*

<table>
<tr><td>Hall to Simon Gray,
3 August 1979</td><td>

My dear Simon,

[…] *Close of Play* has had the most difficult birth of almost any play of my experience. What with the strike, it was a great tribute to you and to the cast and to Harold that it survived.

It has come through well. But it would be idle to pretend that we have been able to give you the advance booking, and the audience building service which we can normally offer a new play. The strike prevented that.

The performances in June only played to 53%. And the first batch in July alarmed us even further by dropping to 43%.

However towards the end of the month, we reached 68%.

Before this, we were regretfully feeling that we would have to finish the play [after] its tour in Dublin. But we have decided to bring it back for 6 performances. It will, I'm afraid, have to finish on 22nd October.

This will have given you 47 performances at the Lyttelton and 15 on tour [and] 30,000 people will have seen your play. And if this depresses you, remember it is the equivalent of a three-month sold out run at the Royal Court.

We believe we are being fair. There are 21 performances from August to mid-October and we have little advance, and little interest at the Box Office. But we try to stand by new plays to the best of our ability.

You know our difficult financial position, and our need to make up the year's losses. So this plan is the best I can do.

I remain proud of the production and glad of the chance to do the play.

On to Dickens I hope.

Best wishes,
    Yours ever,
        Peter

</td></tr>
</table>

Dear Peter,

The letter you wrote me is only the second communication I've received from the National since my play opened. The other was an abusive letter from a member of the public. Yours was equally unexpected, and even more unwelcome. I did hear a few rumours (the source being actors' agents) that the play was coming off in October, but I contradicted them on the grounds that, unlike the proverbial husband, I would be among the first to know. Foolish of me, as it's turned out. My excuse must be that I'm used to better treatment in this kind of situation – perhaps I've been spoiled by West End managements who treat the premature closing of a new play as a matter of some consequence to its author, and thus take the trouble to discuss it with him before actually making the decision.

As for the decision itself:

Close of Play did, indeed, get off to a lousy start, with no possibility of advance bookings, and precious little publicity (closely followed by none at all). In spite of all this it seems now to be finding a substantial audience. My brother reports that the Wednesday matinee was pretty well full, and Harold reports that Tuesday evening's house was packed. (Harold has other things to report – among them the response of the house and the nature of the event itself – but perhaps as these don't count as marketing realities, they are of no value.) The NT launched (if that can be the word) a new play in the most appalling of circumstances; failed to give it any compensating publicity; decided, before it could have any time to establish itself, that it wasn't attracting a sufficient audience; and butchered it just when it was, against all the odds, and no doubt embarrassingly, beginning to do so. All this you've done to a production you claim to be proud of. Furthermore, all you can offer by way of consolation is that we will have played to the equivalent of three months at the Royal Court. Why not go further, and work out that we will have played to the equivalent of two and a half years at the King's Head (or one night at Stamford Bridge?). Or in more realistic marketing terms, to about the same number of performances as *The Rear Column* at the Globe [last year] – an experience that played a large part in bringing me to the National, as you yourself well know.

I believe, possibly selfishly and unrealistically, that if ever a theatre had a duty to stand by a play, the National did with *Close of Play*. To the extent, at least, of holding back to see whether it might make up – as it seems now to be doing – the ground that the situation there deprived it of initially.

During the three months' rehearsal you saw fit to thank me for my 'stoicism' and 'professionalism'. But I simply don't know any 'professional' and 'stoical' way of responding to your letter, and the lack of consideration that seems to have led up to it.

Sincerely,
Dictated by Simon Gray and signed in his absence.

cc Harold Pinter, Judy Daish [Gray's agent]

Hall to Gray,
7 September 1979

Dear Simon,

I found [your letter] one of the most unfair, discourteous, and belligerent I have ever received (and I have received a few).

There seems no point in trying to score off you as you have scored off me by refuting your lists of half truths and unhappinesses. Clearly nothing is going to alter the fact that you believe us cavalier and would prefer to be in the hands of the West End.

We spent nearly £6,500 on extra press advertising *Close of Play*, well above average – and worked our socks off in special editorial publicity. The seven performances of *Close of Play* in September have an advance of 22%.

Perhaps when your hurt has subsided a little (if it ever does) and if my anger abates, we should meet for a drink. But not now.

You know I am passionate about [your writing a play based on the life of] Dickens, which you yourself suggested. If you want to withdraw, do so. I presume you will, and I shall quite understand. […]

Yours ever,
Peter

The dispute over Close of Play *did no lasting damage to Hall and Gray's close and enduring professional partnership and personal friendship. Hall would go on to direct the world premieres of Gray's* Just The Three of Us *(1997),* Japes *(2000) and* Little Nell *(2007), about Dickens's mistress, Nelly Ternan.*

Amadeus (1979)

by Peter Shaffer

Director: Peter Hall

Olivier, 2 November 1979 to 4 June 1981 (129 performances)

In 1977, Paul Scofield was playing the title role in Hall's production of Volpone *and appearing in Harley Granville Barker's* The Madras House, *and Hall was desperate for him to stay on beyond January 1978, writing at least eight times with offers for 1978–79, including Gaev in* The Cherry Orchard; *none were accepted. Then Hall sent Scofield* Amadeus, *which is dominated by Antonio Salieri, the mediocre court composer who becomes obsessively jealous of Mozart's genius in 1780s Vienna.*

Paul Scofield to Hall, January 1979	My dear Peter,

All I can say is that, if I get the chance, I've just got to play that part. I find [*Amadeus*] quite breathtaking & very alarming, & it seems to deal with unspoken areas of feeling, the relationship of truth to love and hate, the topsiturviness of success/failure & so much more. Yes I would like to do it.

So I'll expect further developments – thank you for sending it to me.

Love,
  Paul […]

Hall to Gillian Diamond (casting director), 5 March 1979	I would be grateful if you could call John Dexter at the Savoy.

He seems to want Simon Callow as Mozart – I can't but think that this is a good idea.

John seems to be interested in Brenda Blethyn for Constanze [Mozart's wife]. […]

PH

cc Christopher Morahan

Dexter had allowed 'every detail' of his production of their previous hit, Equus, *to be incorporated into the stage directions of the published text, out of 'affection and regard' for Shaffer. Many subsequent revivals around the world appeared to Dexter simply to have recreated his* Equus *staging.*

After working with Shaffer on Amadeus *for several years, Dexter insisted that he would only direct it with a contract guaranteeing him a share of Shaffer's royalties, not only for the NT premiere, but in all revivals. They argued; Hall mediated.*

Balcombe,
Sussex.

My dear Peter.

Tuesday.

All I can say is that, if I get the chance, I've just got to play that part. I find the play quite breathtaking & very alarming, & it seems to deal with unspoken areas of feeling, the relationship of truth to love and hate, the topsiturviness of success/failure & so much more. Yes I would like to do it.

So I'll await further developments — thank you for sending it to me.

love

Paul.

P.S. I'll drop it in to
P.T.O. the National next time I'm by

Paul Scofield writes to Peter Hall after
reading *Amadeus*

Peter Shaffer,
telegram to John
Dexter, 13 June 1979

IT TRULY SADDENS ME BUT IT IS NOW CRYSTAL CLEAR
TO ME THAT WE MUST NOT WORK TOGETHER YOU HAVE
EVERY RIGHT TO DEMAND CERTAIN TERMS AND I HAVE
EVERY RIGHT TO REFUSE THEM ON THE PRINCIPLE THAT
AS A PLAYWRIGHT I AM NOT PREPARED TO PAY FOR THE
SERVICES OF THE DIRECTOR. I TRULY BELIEVE IT WOULD
BE UNHEALTHY TO EMBARK ON THIS PRODUCTION WITH
YOU FEELING AGGRIEVED OR ME FEELING SIMILARLY.
YOU HAVE CLARIFIED FOR ME ABSOLUTELY THAT IT WILL
BE BEST, ESPECIALLY AFTER THE WRETCHED PRECEDING
WEEKS, TO END IMMEDIATELY THIS SERIES OF PAINFUL
CONVERSATIONS AND DEMANDS. I MUST REGARD THIS
DECISION AS FINAL.

Dexter to Shaffer,
25 June 1979

Dear Peter,

Your telegram was read to me in front of Peter Hall whilst we
were discussing the possibilities of reaching a solution.

Your telex seems to me a mixture of invention and deliberate
misrepresentation.

Now that the affair has ended, I have only one observation to
make at the end of our personal and working relationship. As
I look back on events which have destroyed a friendship I had
always imagined to be lasting, my bewilderment increases. I seem
to have been facing a different personality to that which I had
previously known. […]

It is the loss of this friendship that distresses me more than
the loss of the play, and I suppose the fact that [*Amadeus*] would
not have emerged in its present form were it not for the time and
work we have expended together for the last four years. This I
suppose must be my consolation.

I have heard much in these last months both from your
agent and yourself of your 'agony'. My feelings have never been
discussed. I trust this short resumé will help to clarify them for
you and for the few people who have been unfortunate enough to
be involved. You may rest assured that it will be the last you will
hear from me.

*Dexter never sent this letter – and he and Shaffer never worked together again. Dexter
maintained his relationship with the NT, first by directing Callow as Orlando in* As You
Like It *(Olivier, July 1979).*

Hall took on Amadeus. *Scofield and Callow were joined by Felicity Kendal as
Constanze. The play opened on 2 November.*

Simon Callow
(Mozart) and Paul
Scofield (Salieri)
in *Amadeus*. Photo:
Nobby Clark

Shaffer, postcard to
Scofield, 2 November
1979

Dear Paul,

I find I have no words – only the most halting & average – to tell
you how I feel about you in this play: you are quite <u>sublime</u>. You
are miraculous & incomparable. I am the luckiest author in the
world – and always will acknowledge so.

    Love,
      Peter

Amadeus *played to standing ovations and sold-out houses. Its transfer to Broadway seemed
inevitable.*

Shaffer to Scofield,
4 December 1979

My dear Paul,

How are you? By now no doubt enjoying your holiday. I hope
enjoying it <u>enormously</u> – with an enormousness commensurate
with your triumph and tremendousness in the play! And with my
happiness. […]

The American producers said they were going to send you a
formal telegram inviting you here. That made me <u>very</u> happy. I do
hope you will accept. Our play needs you so much. I can't imagine
– truly I cannot imagine – doing it with anybody else. We made it
together with such love – you and Peter and I – & really above all,
in the end, <u>you</u>, who delivered it.

It was honestly the most satisfying experience of my working
life to watch a character of such complexity being conjured into
such vigorous, <u>palpable</u> life by you. And now I want the whole
world to see you! Or at least New York – where audiences are so
eager and vital. They <u>long</u> for the theatre and great acting: they
lust for it! […]

The play acquires through you an elegant profundity – and
a tragic dimension that is <u>essential</u> to it. Your Salieri is so
absolutely right & thrilling & dangerous & (ultimately also)
pitiable it constitutes for me one of the few utterly achieved
glories of the modern theatre. There. It's said!

I fancy you didn't care for New York much when you were last
here. I know what hardship it is for you to be away from your
home & your haunts. And heavens I understand that. So it is
really with much plucking up of my courage that I write to you
about this at all. […]

Dear Paul: please come here.

Love to you,
Peter

Scofield refused the Broadway offer.

*Ian McKellen was lined up to replace him, with New York previews scheduled to begin
in November 1980 – provided the producers, the Shubert Organisation, could convince
America's exacting Actors' Equity union that McKellen was a big enough star to deprive a
US performer of such a plum part.*

Hall to Ian McKellen,
2 May 1980

My dear Ian,

Equity have blessed you, so we are in business. You are playing
Salieri. Peter and I are cheering.

[We] agree that we have to find an English accented company.

I don't think we shall have a star as Mozart, and I think you are
absolutely right, over-casting of Mozart would distort the play.
We will find somebody.

There is also no question of having English actors as Mozart
and Constanze.

I believe that [the Broadhurst] is a good house for our play. But
I understand your anxiety – it is on the border of being too big for

intimate playing. But I do think it is a big play – it responds – as you've seen from the Olivier – to a big space.

Phone me on your return to London. Peter Shaffer will be here and the three of us will meet. All is set fair. […]

Best wishes,
    Yours ever,
        [Peter]

Hall to John
Schlesinger, 2 June
1980

Dear John,

The NT is riding the crest of a wave, at least in terms of box office.

I am not actually directing – the first real gap in 25 years. The agonies of the rehearsal room are beginning to look highly preferable to the agonies of administration. But [in the autumn] I direct *Amadeus* on Broadway. I'm sure you know the situation – in the same breath you're told that this is a million-dollar production, and that there's no money for anything you want. […]

Yours ever,
    Peter

With Tim Curry as Mozart and Jane Seymour as Constanze, Amadeus *had a four-week try-out in Washington DC, and opened in New York, at the Broadhurst, on 17 December 1980.*

Shaffer, card
to McKellen,
17 December 1980

My dear Ian,

The pleasure has been enormous. The work has been enormous. The benefits & joys – if there is justice – will be enormous too. You have been heroic & extraordinary: I am truly exceedingly and extremely grateful. May you derive from *Amadeus* everything you wish for yourself. Success & honour & happiness & all the pleasure you so richly deserve.

Thank you for being in my play.

Allons!
    Peter

Hall to Alan
Ayckbourn,
20 January 1981

My dear Alan,

I am back from New York covered in glory from *Amadeus*, but whether I shall be covered in dollars or not remains to be seen. […]

Best wishes,
    Yours ever,
        Peter

Dec 18 : 1980

My dear Ian,

The pleasure has been enormous. The work has been enormous. The benefits & joys – if there is justice – will be enormous too. You have been heroic + extraordinary: I am truly exceedingly and extremely grateful! May you derive from "Amadeus" everything you wish for yourself. Success + honour & happiness + all the pleasure you so richly deserve. Thank you for being in my play. Allons! — Peter

Hall would earn hundreds of thousands of dollars from his royalty on Amadeus, *which won Tonys for him, Shaffer and McKellen, and became one of the longest-running plays in Broadway history.*

In London, Scofield, Kendal and Callow left Amadeus *in April 1981, handing over to, respectively, Frank Finlay, Morag Hood and Richard O'Callaghan, for the West End transfer.*

Callow immediately played Verlaine in Christopher Hampton's Total Eclipse *(1968), directed by David Hare, at the Lyric, Hammersmith.*

Simon Callow to Scofield, 27 May 1981	Dearest Paul,

I can't tell you how delightful it was to see you and Joy t'other Monday, though it wasn't the <u>best</u> performance we'd ever given (Monday night <u>plus</u> that audience, ohlala). There were so many things I wanted to ask you about [*Total Eclipse*] – but dressing-rooms and indeed almost everything après show are such hell somehow one can never speak like an ordinary human being. I sometimes so dread meeting people afterwards (unless I'm absolutely sure it was an utterly brilliant show – but how many times in one's life can one claim that?) that I either escape down the back stairs or else talk so much and so fast about anything or everything but the show that people never get a chance to tell me what they thought at all. Poor Hare was [so] mortified that you hadn't seen a very good perf. that he ran away.

I've got spoilt by playing with extraordinary artists, giving people, vibrating presences (by which I mean <u>you</u>, not to put too fine a point on it!). […]

You've been much in my thoughts lately – I do miss our *Amadeus*es (tho glad that they've finished too). […]

Love to you both,
Simon

Two movie producers, Saul Zaentz (an Oscar-winner for One Flew Over the Cuckoo's Nest) *and Ray Stark (recent winner of an Academy Award for career achievement), had been competing for the rights to* Amadeus.

Shaffer to Hall, 19 July 1981	My dear Peter,

Last night I had the most upsetting talk with Maria [Ewing, Hall's wife]. She told me that one of the newspapers had announced that *Amadeus* would be filmed with [Miloš] Forman directing; that both of you were very hurt.

I am extremely sorry. I cannot apologise enough for your learning this news from a newspaper. I have been in a quandary about how to tell it to you for days. It was only very recently that I learnt myself that Robby Lantz [Shaffer's US agent] had virtually agreed a deal with Mr Zaentz, with a view to Forman directing.

Peter, I know how deeply you desired to direct the film. I hope you realise how seriously I pursued your claims with the one producer prepared to take them seriously: Ray Stark. [But] there was clearly no way to secure your appointment. Nor was there any way to secure it with any other producer. This is the absolute, if embarrassing truth.

Stupidly – very stupidly – I dreaded too much being the one to tell you, even though it was my responsibility. I kept putting it off. Then suddenly Maria phoned with the news. I was deeply surprised and badly shaken. Suddenly I realised, like a sleepwalker waking, where my procrastination had led me. In shrinking from causing you a moment of inescapable distress, I had actually caused you much greater distress. Hesitation and drift and over-sensitiveness have resulted in my giving you the pain I was casting about to avoid.

The moral is not only that he who hesitates is lost, but he may also lose things most precious to him: in this case the regard of a man whose huge talent and imagination are the sources of unending joy for him. We made *Amadeus* together. It revived us both. That is our joint and untarnishable pride. I beg you not to let my paralysis of action create a dreadful tension where there should only be love between us. I have done nothing venal, nothing betraying.

Peter, please do not reject my really deep affection for you, nor deprive me of your own which I cherish so much, and which has nourished me so richly.

Love to you – as always.
Peter

Hall to Shaffer, 28 July 1981

Dear Peter,

Please excuse the silence. I needed time. And I must be candid – even if I hurt; because to reach the end of a relationship as rich as ours has been without candour is unthinkable.

I do not accuse you of lying. It's worse in a way: I believe you deceive yourself – and infinitely.

You were cowardly to let me read the news in the paper. It is appalling treatment. And you apologise for it.

But that seems to me insignificant before the main issue. I do not believe that you and Robby ever had the least intention of trying to get me the picture.

At first I thought it was only a question of money: you wanted and expected more money than could ever be raised on me. But now I hear that you are getting no more than the same sort of deal that Ray Stark offered.

No, you didn't think I could do the picture. You are perfectly entitled to think this and to act on it. But you should have said so to my face long ago. It is shabby to be silent.

The play is yours. You wrote it. You could have waited to sell it. You could have insisted on me.

You and Robby have treated me as a beginner, and you've had little respect for my feelings, my strong desire to do the picture or my contribution to the play. I am very, very hurt, although I assure you nobody shall know of it further. I am far too proud.

I hope, though, that you will show this letter to Robby.

I shall continue to do my duty by *Amadeus* to the best of my ability. But that is it. I feel betrayed.

But in the future with others, I beg you to say what you think. Your desire not to hurt, your reluctance to confront unpleasantness, has caused infinitely greater damage.

Ever,
  Peter

McKellen to Scofield,
30 July 1981

Dear Paul Scofield,

I gather that your refusal to return to New York means that you haven't spent a year of regrets every time news filters through about *Amadeus* on Broadway! However, I wanted to share a bit of my pleasure, which has been considerable, since without you, I couldn't be playing Salieri.

Every reporter I meet wants to know how you are and how you were in the part. My sister, who is your greatest admirer, came over to see the play. Her first remark in the dressing-room was: 'Isn't Tim Curry wonderful?' About a quarter of an hour later she gave me my only compliment: 'You know, Ian, you managed to sound like Paul Scofield nearly three times.' I don't know if you've read Shaffer's changes. They were certainly helpful to me. The plot is simpler and there are a few more jokes with which I manage to ingratiate myself with the house. The ease with which you controlled the Olivier audience was something I despaired of matching at the Broadhurst, which incidentally holds as many people – a very wide proscenium and a huge dress-circle. I fling myself into the younger Salieri and try to show a development from youthful, rather fetching ambition to the embittered sophisticate of the later scenes. It's not an easy journey to route out, particularly as Shaffer in Act 2 seems much more interested in Mozart biography than in Salieri's ever more painful dilemma. But, as you can imagine, Peter's staging and the music and the sheer size of the Company are all impressive. And there has really been no opposition on Broadway. Any decent play or acting usually stops Off-Broadway or at Papp's Public Theatre, these days.

I've met the Norwegian and a German Salieri – they think the play's a masterpiece. Do you miss playing it? I've been much relieved to find 8 shows a week perfectly manageable [and] one gets into a routine – but compared with Shakespeare, it's almost relaxing. I had a little voice trouble at the outset but now I find I've plenty of energy to enjoy the city and make some good friends. Each day presents some delight or other. However after 250 performances (and only 65 to go!) I'm ready to return. I turned down a 10-month tour of the USA next year in the hope that I can fit back into England by the autumn. A whole year away is unsettling; but I've enjoyed the chance to be a little objective about home and about myself; to have some attitudes confirmed and others challenged. I saw Alec McCowen the other week here and he was going on and on about his love of

New York: so I asked him for one thing in which London was superior. Unhesitatingly he replied: 'Standards!' And that's it – everyone aspires here to wealth and the status of success, fed by the American dream that anyone can be a star and any star can become President. Which I suppose is a fair alternative to the English equivalent that anyone can become a princess, if she happens to be the daughter of an earl!

But in the Broadway Theatre, money is everything. It allows our management to put up our prices to $35, the very week in which we paid off [the show's capitalisation] in May. It thwarts experiment. And as it intensifies the rewards for the winners, it increases the losses for the rest. Who would want to work permanently in a system which works like LITTLEWOODS in which winner takes all? Of course the real winners are the impresarios. And although I get on well enough with the Shuberts, they don't actually know or care enough about the theatre to encourage me to want to return for a bit. So maybe one day soon I'll be doing another actor the sort of good turn you did me.

Belated congratulations on your initial success, without which I and Frank [Finlay] and the Salieris in Norway, Germany and everywhere else, might never have had a chance.

All best wishes,
Ever,
Ian McKellen

Hall to McKellen, 7 August 1981

Dear Ian,

It was very good to see you and to have the lunch.

You are now playing Salieri with a richness and a detail which is quite masterful. You get better and better.

I found the show in wonderful shape. A whole new strand is visible in it. The play is now also a love story – the love story of Constanze and Mozart. And there is the obverse side – the destructive desire of Salieri. So sensuality has come into the piece. It's quite marvellous.

Love,
Peter

After McKellen's departure, Amadeus *had six more Salieris, including John Wood and Frank Langella, before closing in October 1983.*

The film of Amadeus *(1984) won Oscars for Shaffer (Best Adapted Screenplay), Forman (Best Director) and Zaentz (Best Picture).*

Hall would direct Shaffer's Yonadab *(Olivier, 1985) and, for the RSC,* The Gift of the Gorgon *(1992); they revived* Amadeus *in London and New York in 1998–99, and remained good friends for life.*

The Romans in Britain (1980)
by Howard Brenton

Director: Michael Bogdanov
Olivier, 16 October 1980 to 24 March 1981 (26 performances)

Howard Brenton to Hall, 5 July 1976	Dear Peter,

I've a monstrous idea for a play – I don't want to turn your hair white by writing it baldly down on paper, perhaps we could talk about it soon?

Best wishes,
Howard

Brenton wrote this letter a week before Weapons of Happiness *opened. Hall had already promised him another commission. The 'monstrous' idea was to juxtapose ancient history and contemporary conflict: in the first part, Brenton would present the Roman occupation of Britain in 54 BC; in the second, the present-day British military presence in Northern Ireland.*

Brenton to Hall, 1 August 1977	Dear Peter,

The Romans in Britain

[…] My instinct is to do some reading then, quite quickly, I am into a full first draft of both parts of the play, trying to complete it in six months or so – full of inaccuracies and wild scenes, but getting the weight and nature of the beast. […]

Best wishes,
Howard

Hall, memo to John Russell Brown et al., 23 August 1977	<u>Howard Brenton and *The Romans in Britain*</u>

I think it has enormous potential. It's a two-part play – really two plays to be given on the same evening rather like *Tamburlaine*. It deals with the urge to Imperialism and its consequences.

PH

By autumn 1978, Brenton had completed a two-play version of The Romans… *Early in the first play three young Celts (a pair of foster brothers and Marban, a druid) murder two Irish peddlers. Roman centurions then kill the brothers, and one of the centurions rapes Marban. Hall shared the script with Christopher Morahan.*

Christopher Morahan (Lyttelton Director) to Hall, 31 October 1978	Dear Peter,

I never thought I would recover from the savage imagery and language of the first half, to enjoy the second half as much as I did, and to come away from the whole audacious enterprise so stimulated. He has managed to pack into the writing an extraordinary sense of the way that any present is made by its past.

However I do consider the language and actions of the first play a near parody of the blood and bugger school, a two-finger gesture to the hapless NT audience, and for it to be played on its own in one evening, a sure frightener for the second play. I'd admire the stamina or resilience of those who would return for a second evening. Shouldn't the two plays be tightened for one evening's show? And in the Cottesloe?

CM

Peggy Ramsay to Hall, 4 December 1978

PERSONAL
Private!

My dear Peter,

Regarding our conversation on Friday about [*The Romans…*]: the real problem (and you must tell me if I'm wrong), is the sense of scale. It doesn't have any epic quality about it. I don't think this will matter, provided it is directed as a play about a group of people; but if it were presented in an epic manner I think it could get badly attacked by the critics, as the moment you put characters in Roman clothes the author is equated with Shakespeare, and it must be better than *Julius Caesar*!

I hope you don't think it impertinent of me to mention it so early in the game, but the fact is that this author isn't an epic writer (but thinks he i̲s̲, so one can't talk about this with him). […]

I think you had better throw this letter away when you have read it, although I think it's oblique enough for it not to make any sense to anyone but you.

Warmest regards,
    Ever yours,
        Peggy

As Brenton worked on The Romans… *he also finished a version of Brecht's* The Life of Galileo; *Hall offered its title role to Michael Gambon.*

Brenton to Hall, 1 August 1979

Dear Peter,

Thinking over the possibility of John Dexter as *Galileo*'s director it would be excellent. Peggy gave me a good talking to. ('Gambon, Dexter and you – bizarre, dear! Would you survive it? Find out, dear!' Etc.)

The Romans in Britain is taking yards of stomach wall away but going well. I catch myself grinning at being the father and mother of such a big play.

Best wishes,
    Howard

The Romans… *would be directed by Michael Bogdanov, who spent a week with Brenton in Wales in July 1980, finishing what was now a single play again, still with Marban raped early on. Posters advertised* The Romans… *as 'Not suitable for children'. Hall warned the NT Board it might prove controversial. The Board's ex-officio members included Geoffrey Seaton, chief whip on the Greater London Council (the NT's second-largest funder, after the Arts Council), and the GLC's leader, Horace Cutler, another Tory. Both men saw* The Romans… *preview on 15 October; both walked out before the interval.*

Horace Cutler, telegram to Hall, 16 October 1980

BASED ON LAST NIGHTS PERFORMANCE QUOTE ROMANS IN BRITAIN UNQUOTE IS A DISGRACE TO THE NATIONAL THEATRE. STOP. ITS STAGING SHOWS A SINGULAR LACK OF JUDGMENT ON YOUR PART. STOP. SEVERAL OF THE AUDIENCE LEFT AT THE INTERVAL AND SOME DEMANDED THEIR MONEY BACK. STOP. […] I HAVE NO DOUBT THAT THE GLC WILL BE RECONSIDERING ITS POSITION VIS A VIS THE NATIONAL THEATRE AT AN EARLY DATE.

Geoffrey Seaton to Hall, 16 October 1980

Dear Peter,

I write to register the strongest possible protest at a most disgusting and immature play. I know you warned [the Board] that it would be 'strong meat' but few could possibly have suspected that it would be so devoid of any merit.

I have for some time been pleading the National's financial cause (with some success) with people who have seen the GLC's grant as a fair area for cuts in this difficult financial climate. This play has made that task probably impossible. Indeed the feeling among many members here is that the grant should be suspended forthwith. It may well be that the cheapest thing for the National to do would be to remove this so-called play from the repertoire immediately.

The pressures here are considerable, not on the grounds of censorship but merit. The part which I saw would have disgraced a fourth-form pupil, but I appreciate that views on artistic merit can vary. What must be absolute is that when rates and taxes are being used such plays should not receive support.

Yours ever,
Geoffrey

Hall to Seaton, 16 October 1980

Dear Geoffrey,

[…] The current Olivier repertoire alone contains plays by Ayckbourn, Brecht and Shakespeare, all of them immensely successful. This new play is part of that range. The NT must maintain a commitment to the new as well as the old. New writers today are often outspoken and provocative, and Howard Brenton is a serious and important dramatist with an international reputation.

At Monday's Board meeting I said that I have complete faith in the integrity of the playwright, the director and the play. It is, in my view, an ambitious and remarkable piece of dramatic writing.

We have striven to ensure that nothing is self-indulgent, that it doesn't encourage what it in fact deplores, and that our audiences are warned.

I don't believe in censorship – a view that I think you will share – and therefore don't think that the NT should tell leading dramatists and directors what they should do from an ethical point of view.

Again I am most distressed indeed that you feel the way you do.

Yours ever,
Peter

The Romans… provoked a huge – and, for an NT play, wholly unprecedented – storm in the press and on television. Chairman Max Rayne sought guidance from Sir Derek Mitchell, a Board member since 1977 (and, in the 1960s, principal private secretary to Harold Wilson).

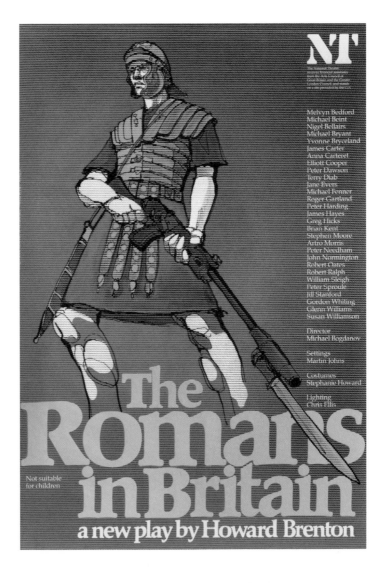

<table>
<tr><td>Derek Mitchell
to Max Rayne,
20 October 1980</td><td>

Dear Max,

The eye of the storm should move on soon. So let us avoid witch hunts at one extreme and votes of confidence at the other.

It is a nasty play. If it had been nasty but good there would be less of a problem. Instead it is nasty and second-rate, which makes it more difficult to argue against those who say it should not have been put on at all.

By second-rate I mean poorly written, confused and immature. I have not seen a [review] that refutes this. Peter has called it 'ambitious and remarkable': well-chosen words, appropriately ambivalent. […]

The Cottesloe was the place for this play if it was to be done at all. All else apart, there are no Guest Nights there: so Horace Cutler and Geoffrey Seaton would not have had the opportunity to walk out.

I have avoided comment on the alleged moral issues. I am against censorship. I <u>am</u> for treading carefully while our roots, including our financial roots, are still taking hold.

Finally, because I think that our only concern now should be damage-limitation I hope that there will be no question of extending the play's run if it degenerates into a *succès de scandale*. We do not need that kind of success.

I am copying this only to Peter.

Ever,
  Derek
</td></tr>
<tr><td>Hall to Ramsay,
28 October 1980</td><td>

My dear Peggy,

Just wanted to say how magnificent Howard has been, and while I don't think the nonsense will be gone immediately, how steady we are all keeping here.

I'm still glad I've done the play. Very glad.

Love,
  Peter
</td></tr>
<tr><td>Ramsay, postcard
to Hall, 1 November
1980</td><td>

Dear Peter,

[…] It seems to me that you did marvels yourself, & I agree it was a good idea – particularly the scandal!

Love,
  Peggy
</td></tr>
</table>

The media furore subsided. But Bogdanov then faced a criminal prosecution, instigated by England's self-appointed guardian of public morality, Mary Whitehouse. Despite the rape of Marban being so obviously simulated, Bogdanov went on trial at the Old Bailey in March 1982, charged with 'procuring an act of gross indecency' between Greg Hicks (Marban) and Peter Sproule (Third Soldier).

Brenton to Hall,
4 February 1982

Dear Peter,

[…] I'm going on the road reading *The Romans…* [at ten theatres]. I'm retaining all the dialogue and incidents but rewriting it as a narrative, so I can tell it as a story.

It sounds a madness, it may be – but I'm confident I can pull it off. I want to raise money for the Theatre Defence Fund [for Bogdanov's legal costs], put the play before an audience again and – very importantly for me – make it clear that the play is not in anyway banned, proscribed or illegal because of the prosecution. Of course I'm close to Michael B. with this and wouldn't do it if he had the slightest doubt.

If you are free, Michael is coming to my last reading at the Phoenix [Leicester], his old theatre of course, on March 12th – would you like to come up with him? We could have a pre-trial celebration? And maybe I'll have cracked the reading by then!

Best wishes,
Howard

The trial collapsed and Bogdanov escaped a possible jail sentence.

Brenton next wrote to Hall at one of the most controversial moments of his NT tenure: after the publication of Peter Hall's Diaries, *which covered, in unsparing detail, his first seven years as Director.*

Brenton to Hall,
30 September 1983

Dear Peter,

Thank you for the record of our meeting in your diary. I'm not used to reading something fair about my work in cold, public print!

I am much indebted to you. Not only for your rock-hard commitment to *The Romans…* during its production and the brouhaha. You have always been straight with me over the four shows I've written for you.

And you, I fear, are about to go off somewhere, to opera or private life, but out of the theatre. I'm afraid I took that as the subtext of your diary: 'Thank you all, sod you all and goodbye.'

If I'm wrong, fine.

But if you are seriously thinking of giving the job up I would like to talk to you. We are from the same background (yer bright grammar school boys of working-class parents). I suspect you do not know your own worth.

Meanwhile – I hope that you are going to bash the National through a new five-year plan. As long as there's a live theatre in this country your work as a director and a manager will be attacked, defended and discussed. So, well done. You have enemies but you also have strong friends. Sleep well of nights.

Best wishes,
Howard

With the previous letter, Brenton enclosed this doctored postcard of Margaret Thatcher standing beside Ronald Reagan.

1981

*Another Country***
by Julian Mitchell

Julian Mitchell's Half-Life *(1977) had premiered at the Cottesloe, with John Gielgud as an elderly archaeology professor. Mitchell's follow-up was a fictionalised account of the 1930s boarding-school days of the spy Guy Burgess.*

Hall to Anthony Jones (Mitchell's agent), 29 January 1981

Dear Anthony,

Another Country has now been fully discussed by the NT's directorate. It caused great interest among us all, and there was particular admiration for the play's courage. I myself particularly liked [its] denouement. But I am afraid that we cannot see a way of fitting it into our repertoire.

> Yours sincerely,
> Peter Hall

Hall copied this to Mitchell, with a covering letter: 'I don't think I can say more without making you feel patronised or insulted. I really am glad to have read it.' Another Country *opened at Greenwich Theatre in November 1981 and made a star of Rupert Everett, as Guy Bennett, the 17-year-old Burgess figure, and did the same for Kenneth Branagh, when, three months after leaving RADA, he took over as Judd, Bennett's Communist friend, for a West End transfer.*

The Hypochondriac (1673)

by Molière

Translated by Alan Drury (1981)
Director: Michael Bogdanov
Olivier, 22 November 1981 to 17 February 1982 (35 performances)

Hall to Michael Bogdanov, 17 February 1981

PRIVATE AND CONFIDENTIAL

My dear Michael,

I must say how very disturbed I am to hear that you want to [set] *The Hypochondriac* in the 1920s [not the seventeenth century].

Had you said to me when we [first] talked that you would <u>only</u> do it if it could be in the 1920s, I really wouldn't have proceeded.

I don't believe in it. And I do not believe that it will bring Molière to our audiences – rather the reverse. It will enable them to escape from an important play by writing it off as a piece of camp theatre.

I am in no position to cancel the production now in view of the ruinous situation of the Olivier.

I can only ask you to think again. [...]

Best wishes.
    Yours ever,
        Peter

Bogdanov, memo to Hall, 19 February 1981

PRIVATE AND CONFIDENTIAL

Peter,

You are a bugger! I shall do as you ask because I know that I can do it. However, this is not to be taken as a once and for all abandoning of my position to bring classical theatre to an audience in a popular form, done in a way I know I can do. We must in future debate each production on the merits of its intentions.

Mike

1982

Guys and Dolls (1950)

Music and lyrics by Frank Loesser
Book by Joe Swerling and Abe Burrows

Director: Richard Eyre
Olivier, 9 March 1982 to 15 September 1984 (289 performances)

Hall watched a dress rehearsal of Guys and Dolls, *the New York-set musical starring Ian Charleson as professional gambler Sky Masterson, Bob Hoskins as small-timer Nathan Detroit, Julia McKenzie as his fiancée, nightclub singer Miss Adelaide, and Julie Covington as the missionary, Sister Sarah, who falls for Sky.*

**Hall to Richard Eyre,
26 February 1982**

Dear Richard,

I think it is going to be quite marvellous, and you are going to have a big success.

You'll know all this already, but it may help harden your resolve if I jot it down. […]

The cast <u>act</u> the songs beautifully. But they are drowned by too loud playing and too heavy orchestration. It is too complex, too evident. The Olivier is a very resonant house and the combined forces of the musicians playing straight at us drowns out the actors.

I'm sure it would be possible to amplify the voices but then you'd lose all the subtlety, and all the humanity. I think the musicians have got to be asked to play much, much quieter, and you've got to thin out the orchestrations. […]

I found a woeful lack of consonants in the cast. You really have to relish consonants to make words audible when singing. […]

Neither Ian nor Julia nor Bob play the arc of the house anything like enough. In one of the duets, Ian didn't look at the left-hand side of the house [so] I never saw his eyes and never really heard him.

The dynamic of the scene changes will need careful study during the previews. At the moment (and please, I <u>know</u> it was only a dress rehearsal), the piece goes soft and soggy on every scene change.

I'm not too sure about the dancing generally yet. It seems to me that since it can't be breathtaking, it has to be acted. […]

I have the impression, although it's early days, that there is a little too much neon.

Having said all this I think it has every chance of being magnificent.

Congratulations.
  Peter

Guys and Dolls *became the most popular NT show of Hall's 15-year tenure – and made Eyre a leading contender to succeed him.*

Way Upstream (1981)

by Alan Ayckbourn

Director: Alan Ayckbourn
Lyttelton, 4 October 1982 to 19 April 1983 (63 performances)

Alan Ayckbourn to Hall, 14 September 1981

Dear Peter,

I'm now in rehearsal [in Scarborough]. It's called *Way Upstream* and is set on (you've guessed it) a cabin cruiser.

I'd sort of like to get it on here before anyone sees it or reads it – if that's OK with you. It's rather different for me and a bit of a technical bugger, to boot.

We're flooding our stage and trying to build a boat that manoeuvres. And <u>real</u> rain. Well, water rain. We may all drown.

When it's on and running rest assured you will receive a) a script and b) an invitation to come up here to judge for yourself. (You will need Wellingtons.)

Love,
Alan

Ayckbourn to Peggy Ramsay, 1 February 1982

My dear Peggy,

[…] I don't want to inundate [the NT] with demands, but we must naturally have approval of [*Way Upstream*] casting.

I am also very anxious that we don't get actors that are too tired. [The National] do seem to have this problem, natural in so large a company, where half their actors are under-worked and the other half nearly dead with exhaustion. When we did *Sisterly* [*Feelings* in the Olivier in 1980] we had to prop some of them up against a wall. […]

Love,
Alan

On board Way Upstream's *pleasure cruiser* The Hadforth Bounty *are two couples: factory boss Keith, his wife June, and his deputy, Alistair, and Alistair's wife Emma. Their river holiday is disrupted by two intruders – the thuggish Vince and his girlfriend, Fleur – who initiate violence and sexual humiliation on an increasingly allegorical voyage.*

Hall to Ayckbourn, 20 April 1982

My dear Alan,

Gillian [Diamond] has told me of your casting session, and it looks an exciting group

One thing does worry me. Derek Newark [as Vince]. I love his intensity, his ability to portray paranoia, and I can certainly hear him tying everybody else up with the nautical terms.

But I just don't think he is glamorous enough, sexy enough to give the centre to your fine play. It's a hard thing to say I know, but I believe it.

The truth of the play stands or falls on the casting of Vince. Derek might give a passable imitation, but not <u>be</u> Vince. Shouldn't we think again?

Best wishes,
Yours ever,
Peter

Ayckbourn to Hall, 24 April 1982

Dear Peter,

[...] I still feel we should not entirely dismiss Derek. However if we can find someone dangerous and packed with sheer animal magnetism, let's grab him but why isn't he in Hollywood?

Love,
Alan

James Laurenson was cast as Vince, alongside Tony Haygarth (Keith), Susan Fleetwood (June), Jim Norton (Alistair), Julie Legrand (Emma) and Nina Thomas (Fleur). They became engulfed in nightmarish technical complications, including faulty hydraulics and leaks in the on-stage water tanks that contained the cruiser. The 12 and 13 August previews were cancelled, the 18 August press night pushed back to 3 September. 'Leaks scupper Ayckbourn launch' read a Times *headline. Ayckbourn had to return to Scarborough, as scheduled, to rehearse his* Intimate Exchanges.

Julie Legrand, Jim Norton, Susan Fleetwood and James Laurenson in *Way Upstream*. Photo: Nobby Clark

<table>
<tr><td>Albe L. Rosen to Hall,
28 August 1982</td><td>Dear Sir Peter,</td></tr>
</table>

I have just heard of your plans to cancel *Way Upstream* due to technical difficulties, and having seen a preview, I must beg you not to withhold this important play from the public.

I found it completely stunning in impact and besides being hilariously funny throughout, it made strong and moving statements on the nature of sexuality, of how we judge and are judged, and on the 'ship of state' we live in. Although the boat demonstrates tremendous feats of stage management (I've worked in the theatre for years and have never experienced a spectacle like it – most impressive, and gigantic gold stars and tranquillisers all round!), it is still basically a sort of 'gimmick' to dazzle with and not the play itself.

Ayckbourn is saying such important things about the truth of human nature. This play must not be scuttled at sea! After all, the Thames is just outside your doors – why not float the boat outside?

Please let others see it. It was the closest to the magical 'catharsis' of the Greeks I've ever experienced – pity, fear, laughter, and a passage beyond life itself. Who needs gimmicks? But we need to see this Ayckbourn.

Yours faithfully,
(Miss) Albe L. Rosen

<table>
<tr><td>Julie Legrand to
Ayckbourn, August
1982</td><td>Dear Alan,</td></tr>
</table>

I was so pleased to get your letter – a happy confirmation that the whole thing has not been a figment of my imagination! – It really is the most peculiar state of limbo that we are all in!

I was delighted, however, to hear from Ernie [Hall, stage manager] that we will be reassembling at the end of September. Surely things will run smoothly this time?!

I think you've shown the most extraordinary patience and I feel terribly ashamed that such a place as the NT should have subjected you to such chaos. […]

It seems miraculous that you have put on another show in the interim – how marvellous, it must have renewed your faith in the theatre! […]

I look forward very much to seeing you soon, under what I hope will be more peaceful circumstances than has been the case recently!

Love,
Julie

Way Upstream finally opened on 4 October – but its technical problems continued, as the show report on the next page shows.

Amidst concerns for the health of actors and stage crew, water samples from the tanks were sent to Professor Ian Phillips at the Department of Microbiology, St Thomas's Hospital Medical School.

1. Late curtain up: The bank had jammed solid at 11.30 a.m. when
   we were about to embark on a boat and bank technical. Work
   continued on it throughout the day and was still not completed
   by curtain up time. We had, however, run through all the Act 1
   bank movements successfully. In addition to this, the water
   in the tank had been drained off because of leaks and then
   refilled.

2. The boat movements were erratic throughout because work on
   the bank prevented a new boat operator(Jem Wilsher being on
   holiday)getting any technical rehearsal at all. Also, boat
   pivot problems with the winch not only made it neccessary
   to interrupt the performance twice in Act 2 by bringing in the
   iron curtain and replacing a slipped cable on it's wheel, but
   also entirely threw out the position of the boat in it's last
   three moves.

3. The performance was interrupted for two minutes at the end
   of the second Act 2 mooring scene and for 4 minutes at the
   end of the Act 2 fight scene for the above mentioned breakdown
   of the upstage pivot winch.

4. Long interval: The bank once again jammed on it's last move
   in Act 1 and had to be worked on in the interval. The pivot
   winch also was worked on in the interval.

5. There was a new speaker in the boat and, again because of
   work on the bank throughout the day, the sound operator had
   been unable to adequately test levels. The first music cue in
   Act 1 was so loud in the boat that neither actors or operators
   could hear what was happening in the play and the speaker had
   to be turned off. A radio cuelight didn't work for the first
   boat move,therefore it was late. The radio headset used by
   the boat operator could not be made to work in Act 1 and I
   was unable to communicate with him.

6. Curtain calls: Because the cable on the pivot winch slipped
   off it's wheel for the third time, we were unable to move the
   boat after it's final Act 2 manoeuvre so we had to scrap
   the set call and line the cast up on the downstage banks.

7. The feeling of the company after the performance was that they
   could not face the prospect of ever having to live through
   such a traumatic performance again.

..........E. Hall..........

Ian Phillips to Tony Bond (NT), 8 February 1983	Dear Mr Bond, Bacteriological Tests on Water Samples […] All the water samples showed heavy contamination with a mixture of organisms. [One,] Aeromonas, has been associated with gastroenteritis. Leaving the question of smell aside, I would not be particularly keen on swimming in the stuff. […] 　　You should add some kind of disinfectant to the water. […] 　　Yours sincerely, 　　Ian Phillips

When Way Upstream's *beleaguered run ended in April 1983, it had entertained 42,000 people, and left Ayckbourn bruised but undaunted.*

Ayckbourn to Hall, 14 January 1984	Dear Peter, Happy New Year to you. 　　I was thinking next of doing a full-scale adaptation of *The Water Babies* but feel I may shelve it temporarily. […] 　　Hope the old building keeps afloat. I really must stop making these jokes. 　　Love, 　　Alan

1983

A Map of the World (1982)

by David Hare

Director: David Hare
Lyttelton, 27 January to 13 August 1983 (66 performances)

The principal character in A Map of the World *is Victor Mehta, an Indian novelist attending a UNESCO conference in Bombay. The play was stage-managed by Diana Boddington, who had been with the NT since 1963.*

Diana Boddington to David Hare, 31 January 1983	My dear David, Just a small note to say 'thank you' for the champagne, and how much I have really enjoyed working with you. As I had been warned about YOU!! How difficult you were!! I was in great fear at our first rehearsal. But I have never seen any of these awful qualities in you!! All I have seen in you are great charm, a wonderful sense of humour, a man who knows what he wants & what he is doing (very unusual these days!!) I have loved every

minute of working with you. I only hope that the play will be a great personal success for you. That I will have the opportunity of working with you again i.e. if you don't ask for someone else!!! After so many years in the theatre it is difficult to name the great Directors, & now you have been added to my list.

My dearest love & wishes to you for a great future – which I know you will have – and may we work together again very soon (that is, if you want to!!).

God bless and luck and thanks,
   x Diana x

Sean Mathias to Hare, 20 March 1983

Dear David,

I've been staring at this piece of writing paper for 20 minutes and it now seems that composing a letter to you is becoming as difficult as starting a new play. So fuck it.

I loved *Map of the World*. It was such a beautiful evening of theatrical craft, intellect and finally, deeply felt passion. The argument [between Mehta and a journalist, Stephen Andrews, about the problems of the developing world] was so convincing, on both sides, that I was artistically and politically as perplexed as I continually seem to be in real life.

I love what you say about 'the writer' – that voice that must speak and thereby may affect and that isolated figure in his bunker. But it was the line of Mehta's concerning 'change' that sent a shadow right across my body; for me the climax of the evening's passion. Thank you for such a stirring evening.

To have seen *Plenty* only six weeks ago [in New York] and now this play, makes me feel most humble as a young man starting out on his writing life. With such inspiration I ought not to complain.

Many thanks and all the best,
   Sean

1984

A new play**
by Alan Bennett

Bennett's film An Englishman Abroad, *about actor Coral Browne's meeting with spy Guy Burgess in Moscow in 1958, was shown on BBC1 on 29 November 1983.*

Hall to Alan Bennett, 10 January 1984

Dear Alan,

May I add to the chorus of praise you have rightly received for your Guy Burgess play?

I have been meaning to write to you all year, and the beauty of that piece has spurred me to actually do it.

I long for some comedy in the Olivier. Some new comedy. I don't mean that you should be invited to put on a clown's cap and be funny. But I'm a little tired of every new play submitted for the Olivier having a cast of hundreds and being historical.

The Olivier is a wonderful place for gestures large and small.

Your writing would work wonderfully well there. Is there ever any chance of a play from you?

Best wishes,
  Yours sincerely,
    Peter

**Bennett to Hall,
18 January 1984**

Dear Peter,

It's so nice to be <u>asked</u>! And I wish I could say that that's just what I've been waiting for and enclose a wonderful, airy comedy by return.

I've started at least a dozen plays in the last three years, all of which have ground to a halt about 20 minutes in. I then abandon them in despair and take to television which I can write because I somehow feel nobody <u>notices</u>.

But I am encouraged by your asking and if I do get anything finished that isn't a vast epic but a tremulous confection of jokes I'll come running across Waterloo Bridge with it.

Thanks too for the compliments about Burgess. We were all slightly taken aback by how much it was liked and how generally. So I have a slight feeling that we got away with it. Still it's such a nice change when one does.

All best wishes,
  Yours sincerely,
    Alan B.

Gloucester Crescent,
London NWI
January 18 1984

Dear Peter,
         Thank you very much for your letter.It's so nice to be
<u>asked</u> ! And I wish I could say that that's just what I've been
waiting for and enclose a wonderful,airy comedy by return of post.
         The truth is I've started at least a dozen plays in the
last three years,all of which have ground to a halt about twenty
minutes in.I then abandon them in despair and take to television
which I can write because I somehow feel nobody notices.
         But I am encouraged by your asking and if I do get anything
finished that isn't a vast epic but a tremulous confection of jokes
I'll come running across Waterloo Bridge with it.
         Thanks too for the compliments about Burgess. We were all
slightly taken aback by how much it was liked generally.So I have a
slight feeling we got away with it.Still its such a nice change when
one does.
               All best wishes,
                  Yours sincerely,
                     Alan B.
                  Alan Bennett

A 'Utopian' play**

by Howard Brenton

Howard Brenton to
Hall, 22 March 1984

Dear Peter,

Not good news. The 'utopian' play I've been trying to write has broken down – again. This is the third attempt. I've got nearer, but the writing I've done over the last nine months has become so weird, poetic, unreal that I have to keep it secret.

This has been going on since 1977. Whether I'm feeding other work off the endless impossibility of writing this subject, I don't know. I've decided to put it aside until next winter after writing the play with David [Hare] about Fleet Street [*Pravda*]. I will damn well get the thing written right in the end. […]

Hope I've not messed you about with the continuing non-appearance of the bloody thing.

I am well, fit and in a good state! Despite having written something through the winter that's not worked.

Best wishes,
Howard

It must be awful 'to have an unrealised play in your system', replied Hall. When Brenton finally delivered in June 1987, with Diving for Pearls, *it was 'not the utopian idea'; instead, the tale of an upper-class prison visitor who falls for a lower-class inmate; she helps him escape and they go on the run. Hall admired 'its strength as a cry of pain and rage' – but turned it down.*

Henry IV: Parts One & Two (1596-97)**

by William Shakespeare

Ronnie Barker believed his 'great stroke of luck' in his twenties had been to act for Hall at the Arts Theatre, London, in 1954–55. With Barker preparing to film a fourth series of BBC comedy Open All Hours, *Hall invited him to play Falstaff in* Henry IV.

Ronnie Barker to
Hall, 17 June 1984

Dear Peter,

I'm afraid I now realise that the length of time required is too great for me to cope with, due to my TV commitments.

By the time we finished rehearsals, I would be into my next series; and I have long ago realised that I cannot give my mind to two jobs at once (not like those far-off days of *Summertime* (Act III) and *Listen to the Wind* (Act I)).

I must, therefore, regretfully put aside any thought of Sir John, and be content with the thought that at least I was asked; an honour which I shall always treasure.

My congratulations on your marvellous career.

As ever,
Ronnie

Hall insisted he could schedule an NT season that allowed Barker to juggle Shakespeare and sitcom: 'It is rare in life when you feel that the actor and the part are one, and you simply have to do this.' Barker was not to be persuaded. He never took another stage role.

Wild Honey (1881?)
by Anton Chekhov

in a version by Michael Frayn (1983)
Director: Christopher Morahan
Lyttelton, 19 July 1984 to 17 August 1985 (125 performances)

Michael Frayn had made his NT writing debut with a translation of The Cherry Orchard, *used by Hall in the Olivier in 1978. Frayn was waiting for his translation of Tolstoy's* The Fruits of Enlightenment *to be staged by Christopher Morahan in the Olivier, in March 1979, when he wrote the following.*

Michael Frayn to Christopher Morahan, 6 December 1978

Dear Chris,

I've now – at last – had a chance to read the *Platonov* text and think about it. I must say there seems to me a great deal of the most marvellous stuff in it – really wonderful scenes. Some of them made me laugh aloud. It's astonishing – Chekhov apparently wrote it when he was still just a second-year medical student. But already he can create characters of all ages who are simply <u>alive</u>. Not all the characters are successful; but the best of them speak their own words, think their own thoughts, and live their own lives. They simply <u>are</u>.

I should very much like to have a go at teasing a workable play out of this material. It will be a monstrous labour. In its present form [the complete text] would run for about seven hours; I think something like 2½ would be more appropriate for what it is. One of the main problems is an uncertainty of tone. The characteristic ambiguity of comic and tragic that Chekhov mastered in his later plays is here (interestingly but disconcertingly) foreshadowed by an uneasy wobbling between comic and melodramatic.

I enclose my [four-page 'Proposal for Reworking the Play']. I know you've done a very successful version before [for BBC television in 1971, with Rex Harrison as Platonov, the dissolute, womanising schoolmaster], I remember it with pleasure. I should like to propose a title. Chekhov left it untitled. It might be a good idea to move on from *Platonov*, partly because last time (as I remember) everyone mispronounced the name most painfully. I should like to suggest *Wild Honey*. The phrase comes from the letter that Platonov received from Anna Petrovna [his widowed lover] in Act Three, which memorably describes the period from the 'wild night' of Act Two as 'a month smeared with wild honey'. I think it captures something about both the wayward sweetness of the sexual intrigues and intense feeling of summer in the play. (One of the most amazing things, incidentally, is the strength and pervasiveness of the erotic feeling throughout.)

In view of your proposed casting: Platonov himself is a wonderful study of middle-aged frustrations and longing, but he does describe himself as being 27. [...]

Perhaps we could meet. I shall be doing jury service until [8 December], but there are usually children here to take a message from about four-thirty onwards.

Yours,
Michael

John Russell Brown, memo to Morahan, 14 December 1978

Platonov

I was glad to see Michael's outline and notes.

a) I think *Platonov* as a title will register with many theatregoers, because of the telly. It would be making a very big statement if we were to call it *Wild Honey*. (Perhaps I'm more alarmed at this because it sounds like an Elizabeth Arden product). [...]

JRB

In 1979, Frayn failed to persuade Hall and Russell Brown to produce his adaptation – written on spec – of Exchange *(1969), Yuri Trifonov's novella about a Muscovite attempting to jump a housing queue. He then turned his attention to a later Trifonov novel.*

Frayn to Hall, 21 October 1981

Dear Peter,

I don't know whether you recall *The House on the Embankment* by Yuri Trifonov. The NT got hold of the Russian text, at my suggestion. I read it, made a careful analysis of its content and cast requirements, and [wrote] at some length to John Russell Brown, saying that if the NT wanted to do it I should be delighted to translate it. My letter was dated 26 February. I have had no reply whatsoever. [...]

No doubt you're endlessly badgered by people like me who have some favourite writer whose cause they wish to promote, after seeing some production on their summer holidays, or reading the original Icelandic text in the British Museum. But [on] 26 February I also enquired about the fate of [*Platonov*]. I made fairly elaborate plans for reducing it to a workable size, which I submitted to Chris on 6 December 1978. No reply was ever forthcoming. I have made various enquiries about it since. Chris told me that the project had been postponed because of casting difficulties. Otherwise not a word. I really do think that if work has been commissioned there ought to be someone on the staff who is responsible for sending some indication of its fate. Unless I hear to the contrary I shall assume that I am now free to offer my projected version elsewhere. [...]

Yours,
Michael

Hall accepted this 'well-deserved' rebuke – and committed to producing Frayn's version. His script reached the NT in August 1983.

Frayn to Hall, 14 February 1984

Dear Peter,

I'm very sorry indeed that you are still unhappy at the choice of *Wild Honey* as a title, and appalled to find that you still think it might be possible to change it [back to *Platonov*]. I have thought long and hard about this, and am quite clear in my own mind that *Wild Honey* is the title I want.

A handful of salient points. […]

2. d) it is <u>a different play</u> – in effect a <u>new</u> play – <u>my</u> play, based upon Chekhov's, after Chekhov, but totally reshaped and rewritten – for the shortcomings of which Chekhov is not responsible. […]

I take no credit for *Wild Honey*; the phrase is in the text. But I know a good title when I see one. I haven't always been able to <u>find</u> one – several of my books and plays have had poor titles. But *Wild Honey* fits my version like a glove.

Any quibbles from critics will be fundamentally about the justification for rewriting the original, and the success of the result. If they don't feel that what they see justifies my high-handedness then they'll quibble anyway. If they like what they see I don't think they'll waste too much anguish over the title.

I'm sorry to be intransigent. I'm not about many things.

Yours,
Michael Frayn

Hall relented. Wild Honey *opened on 19 July, starring Ian McKellen – then 45 to* Platonov's *27.*

Frayn to Ian McKellen, 20 July 1984

Dear Ian,

Thank you once again for your appallingly generous present, and for your no less generous note. I hope it's a good text; but the text has no real existence until it's performed. I don't have to tell you how extraordinary your performance is, because you know from the reception you got last night. I can only say that I was as amazed and appalled and delighted as everybody else – and I was applauding at the end as shamelessly as if I had no connection with the production at all. You take us on a most amazing journey. It's a revelation to me – a double revelation, in fact, of Platonov and of what it's possible for an actor to do.

A night to remember. Thank you.

Yours,
Michael

Wild Honey *won three Olivier Awards, for Morahan (Director), John Gunter (Designer) and McKellen (Actor in a Revival), who was also named Best Actor at the* Evening Standard *awards.*

Michael Frayn writes
to Ian McKellen after
the first night of *Wild
Honey*

```
Dear Ian,

     Thank you once again for your appallingly
generous present, and for your no less
generous note.  I hope it's a good text; but
the text has no real existence until it's
performed.  I don't have to tell you how
extraordinary your performance is, because you
know from the reception you got last night.  I
can only say that I was as amazed and
appalled and delighted as everybody else - and
I was applauding at the end as shamelessly as
if I had no connection with the production
at all.  You take us on a most amazing journey.
It's a revelation to me - a double revelation,
in fact, of Platonov and of what it's possible
for an actor to do.

     A night to remember.  Thank you.

     Yours,
```

Coriolanus (c.1608)

by William Shakespeare

Director: Peter Hall
Olivier, 6 December 1984 to 26 August 1985 (68 performances)

Hall to Ian McKellen,
3 October 1983

Dear Ian,

I much enjoyed our meeting. And tired as I was, I had a little look through *Coriolanus* last night. I would love to do it again. And with you.

I can think of no better way for me of getting back to Shakespeare. […]

Yours ever,
Peter

Having staged Coriolanus *with Laurence Olivier in 1959, Hall now rehearsed with McKellen, Irene Worth as Coriolanus's mother, Volumnia, and, as Aufidius, his adversary-turned-comrade, Greg Hicks, who had acted with McKellen in the late 1970s, at the RSC.*

Greg Hicks, postcard
to McKellen, 1985

My dear friend,

Just once, well more than once but tonight for sure, you take my breath away. You are the alchemist who can mix the Bard's gold. It streamed out of you and showed you the way. That is his genius and yours to let it through.

You <u>must</u> remember wiping your tears away with your handkerchief – here is the boy/man in quintessence. He fights and his mother owns him and destroys him.

This is a note of joyous admiration and joyous acknowledgement.

And sometimes you're human.

x G.

Most of the play was performed in a circular sandpit, which covered much of the Olivier stage. Hall arranged for 100 audience members to sit upstage, on benches around the sandpit, and deployed them as 'citizen actors', urged to their feet by the cast in eight scenes, including the two Roman riots in Act One.

McKellen, memo to Hall, 14 February 1985

After yesterday's matinee, which was a really strong performance indeed, I [asked] the company whether they would support the suggestion I made to you some weeks ago of doing a few performances without the stage audience leaving their seats. I was not altogether surprised when the reaction was unanimous: from Irene and the tribunes through to the soldiers, they were all convinced it would improve the impact of the scenes, particularly in focusing the audience's attention, and make it easier for them individually.

So, now I find myself requesting, on behalf of everybody, that you agree to permit this development at the end of next week when we do *Coriolanus* again.

I do not know what your friends have thought about the audience on stage. I have yet to talk to anybody who thought that their contribution was helpful: most think that they are extremely distracting. It seems to me a logical development of the production as my own performance gets sharper in detail and everyone, I think, grows in confidence (including, of course, the audience now that they have read the reviews), but we should try removing what is generally thought to be a huge obstacle to the effect of the production.

(Dictated by Ian and signed in his absence)

McKellen had caught Hall during a financial crisis. The Arts Council, by imposing a 4 per cent real-terms cut in grant aid for the National, had in Hall's words 'cut our legs off'. On 6 February, the Board implemented an Emergency Plan: up to 100 backstage and administrative staff would be made redundant, and from late April the Cottesloe would close, for five months.

Hall to McKellen, 19 February 1985

Dear Ian,

I find myself in a terrible difficulty. You are asking me to remove the heart of the production – the very reason that I decided I wanted to do the play. I think it <u>does</u> work and I was very pleased with the result.

So you're rather undermining everything I think about the production.

I'm not denying that you and the company have the right to question me. But I have to have time to go into it fully, re-rehearse, reconsider, and re-evaluate. And time is the one thing I don't have. The special Board meetings continue. I have meetings with MPs, journalists galore etc. etc. And today I start [rehearsing] a new production [*Martine* by Jean-Jacques Bernard]. This, in the circumstances, is certainly a mistake. But I have to keep faith with the actors and with the programme.

If I'm going to put on top of this the taking to pieces and re-rehearsals of [*Coriolanus*] as well, then I am not going to serve anybody properly.

Can you give me time? I don't want to cut the audience movement. I don't believe you're right.

And I am concerned that maybe the company are not getting the audience to behave properly if they no longer believe in the production.

Can we talk? I am very worried.

Yours ever
    Peter

McKellen to Hall,
19 February 1985

Dear Peter,

[…] We must talk because I think your production is not as good as you remember it. Re. the matter of the on-stage audience:

1. I ignore them, which is quite easy as I don't meet them very often, but on my first entrance perhaps the heart of the problem is revealed to me when I look down and they give nothing back: they are observers not participators. […]

3. My main reason for talking about it, is that after every performance I talk to friends who have seen the show, and with one, I promise you only one, exception in what is it now 30 performances, they are unanimous that the on-stage audience is a distraction, and a comic distraction at that. You can imagine how disheartening it is when friends want to talk about the odd characters they have spent the evening looking at, instead of talking about the production and the performances of the actors, and certainly many of our on-stage audience are very weird in their looks.

4. All this can, of course, be out-weighed by your own sense of the production, but I feel that we really do need to discuss whether the strong merits of your *Coriolanus* rest with the actors or with the on-stage audience. […]

I am free day and night if you need to phone me at home. I will happily come in to fit in with any free corner of your schedule, and certainly I ought to prepare how to tell the cast on Thursday what you feel about our collective suggestion.

Love,
    Ian

Hall ceded some ground: for performances from late February onwards, the on-stage audience were only urged to act in three scenes.

1985

A Chorus of Disapproval (1984)
by Alan Ayckbourn

Director: Alan Ayckbourn
Olivier, 1 August 1985 to 29 May 1986 (92 performances)

A Chorus of Disapproval *presents Pendon Amateur Light Operatic Society as it rehearses and performs John Gay's* The Beggar's Opera, *under the tyrannical direction of Dafydd ap Llewellyn; the cast includes his wife, Hannah, and newcomer Guy, a guileless widower who somehow ends up playing Macheath, Gay's brutal, bigamous anti-hero. Ayckbourn wanted Michael Gambon as Dafydd.*

Alan Ayckbourn to Michael Gambon, 2 November 1984	Dear Mike,

It's taken four days to raise The Knight and talk to him re. *Chorus.*

[Peter] sounded very anxious to put together some sort of offer that would attract you – and I hope they'll do this without delay.

It was good to see you the other day. I do hope [the filming of] *Absurd* is going well. And that we'll be together at the NT. That would be lovely

See you soon,
A.

Gambon was joined by Maureen Lipman in the BBC1 production of Ayckbourn's Absurd Person Singular.

Maureen Lipman to Ayckbourn, November 1984	Dear Alan,

I read your play for the National, and I want to tell you that I found it brilliant, touching, funny and a wonderful ensemble piece. I would have loved to have been part of it [as Hannah].

However I didn't care for *Mirandolina* [Carlo Goldoni's 1753 comedy about the eponymous, enchanting inn-keeper in Florence], and it seems the two shows come together as a package. I thought about it a lot – and my instinct tells me that you shouldn't go into a large company, unless you are passionate about the play and the part. *Chorus* would have been wonderful with the right part to go with it.

I'm sorry, and particularly sorry not to have worked with you. The play is so good that I should think it's actor-proof – but I hope you get someone terrific for Hannah.

Absurd Person is in the joyous stage where we all find ourselves hilariously funny – I imagine this will soon pass. Michael works

in great detail, which I like a lot, and Nicky [Henson] & I are
beginning to look married at last.

Looking forward to seeing you & you seeing us –

Love,
    Maureen

Mirandolina *was not ultimately revived by the NT. Imelda Staunton played Hannah;
Gambon was Dafydd; Guy was Bob Peck, then 39 and appearing in the Lyttelton in Athol
Fugard's* The Road to Mecca.

*Ayckbourn had 'discovered' Peck in Leeds in 1968, when directing an amateur revival of
his* Mr Whatnot. *Household fame had eluded the actor until – three months into* A Chorus
of Disapproval's *successful run in the Olivier – the BBC broadcast* Edge of Darkness, *a
compelling, six-part thriller with Peck as a gruff detective whose search for his daughter's
killer uncovers a government conspiracy.*

**Bob Peck to
Ayckbourn,
4 December 1985**

Dear Alan,

[…] Glad you're enjoying *Edge…*; it <u>is</u> a big hit, (certainly <u>within</u>
the BBC) but the audience 'ratings' are only about 4.7 million (and
growing). They have some sort of audience rating called 'positive
response' as well, which is apparently unprecedentedly high.

I'm terribly impressed with it when I see it: a lot of good work has
gone into it since we stopped filming a year ago – editing, music, etc.
And I haven't seen the last three episodes before they are screened –
so I'm waiting like everybody else to see what happens next!

'Within the business' the response has been very positive,
warm, excited. I have been to see several agents and they all want
to take me on. However there has been no come-back in terms of
actual tangible <u>work</u>.

But I <u>have</u> to wait and see what happens, give it a chance. I left
the RSC, not to join the National, but to do tele/and/or film. I've
had to wait a year for *Edge* to come out, and I must try to capitalise
on it – which probably will involve me being out of work and
waiting, available. Available you cannot be while working at the
NT: their scheduling is so erratic, sporadic and drawn-out!

TV writing tends to be bland, not good quality, so I'm not
really expecting to be offered anything which will match the
quality (in writing, camera-work, direction) of *Edge*. Therefore I
might have to hold out for film. […]

You were right about my feelings moving [from *Edge…* to
Chorus…] from 'Man of Steel' to 'Tupperware Man'. It was/is a
terrific contrast and good for my soul. […]

I phoned you the other night partly to convey my congrats
[on *Chorus…* being named *Evening Standard* Best Comedy] and
partly to discuss *Chorus…*. Seeing the clip [used for the awards
ceremony] was very instructive, I suddenly saw, briefly the <u>size</u>
of my contribution. I know TV is going to distort the effect of a
theatre performance: but it set me thinking.

I hope the basic reality is there: I feel it is – my contortions are my
<u>own</u> in certain circumstances. But. Is there <u>a better contribution</u>
to be made by a character less geared to eliciting laughter (through

nervous, gauche, incomprehending – shyness, I suppose), but geared more to being still, blank, much less grotesque.

I think I'm asking whether I should <u>move towards</u> a different characterisation in an attempt <u>to tone down</u> my physicalisation, or whether I should <u>just</u> stop going OTT?

If you have the time to read this far you probably <u>don't</u> have time to reply. Must go and hold boy George. Best wishes to you and Heather, from all four of us.

Bob

**Ayckbourn to Peck,
13 December 1985**

Dear Bob,

[…] I presume your alarm was the result of seeing the *Standard* Awards TV clip. If so, well, frankly it didn't do you justice. <u>In no way</u> change your performance radically! Please. Your Guy is real and funny and touching and serious – all the things he should be. The only danger – and it seems to be the one you're in danger of succumbing to, is that you'll feel you're 'not doing enough' – or 'not registering sufficiently'. You are. If you'll remember last time I came, I mentioned the odd bit of funny biz that had been creeping in – and which I felt was gratuitous – and in the end detrimental to the truth of the character – those are the things to beware of – Examine any extra laughs with great <u>suspicion</u>!!

He is the core of the play – to pinch a metaphor from *Edge of Darkness*. I did enjoy all that, by the way.

[…] See you very soon. Have a very happy Christmas all you Pecks.

Love from us,
Alan

Flesh and Blood (1985)**

by Edna O'Brien

**Hall to Edna O'Brien,
30 May 1985**

My dear Edna,

I have read *Flesh and Blood* and I have reflected about how your vision has moved [through your earlier versions] *The Gathering* [and] *Home Sweet Home*, to this play.

You create an extraordinary world. But I must honestly say that I still sometimes feel that the dramatic incidences are grafted on to keep up the tension.

There is much to admire though. You don't want a critique from me; you want an offer to produce the play. And that I can't give.

I know you would wish me to be honest.

Love,
Peter

Flesh and Blood *was produced at Cork Opera House later in 1985.*

*Sabina***

by Paul Schrader

Paul Schrader, the screenwriter of Martin Scorsese's Taxi Driver *(1976) and* Raging Bull *(1980), had been introduced to Hall by Hall's New York agent, Sam Cohn. Schrader, keen to write his first stage play, accepted a commission from Hall for a drama about Sabina Spielrein, patient and lover of Ernst Jung, and her impact on Jung's relationship with Sigmund Freud. It was to be workshopped at the NT Studio – the research and development facility beside the Old Vic, which had opened in 1984 – before premiering on the South Bank.*

**Paul Schrader to Hall,
11 July 1985**

Dear Peter,

Forgive my procrastination. I've put off writing this letter for several months. It's never easy to admit failure.

I can't write *Sabina*. At some point, every great tale beckons its teller. It gently knocks, then calls, speaks, and finally screams – demanding to be written. The author is impelled to obey. From *Sabina* I got not a peep.

It's not the material, it's me. 'Horses for courses,' they say. I'm sure this will prove fertile ground for other minds.

I viewed this bit of history from every vantage point I could imagine. Yet I always saw (after the dust of cleverness had settled) that the story necessarily, inescapably returned to two themes: the birth of psychoanalysis and the women's movement – themes worn smooth by endless and progressively banal debate. There's little original to say about them at the moment. Silence is the proper response.

So much so, that my perverse heart began to lean the opposite direction: my fantasies formed elaborate defenses of Victorianism in an oppressive post-Freudian culture. In fancy, I ranted like Carlyle. There was no room for an original imprint – for <u>me</u> – in the world of Freud, Spielrein and Jung. (Mishima once admitted that he joined the Right because the Left was already full. I empathised.)

I regret making promises, however qualified, I can't keep. I regret long hours of work which yielded no product. Most of all I regret losing the opportunity to work with you. You are a great teacher and I fancy myself a great learner. A workshop with you would have been a highpoint of my creative life.

On the other hand, I'm fortunate: once again I've proved constitutionally unable to write something I wasn't passionate about. For me, struggling to write something unfelt is as impossible – and frustrating – as trying to drive a car sideways. I have been well served by this disability.

And, God, I wanted to write a play. It's something I can do – and do a damn sight better than many others currently wearing critical laurels. That I believe to the end of every follicle. Hopefully, fate will someday test this belief.

Sorry. Perhaps we can meet nonetheless when you are in New York or I in London.

Damn.

Thanks for your support.

PS

(cc Howard Rosenman [Schrader's agent], Sam Cohn)

Schrader has never written for the stage. He was right to predict that Sabina's life would 'prove fertile ground': Christopher Hampton's account of the Spielrein–Jung–Freud triangle, The Talking Cure, *opened at the Cottesloe in 2002.*

The Critic (1779)

by Richard Brinsley Sheridan

Director: Sheila Hancock
Olivier, 12 September 1985 to 12 April 1986 (58 performances)
[in double-bill with Tom Stoppard's revival of his *The Real Inspector Hound* (1968)]

Sheila Hancock first met Hall when she appeared in his production of Edward Albee's All Over *in 1972. When he invited her to act at the NT in 1985 she was 51.*

Sheila Hancock to Hall, 8 January 1985

Dear Peter,

At one point in our recent meeting, you asked: 'What would you like to do?' I answered, as I always do when asked that, with a weak shrug. My new year's resolution is no more weak shrugs, so here goes:

Cleopatra
Beatrice
Lady Macbeth

Nowadays they would usually be cast younger, but I would argue against this. For modern audiences, being left on the shelf and ageing happen much later and to cast, for instance, someone as lovely and blooming as Helen Mirren as Cleo seems to me to have none of the right resonances for today's women.

Any Ibsen, e.g. *Ghosts.*

Any Chekhov, e.g. *Cherry Orchard* or *Seagull.*

Is it too soon to revive [Albee's] *Delicate Balance* with me as Claire?

What about *Entertaining Mr. Sloane*?
I also think Rattigan should be looked at again. […]

Another marvellous play is Tennessee Williams' *Sweet Bird of Youth.*

So there.

If none of these appeals, just get your secretary to send a brief note and I will fire them off at other poor souls who have been foolish enough to ask the same question.

Best wishes for 1985.

Love,
Sheila

My dear Sheila,

[…] I am keen on the Rattigan, and *Sweet Bird of Youth*. But everything is in chaos now because of the bloody Arts Council and the equally bloody GLC. Here we are being kicked around as a political football, and only the people who work here – and our audiences – will suffer.

So I don't know what will happen. Except that in this chaos Ian [McKellen] is making some plans which he tells me might involve you as a director. The idea has my enthusiastic support.

Wouldn't it be wonderful for you to be able to say that we only ask you to act something here because you were directing. I'm ducking.

It was very good to see you.

Love,
     Peter

McKellen and Edward Petherbridge were forming a 17-strong company to perform a play in each NT auditorium. At their invitation, Hancock became the first woman to direct in the Olivier, staging The Critic *with the McKellen/Petherbridge Company, and also playing Julia in* The Duchess of Malfi *(Lyttelton) and Madame Ranyevskaya in* The Cherry Orchard *(Cottesloe).*

I'm sure you will be as relieved as I am to learn that these are positively the last notes I will be giving you – I think. […]

Hang on to the basic truth of the situation in *The Critic* and the plot of the play in *Hound*. As soon as anybody starts to perform solely in order to get a laugh, it becomes tiresome, with the added embarrassment that if the laugh doesn't come you are left very eggy. Some of you will probably feel indignant that I should even say this, but I know myself, as an actress, and certainly from watching as a director, that it is the easiest thing in the world to drift into something that feels real but is in fact mechanical and hollow.

You should not allow the 18th Century style to make your delivery monotonous. It sometimes lapses into a very measured, ponderous tone. Try and orchestrate long speeches and scenes with as much variety of pace, attack and tone as the <u>sense</u> permits. Keep it fluid and light within the context of the grand style.

Enjoy the language in both plays without it becoming artificial. Relish every word. Don't let habit make you be lazy with the text.

Please stick rigidly to the texts. Don't put in the odd words and ums and ahs. You would be amazed how it ruptures the rhythm and offends the ear, and honestly, both Stoppard and Sheridan knew what they were doing and have written with meticulous skill.

At the risk of being a spoil-sport, may I say now that I think it would be disastrous to try to put any jokes in for the last performance in London. It never works and the audience are always made to feel very left out. The best performances are always the ones that you enjoy. The enjoyment has to stem from your pleasure in the plays and your desire to communicate to an audience. It is not a self-indulgent enjoyment, but full of warmth and generosity.

It has given me great joy to watch you perform this play and to see the real deep pleasure that you have given to countless people.

Sheila

1986

The Petition (1985)
by Brian Clark

Director: Peter Hall
Lyttelton, 30 July to 9 September 1986 (29 performances)

Alec Guinness was 71, and, after declining several invitations from Laurence Olivier, had yet to act with the National. Hall sent Guinness a two-hander, The Petition, *hoping he would play Sir Edmund Milne, an ultra-conservative British Army general who spends a morning arguing with his wife over her support for the Campaign for Nuclear Disarmament.*

Alec Guinness to
Hall, 20 October 1985

My dear Peter,

I got the opportunity of reading *The Petition*, which I return with this.

I enjoyed reading it but frankly I think I would be awful casting. The temptation to caricature would be strong with me – some Garrick Club or Athenaeum member with whom I feel scant sympathy. Also I long to play, in the theatre, something extravagant and preferably clownish. You must think I am avoiding you; I assure you that is <u>far</u> from the case.

Yours ever,
Alec

John Mills played Milne. Guinness never appeared at the National.

King Lear (1606)
by William Shakespeare

Director: David Hare
Oliver, 11 December 1986 to 11 November 1987 (100 performances)

David Hare to Hall,
December 1974

Dear Peter,

I would be very angry if you let anyone else [direct *King Lear*]. It's the only old one that interests me, simply because it's so much better than any other play.

> Best wishes,
>   David

Hare finally tackled the play with Anthony Hopkins, soon after his award-winning performance as a South African media tycoon, Lambert Le Roux, in Hare and Howard Brenton's Pravda *(Olivier, 1985). A fortnight before the* Lear *press night, NT associate director Nicholas Wright watched a run-through in its rehearsal room.*

Nicholas Wright to
Hare, 26 November
1986

Dear David,

[…] I was enormously moved by it. I can't imagine the second half has ever been done better. Giving such weight and time to the sub-plots works triumphantly.

   Tony played the second half wonderfully. In the first half I found him sometimes off his voice and rushing the thoughts or the discoveries. The speech starting 'Reason not the need' is one example. It's whenever he hits that staccato barking tone – you know the one I mean. […]

   I don't think the Fool is there yet, and don't know quite how to help, except to say that the lyrical tone Roshan [Seth] sometimes hits seems at odds with the character's realism. But I must say it's nice to see the part given the right balance, not allowed to take over or become a 'turn'.

   Douglas Hodge [as Edmund] could be tremendously good. His diction lacks bite. It's what used to be called 't's and 'd's. One doesn't quite realise what a wit Edmund is, and I think this is something to do with it.

   I don't know when I've been moved so as I was this morning, and I know it will be tremendous. What a wonderful play.

   Nick

Diana Boddington
(stage manager) to
Hare, 20 December
1986

My dear David,

I am writing to you instead of sending you a Christmas card. I just want to say how marvellous it has been to work with you with *Map of the World*, *Pravda*, *Bay at Nice* & now *King Lear*. I have loved every second of it and admire you oh-so-much. You have such understanding of people and knowledge of what you are doing – which is so important. Actors & stage management alike

know when they have been landed with a Dud!! – but all I have
worked [with] on the mentioned shows have said to me 'David
really knows what he's talking about & we think he is wonderful'.
I also think this and I am so thankful that I am leaving on a 'high'.

I loathe the thought of giving up the theatre after nearly 46
years, but I won't, I will keep in touch & wish you all my love &
luck in all you do in the future. Please if in doubt (which I'm sure
you won't be!!) ring me and ask me just anything. I hope to be
available for years!!

My dearest love & wishes, and wishes, to you Darling David (a
word you never use!!).

God Bless and thanks for everything.

Lovingly,
  Diana xxxx

1987

Richard Eyre, NT Director Designate

*On 10 January 1987, Richard Eyre, who had long been Hall's anointed heir, was presented to
the media as his successor. Eyre had been sounded out by Max Rayne several months earlier.*

Richard Eyre to Max
Rayne, 31 August
1986

PRIVATE AND CONFIDENTIAL

Dear Max,

[…] I enjoyed our meeting, and thought it was very fruitful. I
meant to write to you directly afterwards but have been sucked
into the vortex of rehearsals and planning for my musical
[*High Society* at the Haymarket, Leicester]. What follows is an
approximate guide to some of my thinking. […]

The NT must be seen to exist to do a kind of work that can't be
done in the commercial sector: it is an <u>aesthetic</u> choice to work at
the NT. […]

The real question that needs to be asked about the NT is not
'Who is paying what to whom?' but 'Is the work any good? And if
not, why not?'

I'd like to see the policy of the NT remain as diverse and
pluralistic as in the past. At heart I'm a populist. A theatre that
doesn't have an audience doesn't mean a damn. […]

The NT is a large organisation, but not <u>that</u> large. It's not the
BBC or British Rail. It <u>is</u> possible to know everyone who works in
it – it's the size of a moderately large secondary school. It doesn't
have to assume the characteristics of a bureaucracy and lean
towards inertia, facelessness and paper pushing. But it will do so
unless actively prevented from doing so.

Some practical points:

1. Ultimately, I would be answerable for artistic affairs, David [Aukin, already in post as the NT's first executive director] for administration.

2. I would be more than happy to guarantee that Peter's desire to continue to direct plays at the NT is honoured. This is not appeasement; it is a positive desire. It is important that continuity is stressed and I wouldn't like it to appear either for personal or political reasons that I am denigrating Peter's achievements or his talents. I have much to be grateful to Peter for, as does the NT. If I should succeed him, I hope that he will continue to be a professional colleague and a friend. […]

10. I would like to disband Peter's Associates. As a decision-making body they are, at best, a token group, and to many of those inside the theatre, and most people outside, it smacks of a top-heavy directocracy. […]

12. The Olivier is universally agreed to be a very difficult theatre to present plays in. One has to examine the massive absurdity of this phenomenon: it's like saying you have a watering can that's difficult to put water in. We should not be daunted by the fact that the architect [Denys Lasdun] has, at least in the past, been intractable. We work in his building, we <u>know</u> the problems, and the audiences are aware of the problems. Fortunately the problems are soluble – with money and with will.

I know it's easy to make noble assertions about policy and intentions. They can easily vaporise when confronted by reality. I am well aware of the size of the task, and of the daunting possibilities. I lack Peter's public profile, and possibly his Protean energies as well. But I am confident that I could bring to the NT an ability to motivate people to work together, and to tap the huge reserves of energy and invention that lie dormant in any organisation not working at its most efficient. I would direct a great deal, because in the end it's what I enjoy doing most and do best. I would commit myself unreservedly for three years' full-time work at the NT, probably more.

With best wishes,
Richard

*Anything Can Happen!***

by Ken Campbell

Ken Campbell to
Nicholas Wright,
January 1987

Heathrow Airport!

Nicholas,

I'm still working on outline – provisional title: *Anything Can Happen*! It will be for the sevens upwards. There will be a haunted house.

You will have detailed outline in a week.

Help! They're calling my plane!

Love,
Ken Campbell

PS Excitement! I'm on the short list for the next DOCTOR WHO!

Campbell's handwritten, illustrated outline persuaded Wright to commission the play, but it was not produced – and Sylvester McCoy became the seventh Doctor Who.

Campbell would, however, be an important contributor to the Richard Eyre and Trevor Nunn tenures, writing and performing in four Cottesloe shows, including Violin Time *(1996) and* Ken Campbell's History of Comedy *(2000).*

Antony and Cleopatra (1606)
by William Shakespeare

Director: Peter Hall
Olivier, 9 April 1987 to 6 February 1988 (100 performances)

When they worked together at the RSC in the 1960s, Hall had promised Judi Dench that he would one day direct her as Cleopatra.

Hall, memo to Gillian
Diamond et al.,
6 January 1986

I've told Judi of the likelihood of Vanessa [Redgrave] doing Cleopatra [in the West End]. She says if Vanessa does it and it works, she doubts she will want to do Cleopatra. But we agreed to keep this doubt secret until the event, and still go on planning our *A and C*. Should we decide in the summer that it is not to be done, Judi is still coming, and wants to do something else with Tony Hopkins and with me.

In any event, she wants another part, if not two. She would like to do Coward. She asked if *Private Lives* was too jaded.

She would like to do Feydeau [and] anything that's funny.

She's not, for this reason, desperately keen on *The Deep Blue Sea*, though this could figure if it went <u>with</u> an uproarious comedy.

I wondered about any of the Tennessee Williams ladies – though they are hardly funny. […]

I would appreciate speedy help on making up Judi's repertoire. And please keep the Cleo misgivings secret.

A thought: would she be possible casting for David Edgar's [*Entertaining Strangers*]?

Opposite: Anthony Hopkins and Judi Dench in
the title roles of *Antony and Cleopatra*.
Photo: John Haynes

Dench played Cleopatra, opposite Hopkins's Antony, in a sold-out run, winning Evening Standard *and Olivier awards for Best Actress. She also starred in Edgar's* Entertaining Strangers *(Cottesloe), as the owner of a Dorset brewery.*

From April 1985 to February 1988, Hopkins gave more than 350 performances in the Olivier, as Lambert Le Roux, Lear and Antony. In August 1986 he wrote to Hall explaining that he did not want to join a proposed US tour of Antony and Cleopatra *in 1988 because, although he loved working at the NT, he would by then be sated by his 'feast' of acting, would need to 'recharge' for several months, 'and do something light and undemanding and re-establish some TV and film credit'. There was no US tour. Since appearing in David Henry Hwang's* M. Butterfly, *in the West End in 1989, Hopkins has not acted on stage.*

Rosmersholm (1887)
by Henrik Ibsen

Version by Frank McGuinness (1987)
Director: Sarah Pia Anderson
Cottesloe, 6 May to 27 August 1987 (37 performances)

Sarah Pia Anderson to Hall, 5 August 1986	Dear Sir Peter,

I did enjoy our meeting last week, and I wanted to communicate quickly about *Ghosts.*

Ibsen has been in my blood for some time now and at last I think I perceive a way of freeing the work from the Victoriana that has encased recent productions of the earlier plays. It would be excellent if Maggie Smith were interested in playing Mrs Alving [the widow in *Ghosts,* whose adult son has inherited syphilis from his debauched father]. I thought her Hedda was brilliant. And the current repressive moral climate together with the implications of the Aids epidemic would lend immediacy to a production.

I would also like to re-iterate my desire for *Rosmersholm.* It is such a deeply felt and highly wrought play that I feel it would be best served by a powerful small-scale production that could therefore explode from a strong centre.

The prospect of bringing my experience of contemporary theatre to bear on the classics excites me enormously.

Looking forward to your response,
With very good wishes,
Sarah

It soon emerged that Smith did not want to do Ghosts. *By scheduling* Rosmersholm *in the Cottesloe, Hall granted Anderson's wish for a small-scale production, making her only the fifth woman, after Nancy Meckler, Cicely Berry, Di Trevis and Sheila Hancock, to direct for the National in its first 11 years on the South Bank.*

Waiting for Godot (1955)

by Samuel Beckett

Director: Michael Rudman
Lyttelton, 25 November 1987 to 19 July 1988 (110 performances)

Michael Rudman, Notes on Meeting in Paris with Samuel Beckett, 2 September 1987

1. The first impression also became the lasting impression – an extremely courteous Anglo-Irish gentleman, living very near several hospitals and with some grace but with a considerable amount of irritation at experiencing old age [he was 81]. Certainly not senile.

2. He's not bored with [*Godot*] but he is almost certainly tired of answering questions about it. After [80] minutes I apologised for tiring him and he said 'I would have got tired anyway'.

3. He seems very impressed with the fact that Mike Nichols is directing *Godot*, in New York at the Lincoln Center. I told him I had directed *Hamlet* at the Lincoln Center, but he wasn't impressed and, later, when I began to describe the auditorium of the Lincoln Center he declared the interview at an end and called me 'Mr Rudman'. […]

14. He seemed to think that only a playwright could direct his own play with enough care and attention because only a playwright would take sufficient pains. I don't think he believed me when I implied that I would give it as much care and attention as he did. I'm not sure I believe it so maybe I shouldn't have said it. […]

MR

1988

'Tis Pity She's a Whore (1633)

by John Ford

Director: Alan Ayckbourn
Olivier, 3 March to 4 August 1988 (68 performances)

In Ford's blood-drenched tale of incest and murder, the whore of the title is Annabella (Suzan Sylvester in Ayckbourn's revival), whose brother, Giovanni (Rupert Graves), impregnates her, with gruesome consequences; he enters the climactic banquet with her heart impaled on his dagger. Clive Francis, a fine caricaturist, played Vasques, a servant, and drew Ayckbourn a memorable first-night postcard (see overleaf).

Clive Francis's first-night card for
'Tis Pity She's A Whore

Cymbeline (c.1611)
by William Shakespeare

Cottesloe, 17 May to 29 July 1988 (15 performances)
Olivier, 15 September to 23 November 1988 (19 performances)

Hall staged Cymbeline, The Tempest *and* The Winter's Tale *under the umbrella title of* The Late Shakespeares – *his valedictory productions before Richard Eyre became Director on 1 September 1988. On 17 April, a few days before* Cymbeline's *first scheduled preview, Hall sacked Sarah Miles as Imogen, and replaced her with Geraldine James. Miles was married to Robert Bolt.*

Robert Bolt to Hall, 18 April 1988	Dear Peter,

Yesterday morning I wrote you a letter, which congratulated you on Sarah's performance, first seen by me the evening before. Sarah says that you will think I wrote it after yesterday's bombshell, I didn't think you would, but it did show what a vast difference you and I think about her performance. Yours, of course, is the thing that matters.

But to hire a star, whose work you knew, or ought to have known, engage her in publicity, continue her working hard on your notes, tell her that she was getting better, tell her that her verse was impeccable, up to the point when there was only one run-through to go before the technical run-throughs, and then quite simply sack her, it's simply not on, Peter. Think what a body blow you deliver to her growing reputation. I await your reply.

Love,
Bob

Hall to Bolt, 19 April 1988

Dear Bob,

I know what I have done and I wish fervently that I had not had to do it.

Sarah has worked hard and willingly. She had made enormous progress, but I don't believe she has shown herself capable of making the final leap and I have, I'm afraid, lost confidence in her ability to do so.

My only other alternative, which I considered carefully, was to cancel the production entirely. But I felt this was not fair to the other actors, many of whom look to *Cymbeline* for their best part [in *The Late Shakespeares*].

Believe me, Bob, I wish it had never happened. It gives me no pleasure or satisfaction to have had to cause so much unhappiness.

Ever,
Peter

The end of the Hall years

It seems apt to break with chronology and let the last words on Peter Hall's tenure be his, writing to the man who hired and then steadfastly supported him.

Hall to Max Rayne, 4 September 1986

Dear Max,

Please to accept this letter as my formal and firm decision not to continue when my contract expires in just over two years. After a decade and a half in the job new blood must be brought in.

In many ways I am sad to write this. With the establishing of the NT on the South Bank we have shared an extraordinary experience. When you asked me to take on the National for the move from the Old Vic I remember wondering how on earth we could continuously fill, with plays and with people, not one theatre but three. But it is my conviction that we've turned this magnificent building into one of the friendliest and most loved theatres in the country.

We've suffered some storms, not only with damaging strikes but later with something worse – painful subsidy cuts when we had, I think, proved our worth and needed to grow, not to shrink. But in a way I do not regret those bad times. They were challenges which created a strong organisation. […]

Ever,
Peter

The Richard Eyre Years

———

1988–
1997

The start of the Eyre years

When he took charge of the NT, Richard Eyre was 45, with huge producing and directing experience. He had been Director of Productions at the Royal Lyceum, Edinburgh, run Nottingham Playhouse (1974–78), and produced a dozen films in the BBC's Play for Today *strand, also directing scripts by the likes of Trevor Griffiths and Ian McEwan, and, just before taking office, a controversial film about the Falklands war,* Tumbledown, *written by Charles Wood.*

Eyre's one pre-condition for succeeding Hall, to ease the managerial burden, had been the recruitment of David Aukin as the NT's first Executive Director. From autumn 1988 this pair radically reshaped the NT's production departments. The end of the Hall era was further reinforced by the departure of his staunchest, longest-serving ally.

On 30 November 1988, the House of Commons Notice of Motions included the following, backed by MPs representing all three main parties: 'This House wishes to thank Lord Rayne, the outgoing chairman of the National Theatre, for his 17 years' service; and congratulates him on his outstanding stewardship of this world-renowned drama centre.' Richard Luce, the Conservative arts minister, had decided to end Rayne's tenure, and replaced him with Lady Mary Soames, youngest daughter of Winston Churchill.

On 1 December, the NT celebrated Rayne's unstinting support – which included large, anonymous donations – of the building and its staff.

Max Rayne to Eyre, 2 December 1988

My dear Richard,

I cannot thank you enough for last evening's wonderful party, with its so generous hospitality, tributes and gifts. It meant a great deal to my family and myself, notwithstanding the *This Is Your Life* elements of surprise and superlatives. I know your modesty in terms of personal exposure – which I share – but you really did a splendid job: I deeply appreciate it and the warm sentiments will be remembered long after the embarrassment.

I regret only that I was too emotionally affected to do justice to all the splendid efforts of the Executive and Board over my years at the NT, but they are beyond praise and I know that your continued success will produce its own tributes. It is difficult to envisage life after the NT, but I know that Jane and I will always feel part of it and take enormous personal pleasure in the triumphs that undoubtedly lie ahead. I believe, too, that you will enjoy the fullest support from the Board: it is impossible to be associated with the enterprise and not be – or become – wholly partisan.

I am sorry our association was not of longer duration, but hope our friendship will be. With my every good wish, real gratitude and love from Jane & myself to you and Sue.

Yours ever,
Max

Opposite: Richard Eyre in rehearsal for *Hamlet* in 1989. Photo: John Haynes

Eyre had come to regard Rayne as 'a bit of a surrogate father', and they remained good friends until the latter's death in 2003, aged 85. In recognition of the Rayne Foundation's substantial gift to the NT Future redevelopment, a new production building, opened in 2014, is named the Max Rayne Centre.

1989

Hamlet (c.1601)
by William Shakespeare
Director: Richard Eyre
Olivier, 16 March to 13 December (102 performances)

Hamlet was played by Daniel Day-Lewis; Judi Dench was Gertrude. When the production opened, critics were, mostly, unimpressed by Day-Lewis: 'quick Renaissance intellect was notably absent' (Daily Telegraph); strikes 'one consistent note of querulous melancholy' (Evening Standard). Three days later, Day-Lewis and his mother, the actor Jill Balcon, attended the Bafta awards ceremony.

Jill Balcon, postcard to Eyre, 20 March 1989	Dear Richard,

Daniel & I were <u>so</u> happy for you as we lolled & quaffed comfortably through all that Bafta circus. *Tumbledown* was magnificent, &, after a lifetime of *Hamlet* productions yours is THE one. You couldn't do anything that wasn't exciting: full of undreamed of insights & clarity. I could go on and on, but a P.C. limits one like a sonnet, & I don't want you to feel you must reply. It's a smoke-signal of admiration & gratitude for your work and your faith in my dear son. It's wonderful having D. here to spoil a little, & his attitude to his reviews is wholly admirable. I send you love & look forward to my next perf. in April,

Jill

Eyre's Tumbledown *had won three awards, including Best Single Drama.*
In 1988, Day-Lewis had starred in the film Stars and Bars, *adapted by William Boyd from his novel.*

William Boyd to Eyre, 28 March 1989	Dear Richard,

Thanks so much for arranging the *Hamlet* tickets. I would have hated to have missed it in its first flush, as it were. I thought it was a tremendous production. I was completely gripped and engrossed with it – and I don't recall ever having been previously so affected. In fact I was quite drained and exhausted at the end (God only knows how Daniel feels). I thought it was incredibly lucid and clear cut: very confident, too, in the way that you let people just stand and talk. And because it was so clear what was happening I saw just how fallacious it is to look for <u>one</u> Hamlet: that somehow there is one basic theme, or one way of playing it that makes the play click. 'If only we had the combination we could unlock it' sort-of thing. One suddenly sees that all those one-note productions – of Hamlet as Oedipal wimp, or proto-fascist punk, or demented neuro – are so limiting. It may be neat or nifty, but it's tremendously wrong. That's what I liked about Dan's performance – it was admirably complex: strong & weak, clever & guileless etc. etc. You also realised just what a bloody difficult thing it is that the ghost asks him to do: 'Knock off the King, will you?' We blithely accept these conventions – 'any decent son would avenge his dead father' – without contemplating the appalling problems involved, whether pragmatic or emotional. What else did I like? I thought the players & the play within a play were superbly done. And Polonius was excellent. How refreshing to see the 'advice' [to Laertes] scene <u>not</u> played for laughs: you suddenly realise just how sensible his words were.

Anyway, Richard, I thought it was great. [Peter] Kemp [*The Independent*] and [John] Peter [*Sunday Times*] were on the right lines but as usual some of the other hacks must have been at a different play. I sometimes feel that the perfect fate for these types is what they did to the dead pharaohs before embalming them – having their brains drawn out through their noses with a long thin hook.

Love,
Will

Judi Dench, card to Eyre, 29 March 1989

Darling Rich,

I hope you got your [birthday] message on the answering service [yesterday]. <u>Everyone</u> sang – it was a wonderful sight – tho' I thought, slightly under-rehearsed!!

Hamlet is going wonderfully well – people flock round after the show. And they are genuinely <u>knocked out</u>. It's a GREAT Company and everyone works so hard.

It's really been wonderful to work on it – and the only regret about doing it now, is that we don't <u>SEE</u> you, and I miss the laughs.

But it's a HUGE SUCCESS – & that's thanks to <u>you</u>.

Great love,
Jude

On May 30, Eyre told the Hamlet *company, including Ian Flintoff (Marcellus), that Day-Lewis would be leaving the show a few weeks before the scheduled end of his contract in November.*

**Ian Flintoff to Eyre,
June 1989**

Dear Richard,

Just a note, written in the sprit of good fellowship which you've done so much to foster in the Company.

I can only guess at the amount of time, thought, work, concentration and hope that you must have put into *Hamlet* – even before the Company formed. There must be no little sadness for you that Dan is leaving – though directors are often at the back of the sympathy queue.

I just wanted you to know how much support, loyalty, and goodwill exists in the Company backstage – all of whom will, of course, miss Dan and his warmth, dedication and modesty.

I don't suppose there's anything one can do to be helpful (or indeed any need for it), but if there were, morally or practically, I'd very much want to do that.

        Best wishes,
        Ian

**Ernest Hall, stage
manager, *Hamlet*
show report,
5 September 1989**

On the Ghost's exit in Act I Sc. 5 Mr Day-Lewis left the stage and told me that he could not continue the performance. An announcement was made and the audience invited to take an extra interval. The announcement only specified technical problems. After 32 minutes the performance resumed with Mr Northam [Osric] as Hamlet. Mr Bedford played Osric and Mr Nicholas a Switzer. Mr Northam coped brilliantly (not an exaggeration) and received an outstanding reception from the audience.

Absentees, cast changes (with reasons)

    Mr.Day Lewis(Understudies: Messrs.Northam/Bedford/Nicholas)

Remarks

    On the Ghost's exit in Act 1 Sc.5 Mr.Day Lewis left the stage and told me that he could not continue the performance. An announcement was made and the audience invited to take an extra interval. The announcement only specified technical problems. After 32 minutes the performance resumed with Mr.Northam as Hamlet. Mr.Bedford played Osric and Mr.Nicholas a Switzer. Mr.Northam coped brilliantly(not an exaggeration) and received an outstanding reception from the audience.

Stage Manager

Day-Lewis has yet to act on stage again. His understudy, Jeremy Northam, who had been playing Osric, continued as Hamlet before handing over to the actor Eyre had already – before Day-Lewis's walk-out – chosen to replace him: Ian Charleson, star of the film Chariots of Fire *and Eyre's* Guys and Dolls. *Charleson had Aids, and knew that he would struggle with the part's physical demands. He appeared as Hamlet 18 times, his performance praised by John Peter as 'a brilliant exercise in mature judgment: his sombre self-knowledge forms the true substance of his tragedy, and it enables us both to be moved by the experience and to judge it.'*

Charleson's last Hamlet, on 13 November, was given to a full house and a standing ovation; in Eyre's words: 'He acted as if he knew it was the last time he'd be on stage.' He died on 6 January 1990, aged 40.

Keith Baxter, who had played Henry VIII in A Man for All Seasons *on Broadway, and Prince Hal in Orson Welles's film* Chimes at Midnight *(1965), reflected on Charleson's final role, after meeting Eyre in his NT office.*

Keith Baxter to Eyre, 10 August 1995

Dear Richard,

[…] I never told you how much I admired yr. handling of the Ian Charleson crisis. I was a very good acquaintance of Ian's – not an intimate friend, but friends of mine were his intimates, most particularly Richard Warwick. I had met Ian through David Rintoul (who played Claudio when I did Benedick up in Edinburgh for the Lyceum Centenary). And between Rintoul and Warwick I kept in touch with Ian. During the last months of his life – rehearsing and playing *Hamlet* – Ian often asked to come to my house in Sussex. He would walk along the beach with me and talk quite coolly about Death. He would also – you must understand I was like a surrogate father to him – discuss his fears about rejection from the Company. 'I think Richard knows, but he hasn't said anything yet – what shall I do?' All he wanted, needed, was someone rather square and older, i.e. boring, like me – to listen. So I listened. He told me you had been wonderful and writing this now gives me the chance to thank you for that, for him. Just before the run finished at the National he called me on Sunday 'They're going to Hong Kong. I don't think I can do it. Nobody really likes my performance anyway.' I told him to stop feeling sorry for himself and had he seen the *S. Times* that day. He hadn't. I told him to get Patsy Pollock [casting director] to bring him one. 'Why?' I wouldn't tell him – but it was the John Peter review. Ian called me two hours later. 'Richard did it you know, it was <u>all</u> Richard!' I wish I could have seen it, everyone said it was unforgettable and of course Ian's imminent death lent the whole experience a Pirandellian dimension: 'If it be not now …' But I never could see it because I was in my own play at The Vaudeville, and Ian died one Saturday and I couldn't even get to say goodbye to him. […]

Yours ever,
Keith

The March on Russia (1989)

by David Storey
Director: Lindsay Anderson
Lyttelton, 6 April to 10 August 1989 (40 performances)

Between 1969 and 1974, Lindsay Anderson had directed six of David Storey's plays at the Royal Court; he also staged Storey's Early Days *(1980) in the Cottesloe.*

Lindsay Anderson,
postcard to
Alan Bennett,
11 November 1988

Dear Alan,

[…] For good or ill I have committed to doing David Storey's play, which is called *The March on Russia*, in the Lyttelton … Somewhat annoyed at being relegated to the Storey cupboard, but no use struggling against the zeitgeist I suppose.

> A bientôt,
> L.

The March on Russia *is a semi-autobiographical drama set in the retirement bungalow in Yorkshire of the Pasmores, an ex-miner and his wife, joined by their son (a writer and lecturer), and two daughters to celebrate their golden wedding anniversary. Storey had bought his parents a bungalow for their retirement.*

David Storey to Eyre,
9 April 1989

Dear Richard,

Many thanks for your good wishes on the first night: it seems – perhaps it <u>is</u> – such a short time since you wrote offering to do the play. I <u>hope</u> it's been worth it: as for me, I'm grateful for your response and encouragement: I sense it may have given me a new lease of life, coming out of the blue – as these things, to our pleasure, occasionally do. The reviews, I suppose, have to be designated 'mixed' – the bad not condemnatory exactly, the good better than I'd expected. Whether these are enough to keep the play going – having little experience of the National – I've no idea. Artistically, we've achieved all I could have hoped: not easy, but worth it. The first night was the best of any play I recall.

Meanwhile, many thanks again for your encouragement: I <u>hope</u> we'll have the chance to work together again.

> Best wishes,
> David

The Misanthrope

by Molière (1666)

English version by Tony Harrison (1973)
Director: Paul Unwin
Lyttelton, 31 May to 4 November 1989 (54 performances)

Edward Petherbridge played Alceste. Harrison's translation was first performed in the NT's Old Vic Misanthrope *in 1973.*

Edward Petherbridge to Tony Harrison, 24 November 1989

Dear Tony,

[...] Towards the end [of *The Misanthrope*'s run] I began to feel I'd got more secure in the balance between form & content. Of course the form is the content – but one's response to that form is a question of such sophisticated choice. [...]

I got many appreciative letters – especially on tour – not quite <u>all</u> from middle-aged ladies who wanted to rescue me from the pet shop window or Battersea Dogs' Home (more than one reviewer speculated on what breed or cross-breed of dog I might be). Some of the letters were from <u>young</u> ladies! I don't think any failed to write in glowing terms about your translation. [...]

All good wishes,
Edward

Euphoria**

by Peter Nichols

After The Freeway *(1974), Peter Nichols's* Passion Play *(1981) was rejected by Peter Hall and his NT associates, then directed by Mike Ockrent for the RSC, winning the* Evening Standard *award for Best Play. Eyre wanted Nichols to write for the National again.*

Eyre to Peter Nichols, 16 November 1989

Dear Peter,

I have been thinking about the Olivier's repertoire and am very keen that it should contain at least one contemporary play which would express the spirit of the times – the spirit characterised, as it seems to me, by lying, waste and fantasy.

[Would] a play about the secret services (MI5, MI6 etc.) cover that territory? When you think of the £700 million spent annually to no visible effect, the graft, the paranoia and the ludicrous ineptitude (what were the secret service doing in 1982 when the Falklands caught everybody on the hop?). I think some suitably scabrous comedy could emerge. I also think you would write brilliantly around this subject. [...]

I'd love to read your new play, even if you have promised it to another management.

Very best wishes,
    Yours,
        Richard

Dear Richard,

I'm always glad to have subjects suggested and envy the Royal Court writers their chance to evolve plays from real events or themes like The City. I think of myself as a theatre worker rather than a pure writer and only became a solitary playwright because there was no alternative when I started. I'm sure there's a play in the secret services – but I know very little about them. How would one uncover what's by definition kept under wraps?

As for my new play [*Euphoria*], Mike Ockrent wants to direct it and Ian Albery has been encouraging us to get together again, as he liked [producing] *Passion Play*.

Did David [Aukin] say how much we enjoyed [your Cottesloe production of] *The Voysey Inheritance*? A terrific play, perfectly done. […]

All the best,
    Peter

Euphoria *is a satirical, modern-day reworking of the Jekyll and Hyde story: 60-year-old anaesthetist Lloyd Turner discovers a wonder-drug that transforms him into Larry Freeman, a libidinous entrepreneur, 30, who wants to privatise NHS care for the elderly.*

Dear Richard,

[…] On 5th January you rang saying you wanted the NT to do [*Euphoria*]. You also spent time persuading me that the Court isn't as good a launch-pad as the NT. There was no 'maybe' about it. You were positive. Five days later, David rang to confirm that the NT would do it, with or without Mike.

On 23rd January, the four of us met and you surprised Mike and me by suggesting the Olivier. But a month later Mike withdrew, saying he simply couldn't see it working at the Olivier and had unhappy memories of the Lyttelton [where he had directed two productions]. He thought I should stay with your offer. David and I met in his flat and he assured me nothing had changed except that we now had to find a director. We made a list and agreed to a reading.

After the reading in April, we all thought it needed work. I worked on it for a month and this week was called in by David – I assumed to discuss dates. Instead he made pretty clear that you and he don't want to produce it after all. He said the new version was more authorial than ever, that I hadn't done what I'd meant to. I thought I caught the word 'boring'. There was nothing about going back to the earlier draft, which you both loved so much that you instantly offered a production.

I'm not by nature an optimist and I've remained cautious all through. After all, *Passion Play* was rejected by the NT before going to the Other Lot. And *The National Health* would never have gone on without Ken Tynan's pressure on Olivier. But I was pretty sure you and David were as good as your words and I've been telling people that my new play will be on the South Bank soon. To say this leaves me with egg on my face is putting it kindly. Nor did I much enjoy being called in like some schoolboy, given low marks and threatened with expulsion.

I'm sure that, with all your personal and professional problems lately, you've not given much thought to this, but it's only right you should know how I feel: that this is a piss-poor way to treat someone who's had ten plays done in London, eight of them successes.

Sincerely,
Peter

**Eyre to Nichols,
12 July 1990**

Dear Peter,

I am very sorry that I couldn't have been at your meeting with David.

If you feel you have been treated in a piss-poor way I must apologise. You have earned every right to be treated well, and I have every obligation to do so.

My understanding is slightly different from yours and that is clearly at the heart of the problem. I <u>was</u> enthusiastic about the play and the combination of you and Mike was a partnership that had proved very fruitful in the past. When we met, my enthusiasm was qualified by the caveat that the play was still not right and that you and Mike needed to work on it together. This was agreed, and we pencilled in dates. Mike then withdrew, sending us back to base.

We set up the reading in order that you would have the opportunity of hearing the play and discussing it with David. Due to my other commitments I wasn't able to be party to that discussion and in this respect I let you down badly.

You rewrote the play and delivered it. Its arrival coincided with [my] rehearsals for *Richard III* followed by my father's death. Consequently I wasn't able to give the play the consideration it deserved [nor] to join you and David to discuss it. Circumstances rather than bad faith were to blame <u>here</u> at least.

I've now read the new draft and I'm afraid I still don't think the problems have been solved. I would very much like to talk to you about it, but perhaps you feel that enough is enough. I would at least try very hard <u>not</u> to treat you like some schoolboy.

I do acknowledge your resentment and indignation and wish that I hadn't occasioned them. Please let me know if you want to talk.

Very best wishes,
Yours,
Richard

Euphoria has never been professionally produced.

1990

Racing Demon (1990)

by David Hare

Director: Richard Eyre
Cottesloe, 8 February to 18 July (32 performances)
Olivier and Lyttelton: four seasons, August 1990 to November 1994 (128 performances)

Eyre and David Hare had been friends since the 1970s, when Eyre directed Hare's The Great
Exhibition *and produced Hare and Brenton's* Brassneck. *Eyre wanted them to develop a
play for the NT, and Hare, looking back to his visit to the General Synod in York in 1987,
decided to write about the Church of England. He interviewed Anglican clergy who were
practising 'team ministry', small groups within urban parishes.*

David Hare to Eyre,
18 February 1989

Dear Richard

[I'll] send you a copy of my research notes. The background
got more and more interesting. [One Canon described his best
friend] to me as 'a rugby bladder full of luke-warm water' and
'The worst possible person in the parish'.
    I finished an ACT ONE yesterday and am moving on. […]
Hope [*Hamlet*] is going well. […]

All the best,
    David

[P.S.] It is very, very long, & unlike *Secret Rapture* [Lyttelton,
1988], I think it is only a discussion document, rather than a
finished play. We then have to decide where to go with it.

Racing Demon *is set in a south London parish whose Anglican team includes Rev. Lionel
Espy (Oliver Ford Davies), a rector in his fifties; Rev. Harry Henderson (Michael Bryant),
a closeted homosexual who is forced into exile by the threat of a tabloid exposé of his
relationship with an actor; and Tony Ferris (Adam Kotz), their zealous young curate.
Conservative cuts to welfare services oblige them to devote more and more time to social
work, rather than traditional ministry. For the 'crime' of losing interest in administering the
sacrament, Lionel is dismissed by the imperious Bishop of Southwark (Richard Pascoe).*

Peter Hall, postcard
to Oliver Ford Davies,
19 February 1990

Dear Oliver Ford Davies,

Sometimes you see a piece of acting which just <u>is</u>: character, play,
and actor make a seamless whole. It's rare and it's a wonderful
experience – I suppose it's because of it that I work in the theatre.
    Your performance as Lionel is such a piece of work and I just
want to thank you for it. It is marvellous.

Sincerely,
    Peter Hall

Oliver Ford Davies
and Joy Richardson in
Racing Demon. Photo:
John Haynes

The Rev. Richard
Moberly (South
London Industrial
Mission) to Hare,
23 February 1990

Dear David,

Very many thanks for your offer of seats for *Racing Demon*. We
were all impressed, and enjoyed the performance enormously; so
much so in Patricia's case that, seeing Michael Bryant yesterday
in the street, she leapt out of the car and embarrassed him by
congratulating him on his performance.

It has been interesting reading the critics. All that I have seen
have praised the play and the acting, but seem to have given
varying interpretations of what the play is about. John Whale
said that it 'Dealt with the two most important issues facing
the Church – Faith and homosexuality'. Irving Wardle, in the
Independent on Sunday, saw you as holding a neutral position
between Lionel (plus Harry and Streaky) and Tony (plus
Bishops). […]

I agree with Whale that the play portrays the tension between
dogmatic 'fundamentalist' faith on the one hand and openness to
truth and the affirmation and celebration of people as they are on
the other, and that this is a fundamental issue which crops up all
over the world today, both in religious and political terms.

I don't agree that the play 'deals with' homosexuality. It is there
in passing, but so is the 'hetero' variety. The play does seem to me
to talk about sexuality in general in a moving way. […]

Numerous colleagues seem to have been to see the play, and
I listen with great interest as they discuss it. I have heard only
one person question whether Bishops could really behave like
that. […]

Anyway it all seems to have been hugely successful. Very many
thanks.

Yours sincerely,
Richard Moberly

Dear David.

Mike Fink & I saw "R.D" this evening. I think its the BEST play you've ever written — & probably one of the best plays we've ever seen. Everyone is wonderful in it — and Rich has directed it Beautifully. Denn you! I feel so jealous I could SPIT. Can't you write me a musical so that I can sit on a chair in a fur coat & nothing else and sing RUDE songs?

Devotedly —

Mike Juse & Fink.

Judi Dench to Hare,
March 1990

Dear David,

Mike, Fint & I saw [*Racing Demon*] this evening. I think it the
<u>BEST</u> play you've ever written – and probably one of the best
plays we've <u>ever</u> seen. Everyone is wonderful in it – and Rich has
directed it beautifully. Clever you! I feel so jealous I could SPIT.
Can't you write me a musical so that I can sit on a chair in a fur
hat & nothing else and sing RUDE songs?

> Devotedly –
>   Mike Jude & Fints

At the Olivier Awards, Racing Demon *was named Play of the Year, and Ford Davies Actor
of the Year.*

Ford Davies to Eyre,
16 April 1990

Dear Richard,

Just a note to thank you for all your help over *Racing Demon* and
the winning of this strange award. It was the most rewarding
rehearsal experience of my life.
    Condolences on not winning [Best Director] – that I'm sure is
the penalty of high office!
    To the next experiment together …

> Love,
>   Oliver

Racing Demon *went on a regional tour in autumn 1991, with Tony now played by Reece
Dinsdale.*

Hare, fax to Eyre,
27 November 1991

Richard,

I forgot to tell you [one of the] best jokes from the tour. In Bath –
at the reception afterwards:

POSH MAN: Oh you were in the play.
REECE: Yes.
POSH MAN: What a marvellous company.
REECE: Thank you.
POSH MAN: You were all marvellous.
REECE: Thanks.
(PAUSE)
REECE: And it's a wonderful play.
POSH MAN: Mmm.
(LONG PAUSE)
POSH MAN: That's debatable. […]

> D.

Sunday in the Park with George (1984)

Music and lyrics by Stephen Sondheim
Book by James Lapine

Director: Steven Pimlott
Lyttelton, 15 March to 16 June 1990 (116 performances)

Act One of Sunday in the Park with George *shows Georges Seurat finishing* Un dimanche après-midi à l'Île de la Grande Jatte *in 1884. In Act Two, set in 1984, George, Seurat's artist great-grandson, unveils his latest work. In rehearsals at the NT, Stephen Sondheim strongly disagreed with how Steven Pimlott was staging 'Putting It Together', and has recalled how this Act Two song 'depends on there being images of George all over the stage. Steven ignored that and I complained and he did not take it well. There was a real breakdown in communication, culminating in Steven not wanting me to be at the rehearsals.'*

Steven Pimlott to Stephen Sondheim, 17 April 1990

Dear Steve,

Thanks so much for your note. Unfortunately I shall be in Australia when you return to these shores, but I hope you like what you see …

I too am sorry the way the last few days developed. You must have felt very hurt and excluded when I began to distance myself as I did, but I felt it was the only way I could hold on to what I wanted for the show, and had I lost that, then I think we'd have had an ill-born creature up there. We have made different choices, but I believe passionately in their validity.

I need hardly re-iterate my commitment to your work. I think you & James have created a strange, beautiful animal. It seems to move people to the depths of their soul, or to leave them quite cold, in a way which is rather revealing. I love the quirky second act, & if people tell me the ending is sentimental and that life isn't like that, then I tell them well it fucking well should be.

My very best wishes to you. My sincerest thanks to you. My heartfelt apologies to you. And, if I may be so bold, please, keep the torch burning. I love the songs with all my being.

Yours,
Steven

Pimlott was nominated for Best Director of a Musical at the Olivier Awards, where Sunday in the Park… *won Best New Musical.*

Richard III (1592/93)

by William Shakespeare

Director: Richard Eyre

Lyttelton, 25 July 1990 to 18 September 1991 (105 performances)

Eyre and designer Bob Crowley updated the Wars of the Roses to what Ian McKellen, who played Richard, termed 'a fantasy Britain' of the 1930s, in which an ascendant military dictatorship, led by Richard, Buckingham and Catesby, was opposed by an air force chief (Stanley), naval commander (Richmond) and prime minister (Hastings). On a stage devoid of walls, stairs or doors, the historical period was evoked by costumes, furniture and Jean Kalman's lighting.

Simon Callow, card to Eyre, 6 September 1990

Dear Richard,

I thought [*Richard III*] magnificent – the best production I've seen in the Lyttelton, and the best, by far, of the play. Certainly the first time I've known who was fighting whom; first time those ladies have seemed anything other than tedious … you made it a play about England – and England now – not a concerto for a bravura-crazed actor. Brilliant.

> All the best,
> Simon

On Sunday 7 April 1991, the Olivier Theatre hosted the Olivier Awards ceremony, which was televised. The NT won ten of the 20 categories for which its productions were eligible, including Actor of the Year for McKellen, and Kalman for lighting Richard III and White Chameleon. Eyre was nominated as Best Director, but that prize went to David Thacker for Pericles (RSC).

Ian McKellen to Eyre, 8 April 1991

My dear Richard,

Congratulations on your unrivalled success last night. I've never known these ridiculous events to have such a clear message – that the National Theatre is, right now, the centre of British Theatre.

One by one you were personally thanked on camera. Your taste as a patron of a very wide variety of imports was confirmed. The productions you yourself initiated got awards in every department – acting, supporting acting (whatever that is), lighting & set designs.

Set in the Olivier, the whole show belonged to the National. So that the viewers and audience acknowledged that here is where it's at. The only improvement would, next year, be to secure that the party stays here rather than goes off to outside caterers.

The impression I got flicking through the video was that you are the most successful, influential & perceptive producer in the theatre today: that you are now the equal of your predecessors and that after only 2/3 years. It's astonishing.

It's also worrying that your understandable confusion that your work as a director only got a nomination, may blind you to all the rest.

I think it's <u>much</u> more important that you have success as the National Theatre's Director, rather than as a director at the National Theatre. You are carrying the lives & fortunes of 700 people &, however much they might regret that you didn't get up to get an award, they all take huge encouragement from the success of their theatre, which you are running for them.

You <u>must</u> remember & <u>feel</u> this success. Because the worm will turn & you need to have this current harvest for when financial, critical or personal problems impede progress.

Much love,
  Ian

P. S. If you want to indulge yourself – just imagine what Trevor & Thacker felt having to come here & be in <u>your</u> theatre. And where were Hall, Mendes & Noble? Last night they didn't exist.

Alison Smith to McKellen, 17 October 1991

Dear Sir Ian,

I had to write to thank you and your company for *Richard III* at the Alhambra, Bradford, last evening. My husband, David, and I had not been to a live performance as we have been busy bringing up our young daughters – but felt it was time to treat ourselves. For David, a live performance of Shakespeare was a totally new experience – and he was completely carried away. Your performance was electric – I can't tell you how much I admire your ability to so totally take on a character.

You have the ability to lift your audience from their commonplace everyday life into a totally different world, and make them the better because of it.

I feel renewed, revitalised and very privileged to have seen your marvellous performance.

Thank you,
  Alison Smith

The Richard III *tour ended at the Apollo, Oxford, on 2 November 1991.*

David Cornwell (John le Carré) to McKellen, 4 November 1991

Dear Ian,

So Oxford finished and I suppose you feel as flat as I feel when I've done a book – who shall I be next, if anyone? This is just to thank you on my own behalf, & on behalf of all my guests: the village still hums with the excitement; you gave them a night they will never, never forget. For myself, I thought it one of the truly great performances. I go over it again & again in my head, and it remains wonderfully rich, wonderfully stated & controlled, and magical. […]

Best,
  David (Cornwell)

1991

White Chameleon (1991)
by Christopher Hampton

Director: Richard Eyre
Cottesloe, 14 February to 29 August 1991 (74 performances)

In White Chameleon, *Christopher Hampton, born in 1946, lightly fictionalised his boyhood years in Egypt. The play unfolds from 1952 to 1956, and focuses on Chris, son of an English engineer who works for Cable & Wireless in Alexandria, where the family have a servant, Ibrahim.*

Christopher Hampton to Eyre, 1 February 1990

Dear Richard,

[…] As to [my play], or ours, this has not been the best of times. The damned 'flu knocked me on the head for about a month and now I'm going to have to interrupt my routine (alternate note-taking about Alexandria and Vietnam) in order to spend this month on completing the 1st draft of *Bright Shining Lie* [screenplay from Neil Sheehan's non-fiction book about the Vietnam War].

However, I'm now feeling vigorous again ([your *Voysey Inheritance*] made me think a great deal about the necessity for energy in the matter of writing plays, not to mention brood on the fact Granville Barker's gave out at 43) and have cancelled my trip to Australia, which would have swallowed March, in order to soldier on, in the hope of finishing *White Chameleon* some time in June.

I'm very grateful for your patience and tact: only hope it turns out to be justified. This inability to proceed until all technical problems seem to be satisfactorily solved is tiresome but I can't get round it. I think I understand why Beckett wound up writing plays 30 seconds long – at least he could be sure of not including anything irrelevant.

Love to Sue & Lucy & to yourself and good luck with *Racing Demon.*

Yours,
  Christopher

Hampton, fax to Eyre, 12 September 1990

Dear Richard,

The chameleon has landed.

Love,
  Christopher

Napoli Milionaria (1945)

by Eduardo de Filippo

English version by Peter Tinniswood (1991)
Director: Richard Eyre
Lyttelton, 27 June to 16 November 1991 (58 performances)

De Filippo's comedy, which starred Ian McKellen, is set in Naples during the Second World War. On 1 July, the prime minister, John Major, attended with his wife, Norma, and Sarah Hogg, head of his Policy Unit, who had sat on the NT Board from 1988 until earlier in 1991.

Sarah Hogg to Eyre,
4 July 1991

Dear Richard,

Just a quick note to thank you for a marvellously successful evening; a splendid production and a very good party. The boss enjoyed it enormously, as you will have deduced from the fact that he stayed shockingly late. Prime Ministers, like Cinderella, aren't supposed to be out after midnight or their red boxes turn into pumpkins!

I do <u>miss</u> the NT, but it's lovely to watch it with pride. You have made a triumphant success of it.

All the best,
Sarah

Major's two close protection officers had dozed during the first half of the performance, only to be roused by booming air raid sound effects – which they mistook for an assassination attempt, leaping on top of the PM, who quickly sounded an all-clear. Major wrote to NT chairman Mary Soames a week later, observing that 'my detectives have just about recovered from the shock'.

Murmuring Judges (1991)
by David Hare

Director: Richard Eyre
Olivier, 10 October 1991 to 30 May 1992 & 9 September to 20 November 1993
(103 performances)

Murmuring Judges' *intersecting storylines explore the criminal justice system: the police, the prison service and the judiciary, whose representatives include Mr Justice Duddeford (Michael Bryant) and a QC, Sir Peter Edgecombe (Richard Pascoe).*

As part of Hare, Eyre and designer Bob Crowley's research, Benet Hytner QC (father of Nicholas, who had recently made his NT directing debut) had invited them to lunch in the Great Hall of Middle Temple. He saw the play in preview.

Benet Hytner
to David Hare,
10 October 1991

Dear David,

I write with some temerity, this being the first time I have ever written to a playwright about his own play! I thought you might be interested in some of my comments, and my reactions to the play.

First – is it a good play? I am hardly qualified to judge, not being a Drama Critic (!) but simply as one of the bums on one of the seats, I have to say I thought that as theatre it was terrific; in particular the ending of each of the Acts was memorable in itself. Both Joyce and I thought the evening a tremendous theatrical occasion.

I did in fact pluck up courage and crept across to Middle Temple for lunch today. One High Court Judge (young), one circuit judge (young) and one QC had seen the play and all thought it terrific. Another High Court judge to whom I gave a synopsis thought your approach to the Criminal Justice System absolutely right. […]

Surely, I hear you say, are there no carping criticisms of the play, no errors to be corrected, no nits to be picked? Well, yes – but not many, and in the main minor!

I have already told Richard [Pascoe] that whilst I do not recognise myself as the QC he is typical of a particular and odious brand. Joyce and Nick, however, say he is typical of every barrister they have ever met, me included.

Similarly, there will be many judges who will scream (and with justice) 'foul', but I can name a judge whose head the cap would fit. Richard's performance was terrific. He asked me to give him notes; there are none – nor, at lunch, could anyone else think of any improvement that could be made. Similarly, I thought Michael Bryant was wonderful.

If you are interested in some of the constructive suggestions I could make, you would be very welcome to them; on the other hand I understand that dramatic impact would on occasions take precedence over accuracy.

Congratulations on a fine play.

Best wishes,
Ben Hytner

The Madness of George III (1991)

by Alan Bennett

Director: Nicholas Hytner
Lyttelton, 28 November 1991 to 5 March 1994 (209 performances)

Bennett's play dramatises the Regency crisis of 1788–89, prompted by the king's apparent madness. We see George III doted on by Queen Charlotte, resented by a Prince of Wales eager to occupy the throne for good, and treated by four physicians, including fearsome Dr Willis.

Nicholas Hytner had already staged Bennett's hugely popular adaptation of The Wind in the Willows *in the Olivier in 1990. Bennett sent Hytner a revised draft of* The Madness… *in the run-up to rehearsals.*

Alan Bennett to
Nicholas Hytner, 1991

Dear Nick,

Just one or two points about the text. […]

I've very much simplified the Queen bringing the Regency Bill scene. It may be too short now, but it settles the point on whether the King is sane by this time. I think he is, and Willis is right: he's just playing a game. The point that's unresolved in this area is why, when the King is so agitated about the Bill is he seemingly so relaxed in the Lear scene [when he, his equerry, Willis and the Lord Chancellor (Thurlow) read from *King Lear*]. It may not occur to people and, if it does, is swiftly resolved in this version by Thurlow taking him to London. I don't think we should know the King is in the carriage until he gets there and there may be one scene too many. I think it's such a good idea bringing the King to Westminster, it really gives it a lift.

Mrs Fitzherbert [The Prince of Wales' mistress] is unresolved (and unexplained).

Maybe she should just say 'My function is to show that you can be passionately interested in interior decoration, curtains, furnishing etc. without being a RAGING NANCY!' A propos of which the *E. Standard* has been having another go at me. I'm described as 'the virile playwright'.

Love,
Alan

With Nigel Hawthorne as George, heading a cast of 25, Hytner's production opened to packed houses. However, in the NT booking leaflet for 17 January to 7 March 1992, it was allocated only 14 of the 44 performances in the Lyttelton.

Bennett to Anthony
Jones (his agent),
31 January 1992

Dear Anthony,

With doing *Talking Heads* I hadn't paid much attention to the booking programme at the National. I've just looked at it and find we're only going to get eight performances in February … this after two enormous gaps in December and January.

It does seem to me to be a situation bordering on the ridiculous. Richard keeps saying the play's a victim of its own success but had it been the most abject failure it couldn't have fewer performances than it's getting. It may be the victim of someone thinking that it wasn't going to be a success but there's been time to correct that situation and we still seem to be getting the barest minimum.

In addition there hasn't been any proper provision made for any of the cast who want to be in other productions, even after the provincial tour, which is the ostensible reason why they can't be in current productions. Even with any plans for a West End transfer it seems to me we're getting the worst of every possible world. By the time Duncan [Weldon] does transfer the shine will have gone off … but without it having had enough performances to financially compensate for that; the actors will be pissed off and won't want to transfer because they're already under-compensated as it is, and will go on being so in the West End.

The more I look at it, the more it seems to me wasted. I don't want a play that everybody wants to see and nobody does. I don't know what booking periods remain still to be scheduled but I think we should press for more performances than we've been allotted, however many, because at the moment I think we're getting the mucky end of the stick.

I'm sending a copy of this to Nick Hytner.

Yours sincerely,
  Alan

It isn't the royalties – it's just that nobody I know has managed to see it yet – I get so many letters asking for tickets.

Jones forwarded this to Eyre. The play's run was extended, and, after its regional tour proved one of the most commercially successful in NT history, it returned to the South Bank.

Bennett to Eyre,
19 June 1992

Dear Richard,

[…] I saw in the paper *George III* was playing to 99% capacity. Typically I started worrying about the other 1%.

Love,
  Alan

The Olivier and Evening Standard *awards chose Hawthorne as Best Actor. A final Lyttelton season and a three-city American tour were arranged in 1993–94. Hytner then shot Bennett's screenplay,* The Madness of King George, *as his film debut, and Hawthorne was nominated for the Academy Award for Best Actor, ahead of the Oscars ceremony in March.*

Nigel Hawthorne in the title role of *The Madness of George III*. Photo: Donald Cooper

Nigel Hawthorne to Peter Brook, 9 March 1995

Dear Peter,

[…] It was extremely kind of you to write so generously of *The Madness of King George*. I enjoyed making the film more than I can tell you, and feel that all the Oscar hype which has been plaguing me, is perhaps only a temporary circus which will mercifully evaporate by the end of this month. As an actor I resent being placed in competition with my colleagues. It's not why I do it. And, in any case, who is to say who's 'best'? And what does 'best' mean?

Please give my love to Natasha. I was so thrilled to receive your letter. Thank you a million times.

In great admiration,
Best wishes,
Nigel

The Oscar went to Tom Hanks, for Forrest Gump. *But in 1996 Hawthorne won Best Actor at the Baftas, and* The Madness… *took Best British Film. Five years later, Hawthorne joined Hytner for a Q&A session after a screening at Shepperton Studios, where many of the film's interiors had been shot.*

Hawthorne to Hytner,
30 July 2001

My dear Nick,

What a good evening that was. I was rather dreading having to answer questions about *George* – partly because my experience of working with you (and Alan's script) means so much to me that I'm reluctant to share its details with others. It was an extraordinary time for me and, rather like you, I feel it's something I'll never be lucky enough to experience again.

It was a treat to be in your company again and to see some of those members of the cast with whom it had been such a joy to work.

I send you love and every possible good wish for [*Mother Clap's Molly House* in the Lyttelton]. How lucky they all are to be working with you.

> Fondly,
> Nige

1992

Angels in America (1991–92)
by Tony Kushner

Director: Declan Donnellan
Part One: Millennium Approaches (1991)
Cottesloe, 23 January to 7 November 1992 (113 performances)
Cottesloe, 20 November 1993 to 2 July 1994 (49 performances)
Part Two: Perestroika (1992)
Cottesloe, 20 November 1993 to 2 July 1994 (69 performances)

Eyre to Tony Kushner,
22 April 1991

Dear Tony Kushner,

I think various emissaries from the National Theatre (Giles Croft and John Burgess at the very least) will have told you how much I admire *Angels in America* [*Millennium Approaches*]. It's quite the best piece of new American playwriting that I have read for ages – well, since Mamet.

I would be very pleased if we could buy an option on the play for the first British production.

> Very best wishes,
> Yours,
> Richard Eyre

Kushner to Eyre,
30 May 1991

Dear Mr Eyre,

I've been out of town for the last two months, doing *Millennium Approaches* in San Francisco, and so it's only now that I'm able to respond to your incredibly kind letter. I'm very flattered and of course very, very excited (even a little stunned) that the National is interested in the play.

I met with John Burgess in San Francisco, and I explained to him that I was nearly finished with *Perestroika*, the second half of *Angels*. And indeed I have finished it, though it's immensely long and rough. I plan to get it into readable shape over the next month, and I will send it to you as soon as it's ready.

I will also send along the newest draft of *Millennium*, which is tighter and I hope clearer. The production in San Francisco was a difficult one – woefully underfunded – but it's turned out happily; it opened last weekend to great reviews. […]

Best wishes,
Tony Kushner

Kushner, then 34, was shocked by the NT's interest, partly because his A Bright Room Called Day *had been critically mauled in London in 1988.*

Eyre admired Millennium Approaches *for tackling 'McCarthyism, Mormonism, Marxism, the Millennium, homosexuality, Aids, God and angels'. Set mainly in New York in 1985–86, its principals include Prior, 30, a WASP, part-time designer who has Aids; his Jewish boyfriend, Louis; Prior's former lover, Belize, an African American nurse who tends him after Louis walks out; infamous lawyer, and closeted homosexual, Roy Cohn, who also has Aids; Cohn's Mormon protégé, Joe Pitt, and his wife, Harper.*

Perestroika *takes these characters through to 1990.*

John Burgess (NT literary manager – new writing) to Kushner, 28 August 1991

Dear Tony,

I've read *Perestroika* [three times], each time with increasing admiration. Louis and Joe, and Roy and Belize, and Prior and Harper are so vividly alive and now a permanent part of my imagination. They provide such an interesting way of thinking about the world.

As ever,
John

Millennium Approaches *won Best Play at the Evening Standard awards.*

In March 1992, a rave review of Declan Donnellan's Cottesloe production by New York Times *critic Frank Rich (a 'searching and radical rethinking of the whole aesthetic of American political drama') sparked feverish US interest in the upcoming* Angels… *double-bill in Los Angeles.* Millennium Approaches *would also reach Broadway in April 1993, directed by George C. Wolfe.*

Opposite: Joseph Mydell (Belize) and Sean Chapman (Prior) in *Angels in America: Millennium Approaches*. Photo: John Haynes

Kushner to Burgess,
11 July 1992

Dear John,

I'd planned to come to London at the end of July but the fact that
I am still working on *Perestroika* – and need to have it banged into
playable condition within a month – may very well mean that I can't.
     The anticipation surrounding the arrival of *Angels* in LA
and NY has gone beyond feverish to frothing at the mouth – a
backlash is inevitable. And I wish I felt better about Part Two. It's
terribly hard to get right. Whine whine whine. […]

> All my best,
> Tony

Eyre to Kushner,
22 January 1993

Dear Tony,

I look forward very much to receiving *Perestroika*. I have spoken
to various people who saw it in Los Angeles and the general
consensus seems to have been a disappointment with the
production rather than the play. I don't think you should feel
paranoid about the response of those who saw it – there are so
many more important things to feel paranoid about.
     We are still hoping that we can go according to plan and [have
Declan direct both plays this November].
     Very best wishes and very good luck on Broadway.

> Yours,
> Richard

Giles Croft (NT
literary manager),
memo to Eyre et al.,
5 February 1993

DECLAN UPDATE

I have spoken to Declan briefly today.
     He has now read [*Perestroika*] and is least happy with: the
Russian speech; the Louis/Joe seduction scene; Mr Lies/Harper
scene, in fact most of the Harper scenes, and the Mormon
Visitors Centre scene.
     I have said how much I enjoyed it and that some things will need
to be repeated as not everyone will have seen, or will remember,
Millennium. Also, that he won't get everything he wants.

> Giles

Nicholas Wright (NT
associate director),
memo to Eyre et al.,
10 February 1993

PERESTROIKA

I don't see any need to worry about this. I thought it was
extremely entertaining and compulsive. […]
     It's all more taxing scenically than Part One. But the brilliance
far outweighs the problems.

By July, Millennium Approaches *had won the Pulitzer Prize and four Tonys, including
Best Play and Best Director. The Broadway* Perestroika *would go into rehearsal on
16 August.*

Kushner to Declan
Donnellan and Nick
Ormerod (designer),
11 August 1993

Dear Declan and Nick,

I am still struggling with the accursed play. I think I am in the home stretch; I have a lot of work to do in the next five days, but I will be able to start rehearsals in NY on Monday with a script – albeit a script hot off the xerox machine.

I won't bore you with the grimy details of the last two months. Basically I've found myself for the first time ever completely incapable of writing. I've always been a fearful writer and a great procrastinator but this time all my tricks for getting myself started failed me; going into exile and seclusion didn't produce anything other than massive panic, etc. etc.

All of which is just to make you feel pity for me and to crave your indulgence for a few days more. I explained to Giles this morning that I will express the new version to you by the fastest means possible by Monday at the latest. I didn't want to send parts of it because then I would immediately begin waiting for your response and that would upset the very delicate equilibrium I've managed to create – I sound like a dangerous lunatic, don't I? Well in some ways …

The changes in my life since the play opened last January in London have caught up with me; I'm scared about the future, and about the reception of my work in light of the hysterical reception of *Millennium*. This play is a necessary step to get through. And also the amount of sheer noise has made it hard to think clearly. I've begun to learn how to deal with that.

The play is simply a miserably difficult nest of dramaturgical problems, and solving them under any circumstance would not be easy.

The scenic demands are the same – no new locations, and none eliminated. The big difference is that I've scrambled some of the scenes together, so that the play is less scene–scene–scene–scene than it was in LA. At certain points several locations happen on stage at once. I think you'll like it.

Well, rather than spend more time annoying you with description I should go finish the play.

I am really sorry this has taken so long; I know what sorts of horror it visits upon you and the theatre in terms of preparation, and believe me if I could have found a way to avoid this I would have – it wasn't for want of looking. So please forgive. I am very excited about showing you what an absolute LAMB I can be.

Much much much love,
Tony

Croft, fax to
Donnellan, 16 August
1993

Dear Declan,

I have spoken to Tony and though the play isn't complete yet, he is sending today what he has done so far.

As you read this, Tony is probably in the midst of his first day of rehearsals. He sounded nervous as hell.

Love,
Giles

In New York, because Perestroika *endured what Kushner called exceptionally 'arduous and tension-filled technical rehearsals', it opened three days* after *the play's first Cottesloe preview, not two months* before, *as planned.*

<table>
<tr>
<td>

Kushner to Eyre,
3 March 1994

</td>
<td>

Dear Richard,

Everything that's happened since that excruciating week when the play opened here and in London has been mostly a blur. I've been running all over the place, ignoring mail, phone calls, faxes and pretty much every other social obligation except the almighty deadline. I'd thought life was going to get easier – apparently not.

The most pressing business at the moment for me is the screenplays for *Angels*. I spent a week in Paris with [Robert] Altman, sketching out a shape for *Millennium*. He's remarkable, and I think we came up with a good plan, but the whole thing is, for now at least, both frightening and a little loathsome – the last thing I want to do now is rewrite the whole thing. On the other hand, I'm excited about working with him. […]

Declan seems happy, and says the plays are going over well. It sounds unlikely that there will be much more work on *Perestroika*, but that's entirely my fault; Declan's been very willing but it hasn't seemed worth the difficulty … I'm sure the production is fine, and demanding changes feels like opening a can of worms, vis à vis my relationship with DD, which I would like to maintain, since I am very fond of him.

I look forward to talking with you soon.

All my best,
Tony

</td>
</tr>
</table>

Three months later, Perestroika *brought Kushner his second Tony.* Angels in America *eventually became a six-hour HBO mini-series, directed by Mike Nichols in 2003.*

Square Rounds (1992)
by Tony Harrison

Director: Tony Harrison
Olivier, 1 October 1992 to 16 January 1993 (36 performances)

Square Rounds *was 'a chemical pageant', blending dramatic poetry, music, dazzling costume changes and conjuring tricks, to tell the story of Hiram Maxim, one of the inventors of the machine gun, and Fritz Haber, inventor of TNT.*

<table>
<tr>
<td>

Tony Harrison,
postcard to Eyre,
9 April 1992

</td>
<td>

Dear Richard,

You've probably already been supplied by Trish [Montemuro, stage manager] but this is the illustrated, hand-coloured edition. It will be totally different by next week but I need to know that I shouldn't pull the plug or the spigot out on it.

I need the musical input to begin re-shaping.

</td>
</tr>
</table>

I have 2 or 3 days with a random group of women to lay that ghost once and for all. 22–24 April. Vesta Tilley, Ella Shields, the Incomparable Vonetta 'the Only Lady Illusionist, Protean and Quick Change Artiste' with a colourful rousing finale of 'Flags of all Nations'. Many thanks for the encouraging words. I need them.

Love,
Tony

Jim Carter, who had appeared as Agamemnon in Harrison's version of The Oresteia *(Olivier, 1981), was offered the role of Hiram Maxim.*

Jim Carter to
Harrison, 6 May 1992

Dear Tony,

I'm sorry, but I'm afraid that I have some bad news for you – I want to pull out of the *Square Rounds* play.

I've always had reservations about committing myself to eight months at the National – but I thought that my excitement about the project would overcome my fears. I'm afraid that this hasn't happened and that I was finding myself getting gloomier and gloomier at the prospect of tying myself down for so long.

Part of the reason is, to be crude and selfish, that I don't think that Hiram is quite the part I'd hoped it would be for me. I think that Fritz Haber is the centre of the play and that Hiram was a sideshow – added to the fact that [his] having only one arm means that to all intents and purposes, my involvement in any magic would be minimal!

So, painful though this is, I think it's best that I make a clean break at this stage.

It goes without saying that I think the play is potentially fantastic and that I wish you all the best with it.

Also, any help I can give with the tricks – I'd be more than happy to provide.

If you want to talk about this please call me.

All best wishes,
Jim

Carter was Magic Coach to Square Rounds' *cast of 23, which included Paola Dionisotti as Maxim, Sara Kestelman as Haber and another 18 actresses as 'munitionettes'.*

After The Oresteia *and* The Trackers of Oxyrhynchus *(1990),* Square Rounds *was the third of Harrison's NT shows designed by Jocelyn Herbert. During its final rehearsals, Eyre was directing* Suddenly Last Summer *for television.*

Jocelyn Herbert
to Harrison,
16 September 1992

Dearest Tony,

This must be a terribly difficult time for you – and I worry about you a lot. Just wanted to send you my love and if I can help in any way, do give a sign. When under such pressure it is easy to feel totally isolated and lose contact and confidence even with your friends. Incidentally I have a firm belief that once we get on stage a lot of our present problems will be, perhaps not so serious, but also easier to solve – and the strength and beauty of the play will emerge to carry it along.

> Much love,
> Jocelyn

Eyre, postcard to Harrison, 20 September 1992

Dear Tony,

I'm sorry I won't be around this week – at very least to offer you support and encouragement. I'm very proud that the theatre is doing your play – and I <u>know</u> that it will be a remarkable event. I'm thinking of you.

> Courage – and love,
> Richard

David Storey, postcard to Harrison, 20 September 1992

Dear Tony,

Just to say how much I enjoyed yesterday's run-through: the mixture of pugnacity and sensitivity may or may not be 'Yorkshire' or 'West Riding' – or from a northern back street – but it certainly has a very powerful effect on <u>me</u>! I admire (a) what you've attempted and (b) what you've achieved, no end. All my best wishes for the opening – and congratulations! When the Beeston Bugger gets back to Newcastle and his poetry may it be with still greater strength.

> Love,
> David Storey

'It's been a kind of noble disaster, and I couldn't help,' wrote Eyre in his diary after Square Rounds *began playing to very small houses. 'Partly because of [my] being away, and partly because I had made the mistake of urging Tony to do the play before the script was ready.' In November, Harrison won the Whitbread Prize for Poetry, for his collection* The Gaze of the Gorgon.

Herbert to Harrison, 27 November 1992

Dearest Tony,

I rang many times – but didn't realise you had gone to California.

    Wanted to say how glad I am about the Whitbread Prize & hoped it cheered you a bit after the lack of understanding about *Square Rounds.*

    Hope I'll see you when you get back – we haven't had a chat for ages.

> Much love,
> Jocelyn

David Storey's new play, Stages, *opened in the Cottesloe on 18 November. It starred Alan Bates as Fenchurch, a novelist and artist with northern, working-class roots, enduring a mental breakdown in his fifties. Storey was born in 1933 in Wakefield, west Yorkshire, the son of a miner; Harrison was born about a dozen miles away, in Leeds in 1937, the son of a baker.*

Storey to Harrison,
22 November 1992

Dear Tony,

So many thanks for your wonderful letter – your support. I don't know why your coming from Leeds means so much to me – an identification with your origins, without a doubt, the quizzical look you have of the coal-face miner (an undisturbed working-class expression – undisturbed by education, 'culture', and the rest) – and, of course (the key to it) the content of your work: the same upheaval from unpromising roots which, with hindsight, in reality, promised everything. I'm glad I got to know you at this stage of my/your life: there's something struggled-for about it, something confirmatory. The integrity – the authenticity of your writing – so wonderfully independent of that journalese identification of 'the north' – so wonderfully independent of everything – is such a delight and a tonic, such a reassurance, that I wonder at times if I haven't dreamed it up: only to pick up your poems again and get a revivifying and now almost mandatory jolt.

I'm so proud of what you've done (and you're writing better than ever): to dig out what you have done – to magic what you have done – from all that dolorous West Riding crap, to transcend and at the same time not reject (positively, to love) – to move around the world with such ease, and with such confirmatory gestures, does me more good than you can imagine. You've emancipated yourself from your past (as I say, without destroying it) in a way I've never done – and doubt now I ever shall. Because of that, even if I never see you again, simply to know you are there, that you have been there, that you've left a unique record of your 'travels', is good enough for me! Keep moving, pal!

Stages has had its inevitable mixed reception – from 'masterpiece' to 'I'd have been better left in bed': an odd experience, working on it – not least against the invigorating background of *Square Rounds* (a great uplift, still, to see the 'girls' coming in for their word rehearsals): for me it's been the shedding of a skin at the promise of moving on to something new – certainly something different. Hope to see you again. Keep in touch. Many thanks again. Lots of love.

And – it's good to have a brother.

David

Carousel (1945)

Music by Richard Rodgers
Book and lyrics by Oscar Hammerstein

Director: Nicholas Hytner
Lyttelton, 10 December 1992 to 27 March 1993 (130 performances)

In Carousel, *set on the New England coast in 1873 and 1888, the community includes the prosperous fisherman Enoch Snow, a role taken at the NT by Clive Rowe, who is black. On 5 June 1992, four months before rehearsals began, Theodore S. Chapin, executive director of The Rodgers and Hammerstein Organisation, sent Nicholas Hytner a fax – prompted by the objections of Dorothy Rodgers, the composer's 83-year-old widow – insisting that Rowe would be 'inappropriate' casting, partly because the name Snow would appear 'a joke' to the audience.*

Nichols Hytner to
Theodore Chapin,
5 June 1992

Dear Ted,

I've received your fax, and discussed it with Jenny McIntosh [NT executive director].

We have a problem.

Clive Rowe is in the opinion of [everyone] involved in casting *Carousel* the best, if not the <u>only</u>, candidate for Mr Snow. We have seen everybody who can sing the part, and we cannot imagine an alternative.

He is a brilliant artist: a comic actor of great sensitivity (not capable of buffoonery – he's much better than that), he sings well and he answers to the description of the character in the text.

I believe this play is above buffoonery, and above stereotypes. I cannot accept that on the one hand we mustn't cast a black man as a 'buffoon' for fear of misinterpretation; but on the other we mustn't cast him as an 'insider'. Some inconsistency here!

The company <u>will</u> be interracial on all levels. We could not cast the show otherwise. I do not think the character's name will become a joke. If it does, it's the problem of those bigots who laugh, and shouldn't worry us. The NT Company as a whole is multiracial, and the production will be seen in that context.

We cannot in conscience (and arguably in British law) decline to cast an actor on the sole grounds of his colour. There is no question in any of our minds that Clive Rowe is the best man for the part, and I will say again that we've seen everybody. I have never held more exhaustive auditions – even for *Miss Saigon*!

We should talk soonest. I'll be arriving in New York on Monday night.

With very best wishes,
Nick

Hytner met the Rodgers family in New York and, on 18 June, Chapin sent another fax, approving Rowe.

As You Like It (c.1600)**
by William Shakespeare

Emma Thompson had played Princess Katharine in her then husband Kenneth Branagh's film of Henry V *(1989) and had recently finished shooting his* Much Ado About Nothing *in Italy, as Beatrice to his Benedick.*

Emma Thompson
to Eyre, 14 December
1992

Dear Richard,

I'm very sorry that I didn't make it in for a chat today but life is like a Blender at the moment and therefore there's no point in trying to make plans right now – they'd just slip through our fingers. I <u>do</u> know that I would like to do *As You* at some point with Annabel [Arden] directing.

Maybe we could discuss that in the New Year? I don't know if that's the kind of thing you had in mind. Next year I know I'd like to finish writing *Sense & Sensibility*, and to film *Carrington* with Chris Hampton. Other than that I'm very vague except that watching Ken do Hamlet [for the RSC] makes my throat itch for Shakespeare – but that might be a boring idea for <u>you</u>. Unless it was Annabel & a bit different.

Let us meet if at all possible in '93 and think about '94?! It's always good to plant things early and I'd really like to come to the National soon, if you'll have me.

In the meantime, I hope you're enjoying all the successes – many congratulations!

And love,
    Emma

Thompson would win an Oscar for her Sense and Sensibility *screenplay. She has yet to appear at the National.*

1993

Mr A's Amazing Maze Plays (1988)
by Alan Ayckbourn

Director: Alan Ayckbourn
Cottesloe, 4 March to 19 August (66 performances)

Alan Ayckbourn to Genista McIntosh, 14 June 1992

Dear Genista,

MR A'S AMAZING MAZE PLAYS
[…] I am going to need a wonderful sound recordist – and operator(s). The show is to some extent spontaneously decided by the kids and could drive a lesser technician with a nervous disposition to an early grave.

[…]With very best wishes,
Alan

McIntosh was sure the NT could provide 'the right nerveless masochist for your purposes'. Head of Press Stephen Wood asked Ayckbourn to provide a synopsis for the booking leaflet.

Ayckbourn, fax to Stephen Wood, 2 October 1992

It's a bit of a problem how to describe the play. If you just say 'by Alan Ayckbourn' you tend to get a lot of middle-aged [adults] (as we did initially with *Invisible Friends* [Cottesloe,1991]) with not a child to be seen anywhere. They seemed to enjoy it but it was a bit of a shame.

The other way is to call it 'a play for children' which tends to make the whole thing exclusively for children which is also rather a shame. What I would really love would be a mixture of the two, i.e. all ages. It seems to me that not only are these sorts of audience the best to play to, they're also going to have a much better time enjoying each other enjoying it – if you follow me.

'For all the family' sounds a bit like a panto but maybe it's the best there is. We called the last one up here 'a play for children and intelligent adults'. Which made the kids laugh. 'A play for all ages'? 'All age groups?' Something along those lines.

As regards blurb … what about:

An exciting adventure in which we accompany Suzy and Neville (her dog) through countless dark rooms and secret passageways of an old mansion to discover just where villainous Mr Accousticus has hidden his collection of stolen sounds and voices. A great deal of assistance from the audience is required …

See you Monday.

Marketed as 'For children (of 6 upwards) and intelligent adults', Ayckbourn's production featured Judith McSpadden as Suzy and Adam Godley as Neville.

Jeremy Gear to
NT Education
Department, 6 May
1993

Dear Sir,

I enclose reviews of *Mr A's Amazing Maze Plays* from a group of
10- to 11-year-olds [from Hendon Preparatory School]. I haven't
corrected their work, but they do come up with some very
perceptive observations.

    We all enjoyed both the play and the backstage tour. Thank you
very much for all the work which you do for schools.

    Yours faithfully,
      Jeremy Gear

Hendon Preparatory
School pupil 1,
review, May 1993

The way it was written was good because Suzie's mother keeps
saying long words in a muddle. There was too much miming. Mr
Accousticus (the villain) does not like noise but he speaks very
loudly. The best things are the sound effects and the best actor is
Neville (a dog). […]

Hendon Preparatory
School pupil 2,
review, May 1993

I like this Play because this play was not only watching we could
choose which way the girl go (I like story which about Adventure)

    My favourite acter was the dog. He can understand what we
say. I want to have this dog for my pet.

    Bad thing I thought why girl don't change her cloth. (Is it not
dirty?)

    Why Mr A's do not lock his home's door. (Is it not danger?) I
want to visit Theatre again because it is fun!

Arcadia (1993)

by Tom Stoppard

Director: Trevor Nunn
Lyttelton, 13 April to 24 November (116 performances)

*As Director Designate, Eyre had written to Tom Stoppard, embarrassed at having 'only a
handshaking acquaintance with one of the country's foremost playwrights', and hopeful
that Stoppard might one day prefer to have his work premiered by the NT, rather than by
Michael Codron in the West End, as had most recently been the case with* The Real Thing
(1982) and Hapgood *(1988). Eyre got to know Stoppard well after he joined the NT Board
in 1989.*

Tom Stoppard
to Eyre, 20 November
1991

Dear Richard,

I'm awfully slow and I had to stop for 6 weeks to do something
for money – I go back to the play next week.

    Putting the boot in the other court, or back on the other foot
– when do you need to have seen scripts in order to plan the next
bunch of plays? […]

    Tom

The play in question was Arcadia. *Set in Sidley Park, a grand country mansion in Derbyshire, it alternates between 1809, when we meet a 13-year-old mathematical genius, Thomasina, and 1989, when an academic tries to prove that Lord Byron had killed a minor poet in a duel at Sidley Park in 1810. Characters debate Chaos Theory and quantum physics.*

    A pressing question for Stoppard was who should direct: Eyre, or Trevor Nunn, who, while running the RSC, had produced Stoppard's Travesties *(1974) and* Every Good Boy Deserves Favour *(1977), and directed the latter. In June, Stoppard sent* Arcadia *to both.*

    And on 22 June Nunn wrote to Stoppard, noting that he could not remember when he had last been 'so stimulated, provoked and gloriously entertained' by a script. Arcadia *posed 'the most exciting, brain-teasing kind' of challenges for a director. Its cast would all need to be 'exhilarating verbal duellists', who were masters of 'subtext – particularly sexual subtext'. He would love to stage it.*

    Ten days later, Eyre wrote in his diary: 'Tom has decided that Trevor should direct his play … I felt humiliated but I'm not quite sure why.' As producer, Eyre responded to each new draft.

Stoppard to Eyre, 10 December 1992	Dear Richard,

I'm glad you liked the changes. I have not yet desisted, in small ways, but I have desisted from reprinting. The rehearsal script will catch up on all my fiddling. I've got the length down a bit. […] Onward!

Yours,
Tom |

Arcadia *opened in the Lyttelton on 13 April 1993, with a cast including Felicity Kendal, Bill Nighy, Rufus Sewell and Emma Fielding, then aged 25, as Thomasina.*

Emma Fielding, postcard to Stoppard, 13 April 1993	Dear Tom,

<u>Thank you</u> for writing such a magnificent part in a sparklingly beautiful play. I've learnt so much from Thomasina – and from you & Trevor & Robert May [*Arcadia*'s maths consultant] & all the other actors involved. The most wonderful part has been the feeling that we're all sharing something truly extraordinary, multi-faceted etc. etc. but with such warmth, humanity & JOY. I'm beginning to make less & less sense, but to be 13 again has been great. I have been rather overawed by things and I realised I hadn't a) said <u>thank you</u> and b) how privileged I've felt at 10.30 every morning for the past 7 weeks and how I'll no doubt feel till October/August if not longer. I hope I'll be able to do her justice one day. Well – THANK YOU Tom. Have a wonderful evening,

Love,
Emma |

Arcadia *was transferred to the Theatre Royal, Haymarket by Michael Codron, and won* Evening Standard *and Olivier awards for Best Play.*

Opposite: Rufus Sewell and Emma Fielding
in *Arcadia*. Photo: Richard Mildenhall

The Absence of War (1993)

by David Hare

Director: Richard Eyre
Olivier, 2 October 1993 to 19 March 1994 (100 performances)
Presented as *The David Hare Trilogy*, with *Racing Demon* and *Murmuring Judges*

The concluding play in David Hare's state-of-the-nation trilogy, The Absence of War
*drew heavily on his observations of the 'high-pressure hysteria' of the 1992 General Election
campaign, in which Neil Kinnock was expected to oust John Major from Number Ten, only
to suffer a humiliating defeat. Kinnock, a close friend of Eyre, had given Hare access to his
private meetings with the likes of Roy Hattersley (shadow home secretary) and Gerald
Kaufman (shadow foreign secretary).*

*Hare's play gives us a Labour leader modelled on Kinnock, George Jones (John Thaw),
whose promising election campaign is derailed in its closing stages, betrayed by his shadow
chancellor, who, infuriated by George's 'unelected clique' of advisers, leaks a damning
manifesto secret.*

*The play was read at the Studio in January 1993, and Hare showed a revised draft to
Kinnock, who had resigned as leader after the election.*

David Hare, fax to **Eyre, 19 May 1993**	NEIL KINNOCK'S NOTES ON THE PLAY. ONES I THINK VALID HAVE ASTERISKED

*1. At the Cenotaph former prime ministers stand behind prime ministers. […]
 4. [George's] question to the Prime Minister is implausibly long. You'd never get away with it.
*5. Although George would PRETEND to push paper away in Scene Four, he would actually be absorbing everything. (I have to make it clearer it's just a manner.)
 6. The only reason he would not read [Parliamentary Labour Party] minutes was because he was BLOODY THERE. […]
 9. He must not, in speaking of the people's rights, be looking down on them. After 'you can never depend on them' I should add 'that's their right too' to stress his democratic principles. […]
(*?)12. He thinks POWER is their master, not money. The line would become 'power's a simple master in that way'. […]
*20. Labour leader would not go to Salisbury. Use Southampton. Would not go to Taunton. Use Exeter.
*21. Most of all hates impression he was run by a group. If any group ever THOUGHT they were running him, they were wrong. His mistakes were his and his alone. Is this also true of George? It isn't clear. Is the accusation just or not?

Saturday 2 October witnessed a Trilogy *marathon in the Olivier, with an ensemble
company:* Racing Demon *at 10.30am,* Murmuring Judges *at 2.30pm and the press show of*
The Absence of War *at 7.30pm.*

Jocelyn Herbert to
Eyre, 3 October 1993

Dear Richard,

Sorry I didn't see you after the show last night, so just a line to congratulate you on a brilliant production of such a difficult, amazing and unexpected play – unexpected – to see the Labour Party so mercilessly exposed – its bankruptcy & its death – and the whole political scene revealed for the power maniacs and money grubbing horrors they are – 'God help us all' as my father [author and politician A. P. Herbert] would say.

> Much love,
> Jocelyn

Peter Hall, postcard
to Eyre, 12 October
1993

My dear Richard,

Thank you for the superb new David Hare. You're working as a master. As you know, I didn't re-see the other two plays (though I certainly intend to see *Racing Demon* again) but the atmosphere in the audience that night was quite unforgettable. It made [me] proud that you have made such a National Theatre with such plays and such productions.
Thank you.

> Ever,
> Peter

Hare felt The Absence of War *was his best play; its reviews left him 'driven mad by the complete disparity between the audience's reaction & the dismissals in the press' and he insisted that Eyre include* Daily Mail *showbiz columnist Baz Bamigboye's description of the play as 'David Hare's theatrical masterpiece' in the next booking leaflet – even though it was NT custom and practice only to use quotes from drama critics.*

Eyre, despite Herbert and Hall's postcards, and other plaudits, wrote in his diary of going into 'a steady decline' immediately after the Trilogy *opened. He would soon begin taking the anti-depressant, Prozac, and wondered how much longer he should remain as Director.*

Hare, fax to Eyre,
14 January 1994

Dear Richard,

I've been thinking this morning about last night's conversation. Did I dream it or did you ask me to run the National Theatre?

If you've decided you've only got three years to go, then there are two challenges: 1) Artistic 2) Organisational. I feel I wasn't much use to you on 1). I'm as bewildered as you are as to why nobody is writing [plays] about this decade.

What worries me most about our conversation is that you've had five wonderfully successful years because you've always had a sense of purpose about what you are trying to do, and a vigour to reorganise the building. It terrifies me that if you now take your foot off the pedal, all the old problems will recur. What I couldn't bear is to see a period of work in which you were only half as committed as you have been for the last five years. If, as will inevitably happen, the going were to get rough after this period of golden public opinion, nothing would be more disastrous for everyone's morale than to be defending work they didn't believe in. What's been great is that even when we have been under attack in the last five years, it's been for work of which we ourselves were proud. That makes all the difference. [...]

You really have to decide if you're up for a full second lap, or if what you're now talking about is a period of discreet and decorous withdrawal. If it's the second, then in a way the sooner you make that clear to everyone the better. Because then you can call the favours you are owed by Howard [Davies], Deborah [Warner], Nick [Hytner] etc. – all your A-list directors; you can call Nicky [Wright] in and a few others and have a real white-knuckle session on WHERE ARE THE FUCKING PLAYS; you can set new targets for What Are We Going to Do Before I Go? I think everyone will rally if they know what's the context.

If on the other hand you're up for the first – on into a phase of revolutionary activity – and finding NEW writers and NEW directors, and NEW sources of energy, then, equally, you have to make your mind up pretty soon.

What it mustn't be is drift. I drifted for three months from October recovering from the *Trilogy*, but my fortune is that nobody depends on me. You don't have the luxury of drift.

Fraternally,
David

Eyre, fax to Hare, 15 January 1994	Thank you for listening to [my] ravings. I feel better for having talked to a friend about my state of mind, and have crawled out from the Neolithic slime of despair. In fact I now feel rather positive about things.

Don't worry: I won't drift. For a start I'm too vain to <u>let</u> things go, but I'm also too much of a puritan, and if I'm getting paid to do the job I'm going to go on doing it as well as I can.

I am/have been gathering an artistic agenda and have spent many hours recently in white-knuckle meetings with Nick [Wright] and Giles [Croft]. But I still lack a grand project. I'm getting keener and keener on the Irish notion. Have you read *May the Lord in His Mercy Be Kind to Belfast* by Tony Parker. If not you must read it NOW. It's completely brilliant. I'll think more about big follies. Let me know if you have any thoughts. [...]

Notwithstanding banishing drift I still think that another three years is probably enough – for me and for the National. So I do hope to have a final two years of BLAZING ENERGY. It must include at least one HARE play.

Yes, I did ask you to run the NT, in so far as it's in my gift. There's no reason why a writer shouldn't do it and you're the only one who could. But why would you want to?

Thanks again.

Yours,
Richard

Six weeks later, The Guardian *reported that Eyre 'has told his staff he does not intend to seek reappointment when his contract expires' in 1996.*

1994

Broken Glass (1994)
by Arthur Miller

Director: David Thacker
Lyttelton, 4 August 1994 to 14 February 1995 (68 performances)

By 1993, David Thacker had directed six of Arthur Miller's plays, and the pair had become good friends. Broken Glass, *set in Brooklyn in 1938, is the story of a middle-aged Jewish couple, the Gellburgs: Philip (Henry Goodman) and Sylvia (Margot Leicester, Thacker's wife), who suffers an hysterical paralysis after reading newspaper reports of Nazi persecution of Jews in Germany; she is treated, with great care, by Dr Hyman (Ken Stott).*

Arthur Miller, fax to David Thacker, 24 August 1993

Dear David,

Here are all the [script] changes to date.

'Broken Glass' of course refers to the Night of Broken Glass or *Krystallnacht* when Hitler let loose the thugs to smash up the Jews' stores and synagogues. It signified the end of all temporising & the unleashing of pure terror which, incidentally, served to paralyse the West for a long couple of years.

The title, for Jewish people, will also signify the smashing of a glass goblet under the heel of the groom, indicating the sealing of the marriage. But it also signifies the destruction of the Temple by the Romans so that Jews will never forget it. 'If I forget thee O Jerusalem may my right hand wither ...'

Of course the latter connection will probably not be made by non-Jews, but to hell with them.

Alternative explanation of the breaking glass ritual – it means the Redemption of the world. (Maybe through destruction of this world.) Also the breaking with one's former single life & assumption of marriage. Also the breaking of the hymen. Also a noise to drive off the Angel of Destruction who is trying to break up the ceremony. In general, a noise that drives away evil.

After the final curtain I suggest you get up and explain all this. There are more explanations because Jews can never agree or shut up, but these should keep you busy for now.

Hope you had a good vacation.

Arthur […]

Thacker's production went into rehearsal while the world premiere of Broken Glass, *directed by John Tillinger, ran at Broadway's Booth Theatre. The play ends with Philip suffering an apparently fatal heart attack.*

Miller to Thacker,
8 June 1994

Dear David,

Since you have a great actress, is it possible to add one more element? If on rising to her feet [Sylvia] took two or three steps toward [Philip], and suddenly realises that she was walking, and stopped in amazement looking down at her legs, and then looked up in astonishment as the curtain comes down. Wow!

The play here has built a wonderful reputation, the word of mouth is very exciting. Audiences are enraptured, I think, nobody stirs from beginning to end, and the final reception is very big. Business is erratic – most nights are sold out, then it gets sparse for a day or two, then they're busy again. I myself doubt we'll beat out *Perestroika* for the Tony but nobody yet knows for sure.

My best to Sylvia,
Arthur

Four days later, Tony Kushner's Perestroika *won the Tony for Best Play. At the Lyttelton,* Broken Glass *was described in* The Sunday Times *as 'one of the great creations of the American theatre', and nominated for Play of the Year at the Oliviers.*

Miller to Thacker,
31 March 1995

Dear David,

In the event that *Broken Glass* wins the Olivier, would you mind thanking those who have chosen the play, and at the same time express my congratulations to a marvelous cast, designer and composer-cellist, and to David Thacker, a rare director who is both mechanic and poet, visionary and agitator, without whom … well, why go on past the climax? Should it be embarrassing to read effusive compliments to you and your production, you might add that I am inclined to exaggeration albeit as a necessary means to convey the simple truth, namely, that you led your actors straight to the heart of my play. Of course if the play does not win the Award, take solace in being spared having to say all this so late at night.

All best,
Arthur […]

Broken Glass won, as did Stott (Best Supporting Actor). Miller's daughter, Rebecca, watched the Lyttelton production.

Miller to Thacker,
24 April 1995

Dear David,

Rebecca phoned here to say that she was nothing short of astonished by your *Glass* production. Went on and on about it and your work in it. I tried disagreeing but got nowhere. You have a fan for life.

Incidentally, it took the *NY Times* seven days to report the Olivier. There's a certain sense of freedom, however, in being so disliked by the most powerful paper, probably, on the planet.

All best,
Arthur

In 2001, in a series of Platforms commemorating one production from each of the National's first 25 years on the South Bank, Broken Glass *was chosen for 1994. Thacker read the following to an audience in the Cottesloe:*

Miller to Thacker, 7 September 2001

This honour to *Broken Glass* and the actors who brought it to life in England, and David Thacker's direction, offers me a perhaps forgivable opportunity to express some long-held feelings of mine towards the British audience, feelings which might seem mawkish spoken of under other circumstances. Put as simply as I can, I want to thank you for your response to my work over these many years. Like most other playwrights I have, from time to time, had a hard row to hoe with critics, and I have not always fared marvelously with them in England either. But I have always felt a certain warmth and welcome from the English audience that has never failed me; the truth is your feeling for my work has brightened some dark days and helped keep alive my faith in the continuation of theater as a significant art form, not alone for me, but for the world. Thanks. Arthur Miller

1995

The Merry Wives of Windsor (1597)
by William Shakespeare
Director: Terry Hands
Olivier, 26 January to 9 August (77 performances)

Terry Hands, formerly boss of the RSC, was making his National debut with The Merry Wives…, *and, in his* Guardian *review, Michael Billington described 'the strange sensation' that he had been watching an RSC production – an assertion privately challenged in writing by Hands and Richard Eyre.*

Michael Billington to Eyre, 2 February 1995

Dear Richard,

[…] Obviously we could argue over the question 'What is an RSC actor?' But a very large number of the key actors in *The Merry Wives* – Brenda Bruce, Geoffrey Freshwater [and six others] – have spent a large part of their careers with the RSC and are strongly identified with that company. I'm not saying they should never move. But seeing so many of them together [at] the National has – let's say – a jolting effect. Which company are we actually watching?

But behind this – as we both know – is a much larger question to do with the identity of our national companies. What worries me a bit is that no one seems prepared to address this issue. In the past the identity of both [national] companies derived from a quasi-permanent team of resident directors who did the bulk of the work. Now, for whatever reason, that system has dissolved. Both you and Adrian [Noble, RSC artistic director] rely increasingly on a rotating team of freelancers – Sam Mendes, Katie Mitchell, Steven Pimlott, Matthew Warchus are simply the most obvious names – who seem to move happily between the two organisations.

Is this simply the post-Thatcherite ethos? Is it deliberate choice? Is it actually healthy? Is it leading towards an inevitable merging of styles?

I know I am not alone in being concerned. And I'd be happy – either publicly or privately – to carry on the debate.

With all good wishes,
    Michael

cc Genista McIntosh, Stephen Wood

The Masterplan redevelopment

In 1994, the NT had submitted a bid for almost £30 million of National Lottery funding for The Masterplan, the largest redevelopment of Denys Lasdun's building since it opened in 1976.

Eyre to Peter Brook, Anthony Hopkins et al., 2 February 1995

Improving the National

[…] Sir Denys Lasdun's striking modernist design, with its undisguised use of textured concrete throughout, made it a controversial building from the start.

Since [1976], 12 million people have seen a performance here and many more have visited for backstage tours, exhibitions, Platform performances or foyer music, to use the Bookshop, to eat and drink – or just to sit on the terraces and enjoy one of the best riverside views in central London. I have never doubted that the building fulfils its brief: providing optimum conditions for staging a wide range of drama and accommodating up to 2,500 people at any one time. But after 18 years' operation it has become clear that the building is a victim of its own success, and some aspects work less well than others.

Our Masterplan [involves] measures drawn up by our current architects, Stanton Williams, to improve the building. Amongst other things we want to enlarge the foyers. […]

We also propose to demolish the walkway which links the building via Waterloo Bridge to the South Bank walkway system. This will let much daylight into the foyers and also allow freer circulation in the new [pedestrianised Theatre Square]. […]

You will be aware from recent press coverage that Sir Denys Lasdun has mounted a fierce campaign to combat our proposals. Unless we can unlock this particular planning inertia, the building will inevitably enter into a spiral of decline and be unable to fulfil its primary purpose. […]

I would ask you to write [to the Planning department at Lambeth Council] to support the principle of [our] being able to change what has become one of the youngest Grade II* Listed Buildings.

If we are unable to move forward I forecast a dismal and disappointing future for the building and its foyers. […]

Richard

Thirty years earlier, Brook had spent many hours with Lasdun on the NT Building Committee, debating the size and shape of the South Bank auditoriums.

Brook, fax to Eyre, 9 February 1995

For Richard to use as he wishes:

A theatre lives in the present. No production is designed to last. In an ideal world, theatres would be demolished and rebuilt in every decade. A wise architect is one who recognises that a theatre must change and evolve like an airport. His commission can never be to build a monument, nor a memorial.

Peter Brook

The Lottery awarded £28.5m to the NT. But the western terrace and pedestrian link to Waterloo Bridge were left intact.

Dealer's Choice (1995)

by Patrick Marber

Director: Patrick Marber
Cottesloe, 9 February to 22 April 1995 (41 performances)

Patrick Marber had made his name as a stand-up comedian, and a writer and performer on the news spoofs On the Hour *and* The Day Today. Dealer's Choice, *which emerged from a workshop at the NT Studio in November 1993, was his first play. It unfolds through a Sunday night and the early hours of Monday morning in a London restaurant, before, during and after the weekly staff poker game. The players include the restaurateur, Stephen, his gambling-addict son, two waiters and the chef, Sweeney.*

Eyre to Patrick Marber, 25 February 1994

Dear Patrick,

[…] I really enjoyed [watching *Dealer's Choice*] and would love to do it here in the Cottesloe next year. Can we meet soon and talk about it?

Best wishes,
Yours,
Richard

Marber to Eyre, 26 April 1994	Dear Richard, […] I asked Sue [Higginson] if I could come in to the Studio for a week in November to work on the next draft with as many of the cast as are available. She said yes. This would give me the opportunity to do another draft between then and rehearsals. Having done this work I think the play will be in fine shape. […] Best wishes, Patrick

Ray Winstone was cast as Sweeney, who stakes – and loses – cash he had planned to spend on taking his five-year-old daughter to the zoo.

Marber to Ray Winstone, 11 November 1994	Dear Ray, […] On the 28th your call is 11.00. There will be a script for you then which you can read over lunch. We'll do a read through at 2.00. Please note this will be a very casual affair. There is nothing covert about the late arrival of this next draft. I have been hassling the writer for some months to get it done but he seems intransigent. At 5.00 we'll have a friendly game of cards (Dealer's Choice). I suggest you learn how to play poker pretty quick or we'll skin you by Christmas. If you want me to teach you call me. […] The purpose of our time at the Studio is to work on the text and the characters, it is not technically speaking a rehearsal period – I will not be blocking anything. We will probably improvise a bit, maybe create whole new scenes for the next draft, it's completely open. I would ask you to think of it as an opportunity to get the most out of your part, to add, to deepen your role in the play. Please feel free that at all times you can contribute to the process. You are a co-creator of the play – that said, don't expect a royalty. In short, all ideas are welcomed, however shit they may be. The second aspect of our time is a more personal thing; you're going to be stuck with me and your fellow actors for quite a few months. The play is an ensemble piece, the second act [poker game] is murderously hard without mutual co-operation and the production will fail if we don't get on with each other. I don't want to read your autobiography in 20 years' time and find out you hated being in *Dealer's Choice*. In short, please air your grievances at all times. I mean this. The structure of this business often circumvents direct communication between the very people who need to be communicating (i.e. ourselves.) […]

Finally, I'm delighted that you're doing this play and I'm really looking forward to working with you.

Best wishes,
Patrick Marber

Dealer's Choice *transferred to the West End, and was named Best Comedy by the* Evening Standard. *Eyre's letter of 25 February 1994 still hangs, framed, in Marber's office in London, commemorating 'the happy day I began to think of myself as a playwright'.*

Skylight (1995)
by David Hare

Director: Richard Eyre
Cottesloe, 4 May to 25 November 1995 (81 performances)

Skylight *is set in the London flat of Kyra Hollis (Lia Williams), a teacher at a comprehensive, who, over 12 hours, receives unexpected visitors: Edward Sargeant (Daniel Betts), 18, then his father, Tom (Michael Gambon), a millionaire businessman and her former lover. She ended their affair three years earlier, when it was discovered by Tom's wife, who has since died. Tom and Kyra reminisce and argue: she's fervently left-wing; he reveres, and profited from, Thatcherism. They go to bed together; after Tom leaves, the play ends with Edward and Kyra tucking into the luxurious breakfast he's brought from the Ritz.*

During pre-production, designer John Gunter's proposal for a traverse configuration in the Cottesloe, which would necessarily have placed Kyra in an apartment without walls, alarmed Hare; he wanted end-on staging, with a more substantial, realistic set.

Eyre to David Hare, 4 February 1995

Dear David,

I've been thinking that maybe it's sensible if you direct *Skylight*. You have the role of de facto director as it is, so maybe we should formalise it. I can't quite see the point of me doing it – perhaps, as you would say, just to save you the chore, I could have fooled myself up till Friday that I was fulfilling some sort of useful function, but when you phoned John without even talking to me about the design, then I realised that I was at best the butler and at worst the skivvy.

Of course it would be childish of me to withdraw: I like the play very much and the actors. But I'm no longer able to see what I can add to it, and wonderful writer and good friend though you are, you've never given me the impression that your plays could not have been as well served by you as director.

So – if you DO want to direct the play now is the moment to say. I'm sure the actors and John would comply, and you'd have no hassle from the Director of the theatre.

Richard

Hare, fax to Eyre,
6 February 1995

Dear Richard,

I've just got your fax.

Actually, as far as I recall, we've had three major artistic differences in five years. The first was about the set of *Racing Demon* (I was wrong), the second was about the prison scene in *Murmuring Judges* (I was wrong again), and the third was about the sets for *The Absence of War* (I was right). In the last two cases, I learnt it was stupid for us not to debate matters right through. You should have pushed me harder about the [prison] scene, but out of misguided respect you held off. It was left to *Time* magazine to make me face the truth. It prompted from you the perfectly fair complaint 'Oh I see, when 50 million mid-Westerners are told something doesn't work, you fix it, but when I tell you, you take no notice.' From the same motives, I didn't argue enough about the heaviness of the sets for *A. of W.* Our relationship ought to be able to encompass some artistic debate.

Of course I want you to direct *Skylight*, and you'll do it much better than I could, because I'm hoping you'll ADD to it, in the same way you've added to the last three. There is, however, a special problem with this one. Over the years we evolved a style together so that by the time of *The Absence of War* we both saw and heard it clearly as soon as we read it. The Platonic production existed in our heads, and you had to realise it. This one is different. You yourself use the word 'Brookian'. But Brook proceeds by experiment, not by pre-determining. It took me many, many months of struggle to get as far as I have in hitting this new tone and I've proceeded by trial and error. It's not surprising if there's going to be some trial and error in its realisation as well. It's only an instinct, but somehow the traverse formation made [Tom and Kyra's] world seem airy and thin. [...]

Love,
David

Staged end-on, Skylight *was critically acclaimed at the Cottesloe. Hare and Eyre wanted to take it into the West End, but Gambon, who, by late July was alternating between Tom and the title role in* Volpone, *in the Olivier, was evidently hesitant about transferring.*

Eyre to Hare,
1 August 1995

I spoke with Mike. The outcome was inconclusive but not without hope. He started by saying sheepishly that he didn't think he could do more than the 81 performances in the Cottesloe; he said he found it incredibly difficult, had never done anything like it, had to always give it massive energy and concentration, every time he did it was like the first time, etc. He longed for me to let him off the hook, but I gave it to him with all barrels. I told him that I had never worked with an actor as good as him, or seen a performance as brilliant, and that was the view of most people that saw the play. He had done three great performances, I said – in *Skylight*, *Galileo* and *View from the Bridge*. He had an obligation to the public and to himself to let people see him. He once said to me that he couldn't forgive people who wasted their talent; I quoted this back at him. Give us a short season in the West End, I said, or you'll regret it all your life, and you'll break David's heart. You have to make a sacrifice: it may be painful but there are compensations – the glory, the money, the fame, and the satisfaction of exercising your genius will outweigh the pain … He looked rather troubled.

I left it that he would think again. He's got a rest coming up. Trish [Montemuro, stage manager] said his performance last night was the best ever – a man possessed, determined, it seems, to prove for himself that what I'd said to him was true – that he's a great actor.

I don't know what to think, but I'm much more optimistic than I was. I've given it my best shot.

Love to you all,
Richard

Gambon agreed, and Skylight *began a 10-week run at Wyndham's in February 1996, the month in which it was named Play of the Year at the Oliviers. It opened on Broadway on 19 September.*

Michael Gambon, card to Eyre, 19 September 1996

Dear Richard,

I'll never be able to thank you for everything you've given me in the last two years – it's all been a great leg up the ladder.
You are brilliant and I owe you one.

Good luck,
Mike

Michael Gambon (Tom) and Lia Williams (Kyra) in *Skylight*. Photo: Nobby Clark

A Streetcar Named Desire (1947)**

by Tennessee Williams

Keith Baxter and Tennessee Williams were good friends from 1970 until the playwright's death in 1983. In the same letter in which Baxter wrote about Ian Charleson's Hamlet, he also elaborated on his request to Eyre to let him direct Williams's best-known drama.

Keith Baxter to Eyre,
10 August 1995

Dear Richard,

I'm awfully glad I came. It solved many things in my mind. First of all: I know myself how horrible it is to have to deal with good (talented) friends [seeking] work, and finding the right comfortable words of negation is AWFUL. And I'm not even a friend of yours! So I know what a job you must have, with hundreds of friends asking a favour, without my harassing you.

Seeing you, being with you, clarified some things in my mind. I never told you how wonderful I thought your production of [*The Night of the*] *Iguana* was. Tenn would really have loved it. […] [Baxter here recalls Ian Charleson's Hamlet; see pp. 220–21.]

When I left you I reflected on the intolerable demands I had made. Don't worry about it. I loved it when you said very bluntly that one of the perks of being a boss was that you could employ yourself! Quite right. It was impertinent of me to expect you to give me one of Tenn's plays to direct. (But I shall do one sometime: some place. You've no idea how much I miss him.) The irony of Peter [Hall's] insistence on his rights to *Streetcar* would not be lost on Tennessee.

But I don't think I'd be right for the National anyway, I'm such a non-establishment person. Losing my way in the corridors (after leaving you) some rather wispy young man barked a 'Who are you? Where are you going?' and I was peremptorily directed to the elevator while he watched to make sure I left in an orderly fashion. While I was waiting in the canteen I was surrounded by actors – some of whom I knew – and I eavesdropped shamefully and not one was talking about work; or a film he'd/she'd seen, or a ballet, or an opera, or an exhibition. The topics of conversation were: was the Interest Rate going to go up; would rehearsals of [Sondheim's] *A Little Night Music* go into overtime.

I think the National is wonderful. And I can't think of anyone who could humanise it better than you, but I felt in an alien world and probably that's what you feel about me, so I can't blame you! I grew up in a different kind of theatre – romantic perhaps, certainly a theatre where feeling spoke more decisively than intellect and I'm too old to change now. As I left I saw some of the company of *Little Night Music* dispersing, and that wispy young man, who had somehow got to the lobby before me, opened the Stage Door with a pointed gesture of goodbye and I wanted to tell him that Stephen Sondheim had supported my petition for a Green Card 15 years ago – along with Tennessee, and Elizabeth Taylor, and Henry Fonda, and Ethel Merman – and Stephen had

written 'Keith Baxter is one of the 10 best – no five best – actors
in England'. But I didn't say anything. I just murmured thank you
and the wispy boy shut the Stage Door on me.

Thank you for letting me waste your time. And all good wishes,
believe me.

Yours ever,
Keith

Mother Courage and Her Children (1941)

by Bertolt Brecht

Version by David Hare (1995)
Director: Jonathan Kent
Olivier, 14 November 1995 to 30 March 1996 (61 performances)

**Diana Rigg, fax
to David Hare,
1 September 1995**

Dear David,

Plodding over the fields, script in hand, giving my Mother
Courage. So far so good, the sheep seem to like it. […]

Diana

**Eyre to Rigg,
10 January 1996**

Dear Diana

I'd have to be extraordinarily thick-skinned not to realise that I
have offended and upset you. I am mortified and embarrassed –
and ashamed. Perhaps I am guilty of a sin of omission.

Jonathan tells me that you think I am unenthusiastic about
your performance and his production. If this is your impression,
then I'm certainly culpable for failing to express to you my very
considerable admiration for what you've done in *Mother Courage*.

It's not much of an exaggeration to say that you are part of the
reason that I became interested in theatre. I saw you first in *Lear*
1962 and was heart-struck by the production and by you. I've
seen most of your theatre work since then, and I am – not to put
too fine a point on it – a fan. Perhaps this makes me somewhat
bashful in your presence, and I have undoubtedly failed to convey
to you that I think you give a really remarkable performance as
Mother Courage.

Unfortunately it turns out that it is <u>physically</u> impossible to
extend the production because of the problem of storing the
set. […]

I do hope we can resolve our misunderstanding, and if I <u>haven't</u>
said it clearly before – thank you for a great performance.

Best wishes,
Richard

Dear Richard,

Many thanks for your letter. I do, totally, understand why *MC*
has to come off. I love playing it, [and] passionately believe in
the strength of David's adaptation and Jonathan's production to
sweep away all those long-held preconceptions of Brecht being
boring and polemic. So, thank you again, and on –

  Diana

FROM DIANA RIGG

Dear Richard
  Many Thanks for your
letter. I do. totally, understand
why M C has to come off,
and am delighted to learn
that it has a possibility of
an extended life. Not only
do I love playing it. but

passionately believe in the
strength of Davids adaptation
and Jonathans production
to sweep away all those long-
held preconceptions of Brecht
being boring and polemic
So. thank you again, and
on ———

                Diana.

1996

Habeas Corpus (1973) and *Kafka's Dick* (1986)**
by Alan Bennett

In June 1995, Robert Lindsay told Eyre he was hoping to make 'a splash' with a dual debut at the NT, as Iago for director Steven Pimlott, and in Habeas Corpus, *as a sex-obsessed Sussex GP, Dr Wicksteed, ideally with Julie Walters as his wife. Matthew Francis was scheduled to direct the comedy in the Lyttelton that December, but in July Bennett withdrew the rights. 'Perhaps he's right,' wrote Eyre in his diary, 'perhaps it would have been the wrong theatre for it. He's very apologetic.' Francis filled the vacant Lyttelton slot with* Rosencrantz and Guildenstern Are Dead. *Eyre and Bennett talked of revisiting* Kafka's Dick, *whose premiere Eyre had directed at the Royal Court.*

Alan Bennett to Eyre, 30 January 1996

Dear Richard,

I've been thinking about *Kafka's Dick*, mostly in terms of design, trying to see if there was a way of peopling the Lyttelton stage around the central action – which is really that of a small domestic farce. The only way I can see of doing it is to surround the play with <u>implications</u>, use them to fill the space – and that of course is exactly what I don't want. Until the Heaven sequence it ought to be a very conventional play & I can see it working in the Cottesloe but not the Lyttelton which would sink it.

Of course the same problem with the Lyttelton affected *Habeas Corpus*. Now Sam [Mendes] has asked again if he can do it at the Donmar. I want to say yes but I don't want it to be shards of ice in the heart time. You've been so good to me at the National & I can't imagine any happier place to work so if it's going to sour your last two years I'll say no – though I still wouldn't want to do it at the Lyttelton as the script is so sparse the performers wouldn't be able to get on and off the stage.

I wish I didn't have to think about all this in a way. I ought to be flattered but it just makes me feel I'm letting you down or thinking too much about my own reputation or the durability of the plays. Depending on who your successor is going to be I suppose I'm being offered the opportunity of a swansong & turning it down. Actually Swan Song would be a good title for something.

Love,
Alan

Kafka's Dick *was not revived. Mendes directed* Habeas Corpus *at the Donmar that May, with Jim Broadbent and Brenda Blethyn as the Wicksteeds. Robert Lindsay has yet to appear at the NT.*

Stanley (1996)
by Pam Gems

Director: John Caird
Cottesloe, 1 February to 17 August (98 performances)

Thirty years after she submitted The Burning Man *to Kenneth Tynan, and 20 after the rejection of* Piaf *and* Queen Christina, *Pam Gems finally had an original script produced at the NT.* Stanley *follows the artist Stanley Spencer (1891–1959) from around 1930 to 1959, exploring his relationship with his first wife, and the mother of his two daughters, the artist Hilda Carline. Their marriage is disrupted by his hopeless erotic obsession with the lesbian artist Patricia Preece.*

Nicholas Wright, memo to Eyre, Genista McIntosh, Jack Bradley, 29 August 1995	<u>*Stanley* Draft 2</u>
	
	I finished the new *Stanley* thinking again how moving and honest it is and how well Pam G. has handled the language and the milieu.
	  It takes its time getting going: there's a bitty, unfocused feeling about the first 20 pages or so… […]
	  Really I think the Stanley/Hilda nexus is what the play is about, and Patricia is only of interest insofar as she affects it. […]
	  Quite a lot to do, but it could be tremendously good.
	
	  N.

Before rehearsals began, Spencer's daughters and executors, Unity and Shirin, read Gems's script, which shows Stanley abandoning Hilda, in part because motherhood meant she could no longer devote herself only to him.

Pam Gems, card to Eyre, 25 November 1995	Dear Richard,
	
	Just thought you'd like to know that Unity, in the ladies' loo last night, said I might do as I wished with the script & that her & Shirin's only real objection was to the one-ball joke, which seems a fair trade-off, tho' I'll miss it. I will go thro' the script nonetheless & make minor alterations for good will. Thank you for yr. support – sorry it took so long!
	
	  Yours,
	  Pam

Ken Pople, author of Stanley Spencer: A Biography *(1991), was sent a script and invited to talk to the cast, which included Antony Sher in the title role and Deborah Findlay as Hilda.*

Ken Pople to
Angela Fairclough
(stage manager),
14 December 1995

Dear Angela,

It was kind of you to invite me to the theatre and to suggest that you would be willing to give me a credit or acknowledgement in publications about the play. Regretfully I must decline both offers.

The play as written will no doubt provide a frisson of theatricality, but to my mind fails as effective dramatisation. Had it used a theoretical painter called, say, Montmorency, and merely shadowed Spencer's life, there could be no complaint. But his life and relationships have been used by Pam Gems to provide sensationalism through the use of material from painstakingly researched documentary sources; this material has then been re-arranged – distorted to the purist – in the interests of stagecraft. More Ben Travers in fact than Ibsen. I ask myself by what right a playwright takes it upon herself to turn the life, art and vision of a dedicated, admired and recently deceased painter into entertainment without enlightenment. I see no justification.

A visit on my part to provide background information would effect only cosmetic patching. Had I been contacted earlier it is feasible that the result, if handled without sentimentality, might have been more acceptably authentic. In reading the script I was lost from Scene Two of Act One, and never really regained my composure. I append comments which might go some way to explaining my feelings.

Sincerely,
Ken

Stanley packed the Cottesloe and was part-way through a three-month season in New York when it won Play of the Year at the Oliviers.

Trevor Nunn, NT Director Designate

The search for the next NT Director – in the offing ever since Eyre announced early in 1994 that he would not seek to renew his contract in autumn 1996 – moved into gear in November 1995, when NT chairman Sir Christopher Hogg convened a succession committee, chaired by Sir Michael Palliser and including Tom Stoppard.

David Hare to
Michael Palliser,
14 December 1995

Dear Sir Michael,

[…] My principal feeling is it is very important that the appointment be made quickly.

Through no fault of Richard's, a difficult interregnum has followed on his decision to announce his departure over two years in advance. This has left everyone who works at the National in an odd state of uncertainty.

Speed is important for two reasons. You owe it to the many staff who have already had a year of not knowing what their futures are. [...]

I have worked at the National under all three of its Directors. With the benefit of this experience, I ask you to make your ruling priority to choose a real theatre brain, who will reject the dissonant jargon of 'product' and 'marketplace' and who believes that the work on the stage is more important than running some ludicrous PR campaign to 'position the National's public identity'.

If, as I understand, you intend to take until July to decide, I fear a leakage of talent from what has till lately been a very happy theatre.

Yours sincerely,
David Hare

The press had made Sam Mendes, then running the Donmar Warehouse, and Stephen Daldry, boss of the Royal Court, joint front runners (Daldry assumed Mendes to be Eyre's 'chosen heir'), but neither committed to accepting the job.

On 30 January 1996, Stoppard and Hogg had lunch with Trevor Nunn. He was 55 and had been freelance, directing for theatre, opera and film, since stepping down as joint artistic director of the RSC in 1986, with no intention of ever 'taking on another building or company'. But, at a press conference in the Olivier stalls foyer on 7 March 1996, Nunn sat alongside Eyre and Hogg, as Director Designate.

Peter Brook to Trevor Nunn, 7 March 1996

Dear Trevor,

What splendid news! Through the period of dark rumours, I was praying you'd take this task – you are the only person who is able to know what, why, when and how!

Every wish!
Peter

*Fast Food***
by Abi Morgan

Abi Morgan was 27, and had yet to have a play professionally produced, when her attachment to the NT Studio included eight half-day tutorials with the playwright Stephen Wakelam, in which they worked on her script Fast Food.

Stephen Wakelam to Diane Borger (NT Studio), 19 March 1996

Dear Diane,

She was, of all the writers I've dealt with, the most delightful (the first female, though that's incidental). I also think the play she has been writing here at the Studio is the most promising since I worked with Jonathan Harvey. Not so commercial but more ambitious.

We had a gap in the middle where we talked by phone – I working on my play, she on hers. She encouraged and criticised me: a two-way process.

I expect her to produce her play in the next few weeks. It is technically quite complex. Her main problem at the start was how to stage it – a problem that had spoilt the play she wrote previous to her work at the Studio. I think she is well on the way to solving this but will need some time with actors, a director and designer.

In short, hard-working and talented. Maybe more than that. […]

Best wishes,
Stephen

Abi Morgan to Jack Bradley (NT literary manager), 30 October 1996

Dear Jack,

I do have this vision every time we speak on the phone that you are somehow crouched under your desk talking to me while a board meeting carries on around you. It's not just your hushed tone, more a feeling that you are a streak of anarchy and wit floating amongst the powers that be of theatre.

You must have this very odd image of me: one minute I am fending off bolshy [NT] security guards and engineers mending towel dispensers, the next threatening to swan off to France, like a right prima donna. And I say I'm a writer? Stephen keeps telling me I've got to write about my deeply middle-class roots i.e. all the pretensions and none of the cash which the general juggling of life just explained thus represents. I think they'd walk out of the theatre in their hordes.

Just to say once again, thank you for your interest in the play. I'd love to do a week's workshop and trust your instincts implicitly. It is an ambitious play and may be a bit of Emperor's New Clothing i.e. take away the trickery and there is not a lot there, but a week as a springboard to answer some of these questions is a treat. I look forward to it.

Cheers, Jack.
Abi Morgan

Fast Food *was directed by Marianne Elliott at the Royal Exchange Studio, Manchester, in 1999. Morgan would go on to win Bafta and Emmy awards as screenwriter of* Sex Traffic *(2004) and* The Hour *(2011), and her films include* The Iron Lady *and* Suffragette.

1997

Closer (1997)

by Patrick Marber

Director: Patrick Marber
Cottesloe, 29 May to 20 September 1997 (58 performances)
Lyttelton, 16 October 1997 to 3 February 1998 (55 performances)

Closer follows four characters in contemporary London. Dan (Clive Owen in the Cottesloe) writes newspaper obituaries, falls in love and moves in with Alice (Liza Walker), a former stripper. Larry (Ciarán Hinds), a dermatologist, marries Anna (Sally Dexter), a photographer, whose affair with Dan breaks up her marriage and his relationship with Alice – who then has an affair with Larry. Both original pairings reunite again, and separate again.

Roy Waters to Patrick Marber, 30 May 1997

Dear Mr Marber,

As I filed out of the Cottesloe on Tuesday I saw you at the back of the stalls and wanted to convey how much I had been moved by your play but was inhibited by the fact that we are strangers. As soon as I was outside I wished I had at least made some gesture, like thumbs-up.

I have tried in the attached letter to communicate my response to [Jack] the friend who gave me the ticket. It is meant as a tribute. If I am wide of the mark, set it down to my senility. In either case there is no need to reply.

Yours faithfully,
Roy Waters

Dear Jack,

Just a note to thank you for the invitation to *Closer*.

I'm not much good as a theatre companion, as I can never gather my thoughts quickly enough after the curtain has come down to be able to engage in any useful discussion. I am still living in the world of the play, even if it's bad. My responses don't settle in my mind until I've let my thoughts move randomly over the piece on my way home, and then slept on it.

Not that I'm all that much clearer about *Closer* now. I liked it. No: I thought it was very fine. But it left me feeling uncomfortable and drained.

Though I never quite identified with [the characters] as real people, yet I was totally engaged with their feelings: lust, separation, betrayal, resentment, jealousy, violence, vengeance, loneliness, desolation. It was a passionate play, set in a milieu in which passion was destructive. It also seemed to me disturbingly pessimistic, like Strindberg (though without his misogyny).

It was, of course, shatteringly intense, like the later Ibsen. There was Ibsen, too, in the question of the dubious virtue of honesty in human relationships. Neither of the men, who made so much of the need to know the truth, had any idea how to handle it. […]

I can't believe that Patrick Marber simply wanted to unmask us all as mutually emotionally destructive sado-masochists. So what did he want to do? Perhaps the reviews will enlighten me – I fear that I am being obtuse.

The performances seemed to me to be impeccable and the pacing of the piece relentless and powerful.

Thank you again for inviting me to what I believe to have been an important theatrical event.

Sincerely,
Roy

Those reviews were, mostly, raves: 'I'd be astonished if there's a better new play this year' (Daily Telegraph)*; Marber has 'the most assured sense for dramatic rhythm of any English playwright' since Pinter* (Financial Times)*.*

Ciarán Hinds (Larry) and Sally Dexter (Anna)
in *Closer.* Photo: Hugo Glendinning

Dear Patrick,

I want to congratulate you on *Closer* – as a director too, because I think it's wonderful work, but what a brilliant play it is, which I admired in several different ways, most of all for how it feels stripped down without losing its juice – and the structure is so adroit, masterly. I look forward to reading it, it wasn't out when I was there, which was a couple of weeks ago – I wrote then, in the first gush, interfering, with my lit crit, didn't post it, went to Ireland, but it was sheer enthusiasm, I loved every detail and was pleased for the Theayter – that it could do this, provide this, so eat your heart out, Martins and Julians, and so forth; how childish but yes.

Yours,
Tom

With some cast changes, Closer *transferred first to the Lyttelton, then the Lyric on Shaftesbury Avenue, shortly after it won the Olivier for Best Comedy.*

In January 1999, Marber was staying at the Algonquin in New York, ahead of Closer's *Broadway premiere at the Music Box Theatre. The cast was Ciarán Hinds (Larry), Rupert Graves (Dan), Natasha Richardson (Anna) and Anna Friel (Alice).*

Dear Richard,

Rehearsals start on Monday for N.Y. *Closer.* I just wanted to tell you how much your faith in me/my work has changed my life. None of this would be happening if it weren't for you. I'm more grateful than I have the talent to express. […]

Patrick

Marber watched Closer *several times after it opened on 25 March, then flew home to London.*

Dear Anna, Natasha, Ciarán & Rupert,

Greetings from London. I miss you, love you etc. I'm still a bit lagged and frazzled, so apologies for giving general notes rather than absolute specifics, these will follow in a day or so.

I think it's very important that you all meet before every show in the Green Room for five minutes or so at the half. Just to say hi to each other, discuss the previous show etc.

The more in communication you are with each other the better the show will be. Now you're not having daily notes I feel you need to take collective responsibility for what's happening out there. I'm not asking for a nightly 'love-in', just for you four to create a forum for airing your views and getting connected with each other prior to every performance.

Saturday's perf. was slightly lacking in 'love'. The play was dramatically true but a little too cool emotionally.

Don't forget the giddy excitement of strangers falling in love.

Unless you are charmed/besotted/amused by each other in Scenes, 1, 2, 4, 5 we won't feel for you when love comes undone in Scene 6. Similarly, when shit hits the fan in Act 2 always remember that love not <u>power</u> is driving you to behave as you do. The manipulative power games in the play are rooted in desperation and vulnerability – pretty much from the word go. […]

Closer is a play about many things but as a piece of writing it's entirely rhythmic and it's set to a fast beat.

Before you go on, imagine an LP called '*Closer*'… on the label it says 'Play Loud' AND 'Think Quick'. Sometimes it's a case of literally speaking the words faster but mostly it's about giving your character your own intelligence. Trust now that you don't have to get your thoughts in order before you speak them, let them tumble out like they do in real life – unguarded, uncensored, unplayed. You might feel vulnerable but that's what is wanted. In real life we improvise, we never <u>play</u> intentions, we <u>speak</u> them instinctively and we don't ever ACT – because we don't have the time. […]

Enough said. Have fun. Love each other. Speak up.

Make your acting open – we want your genuine human vulnerability.

Be proud of your work, you should be, it's excellent.

And make the play <u>yours</u>. There are 1,000 people out there wanting to have an amazing experience – go get 'em!

Love to you all,
Patrick

Mike Nichols to
Marber, 7 May 1999

Dear Patrick,

Closer in New York is playing even better than it read. I thought the performances were wonderful. Natasha is seriously sexy on top of being so good. I liked all the actors enormously. I think the style in which you're doing it is just right and the idea of piling up the furniture and the detritus [upstage] works extremely well.

There is great power in your play and in your production and the resonance still has me unsettled a month or more after seeing it.

I hope life and work are going well for you. I'm in Los Angeles just starting a picture. Should you get to LA during the next three and a half months I will be here shooting. It would be nice to have another meal.

All the best,
Mike

Nichols would go on to direct Marber's screenplay of Closer, *with Clive Owen (Larry), Jude Law (Dan), Julia Roberts (Anna) and Natalie Portman (Alice). The film was released in the US on 3 December 2004, and soon watched by the writer of Nichols's previous screen project,* Angels in America.

Tony Kushner, email
to Mike Nichols,
12 December 2004

Meister,

I went last night to the 10.30 screening of *Closer* at the local oogaplex.
What a BEAUTIFUL BEAUTIFUL BRILLIANT movie.
Heartbreaking and tough and exquisitely written, and acted, and
above all else, DIRECTED – [using *Così fan tutte* on the soundtrack]
was entirely apposite, it's just like *Così*, clear ice with a smoky fire
burning inside, advanced calculus and Euclidean geometry barely
covering, and then failing entirely to cover, shattering pain. None of
the people have ever been so good before, but that's not surprising,
that always happens when actors work with you. And the script is
very very smart, wise even; I'm jealous. Anyway, it's perfect. My head
is full of images and lines and moments. […]

   And the theatre, by the way, was sold out, as it had been all day,
every show.

   TK

The Invention of Love (1997)
by Tom Stoppard

Director: Richard Eyre
Cottesloe, 1 October to 29 November (28 performances)
Lyttelton, 22 December 1997 to 25 April 1998 (72 performances)

The Invention of Love – *Eyre's final production as Director – revolves around the poet and
classical scholar A.E. Housman (1859–1936), whom Tom Stoppard splits in two, as AEH,
aged 77; and, from ages 18 to 26, as Housman, first seen as an Oxford undergraduate, filled
with unrequited passion for a heterosexual fellow student, Moses Jackson.*
   *We encounter John Ruskin, Walter Pater and Oscar Wilde, who, after his release from jail,
alludes to the play's title: 'Before Plato could describe love, the loved one had to be invented.'*
   After Eyre missed out on Arcadia, *Stoppard promised to let him direct his next play,
hopeful that it would be ready before Trevor Nunn became Director on 1 October 1997.*

Tom Stoppard to
Eyre, 20 May 1994

Dear Richard,

This is the first of who knows how many occasional notes keeping
you abreast. I have designated May, June, July and August for
writing the Housman play. Just now, in comical despair, I counted
up the Housman/Roman books on the table: 85. Really I'm still
reading, and re-reading what I spent January reading and half-
forgot in February. God knows where the play is in all this: not
visible to me yet. I think there is a play somewhere, but I suspect
it may not be as ingratiating as *Arcadia*, in the sense of rattling-
good-yarn or any yarn at all. The fibres are, probably, AEH's
hopeless lifelong love for a heedless hetero; his very witty withering
contempt for rival scholars; the Labouchère Amendment (1885)
under which Wilde was prosecuted, and the Wilde trials and the
homosexual scene in the 1880s/90s generally; and all of that in
opposition to love and sex in the Roman world of the late republic
and early empire. I have a notion that it's really about the idea of a

Golden Age 'back then', always back then, never now. And about biography. And about frustration. *Arcadia* without the jokes or a plot. Now I've used three of my sixteen weeks and I'm nowhere. If you're alarmed, you're not half as alarmed as I am.

Yours,
Tom

**Stoppard to Eyre,
10 November 1994**

Dear Richard,

You must be wondering about Housman. *Hapgood, Indian Ink* and *Arcadia II*, not to mention 3 *Men in a Boat* and [my screenplay for the proposed film of] *Cats*, etc. have obviously put a halt to it and I'm grieved for myself that I never got as far as 'finding' it. This is just to say I feel exactly the same about it as before (i.e. I love it, and want to do it); and to ask you, if it's not a big secret, how long will you be there at the NT?! – Is late '95/early '96 all right?* – you hinted that there was a time limit. *Ind Ink* opens at the end of Feb. and I want to go back to Housman, of course, next.

I hope you're having a good time at the opera [directing *La Traviata* at Covent Garden].

Yours ever,
Tom

* I wish I hadn't said that.

**Stoppard to Eyre,
3 June 1996**

Dear Richard,

I thought I should write you a note at each change of month: my Save the Slot campaign. I keep at it. I'm going away for six days (from Thursday) but taking it with me. I like working in hotels.

My progress is slow – half a dozen pages – because I'm resisting a form which in the end I'll probably have to give in to, that is, I'm resisting some kind of interlocutor between the story/events and the audience. I would prefer the audience to have direct access to the proper story, but the latter has (a) almost nothing by way of a plot and (b) an excess of specialised reference requiring explanation (Latin, textual criticism, Pater, Ruskin, Jowett, Pattison, Wilde, Labouchère, etc.), and the chronology is odd: time and space, and fact and fiction, are necessarily free-form. In a nutshell, I don't know whether I'm writing *Arcadia* or *Travesties* and until I do know, it won't take off. […]

Of course, I'm having a lovely time. I wish all my life was like this, as it is meant to be: two hours in the London Library, among books which have not been withdrawn for years. For a two-line speech. But I'm dreadfully aware of the shadow over me: what is our slot? Can I have till Christmas? November? If earlier, would you be willing to schedule it on the basis of reading the first Act? These are not necessarily unrhetorical questions – you can treat them as rhetorical for as long as may be.

Love,
Tom

**Stoppard to Eyre,
11 July 1996**

Dear Richard,

[…] Well – JULY. 17 pages. Very slow despite dogged application. I think it may have reached the point of ertia if that's a word. I'll just keep going. It's turning into a sort of dream play with lots of characters (but doubling up somewhat). It's slow because there's not much story to tell me what to do next, so I have to be clever every page and a half to stop it sitting down and talking about itself.

No point in saying more for the moment.

Yours,
Tom

Early in 1997, David Hare was completing a biographical play about Wilde's affair with Lord Alfred Douglas, and learned that Wilde featured in Stoppard's latest.

**Stoppard to David
Hare, 26 February
1997**

Dear David,

[…] You mustn't get bothered about my Wilde & your Wilde – you didn't seem to have understood that I keep him off-stage except for one scene (unwritten – and maybe I'll change my mind & not bring him on at all. I wish I knew.) I haven't got as far as him and have many bridges to cross. It's kind of you to offer but I mustn't read your play yet – I'll only envy it, and if it reveals an inch of common ground that would be an inch I couldn't give mine, perhaps. […]

Yours,
Tom

The Invention of Love was sent to Paul Scofield, then starring in Eyre's John Gabriel Borkman revival, but he did not wish to play AEH, despite finding the script 'so wise and witty, and fascinating'.

In mid-April, Stoppard gave Eyre a revised draft, which was sent to Nigel Hawthorne.

**Nigel Hawthorne to
Eyre, 28 April 1997**

Dear Richard,

I expect you will have heard that it isn't possible for me to consider *The Invention of Love*.

Peter Brook rang over the weekend – as Tom did – and it now appears that [Peter's] film is moving forward and that we will be rehearsing it [in] August. It's a project he's been talking about for well over a year now and we've had a number of meetings. Even so, one never knows with films. Having spent over 45 years thinking that theatre people were all vague and hopelessly unreliable, I now acknowledge their dependability and steadfastness and find that the real villains lurk in the film world. It's been a year of perhaps and maybes and the only thing I can do with Peter is hear the positive tones in his voice and, in the absence of a contract, ally myself to them.

I'm very sad to have missed the opportunity of working with you at the National. What an astonishing period it has been. One that has brought you and the building a huge amount of success. I'm sure you must long to be shed of all the administrative responsibility and work on your own projects – even have a decent holiday. But it will be hard for Trevor Nunn to crank himself up to your momentum and I don't envy his taking over.

Your kindness and warmth to me personally, and also to Trevor [Bentham, Hawthorne's partner], I shall always remember.

I wasn't wedded to Tom's play. I felt such an uninformed nincompoop at the end. Longed for him to write more passionately and move away from the intellectually discursive into emotional confrontation. But I suppose that's not Tom, is it? So, perhaps, even if I'd been free to do the play, I would have found it awkward to decide on something so emotionally restrained. But there, that decision was not required of me.

I've missed the chance, and an historic one at that – your final production – of working with you, which is something I've wanted to do for a very long time, and can only hope the opportunity one day will crop up again

Whatever happens, Trevor and I wish you well.

In admiration,
    Yours affectionately,
        Nigel

The Brook/Hawthorne film project did not go ahead. The Invention… went into production with John Wood as AEH and Paul Rhys as Housman.

Stoppard won his fifth Evening Standard New Play award, and, shortly before its West End transfer in November 1998, he thanked Eyre for giving The Invention… 'such legs, and such sights & sounds &, above all, coherence'. By then, for the Almeida, Eyre had also directed The Judas Kiss – David Hare's drama about Wilde.

The end of the Eyre years

Richard Eyre had been knighted in the 1997 New Year's Honours. While The Invention of Love was in preview, he cleared out the Director's office. He described his leaving party on Saturday 27 September as 'the best – and most overwhelming' celebration of his life. The final entry in his published diary sums up a decade of 'plays, productions, meetings, companies, negotiations, despair, joy and endless talk'. The following speaks to the ethos that underpinned his tenure.

Eyre, Report to NT Board, 29 January 1995

I am still filming *The Absence of War* for the BBC and I apologise to the Board for my absence at an important meeting.

Every year we make what one might call an educated guess about our box office targets – it might more accurately be called an act of faith. I believe it is proper for a large-scale publicly funded theatre to set a high goal for attendance, and I would not seek to disguise my disappointment that we have failed to meet that goal in the current financial year. It is always going to be difficult to find the right repertoire for a 1,100-seat auditorium and a 900-seat auditorium. These are not small theatres, designed for an insulated coterie of self-regarding theatre buffs; they are large, in some ways unwieldy, formidable, technically challenging, public spaces.

We demand of ourselves that our work aims at the highest possible artistic standards, and it is rightly demanded of us that the work is popular and accessible. So we tread a tightrope, balancing risk with safety, and ambition with caution. It is never enough just to say 'These are the plays that we want to do regardless of the consequences'. The least and most we can do is to try to do our best work in good faith; if audiences fail to respond we must resist despondency, try again, succeed or as Samuel Beckett said – fail better. […]

Richard Eyre

Ken Campbell, fax to Eyre, 10 February 1997

The Dramatick Fayre
Of Sir Richard Eyre –
Will we see its like again?
No, thinkes Ken.

Ken Campbell

FROM : Campbellken   10 Feb. 1997 10:26PM P1

The Dramatick Fayre
Of Sir Richard Eyre –
Will we see its like again?
No, thinkes Ken.

Ken Campbell.

The Trevor Nunn Years

—

1997–2003

The start of the Nunn years

Trevor Nunn had known Richard Eyre since directing him as Seyton in a student production of Macbeth *in Cambridge in 1962. With great warmth, Eyre introduced Nunn to hundreds of NT staff in the Olivier in June 1997, hoping that 'you transfer the loyalty and the commitment you have shown to me over the past ten years to Trevor.'*

Nunn told his audience that standstill grants from the Arts Council meant the NT was about £1.5 million worse off, in real terms, than three years earlier, and he would therefore have no choice but to programme fewer shows per year than Eyre.

One defining aspect of his tenure would be the volume, and critical and commercial success, of his own productions, including Shakespeare, new plays by David Edgar and Tom Stoppard, and musical revivals (Oklahoma!, South Pacific, My Fair Lady and Anything Goes).

Though it opened just before he became Director, he viewed An Enemy of the People *as 'in spirit, planning', the first show of his regime.*

An Enemy of the People (1882)
by Henrik Ibsen

Version by Christopher Hampton (1997)
Director: Trevor Nunn
Olivier, 19 September 1997 to 20 June 1998 (85 performances)

Ian McKellen had known Nunn since they acted together at Cambridge in 1960, and had played Macbeth and Iago in two of Nunn's most acclaimed RSC productions. In An Enemy…, he was Dr Stockmann, who jeopardises the economy of his home town by revealing that its supposedly revitalising spa waters are poisoned.

Nunn, postcard to Ian McKellen, 19 September 1997	Dearest Ian, Your vigour and invention and inspirational vitality are undimmed after years of film work; it is incredible to me that you still wrestle the tiger with all the unquenchable energy and dissatisfaction for easy answers that I have always found in you. It's wonderful for the NT to have you back, and much more wonderful for me to have you in this nerve-wracking symbolic production. Have a great night, keep it simple and enjoy a triumph which is deeply deserved. Love always, Trevor

Opposite: Andrew French and Trevor Nunn in rehearsal for *The Merchant of Venice*. Photo: Catherine Ashmore

With An Enemy... *still running, and McKellen committed to playing Captain Hook in* Peter Pan *in the Olivier from December 1998, he and Nunn formulated a plan for him to stay on and lead an ensemble in several plays, including Shakespeare.*

Nunn to McKellen, 30 March 1998	Dearest Ian,

Well, I am devastated of course. The decision you have arrived at to do <u>three</u> plays at West Yorkshire instead of two means that I lose you altogether from the first group of plays that our new NT ensemble would be doing at the Olivier and Cottesloe, and your need to do film work later in the year means I lose you from the second phase of that work. So, all that talk we have had about building a company together, and changing the course of the National both artistically and economically, is going to come to nothing.

Obviously, I am puzzled about what West Yorkshire has done to deserve your decision that you are going to realise this dream with them and not with me. What are the plays? What are the parts? What is the lure?

My biggest immediate problem is that I have said to rather a lot of people on the NT Board that I am building a company with you, and I will now have to explain that I had got that wrong.

Obviously, I must go ahead – I am too committed personally and in planning terms to retreat now. But it will seem like a very different kind of adventure without you and one that begins mightily disadvantaged, making do without your leadership and inspiration, and indeed the daily consultation I had imagined we would be sharing.

Let's start talking about the year 2000. Can I stake a claim for the National to have its greatest leading actor back by then, or has Jude already managed to get in ahead of me?

Love <u>always</u> whatever,
Trevor

For Jude Kelly, artistic director of West Yorkshire Playhouse, McKellen played Prospero in The Tempest, *vainglorious actor Gary Essendine in Coward's* Present Laughter *and Dr Dorn in Chekhov's* The Seagull. *Then, after appearing as Magneto, chief villain in* X-Men, *he would spend 2000 filming in New Zealand, as Gandalf in* The Lord of the Rings. *He did not appear at the NT again during Nunn's tenure.*

1998

Ophelia**
by Bryony Lavery

Bryony Lavery had written Ophelia, *a version of the* Hamlet *story, for amateur dramatic groups in Milton Keynes in 1996. Then, in August 1997, came the death of Princess Diana.*

Bryony Lavery
to Jack Bradley,
26 January 1998

Dear Jack,

[…] I have a new idea for a commission. Annie Castledine [director] and I are very keen to do it together. We are both *extremely* excited and want to come in and give you an idea of it!

I enclose a very brief outline. […]

Lots of love.

Yours sincerely,
Bryony

OPHELIA

A proposal for a full-length play about monarchy …

This is *Hamlet*, set in Elsinore, with its existing characters, but in the parallel present. The play focuses on Ophelia … beautiful, popular, seemingly powerless … not quite royal … with a troubled relationship with an ageing, difficult King-in-waiting. […]

There are various political backstage manoeuvrings which shake and topple the existing monarchy … and result in the death of its most popular, most unroyal member … Ophelia… […]

The character Ophelia seems to me to offer an opacity to explore the continuing fascination with Diana. We can investigate the events and behaviours surrounding her death without offending taste.

It should be written, and written soon. It will be fascinating and dangerous and intellectually and emotionally challenging! Perfect!

BRYONY LAVERY – JANUARY 1998

Nunn to Bryony
Lavery, 16 February
1998

Dear Bryony,

[…] I am not convinced that you have found the right vehicle for your Diana play. *Hamlet* is so specific a model and so not about monarchy that it's hard to see why you should place such an enormous obstacle in your path.

Surely *Hamlet* is Shakespeare's play about death, perceived largely through the articulate and disturbed response of a young man somewhere between adolescence and adulthood. […]

I think you are planning to give yourself insurmountable problems. I will be there cheering if you pull it off, but because I don't believe you are on the right track, I have to pass on your proposal. Let's talk about what you might do after that.

Best wishes,
Trevor Nunn

Lavery did not write her Diana play. Her drama about a child murderer, Frozen, *opened at Birmingham Rep in 1998, directed by Bill Alexander, and became her first NT credit when Alexander revived it at the Cottesloe in 2002.*

Copenhagen (1998)
by Michael Frayn

Director: Michael Blakemore
Cottesloe, 28 May 1998 to 27 January 1999 (88 performances)

Jack Bradley, memo
to Richard Eyre,
18 December 1996

Copenhagen – Michael Frayn

The ghosts of physicists Heisenberg, Niels Bohr and his wife Margrethe replay and reflect upon a meeting in Copenhagen in 1941 when the German Heisenberg came to ask his half-Jewish mentor, Bohr, whether the Allied Forces were developing an atomic bomb.

The play is, intentionally, an exemplum of [Heisenberg's] Uncertainty Principle – that even the process of objective observation affects and alters the thing observed – as these figures attempt to identify one another's true motives at that meeting. To this effect, Frayn uses the device of aside as commentary to demonstrate the theory in its application to human relationships.

Whilst this is a deft idea, I found the play static and frankly uninvolving with little actual drama, despite a wonderfully potent idea at its centre. Bohr's moral responsibility of assisting in Los Alamos as against Heisenberg's work for Nazi Germany to produce a nuclear reactor (but not a bomb); the irony that anti-Semitism depleted the German scientific institutions of the very minds who created the nuclear breakthrough for the Allies – these are rich themes. But they are not experienced as drama. It feels like Frayn's device to wed his story to Heisenberg's theory is his very undoing.

Jack

Michael Frayn to Eyre, 20 December 1996

Dear Richard,

Many thanks for your rapid and generous response to the play.

I entirely agree about its needing a small theatre. The Cottesloe would obviously be the best possible place in London, and I'm sorry there's no chance of that [before your time as Director ends]. I've always particularly longed to have something done under your aegis, and I thought there might have been one last hope.

But if you would show it to Trevor I'd be grateful. [...]

Yours,
Michael

From 1975 to 1990, Michael Codron had produced seven of Frayn's original plays, and Michael Blakemore had directed five of them.

Frayn to Michael Blakemore, 23 January 1997

Dear Michael,

A cool response from Michael C. to *Copenhagen*:

'Great stimulation and enjoyment – as well as puzzlement ... The fragility of our existence in the 1940s you have illuminated in a strikingly original fashion. I have to say the states of Complementarity and Uncertainty were hitherto unknown to me. More certain am I, that if there is a definite commitment from Trevor [for] the Cottesloe, it is the right path to choose however long and irksome the wait.' [...]

Yours,
Michael

Blakemore directed Copenhagen *with David Burke (Bohr), Sara Kestelman (Margrethe) and Matthew Marsh (Heisenberg), and it was heralded as a 'brilliant, brave and demanding' play (*Mail on Sunday*), in which Frayn 'made ideas sing and zing' (*Daily Telegraph*).*

Frayn to Nunn, 14 June 1998

Dear Trevor,

[...] Yes, I'm delighted that the play's been received so well – I could only too easily imagine reviews that dismissed it as a dry sixth-form debate. A lot of the credit should go – as reviewers have recognised – to Michael B., for making it work, from the script stage onwards. He's brought it to life in three dimensions, in his dogged, careful, wily way, whilst fully respecting the simplicity and austerity of the convention. Also to the cast, in whom, after all our difficulties, we have been very blessed.

Not everybody by any means could see the force of the piece on paper, but you did, and you stuck with it throughout. We were very cheered by your support, and very grateful for your flexibility in agreeing to stage it in the round, in spite of the difficulties. So thank you. [...]

Yours,
Michael

a new play by
Michael Frayn

COPENHAGEN

David Burke
Sara Kestelman
Matthew Marsh

Director
Michael Blakemore
Designer
Peter J Davison
Lighting Designer
Mark Henderson

Royal National Theatre

Frayn to Lord
and Lady Annan,
3 November 1998

Dear Noel,

I'm absolutely delighted that you and Gabriele both enjoyed *Copenhagen*. I set a great deal of store by your opinions.

I'm rather taken aback by the success. I had long given up the hope of writing another play that would catch people's interest, and by the time I'd finished this one I'd even lost all serious expectation that anyone would ever attempt to produce it. [...]

    Yours,
      Michael

Having won the Evening Standard *award for Best Play,* Copenhagen *transferred to the Duchess Theatre. In 2000 it opened on Broadway with American actors. Frayn won the Tony for Best Play, and Blakemore Best Director of a Play* and *Best Director of a Musical, for reviving* Kiss Me, Kate *– the first such double in the awards' 53-year history.*

Frayn to Nunn,
20 June 2000

Dear Trevor,

[...] Yes, it's remarkable how the tedium of awards ceremonies is reduced, in retrospect at any rate, if you win something. What most particularly pleased me, and lifted the evening to transcendence, was Michael B.'s amazing double-header. He has not had all the recognition he should at these occasions, mostly because he usually does new plays, and no one knows quite what his contribution has been. [...]

    Yours,
      Michael

1999

Harry Potter and the Philosopher's Stone (1997)**
by J. K. Rowling

Jack Bradley, memo
to Nunn, 15 March
1999

Re: FAMILY SHOWS – 2001 and onwards

Harry Potter and the Philosopher's Stone is the new cult children's novel. J. K. Rowling was the hit of the Edinburgh Book fair and children make pilgrimage to King's Cross station in search of the imaginary Platform 9¾ from which Harry departs for wizard's school.

The book is extraordinary, as are the characters who display enduring charm through it and its several sequels. Of course, the [film] rights were pre-sold (in this case to Warner Bros. [although] technically the stage rights are available). I made a preliminary enquiry of the agent Christopher Little. He was very interested to entertain any approach the RNT might make and I thought would be supportive – were you to be interested – in interceding with Warner Bros. on his client's and our behalf. […]

Jack

Bradley to Emma Schlesinger (Christopher Little Literary Agency), 17 February 2000

Dear Emma Schlesinger,

Harry Potter – J. K. Rowling. Thank you for your letter with the unsurprising but saddening news of the stage rights [not being available until October 2006]. I must say with Harry so far only half way through his days at Hogwarts, and a new adventure promised annually, I imagine our enthusiasm for a stage version will be all the sharper by 2006, so I would implore you to consider us first should you wish a stage version to be presented.

In the meantime please convey my warmest wishes to J. K. Rowling, who has made the problem of present buying for my nieces and nephews a thing of the past.

Yours sincerely,
Jack Bradley

Sleep with Me (1999)
by Hanif Kureishi

Director: Anthony Page
Cottesloe, 22 April to 17 July 1999 (44 performances)

Sixteen years after submitting his Dostoevsky adaptation, Hanif Kureishi had made his NT debut with a version of Brecht's Mother Courage *(Cottesloe, 1993) – but he had yet to have an original script produced on the South Bank.*

Hanif Kureishi to Nunn, 4 September 1997

Dear Trevor,

Thanks so much for your lovely letter. It was good of Nicky Wright to speak to you, and your enthusiasm has cheered me up.

I have indeed been writing a play. It is called *Weekend*, and has eight characters. I've done half of it and I'm pretty certain of the rest of it. When I've got through it I'd like to show it to you. I think I'd like to hear it read – or moved about a bit – at an early stage so as to get some sense of what it might sound like, before returning to it.

The National is the place I'd like it to be done. It was the first place I thought of. It is clearly going to be exciting there. I'd love to be involved.

If you like the play and want me to continue working on it, I would accept a commission. But at this stage I don't think there's much point.

As soon as I've got all the way through it I'll show it to you. Thanks again for writing.

All the best,
Hanif

Kureishi's original title refers to the country-house weekend shared by the play's eight characters, including Stephen and Charles, middle-aged friends with successful TV careers, but Sleep with Me *was a much stronger name for this 'enticing comedy of bad sexual manners' (*Evening Standard*).*

The Merchant of Venice (c.1594)

by William Shakespeare

Director: Trevor Nunn
Cottesloe, 17 June to 13 November (55 performances)
Olivier, 29 November 1999 to 10 May 2000 (59 performances)

The Merchant of Venice *featured the NT Ensemble, whose season began with Trevor Nunn's* Troilus and Cressida *in the Olivier in March.*

Nunn to Richard Eyre, 18 January 1999

Dear Richard,

[…] I started last week with my 40 actors engaged for a year. They are a good bunch, and I am pleased with their multi-discipline composition; they include wonderful singers and dancers, and all of them came through the Shakespeare auditions. But I would be the last person to claim that just because they are on long-term contracts, they are as yet an ensemble, and I know that whether they become one or not has no bearing on whether the work is good, or successful. Still, it's something I wanted to try again for myself, so I am happy to have made a start. […]

Think of me, occasionally, working from 9.00am to midnight every day, and smile with relief …

Love as always,
And happy new year,
Trevor

Nunn brought the action of The Merchant… *forward to the 1930s, so that Henry Goodman's Shylock fell victim to prejudice that evoked European anti-Semitism in the run-up to the Second World War.*

**Peter Brook to Nunn,
1999**

Dear Trevor,

What a thrill! Your *Merchant* is one of the best Shakespeare productions I've ever seen – it illuminates every aspect of this normally patchy and unsatisfactory play and discovers an underlying coherence and human meaning that binds it all into a whole. Extraordinary Goodman! Rarest of all, it becomes contemporary not by modernising, but revealing the natural life within the text.

> With congratulations and love,
> Peter

2000

The Improvisatrice or *The Bride of Cape Coast***
by Moira Buffini

Moira Buffini had been attached to the Studio in autumn 1996. Her first three produced plays including the award-winning Gabriel *(1997) and* Silence *(1999).*

**Moira Buffini to Nunn,
25 February 2000**

Dear Trevor,

A year ago, Jack Bradley commissioned me to write a play about the life and death of Letitia Landon [1802–38], a romantic poet who made a disastrous marriage and died in mysterious circumstances in pre-colonial Africa. It's one of the most extraordinary stories I have ever come across.

So far I have written one and a half pages. This is pretty pathetic I realise, but the reasons for my lack of progress are twofold: firstly, the research involved in the story is massive, especially when you start from a position of almost complete ignorance. I have spent weeks in the British Library, reading her many works (none of which are in print) and reading about the life of her husband, George Maclean. I have read about the Romantic movement and Gothic drama – a style which fascinated Letitia and fascinates me. […]

I have the structure of this play and its themes dancing around in my head – and yet I cannot start writing. The play is set in Cape Coast Castle, a former slaving castle built in the 16th century, which still exists, as a museum, on the coast of Ghana. The play, as well as being about a woman facing her own mortality, is also about the clash of three cultures: literary London (Letitia), the military Empire (George), and the ancient culture of the Ashanti people (George's African 'wife' whose name does not survive). This last culture is the one thing I can't find out about just by reading books. The second far more pressing reason I haven't been able to start writing, is that I need to go to Ghana.

I need between £1,000 and £1,500 to get there. Flights and accommodation are pretty cheap – but still beyond my means. The British Council turned down my request for funds. […]

I have high hopes of getting to Ghana over Easter, before it gets too hot and before I begin to lose heart and momentum for writing the play. It's been a frustrating year. I thought I'd write in case you or Jack were able to think of any avenues I have not tried.

Wishing you all the very best,
Moira Buffini

Buffini did not visit the Gold Coast. She set Landon aside and wrote the dark comedy Dinner *(NT, 2002; Wyndham's, 2003). She returned to Landon in 2003 but did not complete the script, partly because she 'could not find a single silver lining in her story', which ended in probable suicide. But the research fed two Gothic tales: Buffini's NT Connections play* A Vampire Story *(2008) and her screenplay for* Jane Eyre *(2011) – 'So Landon has been on a journey with me.'*

House / Garden (1999)
Two linked plays by Alan Ayckbourn

Director: Alan Ayckbourn
Lyttelton [*House*] and Olivier [*Garden*], 9 August to 23 September 2000
(46 performances of both)

House *and* Garden *are set on an August Saturday, with simultaneous – and simultaneously performed – action at the home of Teddy Platt, an adulterous businessman who is hosting the village fête in his garden. Actors shuttled at speed between* House *in the Lyttelton and* Garden *in the Olivier. Nunn watched Ayckbourn's productions in preview.*

Nunn to Alan Ayckbourn, 7 August 2000	Dear Alan,
	I greatly enjoyed both *House* and *Garden*. I think they look very handsome and the actors are superb. It is impertinent for a beginner like me to offer any helpful hints about egg sucking, but both plays seem to be more leisurely in pace than they might be [and] would benefit from a speed run. […]

The [shows'] changes of mood are absolutely not to be erased by rushing through all the shifts in gear. But I think you could challenge everybody, cast and crew, to go up a whole gear, and improve the shining hour yet further.

Deep thanks, and love,
Trevor

Nunn to Ayckbourn, 10 August 2000

My dear Alan,

I am ecstatic about your reviews today, and in particular, the incidence of the word triumph. Well done, mate. Relax, be happy, and give yourself a week off from writing your next five projects.

Love,
Trevor

Like all Ayckbourn's plays, House *and* Garden *were taken up by amateur dramatics groups. In 2004, a director about to tackle them asked her daughter to seek the playwright's advice on her behalf.*

Ayckbourn, email to Rae Bishop, 5 June 2004

Dear Rae Bishop,

How very enterprising of you to do *House* and *Garden*. Indoors and Out, too. Maybe, being further south than we are, you stand a better chance with the weather. I don't think I could ever have risked that in Scarborough!

Tips, hints and pearls of wisdom? […]

All my plays benefit from truthful playing. That is to say, don't let actors get carried away with the idea that it's all a laugh. Try and refer to comedy as little as possible in rehearsals. Oddly, the laughs only come with most of my stuff when the characters are deadly serious. Well, that's not odd really, that's the basis of all good comic playing. […]

Anyway, very good luck.

Very best regards,
Alan

Noises Off (1983)

by Michael Frayn

Director: Jeremy Sams

Lyttelton, 5 October 2000 to 20 February 2001 (67 performances)

In Act One of Noises Off, *a director, stage manager, assistant stage manager and six actors – including leading man, Garry, and ageing, increasingly forgetful Dotty – stumble through a dress rehearsal of a fictitious sex farce,* 'Nothing On'. *Act Two offers a backstage view of a* 'Nothing On' *matinee, as cast and crew's disastrous private lives destroy any vestige of company unity. Act Three shows a disintegrating performance of* 'Nothing On', *from out front again.*

This farce sustained a five-year West End run in the 1980s, but Frayn rewrote substantially for the NT revival, partly in response to the 'irresistible inventions' of Jeremy Sams.

Michael Frayn, fax to Jeremy Sams, 21 September 2000	SEVEN PAGES INCLUDING THIS ONE

Dear Jeremy,

Another go at the other points we talked about. […]

I'm sorry if I was a little uptight this morning. It's always the same with rewrites: everyone wants them – no one likes them when they've got them.

But you're right to keep on at me. […]

Yours,
Michael

Ahead of a transfer to the Piccadilly Theatre in May 2001, Sams rehearsed two new actors – Lynn Redgrave (replacing Patricia Hodge as Dotty, whose role as 'Mrs Clacket', the housekeeper in 'Nothing On', *involves hilarious business with a plate of sardines) and Stephen Mangan (succeeding Aden Gillett as Garry), while the original cast also continued at the Lyttelton.*

Sams, email to Frayn, 15 April 2001	Dear Michael

Lynn and Steve are going to be sensational. It's incredibly hard working with the cast who have to do evening shows as well … no other real way though, because I'm re-inventing quite a few things, all for the better believe me.

Lynn is dazzling with props, therefore on each entrance she brings on more of them to further relish the long-awaited sardines: a napkin, a knife and fork, a pepper mill, a lemon … and they all get a life (and a laugh) in Act Two! She loses her napkin in Act Two. Freddie offers her his bloody hankie as a replacement. She tucks it into her collar at which point he notices its condition and faints. She doesn't notice this, is about to enter, spots the state of the hankie and throws it to him as he enters … he catches it and faints. Belinda enters with Selsdon, asks what's wrong, [Freddie] explains so graphically that he faints again, bringing her down with him. […]

Lots of love from Jeremy

2001

Howard Katz (2001)
by Patrick Marber

Director: Patrick Marber
Cottesloe, 13 June to 19 September 2001 (51 performances)

Ron Cook played Marber's 50-year-old title character: a suicidally disenchanted London showbiz agent whose misfortunes include losing his job; the discovery that his father has had a mistress for many years; and being robbed.

Paddy Cunneen (composer on *Closer*), fax to Patrick Marber, 12 June 2001

Dear Patrick,

OK, it opens tomorrow. There's nothing more to be done except worry it all the way to the finish line. You're probably in need of a [Woodbine], some sleep and a little bit of eleventh-hour ironic pessimism. I don't have any fags and live miles away, so …

It's obviously absolute garbage, and what is the National doing allowing a soap opera like that on stage? The critics will see right through it, you know. What the fuck were you thinking of?

Best wishes for another major hit.

Paddy

Nunn to Marber, 15 June 2001

Dear Patrick,

[…] I wanted to tell you what a really brilliant job you had done, especially with your preview time, tightening, refining, focusing and detailing an already beautiful fluid and imaginative production.

I thought you had come through to the best imaginable version of the play you had conceived, that it takes us to a place that is totally recognisable, but dramatises that despair – personal, professional, social, political, with gimlet accuracy and earns its eventual glimmer of light in the tunnel in a way that is very moving. It's by far the most ambitious thing you've done and I congratulate you on every aspect of it. […]

Love and thanks,
Trevor

Marber to Nunn,
21 June 2001

Dear Trevor,

[…] I really appreciate your comments about the play and the production. I've had a great time working on *Howard Katz* and am proud of the show.

I must admit the critical response has been surprising because to me the play is clearly my best. Then again, what do I know? […]

Best wishes,
Patrick

Nicholas Hytner, NT Director Designate

By spring 2001, it was known that Nunn would not be extending his initial five-year contract, though he would remain in post as far beyond October 2002 as was necessary to give his successor a sufficient run-in to the job. NT chairman Christopher Hogg had begun leading the succession process.

After The Madness of King George, *Nicholas Hytner had made three feature films in America, and continued his stage partnership with Alan Bennett on* The Lady in the Van *(1999). While rehearsing* The Winter's Tale *(Olivier, May 2001), his first NT show for four years, he decided to enter the Directorial race.*

Genista McIntosh to
Christopher Hogg,
25 July 2001

Dear Chris,

I have thought hard before writing this letter. Until now we have communicated quite informally, and I could have taken that opportunity again, but I feel sufficiently strongly about what I have to say to want it to be on record.

I occupy a somewhat privileged position in that several of the key candidates for the post of Director (whether declared or undeclared) are personal friends. I have tried to maintain a professional distance from the process in recent weeks, but there are things I cannot avoid knowing, amongst them the fact that Sam Mendes has finally ruled himself out. I also know that Stephen Daldry continues to equivocate (or certainly did until very recently), and that Nick Hytner has made it unambiguously clear that he wants the job.

I wish to support Nick's candidacy very strongly. It can be said against him that he has no previous experience of running an organisation, but I would make the following points:

- He is a director of proven international reputation with an excellent track record of success in theatre of all kinds and at all scales.
- He has an admirable grasp of the issues facing the National and a clear sense of how he would go about tackling them.
- He has the ability to draw around him a powerful group of collaborators whose strengths would complement his own.
- He has a great deal of support both within the National, where he is well known and respected, and in the outside world.

- He is well-connected and politically astute.
- Above all, he wants and needs to make a serious commitment at this point in his life. I believe this is not because other opportunities are no longer open to him (they are) but because he is properly ambitious both for himself and the National, which he wants to see continuing to make a major contribution to the cultural life of the country.

Nick doesn't know I am writing to you – I'm not even sure how pleased he would be if he did! I am doing so because I believe his case is very strong and because I feel it is absolutely vital that the current uncertainty is brought to an end as soon as possible. In this respect at least I feel sure you and I agree.

With best wishes,
     As ever,
     Jenny

On 14 September, the Succession Committee, including Hogg, would interview five candidates: John Caird, Max Stafford-Clark, Jude Kelly, Howard Davies, and Hytner.

Nicholas Hytner to Hogg, 7 September 2001

Dear Chris,

[…] Allow me to respond to your invitation to write to you by sharing with you some of my thoughts on what might be, in the words of your 1995 document, 'a clear and distinctive vision of the National as a *national* theatre'.

Over the last ten years, any consensus as to what constitutes our national identity has evaporated. The very word *national* is up for grabs, the concept fraught with possibilities. As a nation we think we know who we were, but we need to find out what we're becoming. It's a tremendous time to be a national theatre, an exhilarating challenge to hold the mirror up to the nation. In the reflection, we'll find new generations, new communities, a society bursting with fresh sources of life and energy.We can set the theatrical agenda, create rather than follow fashion.

We talk passionately about renewing our audience; we wonder how we can attract a more heterogeneous crowd; we worry about marketing, ticket prices,image. It all matters, but in the end it's only on our stages that we can galvanise new audiences by addressing them, even buttonholing them, challenging them and entertaining them with reflections of their own experience and expansions of their horizons. And what stages we have! Our two main stages are hungry for big experiences, big statements that embrace every night whole societies of us.

And we have the artists to make the statements. A colony of playwrights emerged in the 1990s. They developed their skills in studio theatres, many of them finding a ferocious life in wildly diverse corners of their own communities. What they had in common was an unabashed desire to reach out to their audience and to entertain them. We must challenge them now to paint on a larger canvas. […]

Meanwhile, new forms of theatrical expression are emerging which we must encourage and explore. We can be as bold about the redefinition of what constitutes theatre as we must be about expanding its subject matter.

None of this is to deny our responsibilities as a classical theatre, but after 25 years on the South Bank, it's hard to think of many unarguably great plays, particularly from the English repertoire, that haven't been done here. We've arrived at a place where we can start to trudge through the cannon all over again with a weary sigh, or we can dedicate ourselves to its rediscovery in the context of our overarching curiosity about what makes the classical repertoire speak now.

I'm confident that the best directors of the current generation will join me in revitalising the classical repertoire. […]

We'll also be energetic in the development of young directors, and we can cast a wider net for them than the net that 20 odd years ago caught me. A relentless insistence on the difficulties of dealing with large stages has shrivelled the aspirations of many directors. They need to be led from the front and encouraged to step up. […]

There's no shortage of talent, both within the NT and without it. I'm determined to liberate it, to engage fully with our permanent staff, to reaffirm for them their faith in their own creativity. […]

It's a wonderful opportunity.

With all best wishes,
Nick

On 24 September, the Board confirmed that Hytner would become Director on 1 April 2003.

2002

The Coast of Utopia (2002)

Comprising: *Voyage*, *Shipwreck* and *Salvage*
by Tom Stoppard

Director: Trevor Nunn
Olivier, 3 August to 23 November 2002 (*Voyage* 56 performances; *Shipwreck* 45; *Salvage* 44)

Nunn to Tom
Stoppard
18 December 2000

Dear Tom,

That was a splendid dinner and a very good opportunity to talk. Four hours have never gone by more swiftly, and I felt much more informed and rooted by the time we parted. […]

You summarised the most viable conclusion by saying that we must stop referring to a trilogy (even though we both know that this is what <u>eventually</u> we are to be dealing with) and instead tell ourselves the project is two plays to open in (relatively) quick succession in the second half of 2001. […]

There are drawbacks. Because of the touring plan for *Hamlet*, and other work he has now agreed to, we would have to proceed <u>without</u> Simon Russell Beale [as Alexander Herzen (1812–70), Russian socialist writer and the plays' central figure]. I fear he will register this as a blow, but yet it isn't possible for me to persuade him to change horses because Herzen in 'the second play' doesn't yet exist.

I am also trying to secure Alex Jennings to play Leontes [in *The Winter's Tale*] for Nick Hytner and then who knows, … possibly a revival of *Speer*, possibly a new production of *The Ruling Class* [by Peter Barnes] – but preferably to play something unrefusable in your two plays. You and I have talked about him being a superb candidate for Turgenev. […]

One voice in my head says, 'Don't be so pusillanimous, go for it' and solve all these problems as they arise. But there is another more cautionary voice (good or bad angel I don't yet know) that counsels delay to protect the special nature of the work.

If, for the sake of argument, we waited until [2002], what would be the gain?. […]

- You would spend 2001 writing Play Two and Play Three, and then revising the whole work once you had got to the end of the epic. […]
- We could cast Simon and Alex having shown them the whole trilogy.

I am arguing against myself here, because the National really needs the excitement of two new plays by you in [2001] – and no alternative would be as good as that. But I am very anxious about handling such an enormous and important project as yours and treating it in a rushed and ill-conceived way. […]

Whatever decision we take, the knock-on effects are enormous and the deadlines are coming up fast.

Have a wonderful Noel and a happy French New year.

Love,
    Trevor

Stoppard to Nunn,
20 December 2000

Dear Trevor,

[…] You say that two new plays by me in 2001 is an excitement the National needs, and that no alternative would be as good as that. Whether this is so or not (and at best it could only be relatively true), I mention it first because – other than my disappointment, directed at myself, of course, not at the RNT – that is the only argument in your letter against delay, and your letter despite itself convinces me that we should wait. I can only hope that I wouldn't incur your wrath, by luring us into a Schedule Chasm, but here are the points I would add in favour of postponement.

Separating the third play would weaken the sense of there being one story – a trilogy.

The casting issue speaks for itself, but surely the greater issue is the added difficulty of securing an actor across two seasons rather than within one season. […]

Finally but perhaps most important, there is the point you made at dinner: just as Play 2 is making me look back at Play 1, I don't think – ideally – I'd sign off on Play 2 until I've written Play 3.

I'm grateful for your willingness to 'go for it' in 2001, but I think the implications of your letter are inescapable, and you're right to be wary of rushing things. […]

Love,
Tom

The postponement would pay off. Set in Russia, Paris and London, The Coast of Utopia *followed Herzen from 1833 to 1868. Stephen Dillane (Herzen) and Guy Henry (Turgenev) were in a 30-strong cast, which shared 70 parts, across 40 locations and nine hours' stage time, and led the* Evening Standard's *Nicholas de Jongh to conclude: 'Nothing of such intellectual ambition, such daring or epic scope has marked the NT's 38-year history.'*

The end of the Nunn years

Trevor Nunn was knighted in the 2002 Queen's Birthday Honours, after a nominations process initiated by the NT's chairman, with a letter to the Secretary of State for Culture, Media and Sport that neatly sums up the achievements of Nunn's tenure.

Christopher Hogg to Tessa Jowell, 18 February 2002

Dear Secretary of State,

I am writing formally as Chairman of the RNT to put forward Trevor Nunn, CBE, as a candidate for the award of Knighthood.

Trevor Nunn was appointed Director of the RNT in March 1996 [and I] was closely associated with the appointment throughout. At the outset the apparent candidates were young with high potential but limited experience for the job and, more important, limited inclination to go for it. It was therefore welcome to the Board to discover that Trevor could be persuaded to undertake a five-year tenure. We gave very careful thought to his age (then 56, now 62) and to all aspects of his previous record. We concluded that he had the capacity, the drive and the standing to lead the NT with at least as much distinction as any of his predecessors but to do it in his own individual way.

So it has proved. The NT has put on some of the most brilliant productions in its history, including several directed by him; awards won have matched or exceeded those of previous eras; a great deal of experimentation has been conducted, including a wonderful ensemble period in 1999/2000; outreach and diversity have been encouraged; and there has been no financial crisis. The record is that of one of the country's greatest theatre practitioners operating at the top of his bent. […]

This letter has been seen and is supported by the NT Board's Nominations Committee (Sir David Hancock, Joan Bakewell and Sue MacGregor). It would not be complete without the addition of one further point which I divulge to you in confidence and on my own responsibility since I have not been authorised to do so. Trevor is likely to have made anonymous charitable donations to the NT totalling more than £2.5 million – which will be by far the largest donation from a single individual in the NT's history.

In surveying the range and quality of his accomplishments over a lifetime's service to theatre, it is difficult to imagine a finer record or one more deserving of the highest recognition.

Yours sincerely,
Chris Hogg

The Nicholas Hytner Years

2003–
2015

The start of the Hytner years

Nicholas Hytner and his executive director, Nick Starr, had first worked together when the latter, then an NT press officer, handled publicity for Hytner's first South Bank show, Ghetto, in 1989.

On taking office in 2003, they introduced a revolutionary ticketing scheme that Hytner called 'an adventure involving everyone, including the audience. A bold and radical way forward [with] a major, non-populist, non-musical repertoire in the Olivier.'

With substantial sponsorship from Travelex, and lower-than-average production budgets, the NT could afford to offer two-thirds of seats in its largest theatre for just £10, for six months of the year. Beginning with Hytner's Iraq War-infused revival of Henry V, *starring Adrian Lester, and also featuring Kenneth Branagh in the title role of David Mamet's* Edmond, *the £10 scheme was a triumph. It broadened and rejuvenated the National's audiences.*

As Hytner has acknowledged, he was fortunate to have started out as Director when the Labour government substantially increased funding for the performing arts: the NT grant went up by an extra £1.5 million for 2004–05, which helped Hytner and Starr to be 'extremely confident' in their programming.

Elmina's Kitchen (2003)
by Kwame Kwei-Armah

Director: Angus Jackson
Cottesloe, 29 May to 25 August 2003 (45 performances)

Simon Block (playwright) to Jack Bradley, 10 July 2002

Dear Jack,

I'm writing with regard to Kwame's play *Elmira's Castle*, sent last week, which I've now read. This is the second play Kwame's sent me. The first, over 18 months ago, felt strained and generally unconvincing [Block had advised him to put it away and start again]. *Elmira's Castle* couldn't be more different. Frankly, it was like reading a completely different writer – [one] who has found exactly what he wants to say and how to say it.

The story is comparatively simple: essentially, that of a good man struggling to run a second-rate business in contemporary Hackney, surrounded by criminal and gangland forces that are proving difficult for both himself and his teenage boy to resist – though for different reasons. But the simplicity of the story is simple in the way Greek drama is simple – not simple-minded but uncluttered and precise. The play knows exactly what it is there to say, and says it directly. Which isn't to say it couldn't be developed further – it could, of course, but only by building on what is already present, not drastically re-thinking it. Why? Well, firstly, the language is striking, rich and true. Secondly, the characters are present and distinctive from the first line – their relationships to one another are compelling and true. Thirdly, Kwame has a story to tell and a passion with which to tell it that comes through every page, and which is followed through to the very last line (which took me by surprise – in the right way – how often can you say that?). It is also unstressfully humorous, and an insight into a world I (and I suspect most white people) know relatively little about: i.e. how the multi-layered black community lives together and feeds off one another, and [may contribute] to the prevention of its own self-advancement (eschewing blame on white culture for a more critical self-examination of black).

There is violence in the play, but [it's not] gratuitous, and is all the more dramatically shocking for being rare – when it occurs it's a genuine jolt.

It was a joy to read (once my ear became attuned to the argot), and a page-turner – I wanted to know what happened to these people, and had a growing sense that something would, and that it wouldn't be good, but without knowing quite what. When it does happen, it is genuinely shocking and feels completely true to the piece. I hate new plays that are all effect and which don't come from any discernible passion to communicate a particular story. This isn't one of those. Of the plays that I've seen read at Studio readings this is better than any I can remember. I've spoken to Kwame and we both agree it needs a lot of work to maximise the potential of the first draft, but it's my belief it's all there to be had. While the second half needs considerable work, the story doesn't fall apart like so many do. Quite the opposite.

Sticking my neck out I would say that with a committed, sympathetic director and a bunch of actors this is a play that would benefit from the experience of a Studio workshop. He's definitely got something, and of all the new plays I've seen, read, or been involved with, this would be a joy to continue to work on. Of course, I may be completely wrong. What happens now?

Regards,
Simon

Kwei-Armah was teamed at the Studio with another playwright, Nick Drake, and director Angus Jackson, who eventually staged the retitled play: Elmina's Kitchen is the West Indian take-away run by Deli (Paterson Joseph), the 'good man' of Block's letter. Kwei-Armah was named Most Promising Playwright by the Evening Standard, *and played Deli on tour and in the West End. His NT triptych, 'chronicling [contemporary] black British experience as I saw it', was completed by* Fix-Up (Cottesloe, 2004), *set in a London bookshop specialising in Afro-Caribbean history, and* Statement of Regret (Cottesloe, 2007), *set in the fictional Institute of Black Policy Research.*

Kwame Kwei-Armah in rehearsal for *Elmina's Kitchen*. Photo: Ivan Kyncl

Democracy (2003)

by Michael Frayn

Director: Michael Blakemore
Cottesloe, 9 September to 30 December 2003 (65 performances)
Lyttelton, 12 February to 30 March 2004 (39 performances)

From 1969 to 1974, Willy Brandt, West Germany's Social Democrat Chancellor, had a dedicated junior aide and, later, personal assistant, Günter Guillaume, who was spying for the East German Ministry of Security, the Stasi. Brandt resigned following Guillaume's unmasking and arrest. In 2001, Michael Frayn set out to dramatise this extraordinary tale.

Michael Frayn to Peter Merseburger, 19 July 2001

Dear Peter,

Sarah [Haffner] told me you were working on a biography of Brandt. What stage are you at?

I've been turning over the possibility of writing some kind of play about the Guillaume affair – more because of its philosophical implications than its political or historical ones, though of course they're all bound up together. I've read, or am reading, some of the most immediately obvious things, but if there was anything by you available it would no doubt supersede the earlier sources. […]

Yours,
Michael

Frayn to Merseburger,
19 September 2002

Dear Peter,

Your book [*Willy Brandt: Visionär und Realist*] is magnificent – an enterprise on a heroic scale that is truly worthy of its subject – and triumphantly brought off.

I skipped some areas that seemed remote from my interests, I have to confess, because it is a very long book and because I want to go back to my play. I shall return to them. But I've learned a lot – some of it requiring me to modify what I've written in the play. There are also one or two things that I'm simply going to steal. I'm on the I-don't-know-how-manieth draft, and whether it's a play or is ever going to become one I still don't know; but I'm going back to work on it now with renewed heart.

So, thank you. […]

Yours,
Michael

Frayn to Michael Blakemore,
24 October 2002

Dear Michael,

I can't tell you how relieved and delighted I am that you think the play might be workable, with the possible exception of the early sections that introduce the characters. I won't look at these again until you've had a chance to re-read it in a week or two's time. Then maybe when you get back we can go through the whole thing line by line.

It's going to depend even more heavily than *Copenhagen* on the director's contribution. Another difficulty: three of the characters are still alive – Schmidt, Genscher, and Ehmke. All the behaviour that the play imputes to them has already been imputed by journalists and historians, but having it put into their own mouths, as it were, may be more than they will be prepared to put up with. […]

Yours,
Michael

Blakemore's Cottesloe production, performed on Peter J. Davison's multi-layered set, filled with desks, chairs and filing cabinets, starred Roger Allam as Brandt and Conleth Hill as Guillaume.

Frayn to Sarah Haffner,
10 September 2003

Dear Sarah,

[…] Press night of *Democracy* last night. It went very well, and all the British reviews so far are good. Rather dusty one in the [*Frankfurter Allgemeine Zeitung*], which (I suppose understandably) seemed to resent my presuming to write about German history. 'Ein sehr englischer Blick… Einsprengsel urenglischen Boulevardhumors… wirken etwas befremdend in diesem urdeutschen Kontext.' ['A very English view … Sprinklings of archetypally English boulevard humour … have a

slightly unpleasing effect in this archetypally German context'].
Still, it's a success. […]

Love,
Michael

Dear Tom,

What an incredibly generous man you are, in every possible
way. I'm quite childishly pleased and touched that you enjoyed
Democracy. I do think Michael's done it well (and of course
not got remotely enough credit from the reviewers), and it's a
terrific cast. Particularly Roger Allam, who seems to me quite
transcendent. This is actually my biggest contribution to the
enterprise – suggesting Roger Allam. Also reminding everyone
that I'd suggested Roger Allam, seeing off various non-Roger
Allam proposals, coming back to the idea of Roger Allam yet
again, crying with sudden inspiration 'Or how about *Roger
Allam?*' etc. I'm astonished every time I see him – by the way
he's Brandt just by standing there – just by sitting there and not
moving a muscle.

I was very disconcerted, on our flight back from New York, to
discover that Simon [Russell Beale] was going to [play George in
Jumpers in the Lyttelton from June 2003], and so was ruled out for
Guillaume. I'd set my heart on him, as on Roger. Well, now we've
got Conleth I think I can master my chagrin enough to come and
see him in yours.

I'm afraid *Democracy* is a very small-scale enterprise, set
beside the heroic scale and sweep of your trilogy [*The Coast of
Utopia*]. That was an amazing achievement. I still can't imagine
how you ever undertook it. Not just the research and the writing
– but having the courage to lay down the keel of such a huge
vessel. I manage to get going only by underestimating the scale
of each new project – by never having any suspicion of how
much research and organisation and reorganisation and sheer
exhausting *thinking* it's going to involve. I can't help having a
jealous suspicion that your talent makes such an enormous
outlay of labour unnecessary. But perhaps there's no way round
it completely even for you. I remember your gesture of relief at
having finished, at that party in the Ivy. […]

Yours,
Michael

Dear Michael,

We were completely gripped by [*Democracy*]. I liked the austerity
– like Euripides in modern dress. But then, the dark suits and ties
became almost exotic. I particularly loved the running conceit
that an individual is a kind of parliament – and that you can
never be sure until you start to speak who will have the upper
hand. As you are obviously aware, there is much in cognitive
psychology bearing this out – the source of our complexity is

this debating chamber of opposing needs. In that respect, you chose your subject matter brilliantly. Such intellectual muscle in the notion of democracy. And it was moving too, especially at the end. We were wet-eyed. I kept thinking how extraordinary it was, that something so intentionally non-representational should be so psychologically real. It's a rich piece of writing, wise and sympathetic to human frailty. And so many interesting contemporary echoes. I doubt Clinton could hold up ten pages … and left parties loving opposition and defeat. Well, at least here it's the right creeping into that position. I can think of no other novelist in any period who's written so well for the theatre. Nor are there many playwrights prepared to do the kind of thinking you do. While I was waiting for Annalena I read your postscript to *Copenhagen*: so much to think about. I also stared at the page called 'by the same author' and thought what a superb body of work you've accumulated. One of your great strengths as a writer is your intellectual curiosity. I like the thought that I could not guess for a minute what you might do, where you might go next. […]

> Best wishes,
> Ian

2004

The History Boys (2004)
by Alan Bennett

Director: Nicholas Hytner
Lyttelton, 18 May 2004 to 26 April 2005 (222 performances)
Recast; recreated by Simon Cox: 5 December 2005 to 1 February 2006 (59 performances)

Alan Bennett to Hytner, 20 October 2003

Dear Nick,

Here's the thing I've been working on. I can't get any further with it so perhaps you could tell me what you think.

The first part is more or less comprehensible but I don't know if you can make sense of the second half. It's full of gaps and repetitions plus lots of odd bits (e.g. the unexplained film endings) which aren't fully worked out.

Don't worry if you think it's pretty hopeless … and no pressure to read it straightaway.

It probably ought to be called 'In the Lost Childhood of Alastair Campbell'.

> Love,
> Alan

October 20 '03

Dear Nick,

Here's the thing I've been working on. I can't get any further
with it so perhaps you could tell me what you think.

The first part is more or less comprehensible but I don'T know
if you can make sense of the second half. Its full of gaps and
reptutionxx repetitions plus lots of odd bits (.e.g the unexplained
film endings) which aren't fully worked out .

Don't worry if you think it's pretty hopeless..and no pressure
to read it straightaway.

It probably ought to be called 'In th Lost Childhood of
Alastair Campbell '.

Love

Alan .

*The History Boys is set mainly in a Sheffield grammar school in the 1980s, as eight boys
are prepared for their Oxbridge entrance exams by two long-serving teachers – Mrs Lintott
(History), the eccentric, inspirational Hector (General Studies), prone to groping the boys
when giving them lifts home on his motorbike – and a much younger newcomer, Irwin
(History), specially recruited by the Headmaster: 'Get me scholarships, Irwin.'*

*On 27 January 2004, Hytner directed a reading of The History Boys at the NT Studio,
featuring Bennett as Headmaster and Hugh Bonneville as Hector; the boys included Samuel
Barnett, Dominic Cooper, Jamie Parker and Russell Tovey.*

**Hytner, notes to
Bennett on second
draft of *The History
Boys*, January 2004**

<u>Alan:</u> some very brutal cuts suggested here –
I reckon we have to lose about 20–25%: [at the Studio] it read at
first half 1:20, second 1:10 – & when you add 10 mins to either half
for laughs/pauses/production – it's pretty long – so forgive me for
going at it!
I've not suggested more small cuts – leaving that to you – tho'
will happily have a look for them if you want!

*Even after Hytner's 'brutal' editing, The History Boys' opening performances still ran at
two-and-a-half hours, plus interval. The class schooled by Clive Merrison (Headmaster),
Richard Griffiths (Hector), Frances de la Tour (Mrs Lintott) and Stephen Campbell Moore
(Irwin) was Barnett, Cooper, Parker and Tovey, joined by Samuel Anderson, James Corden,
Sacha Dhawan and Andrew Knott.*

THE STUDIO

PLAYREADING

Tuesday 27 January 2004 at 10.30am

THE HISTORY BOYS
by Alan Bennett

CAST

Irwin	PAUL READY
Hector	HUGH BONNEVILLE
Headmaster	ALAN BENNETT
Mrs Lintott	LORRAINE ASHBOURNE
Posner	SAMUEL BARNETT
Dakin	DOMINIC COOPER
Scripps	BEN WHISHAW
Rudge	JAMIE PARKER
Lockwood / Boy 3	KIERAN BEW
Tann / Boy 1	CHRISTOPHER SIMPSON
Timms / Boy 4	LEO BILL
Crowther / Boy 2	RUSSELL TOVEY
Director	NICHOLAS HYTNER

Cast list for reading of *The History Boys* at
the NT Studio

Bennett, postcard to
Hytner, 18 May 2004

Dear Nick,

Whenever anybody asks me about the play, as Michael Grandage
did last night, I always say how surprised I was that you saw its
potential last October and straightaway took it on.

This isn't modesty. Nobody else would have seen what to do
with it or helped me shape it in the way you have done – and with
no disagreement or heartache. I haven't had such a good time in
years. […]

Much love,
Alan

Russell Tovey,
postcard to Hytner,
18 May 2004

FOR ME BITCH NICK –
THANK YOU AGAIN FOR ANOTHER HIGHLIGHT IN MY
PROFESSIONAL CAREER SO FAR! YOU'RE AN ABSOLUTE
GEEZER AND SO EXCITING TO WORK WITH – I HOPE IT
HAPPENS AGAIN & AGAIN!! LOADS OF LOVE & LUCK & HUGE
HUGE RESPECT –
RUSS X

James Corden, card
to Hytner, 18 May
2004

Nick,

I just wanted to drop you a card to say thank you for the last 7
weeks. I've had so much fun and enjoyed working with you so
much. I was incredibly nervous on the first day working here with
you, but within minutes I felt completely comfortable. You are
not just a terrific director, but more importantly a lovely man.
You have made this experience so special. Thank you.

All my love,
James Corden xxx

P. S. Good luck!! x

*The History Boys won the Olivier for Best Play, had West End and Broadway runs, and UK
and international tours. Bennett, Hytner, Griffiths, de la Tour, designer Bob Crowley and
lighting designer Mark Henderson all won Tony Awards, a few months before the release of
the feature film adaptation, directed by Hytner with the original cast.*

Stuff Happens (2004)
by David Hare

Director: Nicholas Hytner
Olivier, 10 September to 6 November 2004 (53 performances)

Michael Bryant played more than 50 roles at the National, including prominent characters in all three parts of The David Hare Trilogy, *whose ensemble also included his wife, Judith Coke. Bryant died in 2002, aged 74.*

Judith Coke, postcard to David Hare, September 2004	Dear David,
	
	It seems so very odd that you should be doing [*Stuff Happens* as] one of your 'specials' in the Olivier without my Old Boy. But as I expect you know, there is a portion of his ashes under the front of the stage, so in a way he <u>IS</u> there, putting in his two-pennorth – even if it's only to say 'Bollocks' occasionally, to keep the younger actors on their toes.
	
	     But this card comes with great love and great hopes for the play, from me <u>AND</u> from him.
	
	     Jude Coke x

Stuff Happens *dramatised the build-up to the Iraq War, putting on stage George W. Bush (Alex Jennings), Condoleezza Rice (Adjoa Andoh), Tony Blair (Nicholas Farrell) and other key figures in the US, British and French administrations, and the UN.*

Peter Hall, postcard to Hytner, 19 September 2004	Dear Nick,
	
	Stuff Happens is a milestone. At any other European subsidised theatre, you would be 'let go'. I'm not very proud of the English at this moment, but what you have been allowed to do makes me proud.
	
	     Congratulations.
	
	     Ever,
	          Peter

Helen Mirren, postcard to Hytner and Hare, 2004	Dear Nick and David, I loved *Stuff Happens* – thank you for your brilliant work – it was so beautifully realised. My heart sank at the beginning – all those men in grey suits. 'No sets! No costumes! – never mind – it's good for me' – but you and DAVID and the Actors made an amazing thing – watchable, funny, informative, and absolutely powerfully Dramatic. VERY VERY Brilliant – all love, Helen.

2005

Paul (2005)

by Howard Brenton

Director: Howard Davies
Cottesloe, 9 November 2005 to 4 February 2006 (47 performances)

Howard Brenton to
Hytner, 1 June 2003

Dear Nick,

It was very good to meet you on Friday.
    And I was so, so excited by your positive response to the idea
of a play.
    [Enclosed] is the scenario.

    Best wishes,
        Howard

PS I'm debating whether, instead of an official from the Rome
magistrates, to have it that the Emperor Nero visits Peter
and Paul in the last scene. Traditionally it was during Nero's
persecution that they were executed.
    It has a feeling of Roman contempt that it's a lowly official who
delivers their sentence … but the temptation to write Nero may
be too great!

Nero did appear in Paul, *which brought Brenton back to the South Bank for the first time since* Pravda *closed in 1986 – a gap in which the National had turned down several of his plays, including* Berlin Bertie *and* Doctor Love. *He followed* Paul *with a drama about Harold Macmillan,* Never So Good *(Lyttelton, 2008).*

2006

Oedipus at Colonus (401 BC)**
by Sophocles

Paul Scofield had won a Bafta for Best Supporting Actor as Judge Danforth in The Crucible *(1996), directed by Hytner, who hoped Scofield, now 84, might act at the National for the first time since 1996.*

Paul Scofield, postcard to Hytner, 14 February 2006	My dear Nick,

Oh yes I <u>have</u> thought about *Oedipus at Colonus* – but don't know of any more recent adaptation. Peter Stein is certainly a big incentive, & if you have a version with which you are pleased, I'd love to read it. May I?

It's lovely of you to consider my doing it.

With affection,
Paul

Scofield, postcard to Hytner, 18 February 2006	My dear Nick,

Feeling deeply apologetic & inexcusably culpable I find I have to retract my expression of interest in playing *Oedipus at Colonus* – I'm afraid I responded in a moment of euphoria at being invited by you to do it; being an admirer of long standing, as well as having golden memories of working with you on *The Crucible*.

I'm finding it difficult to contemplate doing a play in the theatre again – whether or not my reluctance will change I don't yet know, but at the moment I truly feel that I just couldn't do it.

But I still feel euphoric that you should have thought of me & asked me.

Thank you so very much.

With much love,
Paul

Scofield did not return to the stage; he died in March 2008.

2007

War Horse (2007)

Adapted by Nick Stafford from a novel by Michael Morpurgo (1982)

Directors: Marianne Elliott and Tom Morris
Olivier, 17 October 2007 to 14 February 2008 and 17 September 2008 to 18 March 2009
(206 performances)

Devised in a collaboration between Marianne Elliott, Tom Morris, Nick Stafford and Handspring Puppet Company, Michael Morpurgo's seemingly unstageable novel about Joey, a horse caught up in the horrors of the First World War, was thrillingly staged, the horses brought to life by puppeteers. Soon after it opened, though nobody could yet predict that it would become the biggest box-office success in NT history, its impact on audiences was clear.

Michael Morpurgo, postcard to Hytner, 20 November 2007

Dear Nick,

What to say? The transformation of *War Horse* has been a <u>supreme</u> moment of our lives. I know what risks you all took, how hard everyone worked to create this phenomenal piece of theatre. Thank you, hugely. The intensity lingers long. Both the sweetness and the pain are unforgettable. You will have made theatregoers out of many thousands of youngsters and reminded the rest of us of the power live theatre has to touch the core of us. Two lives enhanced down here in Devon, tons of others elsewhere. Bravo!

Love,
Michael

*The Pride***

by Alexi Kaye Campbell

Alexi Kaye Campbell's first play, Death in Whitbridge, *was turned down by Jack Bradley in 2006 (it lacked 'the requisite intricacies of plotting to be fully successful'). His follow-up,* The Pride, *alternates between two years: in 1958, Philip, a closeted estate agent married to Sylvia, an illustrator, has an affair with Oliver, a novelist; in 2008 Oliver is a journalist and sex addict, whose actor friend, Sylvia, helps him cope after his lover, Philip, leaves him.*

Hytner to Alexi Kaye Campbell, 22 October 2007

Dear Alexi,

[...] You've caught both periods very well and have created an entirely different texture for each. The dialogue seems authentic and very speakable throughout – and you will know that too many plays are unreadable and unactable from the off because the dialogue doesn't sing. Yours does.

I was very struck by the play's central perception: that there is an equivalent misery in the repression of desire and in the indiscriminate and uninhibited and permanently available fulfilment of it. Though I was glad you suggest the former is the greater evil, and that your modern couple were given the means to work their way through at the end.

I don't think it's a play for the Cottesloe. The Cottesloe needs almost the muscle that the Royal Court Downstairs needs – it's not that much smaller. Your play will work best if the audience are in the same room, and I hope that one of those [smaller] theatres is smart enough to take it. If you want to hear it read, I'd be very happy to fix that at the Studio.

I'm not personally convinced by the almost mystical connections you make between the three characters in the two periods – although there are some excellent theatrical strokes. I'm not sure that you need to suggest that Philip, Oliver and Sylvia are in effect reincarnated (or maybe I've got this wrong!). And it could be usefully shortened. I'm afraid I say this about more or less everything! […]

> With all best wishes,
> Nick

A Studio reading convinced Kaye Campbell that The Pride *needed 'a little scissor job!' In November 2009 it was produced at the 90-seat Royal Court Upstairs – where audience and characters cannot help being 'in the same room' – and won an Olivier for Outstanding Achievement in an Affiliate Theatre.*

2008

Harper Regan (2008)
by Simon Stephens
Director: Marianne Elliott
Cottesloe, 17 April to 9 August 2008 (56 performances)

In Harper Regan, *the title character, 41 and living in Uxbridge, walks out on her boss, her husband, Seth, and their teenage daughter, Sarah, hoping for a final conversation with her dying father in Stockport. Instead, she has intense encounters, including with a student, Tobias, on a bridge; in a hotel room, with a married, internet hook-up, James; in Stockport, a first conversation in two years with her mother; back home, in a tentatively hopeful breakfast with Seth.*

> *Marianne Elliott had directed the premiere of Stephens's* Port *(2002) at the Royal Exchange in Manchester.*

Simon Stephens,
email to Marianne
Elliott, 5 January
2007

Hey,

I'm so glad you liked *Harper Regan*.

Your notes, as ever, were bang on.

I've done a second draft.

By removing the bulk of the references to shoulders alone I cut about four pages!

It's 102 pages now. […]

I tried to cut all [Harper's] adverbs (e.g. 'really, incredibly, totally, completely' etc.) to ground her language. I have, as a writer, a default voice. Which is quirky and adverbial and not true to character. It's adolescent. So sounds great in Sarah and sometimes Tobias but more often jars in Harper.

I tried to clarify who James is, i.e. not a male prostitute. Rather he's somebody who advertises for anonymous sex online. He's a happily married, successful businessman.

With a wife he adores and kids he cherishes.

Who is in a certain amount of fucking despair.

Maybe you're right about it being too bleak.

I spent a lot of time looking at Tobias.

I kind of want to trim back some of his misogyny.

And make their relationship more hopeful.

To suggest the idea that she can affect his life for the good and he, hers.

Similarly, I want her committed to telling Sarah about the truth of adult relationships. There's something positive in that, however difficult it is.

I want to maybe even get the sense that in Seth's final words he's saying 'I love you completely. I know I may never win you back. But, fucked up as I am, and have been, I will break my back trying. Because you're all I want.'

However ironic and harrowing that speech could be I think it works best if it's not one wholly of despair.

I'm going to look at it next week and then send a second draft to you.

I hope to give a copy to Nick [Hytner] at the end of the month. Maybe sooner than that.

And then we'll see.

But I just really want you to direct it. […]

S.

Stephens, email
to Mel Kenyon (his
agent), 26 January
2007

Nick Hytner ended this afternoon's Associates Lunch by telling me and everybody assembled that one of the things he had to decide was when, not if, he was going to do my play.

It was a lovely and enjoyably theatrical moment.

We're probably looking at delaying the production until January 2008.

So that Marianne can do it.

I think this is good for me.

Means I can work on *Pornography* in Hamburg and *Marine Parade* in Brighton and not have three plays in one year. I'm very, very happy!
INVOICE THEM NOW!!!!!! WOO HOO!!!!! […]

S.

Afterlife (2008)
by Michael Frayn

Director: Michael Blakemore
Lyttelton, 3 June to 30 August 2008 (44 performances)

Michael Frayn, email to Stefan Kroner (Frayn's research assistant on *Democracy*), 29 December 2006

Dear Stefan,

A hasty note to say how absolutely terrific the Christian Stückl production of [*Everyman*] is. A revelation of what theatre might be. Superlative performances. Seeing this has given me pause. If I'm going to write this play I've got to do something far more interesting and far better than I was originally aspiring to. I'm both horribly daunted and timidly encouraged.

I think this time I may have bitten off more than I can chew. […]

Yours,
Michael

Frayn's new play was a drama on the last years of the great Austrian–Jewish director and impresario Max Reinhardt (1873–1943). Reinhardt's epic annual stagings of Hugo von Hofmannsthal's morality play Everyman *(1911), in Salzburg in the 1920s and 1930s, and the Nazi persecution that drove him into exile in the US, are at the heart of Frayn's script, with many passages written in verse, to echo the language of* Everyman.

In November 2007, by when Hytner had committed to producing Afterlife *in the Lyttelton, Frayn sent the script to Michael Codron, inviting 'comments, casting suggestions'.*

Michael Codron to Frayn, 27 November 2007

Dear Michael,

In your depiction of Max Reinhardt,
You have made a Work of Art.
I knew that he had filmed The Dream,
With Mickey Rooney, way off beam,
But I was held in total thrall,
By your mastery of it all,
Of course now in my eighth decade,
Of all the projects I have made,
This would be a stunning choice,
To be associated with your unique voice.
What will happen after June?
To give it after-life would be a boon.
Others I know will you pursue,

Can I join that motley crew?
As for actors the great and good,
They will not need to be wooed.
[…]

> Speak soon I hope, love to both,
> Michael

In Blakemore's production, Roger Allam, whose Willy Brandt in Democracy *had so dazzled Frayn, portrayed Reinhardt on a monumental set by that play's designer, Peter J. Davison – but this quartet could not emulate their previous triumph.*

Hytner, email to
Frayn, June 2007

Michael,

I genuinely feel there is something random about many of the reviews. Unmoored to the play – an almost wilful refusal to watch and listen. You haven't let us down. We're all proud of it. It's a terrific play and it is giving a lot of pleasure. The only consequence of the reviews is that we'll be able to do fewer performances than we'd have liked, but it's well sold already so I'm hoping that we can keep it near to full until the end of the summer. I know how battered you must be feeling, and I'm as perplexed as you.

> All best,
> Nick

Frayn to Codron,
June 2007

Dear Michael,

Many thanks for your message. It was kind of you to write, and I was very touched.

I was a bit stunned by the reviews, I have to confess. But I think I have to take them seriously. One can shrug off a few bad notices – tastes differ, after all. But when almost all of them are bad, and when the same kind of disappointment recurs over and over again, I think one has to do a bit of self-examination.

I see (too late!) that I have been carried away by an idea which is not really dramatic – or which at any rate I haven't found a way to make dramatic. I suppose the parallels between Reinhardt's life and [*Everyman*] are really only of literary and anecdotal interest. Reinhardt was an extraordinary man (with something of all of us in him, hugely magnified), but I haven't found another character strong enough to test him, so that his strengths and weaknesses are not really dramatically exposed and explored. Then again, plays about the theatre are a notorious trap. I got away with it once [in *Noises Off*], and I should have stopped there.

One of my regrets is that I intended the play in part as a tribute to Michael Blakemore and to you. There are some slight echoes of Reinhardt in both of you. I hoped in particular that it might be a good last collaboration between Michael and me, perhaps even with you as well if things had turned in that direction. And I haven't brought it off.

I think I had probably retired in any case, but it would have been nice to have walked out of the building with a clock under my arm rather than being hurried out by the security staff. Looking back over my life, I see that about half of the things I have written have been pretty much flops of one sort of another. I had a very bad run in the 1980s and 1990s, when five things went down one after another. But then, from *Copenhagen* onwards, I had a good patch, and got rather out of the way of bad reviews. Probably a debilitating experience. A good bucket of cold water thrown over one is very reviving. It will help to make me a spry pensioner.

Blake: 'Damn braces, bless relaxes.' Claire [Tomalin, Frayn's wife] reads this as meaning 'Down with things that make you tense; three cheers for ones that put you at your ease.' I read it as meaning 'criticism and opposition sharpen you up; praise and approval weaken you.'

Anyway, it was worth writing *Afterlife* just to get your response in verse.

Yours,
  Michael

2009

Mrs Affleck (2009)
by Samuel Adamson

from Henrik Ibsen's *Little Eyolf* (1894)
Director: Marianne Elliott
Cottesloe, 20 January to 29 April 2009 (61 performances)

In 2005, Samuel Adamson wrote a version of Ibsen's Pillars of the Community *(1877), directed by Marianne Elliott in the Lyttelton.* Mrs Affleck *was a radical reinterpretation of* Little Eyolf, *retaining the original scenario – an already strained middle-class marriage is almost destroyed when the couple's nine-year-old son drowns – but transplanting it from 1890s Norway to the English coast in 1955; Rita and Alfred Allmers become Rita and Alfred Affleck.*

Samuel Adamson, email to Mark O'Thomas, 17 June 2010

Dear Mark

Pleased find rather rushed answers to your questions [for your paper on *Mrs Affleck*] below. […]

  3. *The critics were almost all universally hostile to your work on* [Mrs. Affleck] *as opposed to the reception of* Pillars of the Community, *which was lauded. How do you account for this difference in reaction?*

I didn't read the reviews. (I knew the morning after press night it had been badly received, and when you know that, there really is little point exposing yourself to the criticism.) *Pillars of the*

Community was an English version of the Norwegian play, written according to the current fashion of having a playwright work from a literal translation to create a production-specific, actable text. It was faithful to the Ibsen. It was a 'lost' Ibsen, and the critics delighted in the rediscovery. A play that had seemed unperformable got a smashing production from Marianne and found an audience. It was generally a cause for celebration. *Little Eyolf* is not, I think, considered a 'problem play' as *POTC* is. So I suppose it looked like tampering on my part. Did I go too far, or not far enough? Did [the critics] want unadulterated *Little Eyolf*? I don't know. A well-known director said to me when the lights came down on the press performance, 'I'm afraid, Sam, you'll wake up to discover that they've missed the fjords'. So perhaps they simply felt it wasn't justified, that I had bowdlerised a cherished text? But I wouldn't change a word of *Mrs Affleck*, and I think my reimagining was justified. It was an act of love towards *Little Eyolf*. […]

Best wishes,
Sam

England People Very Nice (2009)
by Richard Bean

Director: Nicholas Hytner
Olivier, 11 February to 9 August 2009 (71 performances)

The main action of Bean's comedy is a play-within-a-play, performed by asylum-seekers in a detention centre. It spans centuries of immigration into London: Protestant Huguenots fleeing Catholic persecution in 1689; Irish families escaping the potato famine in the 1780s; Russian Jews driven out by pogroms in 1888; the influx of Bangladeshis in 1971, forced out by floods and civil war; the aftermaths of the 9/11 and 7/7 terror attacks. In each century, a young woman (always played by Michelle Terry) falls for a young man (always Sacha Dhawan) across the racial divide. Bean wanted to make serious points about immigration and assimilation: 'We knew we were having fun with stereotypes, and that some people would be offended.'

Hytner, postcard
to Richard Bean,
11 February 2009

Richard –

All very best luck tonight. And thank you for this amazing play. I've had a <u>ball</u> doing it and I couldn't be happier than I am to see it packing and delighting (and outraging) the Olivier. It's <u>exactly</u> what the National should be doing.

The press is immaterial: it's a triumph.

Love,
Nick

Hours later, Nicholas de Jongh, drama critic of the Evening Standard, *wrote: 'I hated this gross, cartoon history … Its invective is often funny, … but in the slick, cruel, abusive style that Bernard Manning perfected long ago.' Two days later, Hussain Ismail, a Muslim playwright of Bangladeshi origin, based in Tower Hamlets, attacked play and production in a* Guardian *blog post.*

Ruth Brooks, letter
to *The Guardian*,
21 February 2009

Sir,

Having taken a group of year 12 students to Nicholas Hytner's wonderful production of *England People Very Nice*, I simply could not believe the nonsense and misunderstanding in your report ('Satire or stereotype?', 14 February). Among the surnames of my students were Brennan, O'Mahoney, Fahey, Yussuff, Dovidaityle, Ogunde, Oshi-Ojuri and Kong – so yes, I have a fair smattering of 'immigrants', as well as those who would consider themselves simply English.

Not one missed the point of the stereotype – that this was not how the characters were, but how they were perceived and portrayed. All of them recognised that we were laughing at the unacceptable, and at times it was uncomfortable viewing. And yet they acknowledged in post-show discussion that racism like that shown is exactly what they have encountered and indeed, at times, shown support for in their own words and actions. Nor did they, unlike the worthy critics, fail to make the connection with Brecht, who recognised that to challenge an audience, he also had to shock them out of their complacency, and that it was often best done through comedy.

Far from being in the style of Bernard Manning, it is the comedy of *Little Britain*, of Daffyd and Ting Tong, not to mention Fat Fighter Marjorie Dawes – with her all-encompassing prejudices. Perhaps the final section was a warning about the extremism of certain Muslim leaders, but that concern is expressed daily by politicians, teachers and community leaders as well as by Muslim parents. By all means criticise it as a piece of theatre – although we were part of an audience who obviously loved it – but to challenge this play on the grounds that it glorifies racism is frankly ludicrous. This half-term my students will be writing a review of *England People*. My guess would be that while they may not have the erudition of a Mr de Jongh, they will show a great deal more insight and honesty. Perhaps you'd like to publish one or two?

Sincerely,
Ruth Brooks

The Habit of Art (2009)

by Alan Bennett

Director: Nicholas Hytner
Lyttelton, 17 November 2009 to 19 May 2010 (111 performances)

The Habit of Art *is set in an NT rehearsal room, where actors are working on 'Caliban's Day', a fictitious play set in 1972, at the Christ Church, Oxford, residence of W. H. Auden. In 'Caliban's Day', Auden (portrayed by an actor called Fitz) is interviewed by the biographer Humphrey Carpenter (an actor called Donald), then visited by Benjamin Britten (an actor called Henry), whom he has not seen for 30 years; Britten requests help with the libretto for his opera* Death in Venice. *Bennett first shared the script (working title* A and B, *for Auden and Britten) in November 2007.*

Alan Bennett to Hytner, 22 November 2007	Dear Nick,

I thought maybe you should see this before it gets any further. It's very thin still and in parts formless. The Humphrey Carpenter character needs a through story – though that slightly depends on what his family say about him being depicted and whether they can tell me anything about the unity of the books. He may not even have met Auden – not that that particularly matters.

Don't get your hopes up – I think 80 performances for this one might be optimistic. There are also mad things in it, like [a wrinkle on Auden's face] talking – it's the usual thing of my wanting to talk to the audience directly.

Anyway don't worry if it doesn't seem even promising. I've given you the original MS to read. I've photocopied it but the original is easier to cope with. I'll have it back when you've read it.[…]

Love,
Alan

Hytner to Bennett, November 2007	Dear Alan,

It's much more than promising; it's a wonderful portrait of two dying men, neither as popular as they once were, both seeking to connect their art with their lives, both aware of being on the wrong side of fashion. I think you've caught them both brilliantly.

I remember you saying you were having more trouble with Britten's voice than Auden's, but I think you've got him just right. Anything else you want to talk about – I'm here.

But you're definitely onto something.

Love,
Nick

Bennett delivered a revised draft the following spring.

Bennett to Hytner,
9 March 2008

Dear Nick,

Was it for this, you must be wondering, that you were delivered out of Zion.

I've done a bit more to it, though it's quite rough & ready in parts. I imagine you'll have a bit of a backlog but I'm not drumming my fingers (& off to Amsterdam for 3 days on Thursday).

Congratulations on *Major Barbara*. High praise all over!

Love,
Alan […]

The Habit of Art *opened on 17 November 2009, with Alex Jennings as Henry/Britten, and Richard Griffiths – a late replacement for Michael Gambon, who had been taken ill during rehearsals – as Fitz/Auden.*

Richard Griffiths
in *The Habit of Art.*
Photo: Johan Persson

Richard Griffiths,
card to Hytner,
17 November 2009

'You owe it to the rest of us to keep doing what you are good at.'
  W. H. Auden

Dear Nick,

It sounds like it deserves to be the motto universal. Thank you
for thinking of me. You & Alan have wrought, I think, a
masterpiece.
  I wish you joy of it & all thanks,

  Ricardo xx

2010

Really Old, Like Forty Five (2010)
by Tamsin Oglesby

Director: Anna Mackmin
Cottesloe, 3 February to 20 April 2010 (48 performances)

Tamsin Oglesby wrote Really Old, Like Forty Five *after observing 'the sheer loneliness,
redundancy and inactivity' of residents, including her mother-in-law, in a nursing home.
It imagines a mid-twenty-first-century England in which government scientists address
an overwhelming geriatric crisis by developing robot nurses; offering state-assisted
Home Deaths, and drug-accelerated mortality for dementia in-patients. We see these policies
affect three siblings in their seventies and eighties: age-defying Robbie, frail Alice, and Lyn,
whose Alzheimer's destroys her memory and strains her relationship with her daughter, Cathy.*

Jennie Darnell
(director), email to
Tamsin Oglesby,
31 March 2009

Hi, Tamsin.

[…] I enjoyed the play very much and it really gets under your
skin. Very disturbing. I felt a strong sense of unease at the end.
And I like its theatricality.
  I found the first few scenes really funny, was whipped along by
the wit and pace and ideas.
  Quite early on – scene 5 – I felt that I needed to connect with
these characters more. I think that you'd get very good older
actors which will help this sense of familiarisation but I did feel a
lack of intimate interest in them. […]
  End of Act One surprised me – I fear that it lacks a bit of
impact right now – I can imagine the audience needing the house
lights to go up to be confident of applauding.
  Well, because I've given notes in email I feel I've been too
critical […]. It is a very exciting play and addresses ideas in a
brave and funny way (wouldn't expect otherwise).

  Love,
    Jennie x

| Oglesby, email to Darnell, 31 March 2009 | Jennie, thanks so much. Your comments are *hugely* helpful. The gist of my notes from the NT are to do with creating more of a connection and drive between and in the family scenes; I think your need for an emotional connection with them tallies with this. I agree about the end of act one. Hopefully I'll find the right moment/scene/climax because I haven't a clue what it is right now. […] |

It's great to have a third and very perceptive eye on it. I really appreciate the objectivity! […]

Lots of love,
Tamsin x

Hytner agreed to produce the play, which would be director Anna Mackmin's second NT show.

| Anna Mackmin, email to Oglesby, 21 August 2009 | […] I grabbed 20 minutes with [Nick]. He enthused about the play and was very useful on casting. He said don't bother with Maggie Smith [for Lyn], he knows her work commitments. He also loved the idea of Geraldine [McEwan] and hadn't thought of her either. He said we should try Judi [Dench] but felt it was unlikely. He loves Maggie Tyzack. […] And of course we came back to Judy P. |

Please keep all thoughts (big and small) flowing.
I'll keep you in touch.

Love,
A xx

Really Old… went into rehearsal just before Christmas. The cast included Judy Parfitt (Lyn), Gawn Grainger (Robbie), Marcia Warren (Alice) and Michela Meazza as Mimi the robot nurse.

| Mackmin, email to Oglesby, 5 January 2010 | Sorry not to call you yesterday. I worked late and then went into the [NT] sound studio and then had a million emails and then went to bed! |

I worked on the opening and took a baby step with Judy towards what you want. It's a start. The first scene [an argument set in a National Theatre foyer] all fell apart a bit. Just felt like a group of people bickering away with no entry in for the audience!! Better by the fourth go through. Nothing to worry about, or nothing for you to do anything about, just process. […]

Ta xx

| Sebastian Born (NT associate director – literary), email to Oglesby, 22 January 2010 | Hi, Tamsin – I saw a run yesterday. It's in very good shape. The performances are all absolutely cooking and Judy is leading brilliantly from the front. A lot of it is completely hilarious and the robot is fantastic – danger of stealing the show. But it's also trenchant and moving where it should be. […] |

Best wishes,
Bash

Alice's grandson, Dylan, was played by Thomas Jordan, whose mother wrote to Oglesby midway through the run.

Morag Jordan, email to Oglesby, 9 March 2010	Dear Tamsin,

My friend Carrie wanted to tell you how much the play resonated for her – she wrote me the following email:
    It was a very enjoyable and clever mix of reality, family relationships across the generations, futuristic sci-fi, ethical and human issues re. how society might deal with the age/mental health problem (for me a blatant warning of which road <u>not</u> to go down), ageism and trying to appear young, teenage pregnancies, and of course the frightening and worrisome aspects of what it's actually like for those suffering and their relatives, which end up turning the dire situation into a farce. I assumed the scientific element was purposefully exaggerated to be preposterous and yet the message for the officials is to be careful what you sow because you may be the one to reap the results! I was merely left with a huge smile on my face. Whilst I found it very refreshing and funny, I am not sure I would want to take my mum! […]

    Kind regards,
      Morag

Oglesby, email to Jordan, 10 March 2010	Dear Morag,

I absolutely love grass-roots approval! And your friend describes so succinctly what I've tried to do in the play. There's nothing better than good honest audience appreciation and, not actually being there, I miss the feedback sometimes. […]

    Many thanks again,
      Tamsin x

Welcome to Thebes (2010)
by Moira Buffini

Director: Richard Eyre
Olivier, 22 June to 12 September 2010 (44 performances)

Moira Buffini's five-act epic reimagines the Thebes of Sophocles's tragedies as a present-day African state, ruled by a president whose name gave the play its original title, Eurydice.

Moira Buffini, email to Richard Eyre, 25 September 2009	Hello Richard,

[…] Has Bash [Sebastian Born] emailed you? Apparently there is an American play called *Eurydice* coming in to London before mine opens. What are the chances of that?? He's suggesting I think of another title. Blimey.

    Lots of love,
      Moira x

Buffini, email to Eyre, 13 January 2010

Hello, Richard.

I like *Welcome to Thebes.*
Is that OK with you?

Moira x

Eyre, email to Buffini, 13 January 2010

Yes yes yes!

Rx

2011

The Holy Rosenbergs (2011)
by Ryan Craig

Director: Laurie Sansom
Cottesloe, 16 March to 24 June 2011 (70 performances)

Ryan Craig was feeling 'neurotic' about the prospects of his latest script becoming his first original play to open at the NT.

Purni Morell (head of NT Studio), note to Ryan Craig, 2010

I bet you my house that the National will want to produce your play, entitled *The Holy Rosenbergs* (currently entitled, that is).

P. Morell

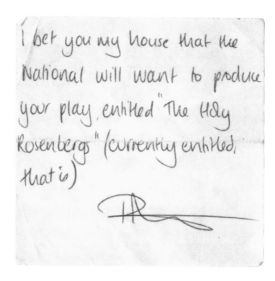

A year later, Craig magnanimously cancelled the bet. But he kept the note.

London Road (2011)

Book and lyrics by Alecky Blythe
Music and lyrics by Adam Cork

Director: Rufus Norris
Cottesloe, 14 April to 27 August 2011 and
Olivier, 1 August to 6 September 2012 (125 performances)

*Alecky Blythe emerged as a leading exponent of verbatim drama: actors performed edited transcripts of her interviews with people caught up in a police siege in Hackney (*Come Out Eli, *2003), and with sex workers (*The Girlfriend Experience, *2007).*

In 2006 and 2007, Blythe interviewed residents of London Road, Ipswich, where Stephen Wright, a forklift truck driver, had been living when he murdered five local sex workers, all women. Paired with Adam Cork on a writers' and composers' week at the NT Studio, she played him her Ipswich recordings. He thought setting them to music could be an 'exciting development' in song composition. Hytner commissioned a full-length piece, which was presented as work-in-progress in May 2008.

Sebastian Born, email to Alecky Blythe, 12 May 2008	Dear Alecky,

I just wanted to say how impressed I was with the work that you and Adam had done here for the past couple of weeks. It's all very exciting.

I think the (musical) form does allow you to be very free to reorganise the material which you've collected in ways which are thematically and narratively interesting. The way forward now seems to be for you to put together an assemblage of the whole thing and then for Adam to compose around that.

What was great about what we saw on Friday was that there were ensemble numbers, scenes, individual arias or duets. You should feel free to push the various forms further, so that, for example, the recitation of the names of the victims becomes a huge and very moving oratorio. […]

All best wishes,
Bash

Blythe's previous verbatim scripts had all been performed using the same method: actors listening to recordings via earphones, and repeating the interviewees' every 'um' and 'ah'. In January 2010, Tom Morris directed actors in a workshop presentation that led Hytner to green-light a full production of London Road, *which Blythe and Cork expected Morris to stage, using the earphones method.*

Blythe, email to Adam Cork, 25 February 2010	I had a very good meeting with Tom a few weeks ago and agreed to lose earphones for performances but he said rehearsals would be carried out with the earphones and I would be very hands on in trying to get the actors to maintain the detail that is there with the earphones. The key thing is authenticity and he said he would very much not want to lose that either. He also said I could of course say no but [in that case] Hytner would probably not schedule it!

Ok, I thought, we really want it to happen at the NT, resources, kudos etc. I trust Tom, he's very collaborative, I'm up for it. Off with the earphones!

THEN I had a meeting with Bash who informed me that Nick is v. keen and … would want to do it in … first half of next year. Great I thought! Oh no, but there's yet another catch. 'Tom is not available until the end of next year so you will have to find another director.' F***! Bash's thinking we should grab the available slot as Nick might change his mind … I'm thinking 'but I've just got my head round this giant obstacle of not using earphones and now you're asking me to put my trust in someone else who probably has never seen my work and hasn't seen how instrumental the authentic delivery of the material is.' Aaahhhhh! 'Don't worry we'll find someone who understands, maybe we'll re-approach Phyllida [Lloyd] or Rufus Norris is very good,' says Bash.

'OK' I say…

I go away and worry about the whole scenario, thinking another director might well … not be so into the whole verbatim side of things as Tom. I write to Tom, tell him I'm gutted but can he suggest a replacement. No word back, hardly surprising.

Yesterday I find myself … having lunch with Andre Ptaszynski, chief exec of the Really Useful Group. I pipe up about our project, 'Oh yes … I heard about that. I'm on the board at the National and in the last meeting out of all the shows Nick's doing next year, *London Road* was the one he got the most puffed up about. He really wants to do it.' Hurrah! …

So Adam, sorry that I have not told you this sooner but I really wanted to bend your ear about it but you've been very busy …

Let me know your thoughts.

Very best,
   Alecky xx

Alecky Blythe (left) and Linzi Hately (right) in rehearsal for *London Road.* Photo: Mark Douet

Norris directed London Road, *in a production named Best Musical by the Critics Circle. It stretched the boundaries of musical theatre: a six-piece band accompanied 11 actors, each portraying a London Road resident, and many other characters, addressing verbatim dialogue and lyrics straight at the audience.* London Road *became a film when Norris directed Blythe's screenplay in 2015.*

One Man, Two Guvnors (2011)
by Richard Bean

Based on *The Servant of Two Masters* by Carlo Goldoni (1746)
with songs by Grant Olding
Director: Nicholas Hytner
Lyttelton, 24 May to 19 September 2011 (92 performances)

Richard Bean, email to Sebastian Born, 25 October 2010	I'd like to send you the first Act of *Servant* by the end of the week because I'm worried that if I spend all of November doing the whole thing and I've got the tone wrong then I've wasted a month.

Bean, email to Born, 4 November 2010	I'm slightly rethinking a couple of the characters so I'll not send you it just yet. Maybe next week if that's OK. Going well. 　　Richard

Bean duly delivered Act One of The Geezer, *his reworking of* The Servant of Two Masters. *Goldoni's Florence in the 1740s was now Brighton, 1963; the servant, Truffaldino, became guileless Francis Henshall. A Londoner who's been fired from a skiffle band, Francis ends up in Brighton, working for both Rachel Crabbe (disguised as her murdered twin brother, Roscoe) and Rachel's beau, Stanley Stubbers – who murdered Roscoe. The ensuing escapades involve a Brighton gangster whose book-keeper, Dolly, fancies Francis, and Lloyd, who runs the pub where Francis serves two elaborate dinners simultaneously – the frenetic high-point of the play's copious slapstick.*

Hytner, email to Bean (cc Born), 14 November 2010	Richard – Thanks very much for the first act. Sorry to have taken a while. 　　Initial thought: when it's good it's terrific. But it often seems to me to be working too hard. The geezer himself is a great success, some of the others seem to me to be in danger of hardening into caricatures that are too extreme. It makes me worry that the play gets submerged by the idea. 　　I need to go through it and be specific. I'll call you tomorrow. 　　All best, 　　Nick

Born, email to Bean, 2 December 2010	[...] I gather that the *Geezer* title has been bounced back in my absence.

Maybe thought just a little too populist for the NT crowd?

All best wishes,
Bash

Bean, email to Born, 3 December 2010	Am I allowed to get into a dialogue with marketing about this. *Geezer* is to me an absolute gift of a title, and we know what a brilliant title can do – *England People Very Nice*.

Richard |

Born, email to Bean, 13 January 2011	Richard – I've just finished the new draft – made me laugh out loud several times. I think you've made the basic plot much clearer, and the characters are really springing to life – dim Pauline, canny Dolly, pretentious Alan and his pretentious dad, Francis, Charlie. The slapstick sequences obviously need to be worked out but will be great – the trunk *shtick* and the two meals set-piece. We just need to sort out the title! I'm quite keen on *The Guy with Two Guvnors* but Nick seems to want the servant connotation in there. […]

All best,
Bash |

Born, email to Bean, 14 January 2011	Just spoke to Nick – he would go with *One Man, Two Guvnors*.
B

Bean, email to Hytner and Born, 8 February 2011	Nick/Bash,

OK, here's the first half rewrite. […]
   All members of the audience in this script are considered to be plants.
      And forward to the second half … […]

Rx |

Hytner, email to Bean and Born, 9 February 2011	Just read it. Brilliant! N x

James Corden would play Francis. Grant Olding, composer for four of Hytner's NT productions, wrote original songs, to be performed live in the show by skiffle band The Craze.

Bean, email to Grant Olding, 26 February 2011	Is James Corden musical? I know he can sing a bit but can he play washboard, whatever?

Rx |

Olding, email to
Bean, 26 February
2011

I don't know how rhythmical he is [as I haven't met him yet].
I mean I'm sure after a couple of sessions with our drummer
he'd be fine – the good thing is that skiffle is quite raw isn't it, so
nothing has to be perfect. But from my experience in trying to
play the spoons last week there's a big difference between playing
something like that and PLAYING it.

     Gx

*With Corden – not ultimately required on washboard (though he did mime xylophone) –
opposite Jemima Rooper as Rachel and Oliver Chris as Stanley,* One Man, Two Guvnors
opened on 24 May.

James Corden in *One
Man, Two Guvnors.*
Photo: Johan Persson

Hytner, postcard to
Bean, 24 May 2011

Richard –

It's an amazing play and an absolute gift. I had no idea it could, or
would, be this funny.
   Thank you!
   It's always a pleasure …

   All very best luck
      love Nick

James Corden, card
to Hytner, 24 May
2011

Nick,

I don't really think I'll ever be able to put into words how much
I have to thank you for. Your faith in me to be able to do this,
your faith in me full stop! I have loved every single minute of this
whole job. Playing this gift of a part, working with you so closely,
it's been a dream come true. Thank you for your wisdom, your
friendship and your guidance. You are a different class to anyone
I've ever worked with. Anytime you call, I'll say yes!

   All my love,
      James x

Ryan Craig, email to
Born, 1 July 2011

Rebecca and I saw it last night. Hilarious. My brain and chest
hurt for a long time afterwards. I was trying to think of the last
time I laughed with that degree of helplessness and I realised it
was the first time I saw the rat poison episode of *Fawlty Towers*.
I think it's really in that league, it's so beautifully handled. So
skilled. It has the feel of a classic.

Bean, email to
Corden, 5 July 2011

Hi James,

[…] Anytime you feel you might need some more ammunition
in the way of new 'ad libs' just ask, I can knock up some options.
From what I've heard you're doing fine without.
   You're doing brilliantly, and I hope you're enjoying doing it.
Looks like you are. How's the knee?

   Richard x

Corden, email to
Bean, 6 July 2011

I'm loving it Richard, every single night. I will never be able to
thank you enough for this part. The only time it isn't fun is five
minutes before and 20 minutes after! […]
   The knee is OK, just hurts a bit. The truth is I think I actually
need to do a bit more (and when I say more, I mean y'no some)
exercise in the day and I'll be better for it.
   All is good though,

   Speak soon,
      James

*The show transferred to the Theatre Royal, Haymarket, where the original cast gave their
final performance on Saturday 25 February.*

Bean, email to Corden, 26 February 2012	I didn't make it in last night, but saw the show report. Looked great.

I gave up my two tickets to some people who hadn't seen it. Somehow felt right, as I'd seen everyone Thursday night. And I've seen it over twenty times.

What a helluva thing it's been.

From the start you were brilliant. I remember my first comments, comedy timing to kill for. And the fun with the impro. has developed.

So many thanks.
Beano x

Most of the original company then took what Corden called 'this ridiculously silly play' to Broadway, where it began previewing on 6 April.

Bean, email to Hytner, 10 April 2012	I think you and I need to have a discussion about the tone of the whole play. The American audience are obviously much more disapproving of the end of the pier saucy filth that is the heart of the play. This is the problem that Olly [Chris] is struggling with. As the flag bearer of filth he's suffering with the audience.

Personally, for this piece, which is a version, it's not me, it's supposed to be entertainment, I'm perfectly happy to compromise and give the audience what they want. As in cutting 'bugger the dolphin'. I'd like to cut 'went out with a virgin once', the same would go for the fart, unless we went for a stupidly big fart. If that doesn't work we cut it altogether.

Corden, email to Bean, 29 April 2012	All going well here still, Neil Simon LOVED it!

Corden was one of five nominees for Best Actor at the Tony Awards on 10 June, up against four Americans: John Lithgow, Frank Langella, James Earl Jones, and Philip Seymour Hoffman, as Willy Loman in Death of a Salesman.

Bean, email to Corden, 10 June 2012	I've got 50 quid on you. Don't screw up.

Rx

Corden, email to Bean, 10 June 2012	I'm afraid you've wasted your money I think! It's all Hoffman. People who don't have votes seem to want me to win though!

He won.

With other actors as Francis, One Man, Two Guvnors *continued at the Haymarket until March 2014, and had three UK tours. It has been performed in translation in dozens of countries.*

2012

The Count of Monte Cristo (1844)**
by Alexandre Dumas
adapted for the stage by Richard Bean

In January 2012, the NT announced that Richard Bean's adaptation of Dumas's 1,200-page novel The Count of Monte Cristo *would open that November in the Olivier, directed by Timothy Sheader.*

Richard Bean, email to Sebastian Born, 23 April 2012	Have you read my first draft of the first half, the one Tim Sheader didn't like, and which Nick [Hytner] has read? If you give me notes on that that'll be three people giving me notes. Rx
Bean, email to Born, 10 May 2012	Tim didn't think my prison scenes were any good, I think they're great and do the job. Could you look at them and give me some idea of what I need to do to satisfy him. Ta. Rx
Bean, email to Born, 13 May 2012	This is my new 'operatic/romantic' first act. It still has much that feels like Bean because it's set in Marseille so there's a lot of grunty working-class folk around. My brief from Tim was to be operatic and raise the stakes. I feel I've done that. If I haven't I don't honestly know what to do. Rx

Five weeks later, 'National Theatre delays Count of Monte Cristo *play' was the headline on a BBC News story, in which Bean conceded: 'I just couldn't get the script to work. It's a difficult task and ... I failed.' The vacant Olivier slot was filled by Sheader's revival of Pinero's comedy* The Magistrate *(1885).*

The Curious Incident of the Dog in the Night-Time (2012)

Based on the novel by Mark Haddon (2003)

Adapted by Simon Stephens
Director: Marianne Elliott
Cottesloe, 2 August to 27 October 2012 (71 performances)

The first-person narrator and central character of Mark Haddon's novel is Christopher Boone, 15, who lives in Swindon with his plumber father, Ed. Christopher has behavioural traits associated with autism: he struggles to interpret body language and faces, likes to be alone and excels at maths. His investigation of the murder of his neighbour's pet uncovers disturbing, adult truths, not least about his mother's 'death'.

Mark Haddon, email to Simon Stephens, 24 September 2008	Dear Simon,
	
	How are you doing?
	    Stupidly busy I presume.
	    Nevertheless and annoyingly …
	    I wondered whether you'd had a look at *Curious*.
	    I sort of presume you've either reread it and think it wouldn't work or you've thought about it and realised it wouldn't work and therefore haven't reread it.
	    Either possibility is fine by me (you have to maintain a Zen-like detachment about these things or you end up being the nursemaid of your own books), but I'm prodding because Toby, my agent, was asking.
	
	Feel free not reply…
	    Mark

Stephens, email to Haddon, 24 September 2008	Or the third option is I've been chasing my tail pointlessly and stupidly and writing a new play for the Royal Court and not had a chance to look at it.
	    Which is careless and annoying and ridiculous of me.
	    And which I'll do my best to remedy within the next two weeks.
	
	I apologise sincerely.
	    Simon

Haddon, email to Stephens, 25 September 2008	Dear Simon,
	
	You're not careless, annoying or ridiculous.
	    I meant it about the Zen detachment so please, don't rush. Having a *Curious* stage adaptation underway would be a fantastic thing but it wouldn't make my own busy life any easier, so … I'm not rushing either.
	
	    Mark

Stephens, email to Haddon, 9 October 2008	*Dog* is even more brilliant on second reading.
	    And very adaptable. I'd love to have a crack at it.
	
	    Simon x

Haddon, email to Stephens, 1 December 2008	Dear Simon,
	
	    […] I (and the world) don't **need** a stage version of *Curious*.
	    The only reason for one is if it's really good and I reckon you could do that.
	    Not least because you really want to.
	    So … don't worry, we'll hang on. […]
	
	    Mark x

Stephens, email to Haddon, 30 May 2009	[…] The only thing I'd say about our meeting next week is that for me it's exploratory.
	    Kind of.
	    I'm finding my approach to your book being the opposite of what one ought to do with a film adaptation. Or so I'm always told.
	    Rather than taking a big line on your book or imposing a vision on it I'm reading it and re-reading it rather slowly.
	    And trying to get inside that moment of your head.
	    And then looking at a stage with it. […]
	
	    Simon

Haddon, email to Stephens, 9 October 2009	Dear Simon,
	
	I think [your script] really works. So much so I wonder why it seemed so difficult to me and everyone else. You've made the difficulty vanish and done it so well you will get absolutely no credit from most people.
	    There's stuff in there I love: the boxes, the train set, and that puppy is going to be a weeper.
	    A proviso: you've used a lot of my prose and there's absolutely nothing wrong with that, but it means my reaction is therefore … odd to say the least (I can no longer read even the novel properly), so trust everything I say with caution and rely more on other people's thoughts.
	    OK, I'm going to leap in with some thoughts – milk them for anything useful or tell me to shut up. Apologies for length. You've fired me up: […]
	    1) I think the first 25pp can be pared down a lot. […]
	    2) You have Christopher talking exactly as he does in the book e.g. doggedly answering every aspect of a question. I think we kind of get the joke and skate over that on the page, but his literalness takes up real time on the stage. I think you can make his replies trimmer and leaner but still in character.
	    3) I think you could remove more of my book, esp. where it's being read out and replace it with pure (often speechless) action even if it's not obvious what's going on, e.g. Christopher in a dark

and silent garden and Christopher lost at the station, i.e. less narrating and more disorienting mystery. […]

> 9) I'm seeing a revolve in my head …
> Oh, fucking shut me up …
> It's great […]

Mark x

By February 2010, Hytner had committed to Marianne Elliott directing Curious… *in the Cottesloe, and Stephens had enlisted Scott Graham and Steven Hoggett of Frantic Assembly to join the team as movement directors.*

The initial opening date, 2011, moved back a year. Elliott cast Luke Treadaway as Christopher. Within the tight confines of the Cottesloe, designer Bunny Christie, video designer Finn Ross, lighting designer Paule Constable and sound designer Ian Dickinson would conjure everything from mathematical formulae to an escalator; Curious *was an exceptionally complex show, technically.*

Marianne Elliott, email to Haddon (cc Stephens), 18 June 2012	Hia Mark, […] Things going OK in rehearsal room so far. Working out how to do scenes physically. And who Christopher is in terms of how expressive he is and what his voice is etc. […] Marianne x
Elliott, email to Haddon and Stephens, 22 July 2012	Hia both, I know we won't get to the first dress on Monday eve. We're behind schedule and it's tough going. There's just so much to do! […] I'm praying we make the 2nd dress. Otherwise first preview will be very interesting indeed. But whatever the case, do remember it will be VERY rough til we can spend the week perfecting. Much love, Mx
Ben Power (NT associate director), email to Stephens, 15 August 2012	Congrats on great reception for *Curious*. Clearly a monster hit – queues for returns snaking round the building … amazing.

Haddon, email to
Elliott and Stephens,
21 August 2012

Dear you two,

Everyone who has seen *Curious* has been totally blown away (and I hear the puppy finally peed last night).

One tiny detail however … which clunked for several people. Since the play is now updated [from the novel]: A is no longer the best grade, A* is, and Christopher would know this. And it's specially noticeable because A-level results came out the other day.

OK, end of annoyance.

I'll go away now.

Lots of love,
    Mark

Luke Treadaway
(Christopher) in *The
Curious Incident of the
Dog in the Night-Time*.
Photo: Manuel Harlan

From the sold-out Cottesloe, Curious… transferred to the Apollo and then Gielgud theatres, for more than 1,600 West End performances. Elliott, Stephens and Treadaway were among the winners when Curious claimed a record-equalling seven Olivier awards.

It opened on Broadway in autumn 2014, won five Tonys (including Best Play and Director) and ran for two years. On 9 December 2016, an NT press release confirmed that Curious… would close in London the following June.

Haddon, email to *Curious…* production team, 9 December 2016	[…] Dear all you wonderful people,

It has been the most incredible … (I am trying *so* hard not to say 'journey') … the most incredible thing. And continues to be an incredible thing in most corners of the known universe.

If I say so myself, my choice of Simon to adapt the book was a stroke of utter blinding genius not least because he wanted Marianne and Frantic

And they in turn wanted *you*. […]

I'm no expert but I strongly suspect that no other play in the West End has ever been loved so completely and so sustainedly. For which … Thank you. Thank all of you.

My only regret is that NT Live never got it to the international space station.

I can probably live with that.

Love,
    Mark

The Effect (2012)
by Lucy Prebble

Director: Rupert Goold
Cottesloe, 13 November 2012 to 23 February 2013 (66 performances)

Following the critical and commercial success of her ENRON (Chichester and Royal Court, 2009), Lucy Prebble's first NT play was a four-hander, in which Connie (Billie Piper), a psychology student, and Tristan (Jonjo O'Neill) fall in love at a research clinic while they undergo a four-week trial of a new anti-depressant, monitored by a female psychiatrist, Dr Lorna James (Anastasia Hille), and her mentor – and ex-lover – Dr Toby Sealey (Tom Goodman-Hill).

Lucy Prebble, email to Rupert Goold and Ben Power, 19 July 2012	So this is a version that at least has an ending …

Though I'm pretty sure we'll do some (ha!) reworking and I'm sorry there are so many spelling mistakes … oh and shit lines etc. Shame.

But at least this is a complete thing if you want to have it for design/production stuff/discussion. Next stage will be major notes I guess and I have to do another pass on the lovers who should be more present tense and defined mostly by their immediate surroundings, I think. And they need to have some of their ground the doctors trespass on cut back.

Also on a re-read I think the depression argument is still a bit facile, full of dodgy turns and not necessarily the most interesting/relevant one. Sigh. But …

At least it's clearly what it's about now and has four real parts. […]

Lxx

Goold, email to Prebble and Power, 19 July 2012

Well done, scribe! Brilliant of you to have it complete. Spent the day with Miriam [Buether, designer] and I really think if we get it right this could be absolutely fucking amazing! […]

Goold, email to Prebble, 25 August 2012 (10.49 pm)

A thought on Dr James: I don't think her breakdown should be, or is, something happening 'on the side' in your head or on the page so I'd keep it in. What's tricky is the old problem of the man who sneezes in Act One, always dead by Act Four. How do we give her a neurological runny nose without signalling too heavily? […]

Prebble, email to Goold, 25 August 2012 (11.42 pm)

I might be going a little signposted for your taste, let's just wait and see with James, I guess. I suspect our first issue will be length; we're getting a little out of control with sheer content. […]

I feel like I'm understanding what the play is about, technically, for the very first time. Emotionally, I have always known. That it's striving for where love and depression touch in their opposition. That depression is an absence of what love is made from just as love is a relief from what depression is made from. But technically, I think there's something else going on. Despite having called it *The Effect* I'm only just seeing that it's so completely about cause and effect in the human. It's an attempt, however clumsily, to look at what IS love or what IS depression by dabbling in what *causes* them. And therefore, happily, located completely in the notions of past and future, the business of our memory, or at least the thing that happened and then what then happened as a result of it. Making memory relevant, in a much more existential way. Does [Dr James's] breakdown/bias cause the disaster on the trial or does the disaster on the trial cause her breakdown and support her bias? With such indivisible questions about what comes 'first' and what comes 'after' how can science ever truly separate a love affair from an anti-depressant effect, for example, themselves forged together and without clear sense of which begat which? How, knowing that life is this reflexive gooey mess between our internal physical state and our external experiences, can we ever control or predict or judge it? The brain's job (and therefore memory's) may be to present a logical case for one or the other as best serves our needs, but can both seemingly contradictory things somehow be true, simultaneously, in one long, reflexive present? And surely the sane response to that insanely quantum disorder is either a breakdown, or the gently accepting focus on simply *doing,* in the space between past and present, that love and care involves.

That must sound ever so pretentious, airy fairy and deluded, but something in it gives me comfort at the moment, though I'm sure it struggles to transcend the page with its ugly weight! This is what happens if I write at night, all clinging to higher notions of meaning to give me faith. Climb climb higher to where you might be safe and beautiful!

Goold, email to Prebble, 26 August 2012 (12.05 am)

That is absolutely beautiful.

Wonderfully clear and profound. The idea of the long reflexive present is very touching and so at odds with Toby and in a way James too. […]

One thing it does make me think about is 'event' as opposed to cause or effect. The cause of Tris and Connie's love may be her bad relationship or his infant abandonment – the past, but the 'event' is their meeting, present feelings, boy meets girl. Is there a comparison to be found in the depression storyline?

Prebble, email to Goold and Power, 29 August 2012

Hi,

So here's something to look at.

It's a bit long and baggy and maybe a bit skippy. I felt a strange deflation as I worked the memory stuff back in, like a clarity was disappearing. But also, as Ben noted, it does feel bigger again, if only in its page length!

If it's a step backwards, that's okay, you can tell me, I feel prepared for that.

There's loads of confusion I can't work out about trying to bring in memory, but it's bloated and unwieldy. I can't work out if I'm not pushing hard enough on argument, or whether actually we are only interested in it all emotionally so it should

Rupert Goold (centre) and Lucy Prebble (right) in rehearsal for *The Effect*. Photo: Ellie Kurtz

be different; more personal, theory-less, and related only to the trial and the relationship between the doctors, instead of all that broader science talk. There's just too much going on.

The very end still feels like a cop-out to me, but I wonder, honestly, if that's only going to be made clear after a reading or even in the [rehearsal] room. My instinct thinks if we accept it's going to be melodrama and high aria at the end, then Tris should be fucked properly at the end and [Connie] leaves with him in a much more damaged way.

I don't know, maybe it feels I haven't done much but I really feel I have. I tried a lot of different things and many of them had unassailable problems, plot wise. I'm really keen to hear something read and to get your help. There's still a motivational problem with Dr James but I think that has made a step, though not sure if it's the right direction!

BLAH BLAH BLAH APOLOGIES DOUBT FEAR EXCITEMENT SHAME etc. [...]

Lxx

Half an hour after the end of The Effect's *second preview, Prebble wrote the following.*

Prebble, email to Goold, Power and Audrey Sheffield (staff director), 7 November 2012 (10.29 pm)	In reference to how it may be baffling and boring audiences, I make the following suggestions: [...] I wonder if the doctors feel so side-lined by DRS2 [their second scene] in writing and staging that we have no emotional investment in them by DRS3. [...] Include one flashback at top of second half [...] Cut Billie's emotional speech at the end of Muller because of its repetition OR cut the whole inner space reference. [...] Lx
Power, email to Prebble, Goold and Sheffield, 7 November 2012 (11.33 pm)	I wasn't in tonight but I don't think anyone is bored or baffled! Everyone I've spoken to is exhilarated, fascinated, moved. (I think a lot of [Lucy's suggestions] are worth doing. Some I have a slightly hysterical reaction to. See below!) [...] *Include one flashback at top of second half.* I REALLY DON'T THINK IT NEEDS IT. WON'T ONE BE MORE CONFUSING THAN SEVERAL? WHAT WOULD IT BE? [...] *Cut Billie's emotional speech at the end of Muller because of its repetition OR cut the whole inner space reference.* PLEASE DON'T CUT THE SPEECH. SHE DOES IT BRILLIANTLY, IT DELIVERS THE HEART OF THE PLAY, A SENSE OF HOPE, OF MYSTERY INTACT IN SPITE OF EVERYTHING. IT IS EXPOSED BUT SO IT SHOULD BE. ALL REAL WRITING ABOUT LOVE IS. BPx

2013

The Amen Corner (1954)

by James Baldwin
Director: Rufus Norris
Olivier, 11 June to 14 August 2013 (48 performances)

In Baldwin's drama about an African-American, Pentecostal church in 1950s Harlem, Marianne Jean-Baptiste played its pastor, Sister Margaret Alexander.

**Rufus Norris,
email to Marianne
Jean-Baptiste,
30 November 2012**

[…] I'm thrilled that you are up for this; if you have the itch for some serious theatre now, it is the most fantastic part for you, and I will do my utmost to make it both an enjoyable and properly full-on time.
    Safe travels and good luck with the raccoons.

    x Rufus

Marianne Jean-Baptiste in *The Amen Corner.*
Photo: Richard Hubert-Smith

Jean-Baptiste, email to Norris, 5 December 2012	[...] Sorry for the delayed response. I've been thawing out and catching up with the family at home [in Los Angeles] before another stint in Toronto next week. My agents are working out the details with the National so things are moving forward.

The raccoons were successful in destroying my honeydew melons but the aubergines are intact!fc Bastards! I wonder how they taste? Roasted raccoon with parsnip and celeriac mash, little truffle drizzle? [...]

M |
| Norris, email to Jean-Baptiste, 5 December 2012 | Bit stringy.

I once had to pick melons for a job, 18-hour days and backbreaking work for a fascist farmer and I've never quite forgiven the melons, so I say be grateful for God's little aubergines. But I am slightly awed by your culinary standards. Do you remember the NT canteen?

Anyway, I'm delighted that things are moving forward. I don't agree with the casting department's hard-line stance on your request for a round of applause every time you enter the rehearsal room, it's entirely appropriate.

x Rufus |
| Jean-Baptiste, email to Norris, 6 December 2012 | The applause on entry is a given and has never had to be part of a negotiation. I am simply astonished that they would suggest Gordon Ramsay over Yotam Ottolenghi for my dietary needs! It's a potential deal breaker!

M |

The Light Princess (2013)

Book and lyrics by Samuel Adamson
Music by Tori Amos

Suggested by a story by George MacDonald
Director: Marianne Elliott
Lyttelton, 9 October 2013 to 2 February 2014 (78 performances)

The Light Princess *had been in development for five years when it opened in the Lyttelton, with Rosalie Craig as Althea, 16-year-old Light Princess of Lagobel.*

Samuel Adamson, email to Matthew Robins (storyboard artist), Marianne Elliott and Rae Smith (designer), 27 March 2013	Hey, Matthew (and SmithElliott),

You're a star. I appreciate this lovely collaborative process. [...]

The writing, the story – dialogue, lyrics and music – is now very explicit and clear on why, psychologically and emotionally, Althea is in the air. [...]

Althea is airborne for two main reasons: |

1) when her mother died, she wanted to chase her mother to heaven. […]
2) she wanted, and wants for three quarters of the show, to escape the bleakness, the woe, the darkness, the hatred and the grief of the world. This bleakness/woe/hatred/grief is exemplified for Althea by the wailing, taunting, jeering Lagobelans. […]

We are in this story to see how it is that she overcomes her childhood retreat [to the air and then the lake].

Althea wants: a family. Her mother back.

Althea wants: to be away from the grief and terror and woe.

Althea thinks: those things are in the air (then the lake).

Althea refuses: to do what others want of her.

Althea is forced (by the lake): to come out of her fantasy hiding places.

Althea gets: what she always wanted.

Love,
Sam x

Adamson, email to Martin Lowe (music director), 3 July 2013

Martino – I don't think we're going to have a complete score by the time we start rehearsals. There will, I'm sure, be mopping up to do, with me taking Tori through plot simplifications, particularly in Act II, that will have musical consequences. […]

I mentioned it to Tori yesterday and she was kind of in denial about it. She has plenty to be getting on with and so do I. […]

Sx

The NT and the creative team hoped the Lyttelton would be the show's springboard to West End and Broadway runs, but it closed on 2 February with neither in prospect. It had received mixed reviews: the Evening Standard *found it 'delicate and sensuous, [with] bursts of thrilling exuberance';* The Guardian *concluded 'it lacks a genuine fairy tale sense of wonder.'*

Shane Thom (stage manager), *Light Princess* show report, 2 February 2014

Comments: Once upon a, once a…

Once upon a time, the Creative team came to watch a glorious production.

It was also watched by an amazing, supportive and enthusiastic audience who stood at the end and gave HUGE cheers, whoops and whistles.

And finally, after 78 performances, the Sealanders and the Lagobelans for the final time came together in harmony and lived happily ever after.

THE END.

Rae Smith (designer), email to Adamson et al., 3 February 2014	Dear Marianne, Tori, Sam and Tim [Levy, producer for the NT],

[…] It was wonderful to catch a brief glimpse of you [yesterday]. […]

What an incredible show!!! And what a world of wonder and beauty that was created. Having not seen it since Press night (down to being a new mum) I was aware of its imperfections, but it is a brilliant beautiful unique and exquisite show and I take it v personally that it is not moving forward … And so I just cried all the way through the last song. Who didn't, right? If not the whole show!!! Mostly because it was so beautiful and mostly because it is so loved by us. […]

All the young ones (6, 7, 9, 10, 14) in my family were completely blown away with it!!!!

With love kisses and respect,
Rae xxxx

2014

Great Britain (2014)
by Richard Bean

Director: Nicholas Hytner
Lyttelton, 30 June to 23 August 2014 (74 performances)

In January 2007, Clive Goodman, royal editor of The News of the World, *was convicted of phone hacking; the newspaper's editor, Andy Coulson, resigned. In January 2011, Coulson resigned after three years as Prime Minister David Cameron's director of communications, blaming media coverage of the hacking scandal, which had widened hugely since Goodman was jailed.*

That May, just before One Man, Two Guvnors *opened, Richard Bean told Hytner that his next play for the NT would be a satirical comedy on the newspaper industry. In July, Rupert Murdoch's News International shut down* The News of the World.

Bean was then contacted out of the blue by Kelvin MacKenzie, who had worked for Murdoch, as editor of The Sun *from 1981 to 1994, and now wished to produce a play about the phone-hacking scandal, which he predicted would 'continue to amaze over the next couple of years'. MacKenzie and Bean had drinks at the Charlotte Street Hotel on 8 September.*

Richard Bean, email to Kelvin MacKenzie, 9 September 2011	[…] I'm thinking hard about it.

Basically, I think some things are possible and some impossible:

STRAIGHT STAGE PLAY – I don't think it's possible to have a straight play about the Murdochs where they are realistically represented, talking about world domination, Cameron, Blair, phone hacking etc. Comedy or tragedy. It would stand or fall on its documentary worth and theatre will always fail on that, unless it's verbatim.

It would be possible to write a straight state-of-the-nation play about those issues but the characters would have different names, they would allude to Murdoch. You could really do phone hacking then. You could do some press baron stuff too, but it would be someone a bit like Murdoch. [It] would not have the documentary tag, and would survive on whether it was enthralling or not. (The only measure of a play's worth in my opinion.)

OPERA – I think it's attractive to do a tragic opera called *Murdoch* about the Murdochs where the Murdochs sing, die, fall in love etc. The ENO would commission that tomorrow, cf *Nixon in China.*

MUSICAL – It would also be possible to do a comedy musical called *Murdoch* or *M.* or *Dial M. for Murdoch.* Satirical, comedy, musical. Possible.

So … I would like to do the state-of-the-nation straight play about the press. […]

I hope this helps your thinking. It's always going to be a long haul from commission to stage. If I'm involved it'll not be up for two years at the very earliest. […]

Richard

Bean, email to MacKenzie, 9 January 2013	Hi Kelvin, and a happy new year to you.

So Nick Hytner has commissioned me to write a play about phone hacking. A state-of-the-nation play on Press, Police, Politics in bed with each other.

I believe it's my round, so if you're up for talking, I'm buying. I'll do a pretty straightforward representation of a fictitious tabloid using hacking to get ahead in circulation and an editor keen on power and influence getting into bed with the Met. Nick must be looking for a brash comedy with enough state-of-the-nation stuff to keep the critics happy.

It won't happen this year because of all the court cases [involving former News International executives].

Your input would be invaluable, but I'd understand if you're sick of the whole thing!

Richard Bean

MacKenzie thought Bean the ideal dramatist for this subject ('A strange mixture of the theatre of the absurd and a slapstick farce'), and answered his questions about the life of a tabloid editor.

By April, Bean had completed a partial draft of Hacked, *in which a ruthlessly ambitious, unscrupulous female news editor on a fictional tabloid hacks phones and colludes with the paper's proprietor, an Irish multi-media mogul; with senior Met police officers; and with a Conservative prime minister (a storyline invoking former* News of the World *editor Rebekah Brooks's friendship with David Cameron). On 7 June 2013, it was confirmed that Brooks, Coulson and others would stand trial at the Old Bailey in September, on charges relating to phone-hacking.*

Hytner, email to Bean, 28 April 2013	Dear Richard,
	
	[…] The lawyers kept laughing when they repeated back lines and scenes that they'd decided didn't give them much legal concern. And they kept saying how much they wanted to see the play. Their advice boiled down to: do it after the Brooks trial and don't worry too much about defamation, though they may pick over a line here and a line there. Which is good. […]
	
	    Love,
	      Nick

Bean, email to MacKenzie, 22 May 2013	The play is going well. I've written a few scenes including a news conference scene where the editor, Wilson, puts in a Kelvin-esque performance. The audience would never think Wilson is you, they'd think he is inspired by you. […] Richard
Hytner, email to Bean, 2 September 2013	After talking to Clive [Coleman, BBC legal correspondent], we postponed the opening till April. The [booking] leaflet deadline is early January, by which time I hope the trial will be over. Nx

Hytner, email to David Yelland (*Sun* editor, 1998–2003), 9 November 2013	Dear David,
	
	It's very good to be introduced to you by Rufus [Norris, NT Director Designate].
	    Would you be up for meeting Richard Bean and me for coffee or lunch? Richard has written a pretty wild satire about the press, the police and the politicians – it would be good to hear some of it first-hand.
	
	    With best wishes,
	    Nick Hytner

Yelland met Hytner and Bean, then attended the NT Studio reading of Hacked *on 19 November.*

Yelland, email to Hytner and Bean, 19 November 2013	Dear Nick and Richard,
	
	Richard's play is very special. […]
	    Overall you have got the newspaper world about right […]
	    I think the way the police merge into the press is brilliant – I think this play is very close to being a *Pravda* and is brilliant. There are things to be done but it is there and you should be delighted.
	
	    More later,
	    David

Hytner, email to
Yelland (cc Bean),
20 November 2013

Thanks so much, David. Your notes seem right on target to me. There's a fine line to be drawn between theatricality, satirical licence and authenticity.

> All very best,
> Nick

The January 2014 deadline for announcing Hacked *in the NT rep leaflet passed with Brooks, Coulson and Co. still in the dock. If the play opened during the trial, the NT would be held in contempt of court. So the National gambled, leaving a blank space in the Lyttelton schedule from June, to be filled, Hytner hoped, with his post-trial-verdict production of* Hacked.

Billie Piper (Paige Brittain, the news editor) led a cast who had to sign non-disclosure agreements before reading watermarked copies of Bean's script. They rehearsed for weeks without information about the play leaking to the media. Still the trial dragged on.

Yelland, email to
Hytner, Bean et al.,
6 June 2014

Nick, Richard et al.,

[…] I have enthused about Billie's performance [in the dress rehearsal].

I've never seen a newsroom staged better and especially that of a tabloid. You have the essence of the small senior 'gang' made up mostly of older greyhairs. […]

The Met: truly accurate, brilliant, brave, funny. […]

The PM: I laughed a great deal … It never happened, it doesn't matter. […]

All in all I think this is superb. I've been privileged to meet you all, especially Richard and the cast, who I think are amazingly gifted.

> See you soon,
> David

Hytner, email to
Yelland et al., 8 June
2014

David, your help has been invaluable. Your encouragement equally so.

Stuck now temporarily in limbo, we intend to do three full dress rehearsals next week on Tuesday, Thursday and Saturday, and hope the jury doesn't keep us waiting too long after that. Though everyone tells us to expect them to be out two weeks. […]

> All very best,
> Nick

Unable to sell tickets, the National held 'invited dress rehearsals' in the Lyttelton, with Hytner coming on stage to warn small audiences that they could not talk or tweet about what they were about to see – or they too might wind up in contempt of court. And Bean wrote an alternate script: one version could be performed only if Brooks were convicted, the other had to be used if the jury ruled 'Not guilty'.

Hytner, email to Billie Piper, 20 June 2014

Hi, Billie –

This is weird, isn't it? The waiting. And the jury isn't sitting today because one of them is ill. They're taking the piss and I want to go round to the Old Bailey and sort them out.

    Hope you're finding things to do…

    Much love,
      Nick […]

On 24 June, the trial ended: Brooks cleared of all charges; Coulson convicted of conspiring to hack phones. The next morning, Hytner and Bean gave a press conference to announce that the play – its title changed overnight from Hacked *to* Great Britain *– would open on 30 June.*

Tom Stoppard, postcard to Bean, 1 July 2015

Dear Richard,

I'm sorry I didn't see you to congratulate you last night – it was a high-octane very funny brilliant evening and a deservedly triumphant climax to your adventure. It's a long time since I was in a theatre with such a buzz. […]

    Yours ever,
    Tom

The end of the Hytner years

Nicholas Hytner called being NT Director 'the most exciting and most fulfilling job in the English-speaking theatre'.

Aside from his work as a director, at an institutional level he and the departing executive director Nick Starr – whom Hytner always credited for much of the NT's innovation during his tenure, and with whom he would soon launch the London Theatre Company, and build its home, the Bridge Theatre – had brought about major change.

For audiences, their legacy is most evident in the Travelex Tickets scheme, which – now priced at £15 – has been running since 2003, and in NT Live, the stage-to-big-screen relays now approaching their tenth anniversary, taking the National's and other theatres' productions to audiences in hundreds of cinemas across the UK and the world. Finally, they supervised the £80 million NT Future scheme, which transformed the NT's riverside architecture, and added new catering, education and production facilities.

Samuel Adamson,
email to Hytner,
21 March 2015

Dear Nick,

I think this coming week is your last at the National. I want to wish you all the very best, send you many congratulations on your extraordinary achievements, and thank you.

I've had the most wonderful times over the past ten years working with you and Marianne on *Pillars of the Community*, *Southwark Fair* [which Hytner directed], *The Alchemist*, *All's Well*, *Saint Joan*, *Mrs Affleck* and *The Light Princess*. Thank you so much for the opportunities to make and to help make this work. And I have countless memories of the superb productions I got to see as a theatregoer. Yours was such a rich and compelling time.

The NT Future redevelopment has made such a difference to the building and to the audience experience: I love the way the theatre beams on the Thames at last.

You will be missed. I know there are exciting things ahead for you and I'm looking forward to seeing what they turn out to be. Good luck!

Love,
　Sam

Hytner, email
to Adamson,
22 March 2015

Thanks so much, Sam. It's very kind of you to say what you say. It's been a pleasure working with you over the years. And I remember *Southwark Fair* with particular fondness.

I think I've got used to the idea of not being there, but Friday will be a wrench whatever ground work I've done.

See you soon.

Love,
　Nick

Overleaf: An exploded diagram showing Denys Lasdun's building after the NT Future redevelopment

The New National Theatre

An exploded diagram illustrating the transformation.

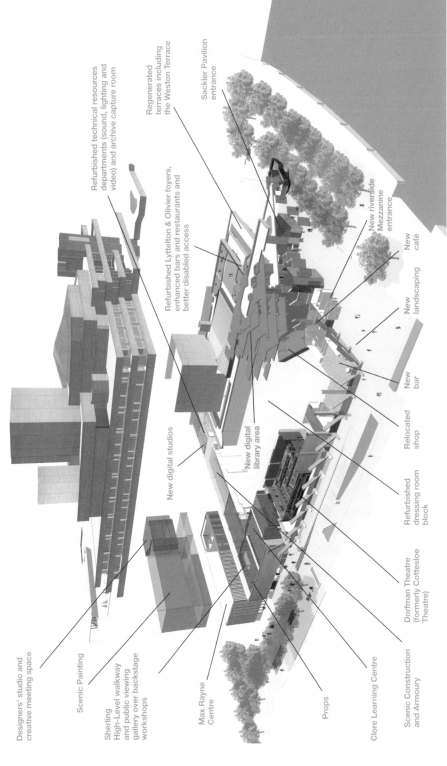

Designers' studio and creative meeting space

Scenic Painting

Sherling High-Level walkway and public viewing gallery over backstage workshops

Max Rayne Centre

Clore Learning Centre

Scenic Construction and Armoury

Props

Dorfman Theatre (formerly Cottesloe Theatre)

Refurbished dressing room block

Relocated shop

New digital library area

New digital studios

Refurbished Lyttelton & Olivier foyers, enhanced bars and restaurants and better disabled access

Refurbished technical resources departments (sound, lighting and video) and archive capture room

Regenerated terraces including the Weston Terrace

Sackler Pavilion entrance

New riverside Mezzanine entrance

New café

New landscaping

New bar

Act 6

The Rufus Norris Years

2015–

The start of the Norris years

On 15 October 2013, as the National prepared to celebrate its 50th anniversary, Rufus Norris was appointed as Director Designate. He was 48, and, as well as staging Death and the King's Horseman *(Olivier, 2009) and* London Road, *had been closely involved in the planning of the rep, as an associate director since 2011. His productions elsewhere included* Festen *(Almeida, 2004; Evening Standard Best Director), and a West End revival of* Cabaret *in 2006. NT chairman John Makinson said the Succession Committee had sought 'a creative director of unimpeachable quality', with 'the summoning power to attract the greatest talents' in UK and international theatre. In 2014, Lisa Burger, then the theatre's chief operating officer, was appointed as its new executive director and has worked alongside Norris since then.*

Everyman (late fifteenth century)
by Anon

Adaptation by Carol Ann Duffy
Director: Rufus Norris
Olivier, 29 April to 30 August to 2015 (68 performances)

Norris, email to Carol Ann Duffy, 6 October 2014

Dear Carol Ann,

We've never met. I'm taking over from Nick Hytner as Director of the NT next April, and would like to throw an idea at you.

I will be directing the first show in the Olivier of the new regime, which starts rehearsing in March next year. I have long been planning a production of a new play, but it has become apparent it's not going to work out. So I'm now looking at an alternative idea, one which is growing on me by the minute, but it does require a close collaboration with a great poet who has an understanding of theatre. For every reason, you are the first person I thought of.

Everyman is arguably the first English play; a morality tale of simplicity but absolute timelessness which has hardly had an outing in the last century, and which could, with the right combination of folk, be a stunning and totally appropriate beginning to what we intend to be a great period in the theatre's history.

Is this something worth having an exploratory conversation about? [...]

All best,
Rufus

Opposite: Rufus Norris in rehearsal for *The Threepenny Opera*. Photo: Richard Hubert-Smith

Hi, Rufus.

An eye-wateringly tight schedule!! Before I consider scaring myself into even considering it, it'd be helpful if you could email me more thoughts … what kind of script you are looking for/how close to the original text, or not/and any other helpful thoughts.

    X Carol Ann

Hi, Carol Ann.

Thank you for getting back so quickly, and for not (yet) ruling yourself out.

I am going to NY on a two-day fundraising duty early tomorrow, and by the time I get back on Thursday I will have a longer answer. I am a totally collaborative practitioner, and any thoughts I have about a project, particularly in its early stages, are very fluid. But my instinctive response is this:

It's most likely a very fresh version, rather than a completely new or significantly expanded entity. It wants to be as if written yesterday, stuffed full of soul and humanity, and maybe a third shorter. God is too brimstone, Good Deeds underwritten, etc. I don't feel it needs a radical conceptual idea. It should be *Everyman*. Spoken now, but timeless.

The production in my head takes place now but with all the same truths as then, is full of life and heart-breaking. It should be English, essentially Christian in its undertow – you only take your good deeds with you when you go – and simple in a very ungeneralised way. Everyman has done most things we all have done, has not killed anyone but his ledger is not well-balanced. God is probably a woman. The cast is as international as London, the music is live and strong, and the whole is highly choreographed naturalism, clear, ephemeral, transient as life. There is a moment where 100 people sing, and a moment where a man and woman are naked in the wind. It's about being human, and is emotionally literate. No lies, no big gimmicks. I've never written like this, it's very liberating! There might be a communal gathering at the beginning, a celebration, where we meet all the characters, so the world is possibly quite small. The stage is big, and probably quite bare. People, words, movement, music, vivid life. The closer you get to death, the more alive you feel.

I do feel this is achievable within the time or I wouldn't be asking. I am, as you can tell, very excited about it, and free-wheeling somewhat. It has the potential, somehow, of being a simple celebration of what a national theatre might be, which is exactly what that play should be. […]

    All best,
    Rufus

Chiwetel Ejiofor in the title role of *Everyman*.
Photo: Richard Hubert-Smith

Norris, email to Duffy,
16 October 2014

Hi, Carol Ann.

I'm attaching a couple of sections of *Everyman* for you to have a first go at.

The first is God's opening speech. I've put in italics lines I think could just be ignored; it's when God is talking as Jesus about how much he suffered for our sakes etc. and it feels too guilt-demanding and overtly religious to me.

The second is where Everyman tries to persuade Fellowship to come with him, and is refused. Fellowship might start as a group and whittle down to one or two by the end of the scene. This may make no difference to how you approach it, but I thought it worth mentioning; in the overly social, lonely days we live in for Everyman to start with a hall full of support and end almost totally alone feels promising.

So here you go, and good luck.

With best wishes,
Rufus

Duffy, email to Norris, 19 October 2014 (1.56 pm)	Hi, Rufus. Emailed GOD yesterday – let me know if it came through OK. x Carol Ann
Norris, email to Duffy, 19 October 2014 (2.07 pm)	Hi, Carol. No sign of God – how peculiar – could you try again? xR
Duffy, email to Norris, 19 October 2014 (2.37 pm)	Any luck?

Norris, email to Duffy, 19 October 2014 (2.47 pm)	I'm afraid to say, I fucking love it.
	    I will look properly later, but it immediately hits a fantastic tone whilst utterly being true, and a wonderful wryness that you do better than anyone.
	
	    x

Duffy, email to Norris, 19 October 2014 (3.16 pm)	Oh nooooo …
Duffy, email to Norris, 19 October 2014 (3.17 pm)	Bear in mind (hoping this puts you off) there will be no time for significant rewrites …

The Red Lion (2015)

by Patrick Marber

Director: Ian Rickson
Dorfman (formerly Cottesloe), 10 June to 30 September 2015 (76 performances)

Patrick Marber returned to the National with two shows in quick succession: he wrote and directed an adaptation of Turgenev's A Month in the Country *(1872), as* Three Days in the Country, *and this opened in the Lyttelton a few weeks after his first original play since* Howard Katz *(2001):* The Red Lion, *a three-hander about the manager, the kit-man, and a talented new striker at a semi-professional football club, set in its home changing room.*

Ian Rickson, card to Patrick Marber, 10 June 2015

Dear Patrick,

Thank you for letting me in, for comradeship, for wisdom, for openness, for honesty, for trust, and writing this wonderful play.

    Love,
       Ian

The next card came attached to a metal plate, about eight inches long and an inch wide, embossed with 'The Red Lion'.

Norris, card to Marber, 10 June 2015

Patrick,

I found this the other week and, of course, thought of you – weathered, hardy, a few dents and a couple of holes but beautiful and true.

    I feel so fucking privileged that you are opening this play here, now, and that we have been so blessed with your company this year. More and more please, you brilliant and gentle man.

    All best tonight,
       Rufus

wonder.land (2015)

by Damon Albarn (creator and music), Moira Buffini (creator, book and lyrics) and Rufus Norris (creator)

Director: Rufus Norris
Olivier, 23 November 2015 to 30 April 2016 (92 performances)

wonder.land *reimagines* Alice in Wonderland *for the Web 2.0 generation: troubled teenager Aly 'disappears' down a virtual rabbit hole as an avatar, Alice. The Albarn/Buffini/Norris collaboration began with the following exchange.*

Norris, email to Damon Albarn, 21 May 2014	D, this is an edited few sketches from Moira's pages [of book and lyrics]. If you want any context call me. Sorry for delay, R
Albarn, email to Norris, 21 May 2014	Getting to grips with words, enjoying the possibilities, will send evidence of aforesaid fun by end of week. X d
Norris, email to Moira Buffini, 21 May 2014	Got this tonight. First ever email I've had from Damon, so it can't be bad. x
Buffini, email to Norris, 21 May 2014	Wow. That's such a relief! […] Yes. We're starting. Good. Mx

2016

The Threepenny Opera (1928)
by Bertolt Brecht and Kurt Weill
Version by Simon Stephens (2016)

Director: Rufus Norris
Olivier, 18 May to 1 October 2016 (83 performances)

Simon Stephens, email to Tom Hughes, 12 January 2016	That's great news [that you're in line to be Rufus's staff director on *Threepenny*]. I'll put in a good word.
	    He is thoughtful. Shy. Dirty. Provocative. He kind of wrestled me in his office. He [is] massively well travelled. He has lived in war zones. He likes the space to think. There are moments when he looks at me like I've had a really good idea and it's when he stops talking and thinks that I know it's been a good idea.
	    He's easily distracted. Beautifully tangential.
	Good fun.
	
	Stephens

Hughes, email to Stephens, 20 April 2016	Hi Simon, […] I've attached today's suggestions for text changes in response to rehearsals. My explanations are in italics. […] Rufus asked me to emphasise again that they are suggestions & that he needs you to honestly respond & to tell us if you think something is a mistake. I'll make sure that he listens to everything that comes back. All love, Tom x
Norris, email to Stephens, 21 April 2016	Hi there big man, So I know from Tom that you weren't too enamoured of some of the suggested cuts/alterations on Tuesday, and I haven't heard about what you made of yesterday's list. There are a handful more today with one little section – going from your cut section of the gang arguing at top of scene 5 into the focus on Jenny – that I'd love you to look at when you're back [from teaching a playwriting course in Inverness], but mostly today it's just been putting in the cuts you suggested. […] It's tricky, trying to respond proactively to the ongoing challenge of cooking this up, without you here. I know that if you were around you'd have taken it all on in your own way and continued to hone it, and I am very aware of how frustrating it must be to just hear from notes, when you can't see the context. I really don't mean to disrespect your marvellous hand in pushing forward, and of course anything we try that isn't yours is a place-holder until you hear it and can make it good. I'm just a little worried about the scale of the task in front of us – the world of it is promising but incredibly time-consuming to uncover – and it would be great to solve as much as possible as we go along. Everyone is very aware that when you hear scenes again you are likely to want to adjust, so there will be no resistance there. I'm also aware that I can be a bit blunt in clumsy pursuit of trying to make it work. Please accept my apologies for that, and feel free to not pull punches if you ever think I'm overstepping in a way that doesn't serve the piece. Hope all is well with you and speak soon, R.
Hughes, email to Stephens, 23 April 2016	[…] I'm finding it so helpful to be at the heart of the process. And to see that anger and fear and disappointment are a part of that. Oftentimes rehearsal rooms feel like a carefully climate-controlled environment. I much prefer this. It's something I like about working with Rufus: there is so little bullshit and social decorum. It's like he's ignored every seminar on working with actors and writers that I've ever been to.

Often because he just doesn't have the time. But there's so much genuine love with that.

At the end of rehearsal today, Rufus looked to Imogen [Knight, choreographer] and I and said 'Smells good, doesn't it?'

And it really does. […] See you next week?

Tx

Stephens, email to Nicholas Hytner, 29 May 2016	Nick, It was lovely to see you on Tuesday. Your energy and enthusiasm galvanised us all. It always has done and will continue to. *Threepenny* has been a long journey and in many ways the hardest job of my career but I am proud of the show that we made in the end. Thank you, all those years ago, for having faith in my ability to make it. Simon x

2017

My Country: A Work in Progress (2017)
by Carol Ann Duffy and Rufus Norris

Director: Rufus Norris
Dorfman, 28 February to 22 March 2017 (20 performances)

Carol Ann Duffy, email to Norris, 3 October 2016 (10.36 pm)	Off to Italy tomorrow (work, but nice work). How are you? x
Norris, email to Duffy, 3 October 2016 (11.08 pm)	Funny you should ask … So the ritual is obviously this. Once every two years I [ask] you to come on board for a mad last-minute ride. This one is less mad, or at least less pressured [than *Everyman*]. After Brexit I got going on a nationwide listening project; we sent gatherers into Glasgow, Derry, Leicester and Merthyr to interview local people about where they live, what they think of UK, referendum, British values etc. There are more going out now to different places, and we'll send the first four back with more focused questions to the five or six most interesting and varied of their interviewees. By December we'll have a ton of stuff.

In January/February I'm going to get seven actors together and
we're going to make a work-in-progress response. It will play in
the Dorfman, then 10 weeks' tour for a week each to the seven
areas and a couple more, and maybe a week in Amsterdam.

The working title is: *My Country (a work in progress)*.

The seven actors will play the gatherers (already fab,
passionate, engaged and in love with their interviewees), as well
as maybe five interviewees each from their area.

The text of the interviewees will be strict verbatim, edited into
themes, divisions, etc. The text of the gatherers will be written;
possibly based on what they are like or what they say themselves,
but possibly more oblique or poetic. Like the angels in [Wim
Wenders' film] *Wings of Desire*, gathering the thoughts of the
nation around this historic moment.

It would be nowhere near the amount of text that you wrote
on *Everyman*, as the bulk would be verbatim, but there would be
some kind of a holding web (or something) woven through. It
would need some [time] in the early part of next [year].

Sorry.

Is this something worth talking you into at all, when you're
back from [your] peaceful idyll?

I adore you, you see.

x

Duffy, email to Norris,	Oh fuck off …
3 October 2016	Yes.
(11.12 pm)	

Playwright Tanya Ronder, Norris's partner, watched the production's first preview on 28 February 2017.

Duffy, email to Norris,	do not touch …
28 February 2017	do not touch that …
(2.37 pm)	do not touch that script until we chat.
	In at 2, but if you're free 1.45 we can chat. Otherwise in tea-break.

Norris, email to Duffy,	Tanya says don't cut or change anything, just direct it better. And
1 March 2017	I always do what she says. So how about we don't change owt for
	tomorrow, but just tidy and drill and shape?
	Yes to 1.45
	x Well done you x

Duffy, email to Norris,	Oooohhhh Tanya … Where have you beeeennnn?
1 March 2017	

Oslo (2016)

by J.T.Rogers

Director: Bartlett Sher

Lyttelton, 15 to 23 September 2017 (23 performances; first preview, 5 September)

First seen in New York, Oslo *dramatises the secret talks between Israel and the Palestinian Liberation Organisation that led to the* Oslo Accords *of 1993. J.T.Rogers sent his friend Ryan Craig the script, shortly before* Oslo *won the Tony for Best Play.*

Ryan Craig, email to J.T.Rogers, 13 May 2017

My God, it's a good play. I mean it's a really good play. I mean I loved it from the very first word to the very last. I was reading it over a cup of English Breakfast Tea in a crowded café and only too late realised I was occasionally slamming the table shouting 'Yes! Yes!!' Like some insane, bookish, bald Meg Ryan. Christ, you bastard. You really bloody nailed it this time. I can't wait for the production. […]

I'm unbelievably proud, brother. You reset the bar now.

Onwards,
   Br. Craig

Opposite: The National Theatre in 2015. Photo: Philip Vile

NT timeline

1904 William Archer and Harley Granville Barker write and privately circulate *Scheme & Estimates for a National Theatre*.

1907 *Scheme* published as *The National Theatre*.

1908 Shakespeare Memorial National Theatre Committee (SMNTC) established.

1909 Donation of £70,000 to the SMNTC capital fund, from financier and mining magnate Carl Meyer.

1913 Unsuccessful House of Commons motion in support of state-subsidised NT.

1914 For £50,000, SMNTC buys freehold on an acre on Keppel Street, London, behind the British Museum, hoping to build a theatre there to open for Shakespeare's tercentenary in 1916.

1916 Keppel St. site becomes home to temporary Shakespeare Hut, which hosts plays and other entertainments for British and ANZAC troops.

1924 British Drama League holds architectural contest for NT designs; £250 prize, won by William Somerville of Toronto.

1930 Granville Barker publishes *A National Theatre*, expanding and revising the 1907 volume.

1937 Purchase of site for NT on Cromwell Gardens, South Kensington, opposite the Victoria and Albert Museum. Granville Barker declines invitation to become first NT Director.

1942 SMNTC and London County Council (LCC) agree land swap: Cromwell Gardens site exchanged for site between Waterloo Bridge and Westminster Bridge.

1946 Joint Council of the National Theatre and the Old Vic established. Arts Council of Great Britain begins using taxpayers' money to subsidise the performing arts, including theatre. Brian O'Rorke becomes NT architect.

1949 Passing of The National Theatre Act, committing £1 million of public funds to building NT on the South Bank.

1951 HM Queen Elizabeth (later the Queen Mother) lays NT Foundation Stone beside Royal Festival Hall

1952 NT site moves along South Bank: now positioned in Jubilee Gardens, next to County Hall.

1955 Drama critics Kenneth Tynan and Richard Findlater hold mock funeral for the NT beside the Foundation Stone.

1960 Joint Council report to Chancellor puts estimated NT building cost at £2.3 million.

1961 Peter Hall expands seasonal Shakespeare Memorial Theatre operations into year-round Royal Shakespeare Company. Laurence Olivier becomes founding artistic director of Chichester Festival Theatre (CFT). Government and LCC commit to building combined South Bank NT and Opera House (new home for Sadler's Wells Opera).

1962 Olivier directs all three productions in opening CFT season, and is appointed first NT Director.

1963 NT Company begins first season at Old Vic, with *Hamlet*. Denys Lasdun appointed architect for combined NT/Opera House complex.

1966 Government scraps South Bank Opera House, obliging Lasdun to design NT as a standalone building.

1967 NT site moves one last time, a few hundred metres east, to its current location, downstream of Waterloo Bridge. Capital cost now put at £5–7 million.

1968 Theatres Act abolishes state censorship of drama.

1969 Construction begins on South Bank NT. Amended NT Act raises government contribution to the theatre to £3.75 million.

1970 Opening of NT's sister theatre, the Young Vic (a hundred metres down The Cut from the Old Vic), created and run by NT associate director Frank Dunlop.

1972 Peter Hall appointed NT Director Designate.

1973 Hall becomes Director on 1 November.

1975 Young Vic becomes independent, severing connections to NT.

1976 28 February: final NT performance at Old Vic. First performances in Lyttelton Theatre (March) and Olivier Theatre (July); HM Queen Elizabeth II officially opens the building (October). Start of early-evening Platform talks.

1977 First performances in Cottesloe Theatre (February).

1979 From mid-March to early May, backstage NT staff strike over pay and working patterns; the dispute costs more than £250,000 in lost ticket sales.

1982 New Education Department mounts first touring production, *The Caucasian Chalk Circle* (Brecht).

1984 NT Studio opens in Old Vic Annexe, concrete building adjacent to the theatre.

1987 Richard Eyre appointed NT Director Designate in January. Party in the Olivier to celebrate Laurence Olivier's 80th birthday.

1988 NT's 25th birthday marked by Queen approving the title Royal National Theatre; she attends anniversary gala in the Olivier. Eyre becomes Director.

1993 Start of inaugural cycle of the NT's Connections festival, which becomes largest youth theatre project in the world.

1996 Trevor Nunn appointed Director Designate in March.

1997 Start of £42 million Masterplan redevelopment of the NT. Nunn becomes Director on 1 October. NT buys the Old Vic Annexe.

1998 First Watch This Space summer festival of outdoor performances on Theatre Square. NT launches its website.

1999 NT2000 project sees the 100 'most significant' plays of the century celebrated in Platforms.

2001 Nicholas Hytner appointed Director Designate in September.

2002 Transformations season (April to September): 13 world premieres in reconfigured Lyttelton and temporary, 100-seat studio, The Loft, in Lyttelton circle foyer.

2003 Hytner becomes Director on 1 April. Launch of six-month Travelex £10 Season in the Olivier.

2007 NT Studio reopens after £6 million refurbishment; its facilities now include NT Archive, education studio and two large spaces for research and development.

2008 National introduces Sunday performances for first time in its history.

2009 Launch of NT Live with broadcast to cinemas of *Phèdre* from the Lyttelton. Sale of millionth Travelex £10 ticket.

2013 As part of £80m NT Future redevelopment, the Cottesloe closes and performances begin in The Shed, a temporary, 225-seat auditorium on Theatre Square. Rufus Norris appointed Director Designate in October. Gala performance in the Olivier, *Fifty Years on Stage*, broadcast live on BBC2 in November.

2014 Studio theatre (formerly Cottesloe) reopens as the Dorfman; alongside it is the new Clore Learning Centre.

2015 Norris becomes Director on 1 April.

Principal characters

All those listed are or were British, unless otherwise stated.

Samuel Adamson (b. 1969), Australian playwright and screenwriter

Damon Albarn (b. 1968), musician and composer

Edward Albee (1928–2016), US playwright

Sunny Amey (b. 1928), New Zealand theatre director; NT repertory manager, 1965–68

Lindsay Anderson (1923–94), film and theatre director

Sarah Pia Anderson (b. 1952), television and theatre director

William Archer (1856–1924), writer and theatre critic

Peggy Ashcroft (1907–91), actress

Eileen Atkins (b. 1934), actress

Alan Ayckbourn (b. 1939), playwright and theatre director

Jill Balcon (1925–2009), actress

Harley Granville Barker (1877–1946), actor, playwright and theatre director

Alan Bates (1934–2003), actor

Keith Baxter (b. 1933), actor

Richard Bean (b. 1956), playwright

Samuel Beckett (1906–89), Irish playwright, novelist, poet and theatre director

Max Beerbohm (1872–1956), essayist and caricaturist

Alan Bennett (b. 1934), playwright and screenwriter

Michael Billington (b. 1939), drama critic and biographer

Michael Birkett (1929–2005), film producer; NT deputy director, 1975–77

Michael Blakemore (b. 1928), Australian actor, writer and theatre director; NT associate director, 1971–76

Alecky Blythe (b. 1972), playwright and screenwriter

Diana Boddington (1921–2002), NT stage manager

Michael Bogdanov (1938–2017), theatre director

Robert Bolt (1924–95), playwright and screenwriter

Sebastian Born (b. 1953), NT associate director (literary), 2007–15

Jack Bradley (b. 1957), NT literary manager, 1996–2007

Howard Brenton (b. 1942), playwright and screenwriter

John Russell Brown (1923–2015), NT associate director (literary), 1973–88

William Boyd (b. 1952), novelist and screenwriter

Glen Byam Shaw (1904–86), actor and theatre director

Peter Brook (b. 1925), theatre and film director

Moira Buffini (b. 1965), playwright and screenwriter

John Burgess (1933–2010), NT literary manager (new writing), 1988–93

Simon Callow (b. 1949), actor, writer and theatre director

Ken Campbell (1941–2008), writer, actor and theatre director

Michael Codron (b. 1930), theatre producer

Judith Coke, actress

James Corden (b. 1978), actor, screenwriter and TV presenter

David Cornwell [John le Carré] (b. 1931), novelist

Tom Courtenay (b. 1937), actor

Noël Coward (1899–1973), playwright, actor, composer and theatre director

Ryan Craig (b. 1972), playwright and screenwriter

Giles Croft (b. 1957), NT literary manager 1990–96

Paddy Cunneen, Irish composer and theatre director

Jennie Darnell, theatre and television director

Oliver Ford Davies (b. 1939), actor and writer

Bette Davis (1908–89), US actress

Judi Dench (b. 1934), actress

George Devine (1910–66), theatre actor, director and producer

John Dexter (1925–90), theatre, opera and film director; NT associate director, 1963–73

Declan Donnellan (b. 1953), film and theatre director and writer

Marianne Elliott (b. 1966), theatre director

Richard Eyre (b. 1943), writer, film, opera and theatre director; NT Director, 1988–97

Michael Feast (b. 1946), actor

Ian Flintoff, actor

Michael Frayn (b. 1933), playwright, novelist and screenwriter

Michael Gambon (b. 1940), Irish actor
William Gaskill (1930–2016), theatre director;
	NT associate director, 1963–65
Pam Gems (1925–2011), playwright
John Gielgud (1904–2000), actor and theatre
	director
Julian Glover (b. 1935), actor
Derek Goldby (b. 1940), theatre director
Clive Goodwin (1932–78), theatrical agent
Rupert Goold (b. 1972), theatre and television
	director
Simon Gray (1936–2008), playwright
Trevor Griffiths (b. 1935), playwright and
	screenwriter
Alec Guinness (1914–2000), actor
Tyrone Guthrie (1900–71), theatre director

Mark Haddon (b. 1962), novelist
Peter Hall (1930–2017), theatre, opera and film
	director; NT Director, 1973–88
Christopher Hampton (b. 1946), playwright,
	screenwriter and director
Sheila Hancock (b. 1933), actress and theatre
	director
David Hare (b. 1947), playwright, screenwriter
	and director
Tony Harrison (b. 1937), poet and playwright
Rex Harrison (1908–90), actor
Ronald Harwood (b. 1934), South African-
	born playwright and screenwriter
Nigel Hawthorne (1929–2001), actor
Lillian Hellman (1905–84), US playwright and
	screenwriter
Katharine Hepburn (1907–2003), US theatre
	and film actress
Jocelyn Herbert (1917–2003), stage designer
Nick Hern (b. 1944), publisher
Greg Hicks (b. 1953), actor
Christopher Hogg (b. 1936), NT chairman,
	1995–2004
Anthony Hopkins (b. 1937), actor
Ted Hughes (1930–98), poet and writer
Nicholas Hytner (b. 1956), theatre, opera and
	film director; NT Director, 2003–15

Derek Jacobi (b. 1938), actor

Elia Kazan (1909–2003), Greek-American film
	and theatre director and producer
Michael Kitchen (b. 1948), actor and television
	producer
Hanif Kureishi (b. 1954), novelist, playwright
	and screenwriter
Tony Kushner (b. 1956), US playwright and
	screenwriter

Denys Lasdun (1914–2001), architect
Bryony Lavery (b. 1947), playwright
Julie Legrand, actress
Oscar Lewenstein (1917–97), theatre and film
	producer
Maureen Lipman (b. 1946), actress and author
Elizabeth Longford (1906–2002), historian
Edith Lyttelton (1865–1948), novelist
Oliver Lyttelton (1893–1972), first chairman of
	the NT, 1962–71

Anna Mackmin (b. 1964), theatre director
Patrick Marber (b. 1964), theatre director,
	playwright and screenwriter
Sean Mathias (b. 1956), actor, theatre director
	and playwright
David Merrick (1911–2000), US theatre
	producer
Arthur Miller (1915–2005), US playwright
Jonathan Miller (b. 1934), theatre and opera
	director
Helen Mirren (b. 1945), actress

Kelvin MacKenzie (b. 1946), editor of *The Sun*,
	1981–94
Geraldine McEwan (1932–2015), actress
Ian McEwan (b. 1948), novelist and
	screenwriter
Ian McKellen (b. 1939), actor
Genista McIntosh (b. 1946), NT executive
	director, 1990–96 & 1997–2002
Christopher Morahan (1939–2017), theatre and
	television director
Abi Morgan (b. 1968), playwright and
	screenwriter
Tom Morris (b. 1964), theatre director and
	producer
Michael Morpurgo (b. 1934), writer, playwright
	and poet

Kate Nelligan (b. 1950), Canadian actress
Mike Nichols (1931–2014), US actor, film and
	theatre director and producer
Peter Nichols (b. 1927), playwright and
	screenwriter
Rufus Norris (b. 1965), theatre and film
	director; NT Director since 2015
Trevor Nunn (b. 1940), theatre, film and opera
	director; NT Director, 1997–2003

Edna O'Brien (b. 1930), Irish novelist,
	playwright and poet
Tamsin Oglesby (b. 1965), playwright
Grant Olding (b. 1974), composer
Laurence Olivier (1907–89), actor, producer
	and film and theatre director; NT Director,
	1963–73

Nick Ormerod (b. 1951), theatre designer

Brian O'Rorke (1901–74), New Zealand-born architect

John Osborne (1929–94), playwright, screenwriter and actor

Bob Peck (1945–99), actor

John Peter (b. 1938), Hungarian-born drama critic

Edward Petherbridge (b. 1936), actor and writer

Ronald Pickup (b.1940), actor

Steven Pimlott (1953–2007), opera and theatre director

Harold Pinter (1930–2008), playwright, screenwriter, actor and theatre director

Joan Plowright (b.1929), actress

Ken Pople, art historian

Ben Power (b.1981), NT associate (now deputy) director

Lucy Prebble (b. 1981), playwright and screenwriter

Kenneth Rae (1901–85), secretary of the Joint Council of the National Theatre and the Old Vic, 1946–62; NT board secretary, 1962–74

Max Rayne (1918–2003), businessman, philanthropist; NT chairman, 1971–88

Margaret (Peggy) Ramsay (1908–91), theatrical agent

Terence Rattigan (1911–77), playwright

Lynn Redgrave (1943–2010), actress

Michael Redgrave (1908–85), actor and theatre director

Ralph Richardson (1892–1983), actor

Ian Rickson (b. 1963), theatre director

Diana Rigg (b. 1938), actress

Bryan Robertson (1925–2002), curator and arts manager

Michael Rudman (b. 1939), playwright, theatre director and producer

Jeremy Sams (b. 1957), theatre director, translator and composer

Paul Schrader (b. 1946), US screenwriter and film director

Paul Scofield (1922–2008), actor

Peter Shaffer (1926–2016), playwright and screenwriter

George Bernard Shaw (1856–1950), Irish playwright and critic

John Schlesinger (1926–2003), film, opera and theatre director

Maggie Smith (b. 1934), actress

Rae Smith (b.1972), theatre designer

Robert Stephens (1931–95), actor

Simon Stephens (b. 1971), playwright

Tom Stoppard (b. 1937), Czech-born playwright and screenwriter

David Storey (1933–2017), playwright, screenwriter and novelist

Michael Stroud (1934–2015), actor

David Thacker (b. 1950), theatre and television director

Emma Thompson (b. 1959), actress and screenwriter

Russell Tovey (b. 1981), actor

Kenneth Tynan (1927–80), drama critic and writer; NT literary manager, 1963–73

Stephen Wakelam (b. 1947), playwright

Irving Wardle (b. 1929), drama critic and biographer

David Yelland (b. 1947), editor of *The Sun*, 1998–2003

Sources

Accessible collections

BL – British Library Manuscripts Collection, London (archives of Peter Nichols, Laurence Olivier and Harold Pinter; and the Lord Chamberlain's Plays)

Bodleian – Special Collections, Weston Library, Bodleian Libraries, Oxford (Alan Bennett Archive)

Churchill – Churchill Archives Centre, Churchill College, Cambridge (papers of Lord Chandos [Oliver Lyttelton])

HRC – Harry Ransom Center, University of Texas at Austin (archives of David Hare, John Osborne and Tom Stoppard)

Hull – Hull History Centre (Papers of Richard Bean)

Leeds – Special Collections, Leeds University Library (Tony Harrison Archive)

NTA – National Theatre Archive, London [some material is restricted access]

V&A – V&A Theatre & Performance Archives, London (archives of William Archer, Peter Brook, Michael Redgrave and Paul Scofield)

York – Borthwick Institute for Archives, University of York (Ayckbourn Archive; The Charles Wood Papers)

Private holdings (not publicly accessible)

NTLDF – National Theatre Literary Department Files, National Theatre Studio, London

(PC) – Personal Correspondence, e.g. Michael Frayn (PC)

Introduction

'boundless expectation, generated by the organisation and the outside world, of what it could provide' – *The National Theatre Story* by Daniel Rosenthal (Oberon Books, London, 2013), p. 845

'We may be the last generation to write to each other' – Larkin, letter to Judy Egerton, quoted in *Selected Letters of Philip Larkin: 1940–1985*, edited by Anthony Thwaite (Faber, London, 1992), p. xi

Prologue: Six Decades of False Dawns

'within the reach of all' – *The Making of a National Theatre* by Geoffrey Whitworth (Faber, London, 1951), p. 28

Granville Barker to Archer, 28 April 1903 – *Granville Barker and His Correspondents: A Selection of Letters by Him and to Him*, edited and annotated by Eric Salmon (Wayne State University Press, Detroit, 1986), p. 43

'unmistakably a popular institution' – Whitworth, p. 53

Hardy to Archer, 1 November 1904 – Whitworth, p. 56

Archer to Trench, 15 December 1907 – Whitworth, pp. 61–62

'produce new plays.' – Whitworth, p. 83

Wyndham to *Daily Telegraph*, 26 March 1908 – Whitworth, p. 92

Shaw to Yeats, 14 July 1913 – *Bernard Shaw: Collected Letters 1911–1925*, edited by Dan H. Laurence (Max Reinhardt, London, 1985), pp. 190–191

Granville Barker to Archer, 4 February 1916 – Salmon, p. 66

Archer to Lyttelton, 25 August 1922 – V&A: Archer THM/368/4/2/9

Beerbohm to Granville Barker et al., 19 February 1923 – *Drama* magazine, April 1923, no. 23, pp. 121–122

'an ideal site for a gibbet' – Whitworth, pp. 135–136

O'Rorke to Rae, 23 November 1946 – NTA: SMNT/6/3/7: Appointment of joint architect 1946–1947

Lyttelton to Rae, 24 December 1948 – NTA: SMNT/3/4: Funding and government assistance to the National Theatre Project, file 1 of 3

Rae to Esher, 29 May 1953 – NTA: SMNT/3/4: Funding and government assistance to the National Theatre Project, file 2 of 3

Olivier et al. to *The Times*, 23 February 1959 – NTA: SMNT/3/4: Funding and government assistance to the National Theatre Project, file 3 of 3

'make my own company, as Number One.' – Rosenthal, p. 40

Olivier to Hall, 3 July 1960; Hall to Olivier, 1 August 1960; Hall to Olivier, 30 January 1962; Olivier to Hall, April 1962 – BL: Add MS 80367

Rogers to Evershed-Martin, 9 August 1962 – BL: Add MS 80303

O'Rorke to Rae, March 1963 – NTA: SMNT/6/3/1: O'Rorke general correspondence 1946–1962

'To Be Renowned' – Rosenthal, p. 66

Harrison to Olivier, 20 March 1963; Olivier to
  Harrison, 23 May 1963 – BL: Add MS 80396
'woefully inadequate' – Rosenthal, p. 65

Act 1: The Laurence Olivier Years

Hamlet (c. 1601)
Olivier to Heeley, 27 May 1963 – BL: Add MS
  80407
Atkins to Olivier, 14 June 1963; Olivier to
  Atkins, 5 July 1963; Atkins to Olivier, 10 July
  1963 – BL: Add MS 80400
Courtenay to Olivier, 20 August 1963; Olivier
  to Courtenay, 29 August 1963 – BL: Add MS
  80394
Hall to Olivier & Plowright, 31 August 1963 –
  BL: Add MS 80367

Uncle Vanya (1899)
Rea to Redgrave, 20 November 1963 – V&A:
  Redgrave THM/31/3/5/183/1; Hatcher to
  Redgrave, 3 June 1964; Redgrave to Hatcher
  – V&A: Redgrave THM/31/3/5/172/7
*Note: Hatcher's letter is dated 'Wednesday
  11.45pm'. Uncle Vanya was performed on
  Wednesday 3 June, allowing for Redgrave to
  receive letter and then reply on 8 June. I have
  assumed 3 June is correct date.*

The Recruiting Officer (1706)
All correpondence in this section – BL: Add
  MS 80395

Play (1963)
Tynan to Devine, 31 March 1964 – *Kenneth
  Tynan: Letters*, edited by Kathleen Tynan
  (Random House, New York, 1994), pp. 292–
  293; Devine to Tynan, 9 April 1964 – *The
  Theatres of George Devine* by Irving Wardle
  (Jonathan Cape, London, 1978), pp. 207–
  208; Olivier to Devine, 12 April 1964 – BL:
  Add MS 80367; *'too fucking tasteless for
  words'* – *Tynan: Letters*, p. 293 (note)

Othello (c. 1604)
'go into blackface' – Rosenthal, p. 77
McEwan to Olivier, 8 April 1963; McEwan to
  Olivier, 15 April 1963 – BL: Add MS 80401
to consider her for Desdemona (Bloom to
  Olivier, 4 June 1963) – BL: Add MS 80400
Olivier to Bloom, 11 June 1963 – BL: Add MS
  80303
Plowright to Olivier, 20 March 1964 – *And
  That's Not All* by Joan Plowright (Weidenfeld
  & Nicolson, London, 2001), pp. 124–125
'People nicknamed the play "Mr Lear"' – *Life*
  magazine, 1 May 1964, p. 91

Brook to Tynan, 21 May 1964 – V&A: Brook
  THM/452/3/172; Olivier to Brook, 26 May
  1964 – V&A: Brook THM/452/3/119

Hay Fever (1925)
All correspondence in this section – BL: Add
  MS 80407, except:
'to play the middle-aged Judith Bliss' (Olivier to
  Evans, 20 May 1964); Evans to Olivier, 21
  May 1964 – BL: Add MS 80400
'Albanian telephone directory backwards!' –
  Maggie Smith: A Biography by Michael
  Coveney (Weidenfeld & Nicolson, London,
  2016), p. 88

The Royal Hunt of the Sun (1964)
kind of play the RSC were not interested in –
  Simon Callow, memorial service for Peter
  Shaffer, Olivier Theatre, 30 March 2017
Hall to Olivier, 17 April 1961 – BL: Add MS
  80367

Dingo**
All correspondence in this section – BL:
  DINGO LC CORR WB 29/1964, except:
Tynan, memo to Olivier, 11 February 1965;
  Ramsay to Tynan, 22 April 1965; *'gave up
  hope and withdrew it'* (Ramsay, letter to
  John Arden and Margaretta D'Arcy, 5 May
  1967 – *Peggy to her Playwrights: The Letters
  of Margaret Ramsay, Play Agent*, selected
  and edited by Colin Chambers (Oberon
  Books, London 2018); Plaschkes to Wood,
  28 November 1967 – York: Charles Wood
  (CW/2/27/2)

The Crucible (1953)
Olivier to Miller, 15 August 1964; Miller to
  Olivier, 17 August 1964 – BL: Add MS
  80405
Redgrave to Olivier, 2 August 1964 – BL: Add
  MS 80402
Hatton to Olivier, 19 August 1964; *'offer his
  services'* (Olivier to Hatton, 21 August 1964)
  – BL: Add MS 80394
the best Crucible he had ever seen (Olivier, letter
  to Anthony Gambrill, 24 February 1965) –
  BL: Add MS 80405

Much Ado About Nothing (c. 1598)
All correspondence in this section – BL: Add
  MS 80397

Virtue with Bottles**
NTLDF: Ken Campbell folder

Black Comedy (1965)
All correspondence in this section, including
  'surely a good thing too' (Shaffer to Olivier &

Joan Plowright, 5 August 1965) – BL: Add
MS 80404

A Bond Honoured (1966)
Osborne to Tynan, 4 November 1963; Tynan to
Osborne, 5 November 1963; *On 22 May 1964,
Peter O'Toole and Paul Scofield were being
'heavily discussed'* (Tynan to Osborne, 22
May 1964); Osborne to Tynan, 29 May 1964
– HRC: Osborne 28.1

Olivier to Guinness, 28 August 1964; Guinness
to Olivier, 8 September 1964 – BL: Add MS
80395

Fitzpatrick, 12 May 1966 – NTA: *A Bond
Honoured* production box (Rights File)

Nellie Osborne, telegram to Osborne, 7 June
1966; Osborne, telegram to Wardle, 8 June
1966; Wardle to Osborne, 8 June 1966;
Osborne, telegram to Wardle, 9 June 1966;
Olivier to Osborne, 17 March 1967; Osborne
to Stephens, 10 June 1970; Stephens to
Osborne, 11 June 1970 – HRC: Osborne 28.1

The Burning Man**
All correspondence in this section – NTLDF:
Pam Gems folder

The Dance of Death (1901)
'had turned down The Royal Hunt of the Sun'
(Olivier to Scofield, 4 December 1963);
Olivier to Scofield, 13 May 1964; Scofield to
Olivier, 7 July 1964 – BL: Add MS 80399

Olivier, cable to Bergman, 7 February 1966;
'very happy and honoured' (Bergman, cable
to Olivier, 11 February 1966); Olivier to
Byam Shaw, 15 February 1966; Byam Shaw
to Olivier, 20 February 1966 – BL: Add MS
80405

Olivier to Lyttelton, 23 February 1967 –
Churchill: CHAN_II/4/13

Rosencrantz and Guildenstern Are Dead (1966)
Olivier, postcard to Petherbridge, 11 April 1967
– Edward Petherbridge (PC)

Goldby to Olivier, 12 April 1967 – BL: Add MS
80413

Merrick, cable to Olivier, 4 May 1967 – NTA:
Rosencrantz and Guildenstern Are Dead
production box (Rights File)

Glover to Olivier, 4 July 1967 – BL: Add MS
80395

Goldby to Olivier, October 1967; Stoppard to
Olivier, 5 November 1967 – BL: Add MS
80413

Olivier to Petherbridge, 2 May 1970 –
Petherbridge (PC)

Lord Olivier?
Wilson to Olivier (both letters) – BL: Add MS
79864

Olivier to Wilson – Churchill: CHAN_II/4/13

Three Sisters (1901)
'with a mouse between its teeth' – Rosenthal,
p. 116

All correspondence in this section – BL: Add
MS 80396

As You Like It (c. 1600)
Parker to Olivier (both letters) – BL: Add MS
80397

Tynan/McCartney exchange: *Tynan: Letters*,
pp. 359–360

All other correspondence in this section,
including *'with great reluctance'* (Olivier,
cable to Dexter, 26 January 1967) – BL: Add
MS 80403

Tartuffe (1664)
'Scofield was then studying' (Olivier to Guthrie,
26 June 1964); *'with not having you here'*
(Olivier, telegram to Guthrie, 5 November
1966); Olivier to Guthrie, 30 March 1967;
Guthrie to Olivier, 7 April 1967; Guthrie to
Olivier, 23 November 1967 – BL: Add MS
80417

Gielgud to Sterne, 10 January 1968 – *Gielgud's
Letters: John Gielgud in His Own Words*,
edited by Richard Mangan (Weidenfeld &
Nicolson, London, 2004), p. 343

Oedipus (55–60 AD)
All correspondence in this section: V&A:
Brook THM/452/4/34, except:

Sunny Amey, memo to Olivier et al., 12 October
1967; *'at the request of the audience'* (Rae to
Mrs Maunsell, 1 May 1968); *'being a snake for
three weeks'* (unsigned memo: replies from
Oedipus actors, 6 May 1968) – BL: Add MS
80412

*Note: Hughes, in his fourth letter to Brook,
writes 'as Apollo founded Delphi after killing
the great snake there (which was Dionysus)'.
Apollo killed Python, the dragon which
guarded Delphi but has no evident connection
to Dionysus* (Oxford Classical Dictionary,
p. 68).

to make curtain-up at the Old Vic at 2.15pm –
Jenny Beavan, email to Daniel Rosenthal, 4
January 2018

An autobiographical new play** by Dennis Potter
Tynan, memo to Olivier, 16 July 1968 – *Tynan:
Letters*, p. 415

Goodwin to Tynan, 6 November 1968 –
NTLDF: Dennis Potter folder

The Way of the World (1700)
All correspondence in this section – BL: Add MS 80417

The National Health (1969)
Olivier to Nichols, 24 May 1967; Nichols to Olivier, 31 May 1967 – BL: Add MS 80411
Hewlett to Nichols, 27 February 1969 – BL: Add MS 78970
Olivier to Howerd, 24 February 1969; *a prior commitment to make a film* (Howerd to Olivier, 21 April 1969) – BL: Add MS 80396
Peter to Nichols, 17 October 1969 – BL: Add MS 78970
Nichols to Olivier, 23 October 1969 – BL: Add MS 80411
Habermel to Nichols, 15 November 1969 – BL: Add MS 78970
Olivier to Blakemore, 24 November 1969; Blakemore to Olivier, 11 December 1969 – BL: Add MS 80411
'carried on by enemies within *the company'. – Diaries: 1969–1977* by Peter Nichols (Nick Hern Books, London, 2000), p. 102
Olivier to Nichols, 2 February 1971; Nichols to Olivier, 10 February 1971; Ramsay to Olivier, 5 March 1971 – BL: Add MS 80411

The Merchant of Venice (c. 1594)
Tynan to Olivier, 28 April 1969; Welles to Olivier, 29 April 1969 – BL: Add MS 80410
Scofield to Olivier, 31 May 1969 – BL: Add MS 80399
Miller, postcard to Olivier, December 1970 – BL: Add MS 80410

Baron Olivier of Brighton
All correspondence in this section – BL: Add MS 79864, except:
Olivier to Sylvestre – Cleo Sylvestre (PC)

The Two-Character Play (1967)**
NTLDF: Tennessee Williams folder

The Captain of Köpenick (1931)
Lyttelton to Scofield, 10 March 1971 – V&A: Scofield THM/397/2/16_1_of_2
All other correspondence in this section – BL: Add MS 80399, including: *offering Alceste in* The Misanthrope *(in Tony Harrison's new translation), Brutus in* Julius Caesar *and Gaev in* The Cherry Orchard (Olivier to Scofield, 11 February and 8 March 1972); *'rather crude cracker'* (Scofield to Olivier, 24 February 1972)

Jumpers (1972)
'green with envy' (Olivier to Neville, 5 October 1971) – BL: Add MS 80398

Bates to Olivier, 15 October 1971 – BL: Add MS 80408
Olivier to Louise Purnell, 15 October 1971 – BL: Add MS 80402
Stoppard to Olivier, 9 May 1972; Olivier to Stoppard, 2 April 1973; *'the new NT will have its eye on me'* (Stoppard to Olivier, 22 April 1973) – BL: Add MS 80408

Peter Hall, NT Director Designate
'wanted to be seen to be free' – Rosenthal, p. 180
'death or retirement' – Rosenthal, p. 186
Rayne to Olivier, 12 April 1972; Olivier to Rayne, 12 April 1972 – BL: Add MS 80365
Quilley to Olivier, 18 April 1972 – BL: Add MS 80398
Olivier to Rayne, 7 May 1972; Rayne to Olivier, 8 May 1972 – BL: Add MS 80365
Hall to Olivier, 10 July 1972 – BL: Add MS 80361

Equus (1973)
Tynan to Dexter and Shaffer, 16 July 1973 – *Tynan: Letters*, p. 531
Tynan to Dexter, 23 July 1973 – *Tynan: Letters*, p. 532
Dexter to Plowright, 1 October 1974 – *The Honourable Beast: A Posthumous Autobiography* by John Dexter (Nick Hern Books, London, 1993), p. 84

The Bacchae (405 BC)
BL: Add MS 80400

The end of the Olivier years
'a distinct overtone of "follow that"' – Rosenthal, p. 209
'quite well because I'm so angry' – Rosenthal, p. 220

Act 2: The Peter Hall Years

The Party (1973)
Tynan to Hall, 29 September 1973 – *Tynan: Letters*, pp. 533–534
Hall to Tynan, 3 October 1973; Dexter, memo to Hall, 9 October 1973 – NTLDF: Trevor Griffiths folder

The Tempest (1610)
Gielgud's Letters, p. 389

The National under fire
'although pretending not to be' – Peter Hall's *Diaries*, edited by John Goodwin (Oberon Books, London, 2000), p. 135
Mirren to Birkett, 29 December 1974 – NTA: MB14
Hall to Eyre, 22 September 1975 – NTA: D12

The Freeway (1974)
Nichols to Blakemore, 10 January 1974 – Michael Blakemore (PC)

Blakemore to Nichols, 13 January 1974 – BL: Add MS 78694

Hall to Blakemore, 17 May 1974 – NTA: D10 (Michael Blakemore)

Nichols to Hall, 21 August 1974 – BL: Add MS 78694

thanked him for his 'utter professionalism' (Hall, postcard to Nichols, 1 October 1974) and remaining correspondence in this section – BL: Add MS 78694

Happy Days (1960)
Ashcroft to Hall, 31 May 1974 – NTA: D22 (Peggy Ashcroft)

Hall to Beckett, 18 February 1976; *'unfortunate composition'* – NTA: D14 (Samuel Beckett)

No Man's Land (1975)
All correspondence in this section – BL: Add MS 88880/6/2, except:

Gielgud to Worth, 14 February 1975 – *Gielgud's Letters*, p. 393; Gielgud to Worth, 29 April 1975 – *Gielgud's Letters*, p. 394

Queen Christina**
All correspondence in this section – NTLDF: Pam Gems folder

The Rape of the Sabine Women (1885)**
NTA: D23 (Rex Harrison)

Watch It Come Down (1975)
Hall to Osborne, 7 August 1974 – HRC: John Osborne 33.6

'and committed to producing' (Hall to Osborne, 20 August 1974); *'I think he would be very good'* (Hall to Osborne, 25 October 1974); Bates to Osborne, November 1974; Hall to Osborne, 7 November 1974; Hall to Osborne, 10 June 1975 – HRC: John Osborne 33.6

Osborne to Hall, 11 June 1975 – NTA: D16 (John Osborne)

Hall to Osborne, 13 June 1975; *'play Ben at the Old Vic for only three weeks'* (Hall to Osborne, 22 September 1975); Hall to Osborne, 18 January 1976; Osborne to Hall, 20 January 1976 – HRC: John Osborne 33.6

All remaining correspondence in this section: NTA: D16 (John Osborne), except:

Osborne to Robin Dalton, 10 May 1976 – Gordon Dickerson, attachment with email to Daniel Rosenthal, 5 February 2018; *'we exploded'* – *Talking Theatre: Interviews with Theatre People* by Richard Eyre (Nick Hern Books, London, 2009), p. 50

Michael Blakemore resigns
All correspondence in this section, including *'disturbed' by his resignation* (Pinter to

Blakemore, 27 May 1976) – Michael Blakemore (PC)

Weapons of Happiness (1976)
All correspondence in this section, including: *this 'magnificent' script* (Hall to Brenton, 10 June 1974) – NTA: D14 (Howard Brenton), except: Russell Brown to Hall, 5 July 1976 – NTA: MB3

Blithe Spirit (1941)
V&A: Scofield THM/397/2/21/1 of 2

The Royal Opening
NTA: MB10

Counting the Ways (1976)
Albee to Hall, 13 December 1976 – NTA: D14 (Edward Albee)

Hall, postcard to Bryden, 28 December 1976 – NTA: D11 (Bill Bryden)

Hall to Albee, 5 January 1977 – NTA: D14 (Edward Albee)

Albee to Hall, 2 March 1977 – NTA: D10 (*Counting the Ways*)

A new play** by Ted Hughes
NTLDF: Ted Hughes folder

Tales from the Vienna Woods (1931)
Ramsay to Hall, 10 December 1976 – NTA: D15 (Christopher Hampton)

'placed on Horváth's grave' – Zoe Wilcox, email to Daniel Rosenthal, 8 December 2009

Bedroom Farce (1975)
Hall to Ayckbourn, 29 August 1973; Ayckbourn to Hall, 3 September 1973; Hall to Ayckbourn, 9 July 1974; Ayckbourn to Hall, 23 July 1974; Hall to Codron, 13 September 1974; *'I cannot see being granted if it were the other way around!'* (Codron to Hall, 19 September 1974); Ayckbourn to Hall, 22 March 1977; Hall to Ayckbourn, 9 June 1975 – NTA: D14 (Alan Ayckbourn)

'rehearsal in Scarborough on 26th May!' (Ayckbourn to Hall, 14 February 1975) – York: Ayckbourn (Aisle 33, Bay 7, Shelf 6, Box 7: 89/18 Correspondence – RNT/Peter Hall 1970s–1984)

Ramsay to Ayckbourn, 10 June 1975; Hall to Ayckbourn, 21 March 1977; Kitchen to Ayckbourn, 31 March 1977; Ayckbourn to Hall, 10 June 1977; *'been acted on instantly'* (Hall to Ayckbourn 14 June 1977); Hall to Ayckbourn, 12 July 1977; Hall to Ayckbourn, 18 July 1977; Hall to Ayckbourn, 6 September 1977; Stroud to Ayckbourn, 26 July 1978; Hickson to Ayckbourn, 12 January 1980 – York: Ayckbourn (*Bedroom Farce*: Aisle 33, Bay 4, Shelf 4, Box 6)

Julius Caesar (c. 1599)
Gielgud to Olivier, 24 September 1969 –
  Gielgud's Letters, p. 348
Hall to Birkett, 1 December 1975; Birkett to
  Hall, 3 December 1975; Birkett to Hall, 27
  May 1976; Hall to Schlesinger, 26 July 1976;
  Schlesinger to Hall, 29 July 1976 – NTA: D13
  (John Schlesinger)
Gielgud to Worth, 17 February 1977 – *Gielgud's
  Letters,* p. 410
Gielgud to Ralph and Meriel Richardson, 24
  March 1977 – *Gielgud's Letters,* p. 413

*Piaf***
for Julie Covington (Goodwin to Russell Brown,
  24 March 1977); Russell Brown to Hall, 14
  April 1977 – NTLDF: Pam Gems folder

Notes from Underground (1864)**
NTLDF: Hanif Kureishi folder

State of Revolution (1977)
Ramsay to Hall, 26 September 1975 – NTA:
  D14 (Robert Bolt)
Hall to Morahan, 5 May 1977 – NTA: D12
  (Christopher Morahan)
Bolt to Hall, 3 January 1978; Hall to Bolt, 24
  January 1978; Bolt to Hall, 21 December 1978
  – NTA: D14 (Robert Bolt).
*Note: In his 21 December letter, when Bolt writes
  'the man in "Brideshead" with the other man
  who liked to have Dickens read aloud to him
  daily', he mistakes Evelyn Waugh's* Brideshead
  Revisited *for* A Handful of Dust.

The National under fire – again
NTA: D22 (Peggy Ashcroft)

Plenty (1978)
Hare to Hall, March 1977 – NTA: D12 (David
  Hare)
Hall to Rigg, 21 March 1977 – NTA: D22
  (Diana Rigg)
Hallifax to Hall, 30 March 1977; Hare to Hall,
  April/May 1977; Hare to Hall, 5 June 1977 –
  NTA: D12 (David Hare)
Nelligan, note to Hare, April 1978 – HRC:
  David Hare 13.3
Hall to Hare, 21 December 1978 – NTA: D12

Betrayal (1978)
All correspondence in this section – BL: Add
  MS 88880/6/3, including: '*Ian McShane and
  Martin Shaw*' (Pinter to Gillian Diamond,
  28 March 1978); '*not suggested, Michael
  Gambon*' (Pinter to Hall, 14 June 1978)

The longest strike
Elliott, statement to employees, 21 March 1979;
  Unsigned memo, 26 March 1979 – NTA:
  ME12: Folder 3
Pate, memo to Elliott, 26 March 1979; Shop
  stewards to Elliott, 30 April 1979; R. C.
  Osborn to Elliott, 30 March 1979 – NTA:
  ME 12: Folder 1

Close of Play (1979)
All correspondence in this section – BL: Add
  MS 88880/6/3

Amadeus (1979)
'*at least eight times with offers for 1978–79*' –
  V&A: Scofield THM/397/22/2/1 of 2
Scofield to Hall, January 1979 – NTA: D23
  (Paul Scofield)
Hall to Diamond, 5 March 1979 – NTA: D12
  (Christopher Morahan)
'*not only for the NT premiere, but in all revivals*' –
  Rosenthal, p. 295
Shaffer, telegram to Dexter, 13 June 1979 –
  Honourable Beast, pp. 216–217
Dexter to Shaffer, 25 June 1979 – *Honourable
  Beast,* pp. 217–218
Shaffer to Scofield, 2 November 1979; Shaffer
  to Scofield, 4 December 1979 – V&A:
  THM/397/2/24/2/1_of_2
Hall to McKellen, 2 May 1980 – NTA: D23 (Ian
  McKellen)
Hall to Schlesinger, 2 June 1980 – NTA: D13
  (John Schlesinger)
Shaffer, card to Ian McKellen, 17 December
  1980 – Ian McKellen (PC)
Hall to Alan Ayckbourn, 20 January 1981 – D14
  (Ayckbourn)
Callow to Scofield, 27 May 1981 – V&A:
  Scofield THM/397/2/26/3
Shaffer to Hall, 19 July 1981; Hall to Shaffer, 28
  July 1981 – NTA: D16
McKellen to Scofield, 30 July 1981 – V&A:
  Scofield THM/397/2/26/1
Hall to McKellen, 7 August 1981 – McKellen
  (PC)

The Romans in Britain (1980)
All correspondence in this section – NTA: D14
  (Howard Brenton), except: Cutler, telegram
  to Hall, 16 October 1980; Seaton to Hall, 16
  October 1980; Hall to Seaton, 16 October
  1980; Mitchell to Max Rayne, 20 October
  1980 – Derek Mitchell Papers (not in NTA)

*Another Country***
All correspondence in this section – NTLDF:
  Julian Mitchell folder

The Hypochondriac (1673)
All correspondence in this section – NTA: D11
(Michael Bogdanov)

Guys and Dolls (1950)
NTA: D11 (Richard Eyre)

Way Upstream (1981)
All correspondence in this section – York:
Ayckbourn (*Way Upstream*: 37 – Aisle 33, Bay
4, Shelf 7, Box 2), except:
Phillips to Bond (NT), 8 February 1983 – NTA:
PO/2/1/29
Ayckbourn to Hall, 14 January 1984 – NTA:
D14 (Alan Ayckbourn)

A Map of the World (1982)
All correspondence in this section – HRC:
David Hare 33.7

A new play by Alan Bennett
All correspondence in this section – NTA: D14
(Alan Bennett)

A 'Utopian' play by Howard Brenton
All correspondence in this section – NTA: D14
(Howard Brenton), including *'unrealised play
in your system'* (Hall to Brenton, 26 March
1984); *'not the utopian idea'* (Brenton to Hall,
3 June 1987); *'pain and rage'* (Hall, memo to
Richard Eyre, David Aukin et al., 11 June
1987)

Henry IV: Parts One & Two (1596-97)**
Barker to Hall, 17 June 1984; *'you simply have to
do this'* (Hall to Barker, 2 July 1984) – NTA:
D23 (Ronnie Barker)

Wild Honey (1881?)
Frayn to Morahan, 6 December 1978 – Michael
Frayn (PC)
Russell Brown, memo to Morahan, 14
December 1978 – NTLDF: Michael Frayn
folder
to produce his adaptation – written on spec – of
Exchange *(1969)* – Rosenthal, p. 373
Frayn to Hall, 21 October 1981; *'well-deserved'*
rebuke (Hall to Frayn, 3 November 1981) –
NTA: D15 (Michael Frayn)
reached the NT in August 1983 (Gordon
Dickerson to Hall, cover note, 5 August
1983) – NTLDF: Michael Frayn folder
Frayn to Hall, 14 February 1984 – NTA: D15
Frayn to McKellen, 20 July 1984 – McKellen
(PC)

Coriolanus (c. 1608)
All correspondence in this section – McKellen
(PC), except: *'cut our legs off'* – Hall to
Christopher Morahan, 17 December 1984 –
NTA: D12 (Christopher Morahan)

A Chorus of Disapproval (1984)
All correspondence in this section – York:
Ayckbourn (Aisle 33, Bay 4, Shelf 3 Box 1)
Ayckbourn had 'discovered' Peck in Leeds – Lyn
Gardner, *The Guardian*, 8 April 1999

Flesh and Blood (1985)**
NTA: D16 (Edna O'Brien)

*Sabina***
NTA: D16 (Paul Schrader)

The Critic (1779)
Hancock to Hall, 8 January 1985; Hall to
Hancock, 21 January 1985 – NTA: D12
(Sheila Hancock)
Hancock, notes to *Hound/Critic* Company, 8
April 1986 – McKellen (PC)

The Petition (1985)
NTA: D23 (Alec Guinness)

King Lear (1606)
Hare to Hall, December 1974 – NTA: D12
(David Hare)
Wright to Hare, 26 November 1986;
Boddington to Hare, 20 December 1986 –
HRC: Hare 33.3

Richard Eyre, NT Director Designate
Eyre to Rayne, 31 August 1986 – NTA:
DM/1/8/1

*Anything Can Happen!***
NTLDF: Ken Campbell folder

Antony and Cleopatra (1606)
Hall, memo to Diamond et al., 6 January 1986 –
NTA: D22 (Judi Dench)
're-establish some TV and film credit' (Hopkins to
Hall, 31 August 1986) – NTA: D23 (Anthony
Hopkins)

Rosmersholm (1887)
Anderson to Peter Hall, 5 August 1986 – NTA:
D11 (Sarah Pia Anderson)

Waiting for Godot (1955)
NTLDF: Samuel Beckett folder

'Tis Pity She's a Whore (1633)
York: Ayckbourn (79 - Aisle 33, Bay 7, Shelf 5,
Box 5)

Cymbeline (c. 1611)
All correspondence in this section – NTA: D22
(Sarah Miles)

The end of the Hall years
Hall to Rayne, 4 September 1986 – NTA:
DM/1/8/7

Act 3: The Richard Eyre Years

Rayne to Eyre, 2 December 1988 – Richard
Eyre (PC)
'a bit of a surrogate father' – Rosenthal, p. 427

The March on Russia (1989)
Anderson, postcard to Bennett, 11 November
1988 – Bodleian: MS. Bennett 179_1
Storey to Eyre, 9 April 1989 – Eyre (PC)

Hamlet (c. 1601)
All correspondence in this section – Eyre (PC),
except:
Hamlet show report, 5 September 1989 – NTA:
RNT/SM/2/4/63
'the last time he'd be on stage' – Rosenthal, p. 446

The Misanthrope (1666)
Leeds: BC MS 20c Harrison/05/EPE

Euphoria★★
All correspondence in this section – NTLDF:
Peter Nichols folder

Racing Demon (1990)
Hare to Eyre, 18 February 1989 – Eyre (PC)
Hall, postcard to Ford Davies, 19 February
1990 – Oliver Ford Davies (PC)
Moberly to Hare, 23 February 1990; Dench to
Hare, March 1990; Frayn to Hare, 27 March
1990 – HRC: Hare 34.6
Ford Davies to Eyre, 16 April 1990; Hare to
Eyre, 27 November 1991 – Eyre (PC)

Sunday in the Park with George (1984)
'not wanting me to be at the rehearsals' –
Rosenthal, p. 456
Pimlott to Sondheim, 17 April 1990 –
Rosenthal, p. 457

Richard III (1592/93)
'a fantasy Britain' of the 1930s – Rosenthal, p. 467
Callow to Eyre, 6 September 1990; McKellen
to Eyre, 8 April 1991 – Eyre (PC)
Smith to McKellen, 17 October 1991; Cornwell to
McKellen, 4 November 1991 – McKellen (PC)

White Chameleon (1991)
All correspondence in this section – Eyre (PC)

Napoli Milionaria (1945)
Hogg to Eyre, 4 July 1991; *'just about recovered
from the shock'* (Major to Soames, 8 July
1991) – Eyre (PC)

Murmuring Judges (1991)
HRC: Hare 32.3

The Madness of George III (1991)
Bennett to Hytner, 1991 – Bodleian: MS.
Bennett 145

Bennett to Jones, 31 January 1992; *Jones
forwarded this to Eyre* (Jones to Eyre, 3
February 1992); Bennett to Eyre, 19 June
1992 – Eyre (PC)
Hawthorne to Brook, 9 March 1995 – V&A:
Brook THM/452/3/60 to 116
Hawthorne to Hytner, 30 July 2001 – Hytner
(PC)

Angels in America (1991–92)
All correspondence in this section – NTLDF:
Tony Kushner folder
'Aids, God and angels' – *National Service: Diary
of a Decade* by Richard Eyre (Bloomsbury,
London, 2003), p. 141
'tension-filled technical rehearsals' – Rosenthal,
p. 532

Square Rounds (1992)
Harrison, postcard to Eyre, 9 April 1992 – Eyre
(PC)
Carter to Harrison, 6 May 1992 – Leeds: BC
MS 20c Harrison/05/JCA
Herbert to Harrison, 16 September 1992 –
Leeds: BC MS 20c Harrison/05/JOH
Eyre to Harrison, 20 September 1992 – Leeds:
BC MS 20c Harrison/05/REY
Storey, postcard to Harrison, 20 September
1992 – Leeds: BC MS 20c Harrison/05/DSO
'before the script was ready' – *National Service*,
p. 196
Herbert to Harrison, 27 November 1992 –
Leeds: BC MS 20c Harrison/05/JOH
Storey to Harrison, 22 November 1992 – Leeds:
BC MS 20c Harrison/05/DSO

Carousel (1945)
'a joke' (Chapin to Hytner, 5 June 1992); Hytner
to Chapin, 5 June 1992; *18 June, Chapin sent
another fax* – NTA: McIntosh 1996/Box
O_52/02 10-5.1

As You Like It (c. 1600)★★
Eyre (PC)

Mr. A's Amazing Maze Plays (1988)
All correspondence in this section, including
'for your purposes' (McIntosh to Ayckbourn,
17 June 1992) – York: Ayckbourn (Aisle 33,
Bay 4, Shelf 4, Box 5)

Arcadia (1993)
'one of the country's foremost playwrights' (Eyre
to Stoppard, 10 December 1987) – HRC:
Stoppard 131.3
Stoppard to Eyre, 20 November 1991 – Eyre
(PC)
sent both men the script (Stoppard to Eyre, 12
June 1992) – Eyre (PC)

'*particularly sexual subtext*' (Nunn to Stoppard, 22 June 1992) – HRC: Stoppard 131.1
'*I'm not quite sure why*' – *National Service,* p. 191
Stoppard to Eyre, 10 December 1992 – Eyre (PC)
Fielding, postcard to Stoppard, 13 April 1993 – HRC: Stoppard 42.6

The Absence of War (1993)
All correspondence in this section – Eyre (PC), including '*disparity between the audience's reaction & the dismissals in the press*' (Hare, postcard to Eyre, 23 October 1993); *to use quotes from drama critics* (Eyre, fax to Hare, 24 October 1993)
'*a steady decline*' – *National Service,* p. 232
'*to seek reappointment when his contract expires*' – *The Guardian,* 28 February 1994

Broken Glass (1994)
All correspondence in this section – David Thacker (PC)

The Merry Wives of Windsor (1597)
Eyre (PC)

The Masterplan redevelopment
All correspondence in this section – NTA: Eyre 110/97 (Box 3)

Skylight (1995)
All correspondence in this section – Eyre (PC)

Dealer's Choice (1995)
All correspondence in this section – Patrick Marber (PC)

A Streetcar Named Desire (1947)**
Eyre (PC)

Mother Courage and Her Children (1941)
Rigg, fax to Hare, 1 September 1995 – HRC: Hare (uncatalogued)
Eyre to Rigg, 10 January 1996; Rigg to Eyre, January 1996 – Eyre (PC)

Habeas Corpus (1973) and Kafka's Dick (1986)**
to make 'a splash' (Lindsay to Eyre, 11 June 1995) – Eyre (PC)
'*He's very apologetic*' – *National Service,* p. 296
Bennett to Eyre, 30 January 1996 – Eyre (PC)

Stanley (1996)
Wright, memo to Eyre, 29 August 1995 – NTLDF: Pam Gems folder
Gems, card to Eyre, 25 November 1995 – Eyre (PC)
Pople to Fairclough, 14 December 1995 – NTA: *Stanley* RNT/PO/1/1/162

Trevor Nunn, NT Director Designate
Hare to Palliser, 14 December 1995 – HRC: Hare (uncatalogued)
'*chosen heir*' – Daldry to Eyre, 21 February 1996 – Eyre (PC)
'*taking on another building or company*' – Rosenthal, p. 569
Brook to Nunn, 7 March 1996 V&A: Brook THM/452/3/60 to 116
Nunn, fax to Eyre, 8 March 1996 – Eyre (PC)

Fast Food**
All correspondence in this section – NTLDF: Abi Morgan folder

Closer (1997)
All correspondence in this section – Patrick Marber (PC)

The Invention of Love (1997)
All correspondence in this section, including '*so wise and witty, and fascinating*' (Scofield to Eyre, 26 January 1997); '*above all, coherence*' (Stoppard to Eyre, 8 October 1998) – Eyre (PC), except:
Stoppard to Eyre, 3 June 1996 – NTA: Directors Office 52/02 (Box 2: 1 of 3)
Stoppard to Hare, 26 February 1997 – HRC: Hare (uncatalogued)

The end of the Eyre years
'*despair, joy and endless talk*' – *National Service,* p. 422
All correspondence in this section – Eyre (PC)

Act 4: The Trevor Nunn Years
'*over the past ten years to Trevor*' – Rosenthal, p. 595
'*in spirit, planning*' – Rosenthal, p. 597

An Enemy of the People (1882)
All correspondence in this section – McKellen (PC)

Ophelia** by Bryony Lavery
All correspondence in this section – NTLDF: Bryony Lavery folder

Copenhagen (1998)
All correspondence in this section – Frayn (PC), except: Bradley, memo to Eyre, 18 December 1996 – NTLDF: Michael Frayn folder

Harry Potter and the Philosopher's Stone (1997)**
All correspondence in this section NTLDF: J. K. Rowling folder

The Merchant of Venice (c. 1594)
Nunn to Eyre, 18 January 1999 – Eyre (PC)

Brook to Nunn, 1999 – V&A: Brook
THM/452/3/60 to 116

The Improvisatrice or *The Bride of Cape
Coast***
Buffini to Nunn, 25 February 2000 – NTLDF:
Moira Buffini folder
'silver lining in her story'; *'on a journey with
me'* – Buffini, email to Daniel Rosenthal, 27
March 2018

House / Garden (1999)
All correspondence in this section – York:
Ayckbourn (Aisle 33, Bay 4, Shelf 3 Box 2)

Noises Off (1983)
'the radical criticisms and irresistible inventions'
– *Noises Off* (Methuen, London, 2000),
Author's Note
All correspondence in this section – Frayn (PC)

Howard Katz (2001)
All correspondence in this section – Marber
(PC)

Nicholas Hytner, NT Director Designate
All correspondence in this section – NTA:
19/17 Christopher Hogg Papers

The Coast of Utopia
All correspondence in this section – HRC:
Stoppard (uncatalogued)

The end of the Nunn years
NTA: 19/17 Christopher Hogg Papers

Act 5: The Nicholas Hytner Years

'non-musical repertoire in the Olivier' –
Rosenthal, p. 691
'extremely confident' – Rosenthal, p. 691

Democracy (2003)
All correspondence in this section – Frayn (PC)

Elmina's Kitchen (2003)
Block to Bradley, 10 July 2002 – NTLDF:
Kwame Kwei-Armah folder
'black British experience as I saw it' – Rosenthal,
p. 710

The History Boys (2004)
Bennett to Hytner, 20 October 2003; Hytner,
notes to Bennett, January 2004 – Bodleian:
MS. Bennett 163
Bennett, postcard to Hytner, 18 May 2004;
Tovey, postcard to Hytner, 18 May 2004;
Corden, card to Hytner, 18 May 2004 –
Hytner (PC)

Stuff Happens (2004)
Coke, postcard to Hare, September 2004 –
HRC: Hare (uncatalogued)

Hall, postcard to Hytner, 19 September 2004;
Mirren, postcard to Hytner & Hare, 2004 –
Hytner (PC)

Paul (2005)
Brenton to Hytner, 1 June 2003 – NTLDF:
Howard Brenton folder
turned down several of his plays, including Berlin
Bertie *and* Doctor Love – NTLDF: Howard
Brenton folder

Oedipus at Colonus (401 BC)**
All correspondence in this section – Hytner
(PC)

War Horse (2007)
Hytner (PC)

The Pride**
All correspondence in this section, including
'to be fully successful' (Bradley to Kaye
Campbell, 11 April 2006); *'a little scissor
job!'* (Kaye Campbell, email to Hytner, 19
December 2007) – NTLDF: Alexi Kaye
Campbell folder

Harper Regan (2008)
All correspondence in this section – Simon
Stephens (PC)

Afterlife (2008)
All correspondence in this section – Michael
Frayn PC, including *'comments, casting
suggestions'* (Frayn to Codron, 26 November
2007)

Mrs Affleck (2009)
All correspondence in this section – Samuel
Adamson (PC)

England People Very Nice (2009)
'some people would be offended' – Rosenthal,
p. 788
Hytner, postcard to Bean, 11 February 2009 –
Hull: U DRBE/2/10

The Habit of Art (2009)
All correspondence in this section – Hytner
(PC), except:
Hytner to Bennett, November 2007 – quoted
in *Alan Bennett and The Habit of Art* (Dir:
Adam Low), transmitted on More 4, 27
November 2010

Really Old, Like Forty Five (2010)
'redundancy and inactivity' – *Daily Telegraph*, 5
February 2010
All correspondence in this section – Tamsin
Oglesby (PC)

Welcome to Thebes (2010)
All correspondence in this section – Moira
    Buffini (PC)

The Holy Rosenbergs (2011)
Ryan Craig (PC)

London Road (2011)
'exciting development' – Rosenthal, p. 814
All correspondence in this section – Alecky
    Blythe (PC)

One Man, Two Guvnors (2011)
All correspondence in this section – Richard
    Bean (PC), except:
Hytner, postcard to Bean, 24 May 2011 – Hull:
    U DRBE/2/45
Corden, card to Hytner, 24 May 2011 – Hytner
    (PC)
'this ridiculously silly play' – *The Guardian*, 11
    June 2012

The Count of Monte Cristo (1844)**
All correspondence in this section – Bean (PC)
'National Theatre delays Count of Monte Cristo
    play' – BBC News, 20 June 2012 (https://bbc.
    in/2qnT6Yq, accessed 10 April 2018)

*The Curious Incident of the Dog in the
Night-Time* (2012)
All emails in this section – Stephens (PC),
    including *'Stephens had enlisted Scott Graham
    and Stephen Hoggett'* (Stephens, email to
    Graham and Hoggett, 28 January 2010)

The Effect (2012)
All emails in this section – Lucy Prebble (PC),
    except: Prebble, email to Goold, 25 August
    2012 (11.42pm); Goold, email to Prebble, 26
    August 2012 (12.05am) – Rupert Goold (PC)

The Amen Corner (1954)
All emails in this section – Rufus Norris (PC)

The Light Princess (2013)
All correspondence in this section – Samuel
    Adamson (PC)
springboard to West End and Broadway runs –
    Adamson, email to Daniel Rosenthal, 18
    March 2018

Great Britain (2014)
All correspondence in this section – Bean (PC),
    including *'continue to amaze over the next
    couple of years'* (MacKenzie, email to Bean,
    2 September 2011) and *'theatre of the absurd
    and a slapstick farce'* (MacKenzie, email to
    Bean, 9 January 2013), except:
Stoppard, postcard to Bean, 1 July 2015 – Hull:
    U DRBE/2/47

The end of the Hytner years
All correspondence in this section – Adamson
    (PC)

Act 6: The Rufus Norris Years

'summoning power to attract the greatest talents'
    – Rosenthal, p. 844

Everyman (late fifteenth century)
All emails in this section – Norris (PC)

The Red Lion (2015)
All correspondence in this section – Marber
    (PC)

wonder.land (2015)
All emails in this section – Buffini (PC)

The Threepenny Opera (1928)
All emails in this section – Stephens (PC)

My Country: A Work in Progress (2017)
All emails in this section – Norris (PC)

Oslo (2016)
Craig (PC)

NT timeline

An important source for this timeline is 'Stage
    by Stage', which can be downloaded at
    www.nationaltheatre-org.uk/about-the-
    national-theatre/history

Permissions

Correspondence

Correspondence from the following individuals is their copyright and appears by their kind permission:

Samuel Adamson, Sarah Pia Anderson, Eileen Atkins, Alan Ayckbourn, Keith Baxter, Richard Bean, Jenny Beavan, Alan Bennett, Michael Billington, Michael Blakemore, Alecky Blythe, William Boyd, Howard Brenton, Peter Brook, Moira Buffini, Simon Callow, Jim Carter, Michael Codron, Judith Coke, James Corden, David Cornwell, Tom Courtenay, Ryan Craig, Paddy Cunneen, Jennie Darnell, Oliver Ford Davies, Judi Dench, Carol Ann Duffy, Marianne Elliott, Richard Eyre [letters to: Max Rayne, 31 August 1986; David Hare, 24 October 1993, 15 January 1994, 4 February 1995 & 1 August 1995; email to Moira Buffini, 13 January 2010], Michael Feast, Emma Fielding, Ian Flintoff, Clive Francis, Michael Frayn, Michael Gambon, Julian Glover, Rupert Goold, Mark Haddon, Christopher Hampton, Sheila Hancock, David Hare, Tony Harrison (© Tony Harrison, reproduced by permission of Faber & Faber Ltd), Ronald Harwood, Nick Hern, Greg Hicks, Christopher Hogg, Sarah Hogg, Morag Hughes, Tom Hughes, Benet Hytner, Nicholas Hytner [letters to: Theodore Chapin, 5 June 1992; Christopher Hogg, 7 September 2001], Derek Jacobi, Marianne Jean-Baptiste, Michael Kitchen, Hanif Kureishi (© Hanif Kureishi, used by permission of The Wylie Agency (UK) Limited), Tony Kushner, Bryony Lavery, Julie Legrand, Maureen Lipman, Anna Mackmin, Patrick Marber, Sean Mathias, Ian McEwan, Genista McIntosh, Ian McKellen, Helen Mirren, Abi Morgan, Michael Morpurgo, Kate Nelligan, Peter Nichols, Rufus Norris [emails to Marianne Jean-Baptiste, 30 November and 5 December 2012], Edna O'Brien, Tamsin Oglesby, Grant Olding, John Peter, Edward Petherbridge, Joan Plowright, Lucy Prebble, Ian Rickson, Diana Rigg, Jeremy Sams, Paul Schrader, Maggie Smith, Rae Smith, Simon Stephens, Tom Stoppard, Emma Thompson, Russell Tovey, Stephen Wakelam, Irving Wardle, David Yelland.

The correspondence of the following individuals appears by kind permission of, and is the copyright of, the estates or individuals or trusts identified in brackets; the editor and publishers thank them for their generosity and co-operation:

Edward Albee (The Estate of Edward Albee); Lindsay Anderson (University of Stirling Archives); Jill Balcon (Estate of C. Day-Lewis and Jill Balcon); Harley Granville Barker (The Society of Authors as the Literary Representative of the Estate of Harley Granville Barker); Diana Boddington (Claudia McKelvey); Letters by Robert Bolt to Peter Hall (Peters Fraser & Dunlop [www.petersfraserdunlop.com] on behalf of the Estate of Robert Bolt); Ken Campbell (Daisy Campbell); Noël Coward (NC Aventales AG – Successor in title to the Estate of Noël Coward); Pam Gems (The Trustees for the Literary Estate of Pam Gems); John Gielgud (The Trustees of the Sir John Gielgud Charitable Trust); Simon Gray (The Estate of Simon Gray); Alec Guinness (The Estate of Alec Guinness); Peter Hall (The Royal Shakespeare Company and Nicola Hall, for his correspondence 1960–63; Nicola Hall, for his correspondence post-1989); Rex Harrison (The Estate of Rex Harrison); Nigel Hawthorne (Trevor Bentham); Lillian Hellman (George Lane, agent for The Estate of Lillian Hellman); Jocelyn Herbert (Sandra Lousada for the Jocelyn Herbert Estate); Ted Hughes (© the Estate of Ted Hughes; reproduced by permission of Faber & Faber Ltd); Elia Kazan (Frances Kazan); Elizabeth Longford (Estate of Elizabeth Longford); Arthur Miller (Letters to Laurence Olivier and David Thacker by Arthur Miller. Copyright © Arthur Miller 2004 Literary and Dramatic Property Trust, 1964, 1993, 1995, 2001, used by permission of the Wylie Agency (UK) Limited); Derek Mitchell (Sarah Roberts); Laurence Olivier [correspondence from 1960–62] (Lady Olivier & Richard Olivier); John Osborne (Gordon Dickerson on behalf of The Arvon Foundation); Bob Peck (Jill Baker); Steven Pimlott (Daniela Bechly); Ken Pople (David Pople); Peggy Ramsay (The Peggy Ramsay Foundation); Terence Rattigan (The Sir Terence Rattigan Charitable Trust); Max Rayne (The Estate of Lord Rayne); Bryan Robertson (The Bryan Robertson Trust); John Schlesinger (Michael Childers); George Bernard Shaw (The Society of Authors, on behalf of the Bernard Shaw Estate); Paul Scofield (Martin Scofield); Peter Shaffer (the estate of Peter Shaffer c/o Macnaughton Lord Representation); Robert Stephens (Patricia Stephens); David Storey (The Storey Family); Michael Stroud (Christopher Brown); Harold Wilson (Crown copyright, published under Open Government licence).

With the exception of those items of correspondence listed against their names on p. 388, all correspondence from the National Theatre's Directors (Laurence Olivier, Peter Hall, Richard Eyre, Trevor Nunn, Nicholas Hytner and Rufus Norris) is copyright of the National Theatre and is used by kind permission of the National Theatre Board, as is correspondence from the following:

Sunny Amey, Jean Benedetti, Michael Birkett, Michael Bogdanov, Sebastian Born, Jack Bradley, John Burgess, Giles Croft, John Dexter, Michael Elliott, Derek Goldby, Ernest Hall, Christopher Morahan, Purni Morell, Rufus Norris, Trevor Nunn, Laurence Olivier, Tom Pate, Ben Power, Kenneth Rea, Michael Rudman, John Russell Brown, Shane Thom, Kenneth Tynan and Nicholas Wright. The unsigned memo, 26 March 1979, on p. 158 is copyright of the National Theatre.

Facsimiles

Image copyright for all facsimile reproductions (cards, cast list, diagram, letters, memos, postcards, show reports) is copyright of the National Theatre, except for the following: © Daniel Rosenthal: p. 2, front cover of *Scheme & Estimates ...*. British Library, London, UK © British Library Board, All Rights Reserved/Bridgeman Images: pp. 78–9, Maggie Smith, letter to Laurence Olivier; p. 89, Terence Rattigan, telegram to Laurence Olivier. © Harry Ransom Center, The University of Texas at Austin: p. 153, Kate Nelligan, note to David Hare; p. 228, Judi

Dench, card to David Hare. © Ian McKellen: p. 169, Peter Shaffer, card to Ian McKellen; p. 194, Michael Frayn, letter to Ian McKellen. © The Borthwick Institute, University of York: p. 212, Clive Francis, postcard to Alan Ayckbourn (reproduced from an original in the Borthwick Institute; Ayckbourn, Box 161). © Richard Eyre/Chestermead Limited: p. 268, Diana Rigg, postcard to Richard Eyre; p. 282, Ken Campbell, fax to Richard Eyre. © The Bodleian Libraries, The University of Oxford: p. 313, Alan Bennett, letter to Nicholas Hytner (Shelfmark: MS. Bennett 163/1, fols. 1r). © Ryan Craig: p. 332, Purni Morell, note to Ryan Craig.

Photographs and posters

Illustrations on the pages listed have been used by kind permission of the copyright holders as shown:

© Chris Arthur: p.ii. © Catherine Ashmore: pp. vi, 284. Design and photography by Richard Bird: p. 113. Design by Richard Bird © National Theatre: p. 177. Copyright © Michael Childers: pp. 93, 145. Copyright © Nobby Clark/Arena PAL: pp. 102, 166, 184, 265. Copyright © Donald Cooper: p. 238. Copyright © Zoë Dominic: pp. 18, 43, 62, 72. © Hugo Glendinning: p. 275. © Manuel Harlan: p. 344. © John Haynes/Bridgeman Images: pp. 209, 216, 227, 241. © Richard Hubert-Smith: pp. 349, 360, 364. © Ellie Kurtz: p. 347. © Ivan Kyncl/Arena PAL: p. 309. Copyright © Angus McBean: pp. 23, 24. Copyright © Michael Mayhew: p. 156. Design by Michael Mayhew © National Theatre: p. 290. © Richard Mildenhall: p. 253. © Johan Persson: pp. 306, 328, 337. © Philip Vile: p. 371. © Helen Warner: p. 334.

All National Theatre copyright material is used by kind permission of the National Theatre Board.

Index